Wechsler Individual Achievement Test®
Second Edition

Scoring and Normative Supplement for
Grades PreK–12

THE
PSYCHOLOGICAL
CORPORATION®

A Harcourt Assessment Company

THE
PSYCHOLOGICAL
CORPORATION®

A Harcourt Assessment Company

Published by The Psychological Corporation • 19500 Bulverde Road • San Antonio, TX 78259, USA

Printed in the United States of America

1 2 3 4 5 6 7 8 9 10 11 12 A B C D E

Visit our Web site at www.PsychCorp.com

Contents

Appendix C. Grade-Based Normative Tables

Appendix D. Additional Grade-Based Normative Tables

Appendix E. Age-Based Conversion Tables

Appendix F. Age-Based Normative Tables

Appendix G. Additional Age-Based Normative Tables

Appendix H. WIAT–II Scores Predicted From the WPPSI–R, the WISC–III, and the WAIS–III Scores

Appendix I. Predicted-Achievement Method: Differences Required for Statistical Significance and Differences Obtained by Linking Samples

Appendix J. Simple-Difference Method: Differences Required for Statistical Significance and Differences Obtained by Linking Samples

Appendix K. Supplemental Tables

References

Introduction

The *Wechsler Individual Achievement Test–Second Edition* (WIAT–II) is a comprehensive, individually administered test for assessing the achievement of children, adolescents, college students, and adults who are in Grades Pre-kindergarten (PreK) through 16 or who are aged 4 through 85 years. The WIAT–II is a revision of the *Wechsler Individual Achievement Test* (WIAT; The Psychological Corporation, 1992). The WIAT–II can be used to comprehensively assess a broad range of academic skills in reading, mathematics, written language, and oral language, or to test only in a specified area of need. The WIAT–II *Examiner's Manual* provides the necessary information about the development of the revised instrument; the step-by-step administration, recording, and scoring of the subtests; guidelines for the interpretation of test scores; and suggestions for intervention. The *Examiner's Manual* also reports data about the standardization sample and evidence of the test's reliability and validity. For the convenience of the examiner, all of the scoring examples and guidelines and normative information is in either the *WIAT–II Scoring and Normative Supplement for Grades PreK–12* or the *WIAT–II Supplement for College Students and Adults.*

This supplement contains the scoring guidelines and normative data specific to examinees in Grades PreK–12 or aged 4–19 years. Although most of the necessary information to administer and score items is included in either the stimulus booklets or the record form, additional examples of scored responses are provided in Appendix A of the supplements. The scored responses are guides for the examiner, as he or she becomes more familiar with the scoring criteria. Examiners may wish to first score a response that has been included as an example, then compare their assessment to the recommended scoring.

The normative data includes grade-based and age-based standard scores, percentile ranks, normal curve equivalents (NCEs), stanines, and confidence intervals for each of the subtests and composites. Age and grade equivalents are provided for each subtest. Additionally, normative data is available for the conversion of supplemental raw scores to quartile-based scores (with the exception of the Alphabet Writing score, which is converted to a decile score).

The WIAT–II test was standardized on a nationally representative sample of children aged 4:0 to 19:11 during the 1999–2000 and 2000–2001 school years. Additionally, a subset of the standardization sample was administered the Wechsler Intelligence Scales. The *Wechsler Preschool and Primary Scale of Intelligence–Revised* (WPPSI–R; Wechsler, 1989) was administered to 199 children, the *Wechsler Intelligence Scale for Children–Third Edition* (WISC–III; Wechsler, 1991) was given to 775 children, and the *Wechsler Adult Intelligence Scale–Third Edition* (WAIS–III; Wechsler, 1997) was administered to 95 high school students aged 16–19 years. The college and adult sample was collected during the same period, and a subset of the college and adult sample was administered the WAIS–III.

The WIAT–II scores that are predicted from the WPPSI–R, the WISC–III, and the WAIS–III (i.e., Full Scale IQ, Verbal IQ, Performance IQ, Verbal Comprehension Index, and Perceptual Organization Index) are presented along with the differences that are required for statistical significance and the differences that were obtained from the linking samples. For examiners who choose to use the simple-difference method, information about the differences that are required for statistical significance and base rates are also included.

Supplemental tables include ipsative data about the differences between the composite scores, the differences between single subtest scores and the average of subtest scores required for statistical significance, the cumulative percentages of the standardization sample that obtained various discrepancies, and the differences between subtest scores required for statistical significance. Lastly, information on the intercorrelations of the WIAT–II subtest and composite scores and the Wechsler IQ scores and data for the intersubtest scatter are included.

Scoring Examples and Guidelines

A

Appendix A.1.
Reading Comprehension

The sample responses for each of the following items were selected from the standardization sample to represent a comprehensive list of possible responses and scores. Evaluate the sample responses to determine if the examinee's response should be scored 2, 1, or 0 points. If the examinee's response is *not* included in Stimulus Booklet 1, or in the sample responses listed in this appendix, determine the appropriate score by choosing the sample that is comparable to the examinee's response, or by determining if the examinee's response is within a specified guideline. All guidelines appear in parentheses. Responses that should be queried are noted with a **(Q)**. Query by saying, **Tell me more.**

Item 10. What can students bring to school on pet day?

2 points: (Response must include dogs, cats, *and* birds.) • dog, cat, or bird

1 point: dog **(Q)** • cat **(Q)** • bird **(Q)** • pets **(Q)** • animals **(Q)** • only 1 pet **(Q)**

0 points: fish • Spot

Item 11. Josie has a bird. How should she bring it to school?

2 points: in a cage • put it in a cage

1 point: in a box with holes

0 points: in a backpack • in your pocket • on Pet Day

Item 12. What will happen if Tim has the best pet for Pet Day?

2 points: He will get a prize. • He will win a prize.

1 point: He will win. • He will get a ribbon.

0 points: He will win a pet.

Item 13. Jody wants to bring 3 pets, but her teacher said, "Look at the poster." Why do you think her teacher said that?

2 points: You are only allowed to bring one pet. • You are only supposed to bring one to school. • The teacher said that you can only bring one pet.

1 point: That would be too many. **(Q)** • So it won't be crowded. **(Q)**

0 points: because the animals will fight

Item 14. What does *"pets must be on a leash"* mean?

2 points: (Response must describe what a leash is *and* its purpose.) • on a rope so they don't run away • on a rope so they don't fight

1 point: (Any response that indicates a restraint is required to participate *or* describes what a leash is.) • because they might go somewhere or run away • they must be tied up • hold them by a leash so they can't get away **(Q)** • that your dog or cat should be on a leash so that it doesn't go running around the classroom • you have to have a collar with a rope hanged onto it • so they can't get loose

0 points: dog • cage

Item 16. What do the people want to do?

2 points: (Response must refer to tree *and* park.) • plant/put a tree in a park

1 point: to plant a tree • plant (**Q**)

0 points: plant the seeds • play in the park

Item 19. What did Lee see first?

2 points: a duck • a duck in the water

1 point: water

0 points: a frog • a duck and a frog

Item 20. Where does the Baobab tree grow?

2 points: in dry African lands

1 point: in dry lands/places • in the same place elephants live

0 points: in the ground • in the grass • in the forest

Item 21. When does the tree get leaves?

2 points: when it rains twice a year • when the rainy seasons come

1 point: two times a year

0 points: in the summer • in the spring

Item 22. Why do elephants dig holes in the tree?

2 points: (Response must make reference to chewing wood *and* that the wood is damp.) • so that they can chew on the soft damp wood inside • the wood is damp and soft and chewy

1 point: so they can chew on the soft wood inside • because they are hungry/thirsty • to get food • to eat it

0 points: so they can get the wood

Item 23. What are two ways that people use the Baobab tree?

2 points: (Response must refer to storage *and* living in the tree.) • to store water in it, and they live in it • they use it to store water and food in, and sometimes they live in the hollow part • People store water or food in the trunk, and live in the hollow tree.

1 point: to store water and food in • to live in

0 points: they come because of the elephant • People think it's growing. • to chew the wood • hide in when it rains

Item 24. What does the word *hollow* mean in the story?

2 points: there is no insides • that it is empty • nothing in it

1 point: a hole (**Q**) • the center of the tree (**Q**)

0 points: something hard • it was wood inside • really hard • wood • dry

Item 25. What would be a good title for this story?

2 points: How the Baobab Trees Live • The Baobab Tree Grows • The Baobab Tree

1 point: How the Baobab Trees Are Used • Trees in Africa • A Funny Tree • A Tree That People Live In

0 points: The Tree • A Funny Bamboo Tree • Trees

A

Item 27. What animal is this about?

2 points: elephant

1 point: Dumbo • (any other character name for an elephant)

0 points: rhino

Item 28. What does the story tell us that Tamiko liked to do?

2 points: (Response must indicate that she liked washing *or* cleaning in general.) • She liked to clean.
• (to) clean • liked everything to be very, very clean • loved to have everything clean
• cleaning and shining

1 point: She liked to wash her dog.

0 points: to look at the stars • mop in the sky

Item 29. What happened to Tamiko's dog?

2 points: (Response must indicate the dog became bald from being washed.) • She washed him until
he was bald. • She cleaned it until it was bald.

1 point: (Response indicates only that the dog was washed *or* became bald.) • She cleaned him.
• He got bald.

0 points: He was left on the ground. • He was sad. • He ran away.

Item 30. What did Tamiko do before she went to Toko Town?

2 points: She made everything clean. • She shined her house. • She cleaned the whole house.

1 point: She mopped the floor. • She tidied up.

0 points: She shined the stars. • She cleaned the moon and stars.

Item 31. How did Tamiko get to the stars?

2 points: Some wind picked her up. • A gust of wind picked her up. • A gust picked Tamiko up
and carried her to the starry sky.

1 point: a storm

0 points: She flew. • She rode her mop/broom.

Item 32. What does the word *familiar* mean in the last sentence?

2 points: (Response must make reference to something seen before, known well, *or* recognized.)
• something you've seen before • something you've encountered before • you have
seen something before but not for a long time and you see it all over again • you know it
very well • you recognize it because you've seen it before

1 point: the same as last time (**Q**)

0 points: they weren't sure about it • a same smile • it is curved like our face except on only one
side of it • it's different

Item 33. Why are the stars brighter now than ever before?

2 points: (Response must make reference to Tamiko *and* that she cleaned/polished them.) • She
cleaned the stars. • because Tamiko went up to the stars and was mopping up there and she
mopped a star • because she polished them • because she went up there and cleaned and
shined the sky

1 point: because Tamiko is there • they're clean (**Q**)

0 points: because the moon came out

Item 34. How does a cricket make a chirping sound?

2 points: (Response must make reference to wings *and* rubbing them together.) • with its wings rubbed together • by rubbing its wings together

1 point: by its wings

0 points: with its leg • with its back legs • uses its legs against its wings • rubbing them together (**Q**)

Item 35. Which of the sentences in the story tells an opinion?

Do not give partial credit.

2 points: (Response must refer to the first sentence.) • Everyone likes to listen to crickets chirp. • the first sentence

0 points: (Response indicates any other sentence.)

Item 36. Where are a cricket's eardrums?

2 points: under their front legs

1 point: under its feet • undcr its legs (**Q**)

0 points: with their feet • their legs • in their ears • in their heads

Item 37. What do some people believe about crickets that is not true?

2 points: They rub their legs together to make the noise.

1 point: They don't use their wings to make noise. • They are good luck.

0 points: They can't fly. • They can't hear. • They fly with their wings.

Item 38. What is the meaning of the word *dispatch* in the passage?

2 points: it carries a message to their brain

1 point: go to (**Q**)

0 points: a message to the cricket's brain • talk to the other cricket • like a message

Item 39. How does a cricket use its legs to hear?

2 points: (Response must include accurate mention of at least *two* of the following: eardrums, picks up sound waves, dispatch to the brain.) • It picks up sound waves and works like its ear drum. • They pick up sound waves from the air and dispatch a message to their brain.

1 point: under its front legs are its eardrums • because of the things like our eardrums under their legs • It sends a message to the cricket's brain. (**Q**) • They have a flat round place on their front legs. • use their legs to hear at the spot (**Q**)

0 points: that chirping noise helps him hear • so they can hear and move • to hear

Item 41. What did the campers think they had seen?

2 points: an evening star • a bright evening star

1 point: a bright star • a star

0 points: The brightest planet was Venus. • Venus

Item 43. What animal is this about?

2 points: a rabbit • bunny

1 point: the Easter bunny • Peter Rabbit • (any other character name for a rabbit)

0 points: frog

Item 44. What will it do if it sees you?

2 points: He'll hop away.   •   It will hop away.

1 point: run away

0 points: hide

Item 45. Where did the dragon live?

2 points: (Response must include at least *two* of the following: Korea, lake, mountain.)   •   in a small lake beside a (small) mountain   •   by the lake in the mountain   •   by a lake in Korea

1 point: He lived over by a lake.   •   by a small lake and a small hill   •   on a mountain

0 points: by the river   •   by a hill

Item 46. What did the man want?

2 points: (Response must include a reference to living, mountain, *and* [large] size.)   •   He wanted to live by a large mountain.   •   to live by a higher mountain   •   to live on a large mountain

1 point: He wanted a house by the mountain.   •   He wanted a larger mountain.   •   He wanted the mountain to be bigger.   •   He wanted to build a house on the large mountain.

0 points: to live with the dragon as neighbors and make the lake bigger

Item 47. What does *cooperated* mean in this story?

2 points: (Response must include working together to mutual advantage.)   •   to work together either to meet a goal or so they both end up with something

1 point: They worked together and got along.   •   They were glad they worked together.   •   helps   •   to help somebody

0 points: They waited until they got the mountain larger.   •   they did what the man said   •   they were glad they had   •   that they got together and get along   •   get along

Item 48. What made the dragon's lake larger?

2 points: (Response must focus on the lake [not the mountain] *and* indicate the removal of something that impacts size.)   •   The rocks came out and there was more room in the lake.   •   when the man and dragon took out the rocks and sand   •   taking rocks out of the lake   •   He was taking all the rocks and mud out.   •   when they took the rocks away   •   taking out mud and stones

1 point: They kept digging in the mud and putting it on the mountain and it got bigger.   •   it rained

0 points: the stuff that the man had brought to help him   •   the man and the dragon

Item 49. What lesson could be learned from this story?

2 points: (Response must refer to the mutual benefit of cooperation.)   •   When two people cooperate, things get done that make them both happy.   •   By cooperating, everyone can get what they need.

1 point: (Response refers only to friendship *or* cooperation.)   •   If you have a friend you can cooperate with them and live by them.   •   You should cooperate.   •   If you work together you can complete many things.   •   If you cooperate, you will be glad you did.   •   cooperate   •   If you cooperate, you can be good friends.

0 points: to help somebody when they're in need   •   to be friendly   •   helping is also nice   •   Having good neighbors is something good to have.

Item 51. What in the popcorn makes it pop?

2 points: a little bit of water • water

1 point: heat • steam

0 points: the microwave • cooking it

Item 52. What does the word *erupt* mean in the last sentence?

2 points: to get bigger and explode • it kind of bursts • pop-out and turn into popped corn

1 point: to go through and make it pop

0 points: to change • to develop and go everywhere • grow longer • When you heat up something it causes a fire.

Item 54. Why did the milk fall down?

2 points: The dog jumped around and hit it. • The dog hit the table and it caused the milk to fall.

1 point: It bumped into the kitchen table. (**Q**)

0 points: the dog • table broke • it spilled

Item 55. Why won't the shirts shrink when cleaned?

2 points: it is 100% preshrunk cotton • because they're already preshrunk

1 point: because it says they are washable

0 points: they have cotton in them • they are premium • it's 100% cotton

Item 56. How should the shirts be cleaned?

2 points: in the washing machine • machine washable

1 point: soap and water (**Q**)

0 points: by hand

Item 57. The shirts are made of what material?

Do not give partial credit.

2 points: cotton • preshrunk cotton • 100% cotton

0 points: premium • specify • shirt material

Item 58. Why does the Ollie Owl shirt cost more than the other two shirts?

Do not give partial credit.

2 points: the sleeves • the long sleeves

0 points: Ollie Owl is famous.

Item 59. What three ingredients must you have to make Gobbledeeglue?

2 points: (Response must include in any order: Borax [powder], [white] glue, *and* water.)

1 point: (Response must include any three things listed in the passage.) • water, glue, powder • the glue, a cup, a spoon • water, powder, food coloring

0 points: glue • a cup • food coloring

Item 60. Why must you do Steps 1 and 2 before you can do Step 3?

2 points: If you put them all in at the same time, the Borax might not dissolve. • If you put them all in the same bowl, the Borax might not dissolve.

1 point: that's the order **(Q)** • so it will come out right **(Q)** • if you don't , then you won't have the items ready—it will ruin the whole experiment **(Q)** • to make sure that it dissolves **(Q)**

0 points: because they came first **(Q)** • they're first **(Q)** • because when you mix the glue and water together, you must add the Borax powder for 3 minutes • might not know what to do • so you can make it easier • you need to stir it first • have to mix the other ingredients first

Item 61. How does Gobbledeeglue change after step 4?

2 points: the color changes

1 point: food coloring **(Q)** • add food color

0 points: you have to leave it alone for 3 minutes • it hardens • it bounces

Item 62. What do you do right after the first time you put Gobbledeeglue on a sheet of plastic?

2 points: leave it alone • let it sit • leave it on the plastic

1 point: watch it **(Q)**

0 points: see what happens next • You pick it up and roll into a ball.

Item 63. What would you predict would happen if you tried to pull Gobbledeeglue apart?

2 points: bounce back together like elastic

1 point: it would/would not tear (either is a feasible prediction based on the information provided) • it will/will not pull apart (either is a feasible prediction based on the information provided) • it'll be hard like the inside of a ball

0 points: it might be sticky and you might have to wash your hands • it would make a mess • it won't be the way it's supposed to be • it'll fall apart • it'll get sticky • it'll crack • it probably would go everywhere

Item 64. What is the meaning of the word *dissolved* in Step 2?

2 points: melt into the water • it disappears in the water because it gets really small

1 point: spread **(Q)** • it's apart • go into it like water on a sponge • mixes in so you can't see it

0 points: until it is thick • let it react—let it get all of its thing • turns from something hard to something soft

Item 66. Why should you be prepared before you begin assembling the model?

2 points: the glue will dry before you get parts together • glue will dry while you are going to get something

1 point: so you will not have to get up • because it is a short drying time • so you don't have to stay forever and work quickly

0 points: so it can dry fast **(Q)** • the glue might dry on your hand

Item 68. What did John need to do first?

2 points: think about reasons for being on the team • think about reasons for wanting to be on the team

1 point: think about his reasons **(Q)** • to think

0 points: wait • the coach • he had to wait until the coach answered about his reason • try out for the team

Item 69. What question had the coach probably asked John?

2 points: Why do you want to be on the team? • What are your reasons for wanting to be on the team?

1 point: if he really wanted to be on the team • to think about his reason for wanting to be on the team

0 points: Are you ready to play right this time? • Do you think you made the team?

Item 70. About how old is Michael?

Do not give partial credit.

2 points: 8–13 (years old)

0 points: (Response indicates any other age.)

Item 71. What is different about Michael's appearance?

2 points: When he was born he had a defect; his bones were not formed. • The bones in his face don't grow right. • His bones didn't grow right.

1 point: He has birth defects.

0 points: He has a big heart. • He has changes. • He had already raised $50,000 for charity.

Item 72. What is the main reason Michael says he wants to help other people?

2 points: (Response must include a broad-reaching *or* general reason.) • It'll make the world a better place. • He wants a better world.

1 point: (Response includes any specific reason.) • so he won't feel sorry for himself • He doesn't want them suffering like he has. • He doesn't want to think of himself first.

0 points: so people won't end up like him • so everybody can be happy • there are other people in more difficulty than him • he wants other people not to have tragedy • to help the children at the hospital • wants to help people suffering

Item 73. What does the word *compassion* mean in this story?

2 points: (Response must include a feeling of caring *and* the emotional response involved, such as wanting to do something for that person.) • that he cares about the others more than himself and he wants others to have a better life

1 point: thinking of other people • he cares about it **(Q)** • he cares **(Q)**

0 points: dreams • his thoughts • you like someone • love

A

Item 74. What is the main idea of this passage?

2 points: (Response must indicate that although Michael has a problem of his own, he still wants to help people less fortunate than himself *or* one must not judge a book by its cover.) • Michael has a defect and he doesn't think about himself, he thinks about others. • He has a problem but he wants to help people with worse problems. • not to judge others by their appearance as they can be really nice people • not to judge a book by its cover

1 point: that he helps other people • it is about charity for other children • he doesn't stay sad because of the way he looks • how Michael helped many people

0 points: not to feel sorry about himself • he raised $50,000

Item 75. Who is Kwawar?

Do not give partial credit.

2 points: their god • a Great Spirit that made the earth • the Great Spirit • a god • God

0 points: a turtle • a Native American • a ghost

Item 76. In all, how many Turtle Brothers were needed to fulfill Kwawar's request?

Do not give partial credit.

2 points: 7

0 points: any other number

Item 77. What caused the mountains to arise?

2 points: He placed dirt over the shells.

1 point: the earth **(Q)** • the bulrushes

0 points: the Great Spirit, he inserted fingers into the soil • because the earth began to tremble • Kwawar became restless

Item 78. What natural event does the Turtle Brothers' quarrelling explain?

2 points: an earthquake

1 point: landslides • the land shakes

0 points: floods • war • shaking **(Q)**

Item 79. What great gift did Kwawar give the Turtle Brothers?

2 points: to have formed California on their backs • He gave them the responsibility of bearing California.

1 point: to be California mountains

0 points: they got to help him • they learned to get along • they were proud

Item 80. What is the meaning of *contemplated* in the story?

2 points: thought about long and hard • he was thinking and deciding, trying to remember • meditated about

1 point: they tried to figure out what happened • thought up

0 points: to create something • deciding/decided • assuming • planning/planned • to create land • made up his mind • discovered

A

Item 82. Tell in your own words what has happened as a result of the avalanche.

2 points: All the cars stopped when the snow came down on the road. • road was covered with debris and traffic stopped • it probably caused a traffic jam because of the stuff on the road

1 point: it covered the road with debris • it blocked the road and there's debris on the road

0 points: it came tumbling down the hillside (**Q**) • covering the road (**Q**) • Traffic had to stop so the road crew could clean the road off. • rocks fell down and everybody stopped so they wouldn't get hit

Item 83. What does the word *debris* mean in this sentence?

2 points: covering road with rocks and rubble • ruined houses, wood, and stuff • rocks, sticks, mud, snow • dirt, grass and stuff that came down with the avalanche • sticks, dirt, gravel

1 point: snow • rubbish

0 points: pieces of something like metal from an airplane • rocks or any matter that people don't want • a tree was throwing sticks off

Item 85. What does the word *fancy* mean in this sentence?

2 points: they like something else better • they like • they like it best

1 point: enjoy

0 points: nice • nuts, grains, and seeds • something nice and very expensive

Item 87. Why did the track meet end earlier than expected?

2 points: (Response must refer to bad weather *and* the cancellation of the long distance events.) • bad weather and long distance events were cancelled • because of the weather and long distance events were cancelled

1 point: (Response includes a reference to either bad weather *or* the cancellation of the long distance events.) • because of the weather

0 points: it was over

Item 88. What does the word *inclement* mean in this sentence?

Do not give partial credit.

2 points: bad weather • bad • not perfect—rainy • rough • stormy

0 points: like, it got really hot • suddenly • unexpected • weather the people aren't used to, like if they are used to hot, it feels real cold

Item 89. What were two dangers encountered by the family on their journey?

2 points: (Response must include at least *two* of the stated or implied dangers.) • faced a grizzly bear and attacked by outlaws • bears and harsh wilderness

1 point: (Response includes at least *one* of the dangers.) • grizzly bears • hiked in the cold in the wilderness

0 points: it was cold

Item 90. According to Diana, why doesn't Charlie want to go to the Yukon?

2 points: because it was his father's dream • He doesn't want to follow his father's dreams.

1 point: he's a rebel • because his father made him go

0 points: he dislikes his father • to find gold • he knows it will be really hard • he wasn't certain

Item 91. According to the reviewers, what are two main themes or ideas in *Yukon Gold*?

2 points: (Response must refer to wilderness adventure *and* family conflict.) • Two teenagers fighting for independence as they travel and find adventures along the way.

1 point: (Response includes at least *one* of the themes.) • It is about a family who wants to follow the father's dreams, and them having a good time. • The family encounters many dangers, and the father is attacked by a grizzly. • it's really dangerous and they barely survive • getting attacked by grizzlies and looking for gold

0 points: Yukon gold, the North American Press Services • journeys and going places • His children don't want to go because they are afraid there are too many dangers.

Item 92. Diana gave *Yukon Gold* four stars although Gary gave it two. What did Gary dislike about the movie?

2 points: The story was hackneyed, and the ending held no surprise. • that the hackneyed ending holds no surprise • The story was too predictable. • The ending holds no surprises.

1 point: that it held no surprises (**Q**) • the ending

0 points: the story of two teenagers fighting • he doesn't like adventure movies

Item 93. What is the meaning of the word *hackneyed* in Gary's review?

2 points: overused • same story ending as in other movies

1 point: it didn't hold any surprises and wasn't very surprising

0 points: not very good • something could happen suddenly • ruined • not enjoyable • not very exciting • boring

Item 94. What is the meaning of the word *records* in the first paragraph?

2 points: (Response must refer to preserved information.) • a documentary of the past • the oldest written recordings • papers kept after a period of time • anything written down at that time • information written down a long time ago • things written down about history • annals • something people have written and kept

1 point: (Response refers to information only without a reference to the past.) • tablets of written information • something information is kept on • sources (**Q**) • books • facts • writing that can be looked up • what they found that had been written down • written tabulations • an account of what happens • 3,500 year old clay tablets

0 points: old proverbs • written or spoken language

Item 95. Where do you think Ben Franklin found the proverbs he included in *Poor Richard's Almanack*?

2 points: heard from people and from his family (mom, etc.) • from other people, or made them up, or brought from England

1 point: some of his friends said them to him • from the Bible • he heard them (**Q**)

0 points: in the summer • he wrote them himself • he made them up himself • he was taught them

Item 96. What do you think *Haste makes waste* might mean?

2 points: (Response must refer to haste *and* waste.) • If you hurry too much you might do it wrong and have to do it all over again—and that's a waste of time.

1 point: If you're in a hurry, you'll probably forget something. • If you go too quickly, then you won't do well.

0 points: If you don't like it or use it, it's wasted.

Item 97. Why do you think most people like proverbs?

2 points: easy way to understand life • helps you with everyday life • so you can prove a point easier • they are wise things • words of wisdom

1 point: they are short, easily remembered, thought of as true • they are easy to remember and widely accepted as true • because they're short

0 points: they are old

Item 98. Which of the proverbs mentioned in the passage is a comment on modern technology?

Do not give partial credit.

2 points: garbage in, garbage out

0 points: a stitch in time saves nine • a picture is worth a thousand words

Item 100. How are mammals and saurian different?

2 points: Mammals are warm blooded, but saurian blood corresponds with the cold or warm (cold-blooded). • Mammals maintain a constant body temperature, but the temperature of the saurian changes relative to the environmental temperature. • saurian change with environment; mammals keep same body temp

1 point: their body temperatures (**Q**) • their temperatures (**Q**)

0 points: they don't change but the other ones do

Item 102. What does the sentence tell you that the great Dust Bowl was?

2 points: a big drought in middle and southern parts of the U.S. • On the plains when it stopped raining, it was dry and dusty. • something that happens when it quits raining

1 point: dust storms • sand storms

0 points: raining in large parts of Kansas, Colorado, New Mexico, and Texas • period of time when it rained a lot • lots of raining • a football game

Item 103. For what primary reason did Kristi's mother want her daughter to skate?

2 points: to strengthen her frail legs

1 point: to make her stronger

0 points: for the Olympic gold

Item 104. How does the definition of *routine* in the first paragraph differ from that in the next paragraph?

2 points: 1st, is a routine of how she would get up, her daily routine; 2nd, involved her coaches and her routine on ice.

1 point: things you do every morning at chosen intervals (**Q**) • 1st, talks about her hard work, what she did; 2nd, she said what she did was perfect and easy on the eyes to watch • 1st was grueling, the 2nd captivated her audience (**Q**)

0 points: it's a different year

Item 105. Why was Kristi's workload double that of other skaters?

Do not give partial credit.

2 points: She was in singles and pairs competition. • She competed in two events.

0 points: because she had a partner helping her • because she had frail legs • because she also wanted to be on the Olympic team • She had to wake up at 4:00 every morning to practice and then do her school day.

Item 106. Who won the pairs gold medal at the 1990 Nationals?

2 points: Kristi and Rudy

1 point: Kristi and her partner

0 points: Rudy • she did

Item 107. How was Kristi able to compensate for her athletic limitations?

2 points: by her grace and consistency

1 point: grace • consistency

0 points: she had frail legs—but overcame it and then strengthened them • she kept trying • by practicing so much

Item 108. What is the meaning of the word *demise* in this story?

2 points: destruction • the reason that they are gone or not here anymore • disappearance • killing off • for their lowering in population—death of many

1 point: perish

0 points: a whale is dying

Item 109. In what two ways have people been the primary reason for the whales' demise?

2 points: (Response must include a reference to whales being hunted for commercial gain *and* whales getting caught in nets and starving.) • hunt them for commercial gain and if fishing, they may get caught in the net

1 point: (Response includes *only* one of the reasons.) • hunting and fishing • being hunted

0 points: throwing trash in the water • pollution

Item 110. Why is it important for us to know about the struggles of the humpback whales?

2 points: so then we support saving them since we are the only way they can be saved

1 point: They are on the endangered species list. • If we don't take care of them, we will lose them. • because they are a part of our ecosystem

0 points: because whales are mammals too

Item 111. What two things might happen if a whale is caught in a fishing net?

2 points: (Response must refer to drowning *and* starving.) • Larger whales would break out, but if they couldn't get the net off, they would starve and they could drown, and they can't produce oxygen under water.

1 point: starve • flippers might get caught so will have to cut net off or they drown

0 points: He could pull the boat under.

Item 112. According to current studies, what is likely to happen to the humpback whale in the future?

2 points: If people take action, their numbers will increase. • promising recovery

1 point: They will be protected better.

0 points: be extinct

Item 114. What is the most likely reason for the changes in the peach prices during the year?

2 points: (Response must refer to supply *and* demand.) • The more peaches the lower the price, the less peaches the higher the price—based on the growing season.

1 point: (Response refers to either supply *or* demand.) • When more peaches are being sold, the stores can charge less. • at the height of the season more people want them

0 points: because sometimes it is good growing conditions for peaches and sometimes it's bad times • in the beginning, very high and not a lot of peaches; at the end, very high too, in the middle they have a lot and keep producing • when the peach season was at its height, there were plenty of peaches so they charged more at the end when peaches were dying • in/out of season (**Q**)

Item 115. If today's zoo admission is $4.00, what was zoo admission in January 1993?

Do not give partial credit.

2 points: $3.00 • three • a dollar less

0 points: (Response indicates any amount other than $3.00.) • less than now

Item 116. What is the main reason Tom gives to support his position?

2 points: (Response must state a cause and effect relationship between the last price increase *and* a decline in zoo attendance.) • the correlation between previous raises of ticket price and the decline in patronage of the zoo

1 point: (Response indicates that zoo attendance has dropped but does not state a reason.) • The number of people visiting the zoo declined.

0 points: the attendance will go down • If you increase the price, less people will come, and as that continues, less people will be coming every year (this *is* Tom's position). • He feels that if they do increase admission prices, attendance will drop off. • zoo's attendance would go down, people go to other places and lose money in the long run

Item 117. When he says *take up the slack* in his sentence, what does Tom mean?

2 points: find new ways to meet the same goals • to account for the money that the zoo would have made if the prices had been raised • When they find themselves not making as much money from tickets, they can make the money up through concessions.

1 point: to help something like to assist it in an area where something is lacking • compensate

0 points: it doesn't matter if the prices are low, the zoo can handle it

Item 118. Tanisha uses the word *acquisitions* in her letter. What does it mean?

2 points: the bringing in of new animals to the zoo • she means to get new animals

1 point: something bought or gained in some way that you end up owning them • acquire them (**Q**) • to make additions (**Q**)

0 points: projects for new animals • facilities • new cages • exhibits • housing for the animals • different kinds of things for the animals • they need some food • animals • new attractions

Item 119. According to Tanisha, what three things might happen if zoo prices are not raised?

2 points: (Response must include at least three results.) • loss of education, other zoos will get the animals, the zoo may have to close, the families will go somewhere else • zoo will have to close or sell animals and people would look elsewhere for entertainment

1 point: (Response includes one *or* two results.) • they won't be able to get more animals and might have to sell the ones they have • the zoo might close and they won't give a raise to the employees

0 points: people bring in food and don't pay for zoo, everyone loses the animals because of cost of food, and a small price will justify the zoo's need **(Q)**

Item 121. What has happened to the king?

2 points: he died • The king has died.

1 point: he's no longer in power, something happened **(Q)** • His reign ended with his destruction.

0 points: give up his seat • sentence was up • the king's reign ended with the dismiss **(Q)** • impeached • resigned • voted out • his reign ended

Item 122. What would you predict might happen as a result of the event described?

2 points: somebody else could take over, either his son or the group of people that killed him • the group that won could take over the kingdom • a new king would be crowned

1 point: there would be some change in the form of government

0 points: he wouldn't be king anymore • perhaps people weren't happy with the old forms of ruling

Item 123. What was the first discovery of the Central Asiatic Expedition?

2 points: they found a collection of dinosaur skulls

1 point: fossils • dinosaur skeletons

0 points: whales off Alaskan coast • dino eggs

Item 124. Tell three adventures Andrews had experienced before going to the Gobi desert.

2 points: (Response must include at least *three* adventures.) • hunting whales (off Alaskan coast), accosted by Manchurian bandits (in China), searching remote regions in Tibet for museum specimens • hunting whales, fighting in China, specimens in Tibet and Burma

1 point: (Response includes only *two* adventures.) • he hunted and worked for the museums

0 points: the mystery and danger of his hunt; the whole thing across then E. China; search for a tribe **(Q)**

Item 125. Where did the scientists discover the dinosaur eggs?

2 points: (Response must include a specific reference to Flaming Cliffs.) • the dunes, Flaming Cliffs • Flaming Cliffs

1 point: dunes—Gobi desert • loose rock and sand of the dunes • Mongolia • Asia

0 points: in the desert • in China

Item 126. How did Andrews' expedition alter scientific knowledge?

2 points: They proved conclusively that dinosaurs laid eggs.

1 point: the discovery of modern bones from Andrews and dinosaurs laying eggs • found dinosaur eggs • first eggs found • dinosaurs (dinos) lay eggs

0 points: proved dinosaurs existed • they searched for what they were looking for • it proved that dinosaurs existed

Item 127. What is the meaning of the word *brigands* as used in the passage?

2 points: outlaws • bandits • highwaymen • thieves • pirates

1 point: snipers • killers • terrorists • rebels

0 points: some kind of native people who already live there and who are ready to attack (**Q**) • some kind of animal or tribal people • headhunters • tribes • Mongolians • army men

Item 129. What is the meaning of the word *longevity* in this sentence?

2 points: You are able to live a long time.

1 point: how long you live, lifespan • the amount of time something lasts, length of time

0 points: length

Item 130. Describe the trend reported in this sentence.

2 points: People are living longer than previously. • Over time, lifespan on the whole increases. • As time continues, people on the whole are living longer. • More people are living longer than at the turn of the century.

1 point: More people are living to age 65 now.

0 points: tells how long people live now (response does not explain how long)

Item 131. At what life stage is a person likely to begin a career?

2 points: Building the Nest • 20's Building the Nest

1 point: the twenties

0 points: (any other stage)

Item 132. What is the main theme of the "Mid-life Rebirth" developmental tasks?

2 points: (Response must include change or reevaluation *and* the accompanying action.) • a reexamining of one's self, awareness of middle age, looking at emotions, spirituality, reestablishing selves

1 point: (Response includes either change *or* action.) • instability • remodel life structure • redefining yourself • adjusting to life's limitations • revision • physical energy, emotions, new friends, change in careers, sense of loneliness, dependence, questions • asking deep questions of spiritual issues, a re-birth, a mid-life crisis • they may feel stuck in one place and do crazy things

0 points: self acceptance • realizing you're growing older • finding yourself • to settle down

Item 133. Although Rachel was recently promoted to manager of her office, she is questioning her choice of careers and regrets that she never pursued her dream of composing music. At the same time, she is reluctant to quit her job because she recently bought a new home. What developmental stage is Rachel probably in?

2 points: Looking Around • 30's Looking Around

1 point: the 30's

0 points: (any other stage)

Item 134. What might happen if a person did not accomplish the developmental tasks of the "Breaking Loose" stage?

2 points: They may never become their own person, have a stable career or their own set of morals.

1 point: drifting • be a burden on their family • find it difficult to settle down • the other stages would be behind • living at home, attached to family, lifestyle would change and be repetitious • be very attached to parents, afraid to go out, strongly attached to what they've been taught, narrow minded • probably have a hard time doing things from building nest on • probably wouldn't be able to function in society as well

0 points: They would stay in that stage. • wouldn't be successful • insecure • never grow up • no responsibility • low self-esteem • might have emotional turmoil • unsatisfied • immature

Item 135. If the last life stage called "Deepening Wisdom" were added to the chart, what would you predict two of the developmental tasks would be?

Responses fall into approximately 8 categories. To score 2 points, the response must refer to at least two categories. A 2-point response will be rare. A response that refers to only one of the categories is scored 1 point.

Category 1. (Positive) Resignation/Realization/Acceptance of self/life: People would realize the meaning of their lives and what was important. • acceptance of choices that have been made in the past and greater emphasis on spiritual issues • acceptance of one's self worth • satisfaction with life's work

Category 2. (Negative) Resignation/Realization/Acceptance of self/life: dependency, approaching death, failing health • have someone take care of you • resignation that all the things they had hoped for in their lives weren't going to happen • acceptance of physical losses • dealing with a medical condition

Category 3. Enjoyment of life: be happy and content • enjoy kids, travel • You would slow down and take life as it comes. • feel good about oneself, no longer need for competing on the ladder of success • live out missed opportunities • happiness • leisure time • to focus on family and enjoy the simple pleasures of life more • appreciate life • enjoy life

Category 4. Death (preparation for, dealing with, acceptance): preparing for your mortality and loss of friends • sense death • preparing for death and resolving issues that were never closed • approach death without being afraid • selling your possessions and make plans for your demise • write will and plan funeral

Category 5. Seeking knowledge (spiritual and otherwise): seeking knowledge, analyzing knowledge, passing on knowledge • seeking deeper wisdom • passing on knowledge that is learned to others • exploring hobbies and interests • more study and spiritual research • using the knowledge you gained over the years to reassess your thoughts • passing on knowledge that is learned to others • continue on in education • go back to school, philosophize more • focus on new hobbies • look at new religious interests • analyze life • writing a book • passing on experiences • learning from mistakes • passing on life's lessons to grandchildren • giving advice

Category 6. Thinking/Reflection/Introspection/Retrospection: looking back on life • search for life's meaning • thinking about whether you are living life the way you're supposed to be living it, a lot of thinking • reflecting on life's experiences • more spiritual research • introspection

Category 7. Serenity (peace, patience, spiritual enlightenment): spiritual awareness • patience • sense of fulfillment, security

Category 8. Focus on family or others: focus on people instead of possessions and power, select a few good friends • importance of family

Item 136. What is a *fissure* as described in the passage?

2 points: a break in the rock • a slit in the rock • a crevasse or niche

1 point: a space in rock **(Q)** • a nick in stone • an indentation or hollowed-out part of stone

0 points: an overhang

Item 137. What suddenly made this rock climb so difficult?

2 points: suddenly a really huge, rocky thing they had to climb • because of how high and steep it was

1 point: they were tired • fatigue and elements (the wind)

0 points: the switchbacks • fear

Item 138. What was the most important thing the women had to overcome in order to scale the rock?

2 points: their fatigue • their fatigue and they might have been frightened to climb it

1 point: the escarpment • the wind • backpacks • finding hand-holds

0 points: heights • difficult to overcome obstacles • their confidence • determination • couldn't do it • fear

Item 139. What kept the women from turning back when they saw the sheer surface of the rock?

2 points: really determined—had already gone a significant distance and didn't want to turn around

1 point: that she was almost there • They had hiked five miles and 6000 ft. and they were not going to turn back.

0 points: there was no way down • They were afraid they'd fall.

Item 140. Why did Angela refuse to look at Sherry as she approached the summit?

2 points: looking down would prevent her from achieving her goal • very focused on herself • needed to concentrate on getting herself to the top

1 point: so she wouldn't look down

0 points: because she was right behind her • because she is scared of heights

Appendix A.2.
Written Expression

The Written Expression subtest is organized so that the most appropriate items are administered to an examinee according to grade. Examinees in Grades PreK–K are administered *only* Alphabet Writing. Examinees in Grades 1–2 are administered Alphabet Writing, Word Fluency, and Sentences. Examinees in Grades 3–6 are administered Word Fluency, Sentences, and Paragraph. Examinees in Grades 7–16 are administered Word Fluency, Sentences, and Essay. The design of the record form helps examiners track the scores that are added to calculate the total raw score for a specific grade.

Alphabet Writing

The Alphabet Writing score is based on the number of correct letters written in 15 seconds. Score 1 point for each correctly formed and sequenced letter. Sequencing is established in reference to the last correctly formed letter. To be in sequence, a letter needs only to appear in its appropriate alphabetical order in reference to the previous, correctly formed letters. **Sequencing is scored so that the examinee will receive the most possible credit for correctly formed letters.** Do not give credit for the letter *a* that is written as the model. Score 0 points for a letter:

- written in cursive, out of order, or reversed (i.e., written backwards);

- that cannot be recognized out of context;

- written as a capital (uppercase) letter;

- that is the letter *a*;

- that does not meet the letter formation guidelines that follow.

Refer to the following guidelines and examples to determine the correct formation of each letter. Examples of scored Alphabet Writing responses follow.

For examinees in Grades PreK–K *only*, the Alphabet Writing total raw score is converted into a supplemental score. Transfer the Alphabet Writing total raw score to the Supplemental Score Conversion Worksheet and convert it to a decile. Transfer the decile to the space provided in the Summary Report.

For examinees in Grades 1–2, the Alphabet Writing score is *not* a supplemental score; rather, it is a raw score (maximum of 25) that is added to the other items in the subtest to calculate the Written Expression total raw score.

Alphabet Writing Scoring Rules

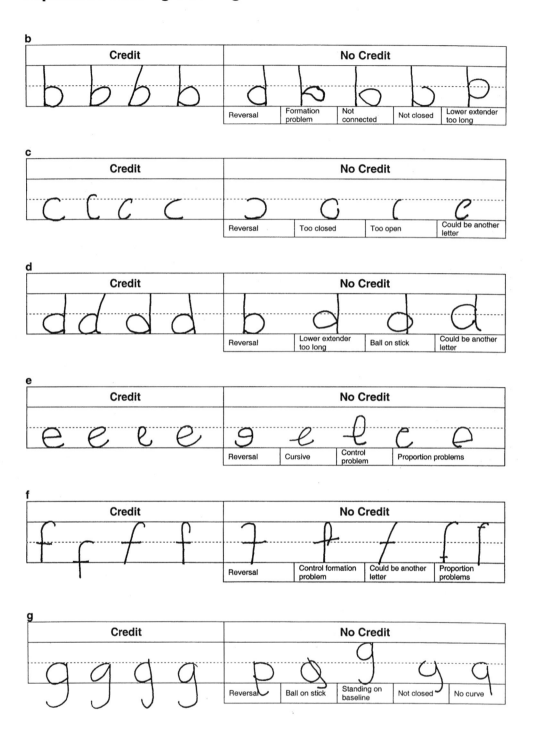

b

Credit	No Credit				
	Reversal	Formation problem	Not connected	Not closed	Lower extender too long

c

Credit	No Credit			
	Reversal	Too closed	Too open	Could be another letter

d

Credit	No Credit			
	Reversal	Lower extender too long	Ball on stick	Could be another letter

e

Credit	No Credit			
	Reversal	Cursive	Control problem	Proportion problems

f

Credit	No Credit			
	Reversal	Control formation problem	Could be another letter	Proportion problems

g

Credit	No Credit				
	Reversal	Ball on stick	Standing on baseline	Not closed	No curve

Alphabet Writing Scoring Rules

h

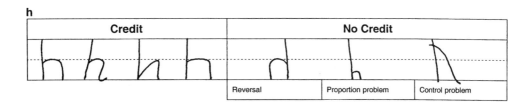

Credit	No Credit		
	Reversal	Proportion problem	Control problem

i

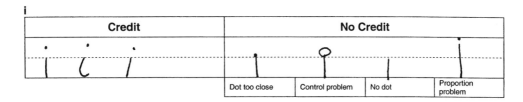

Credit	No Credit			
	Dot too close	Control problem	No dot	Proportion problem

j

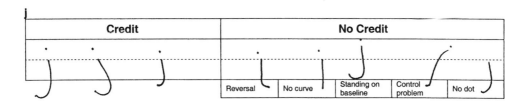

Credit	No Credit				
	Reversal	No curve	Standing on baseline	Control problem	No dot

k

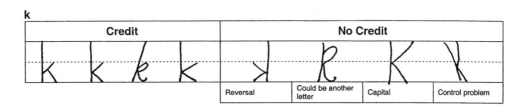

Credit	No Credit			
	Reversal	Could be another letter	Capital	Control problem

l

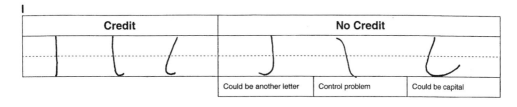

Credit	No Credit		
	Could be another letter	Control problem	Could be capital

m

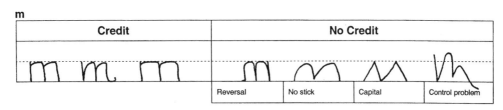

Credit	No Credit			
	Reversal	No stick	Capital	Control problem

Alphabet Writing Scoring Rules

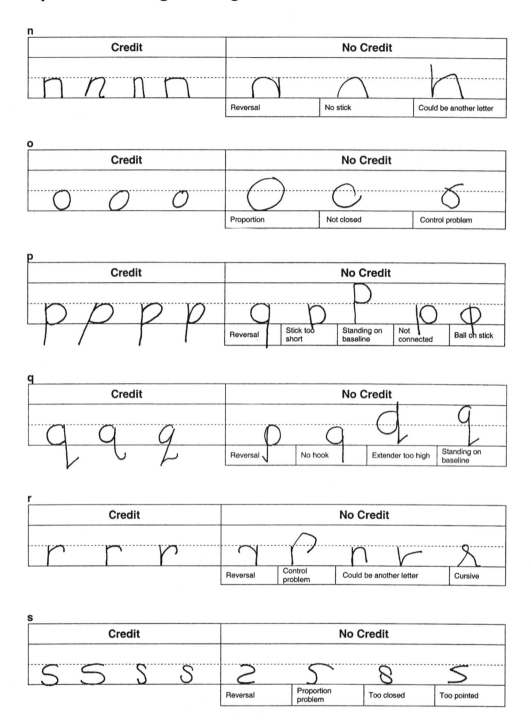

Alphabet Writing Scoring Rules

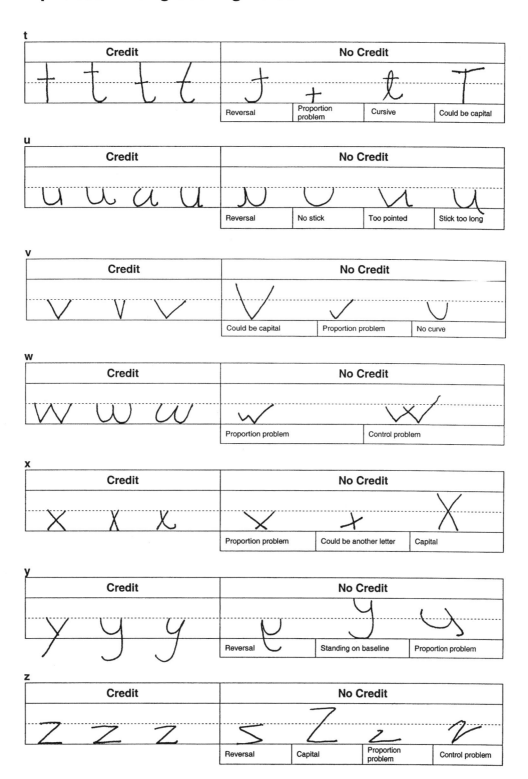

t

Credit	No Credit			
	Reversal	Proportion problem	Cursive	Could be capital

u

Credit	No Credit			
	Reversal	No stick	Too pointed	Stick too long

v

Credit	No Credit		
	Could be capital	Proportion problem	No curve

w

Credit	No Credit	
	Proportion problem	Control problem

x

Credit	No Credit		
	Proportion problem	Could be another letter	Capital

y

Credit	No Credit		
	Reversal	Standing on baseline	Proportion problem

z

Credit	No Credit			
	Reversal	Capital	Proportion problem	Control problem

A

Alphabet Writing Scoring Example With Record Form

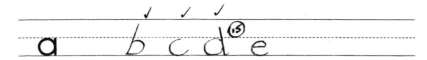

Written Expression					Grades PreK–6

Alphabet Writing ⏱ Record at 15 seconds	Score	Grades PreK–K	Grade 1	Grade 2
Grades PreK–2 ➡ 1. Letter written at 15 seconds _d_ Grades PreK–K STOP	max = 25	**3**	Item 1	Item 1

Grades PreK–K Total Raw Score

Alphabet Writing Scoring Example of Sequencing

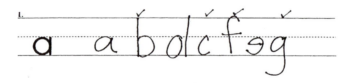

In the Alphabet Writing Scoring Example With Record Form, the examinee correctly formed the letter *d* at 15 seconds and received a score of 3 points. In the Alphabet Writing Scoring Example of Sequencing, the examinee did not receive credit for the letter *d* because it was incorrectly formed *and* out of sequence. The letter *c* restored the sequence and received credit. The letter *f* received credit because it was appropriately placed in sequence after the letter *c*. The letter *e* received no credit for being out of sequence and reversed. If the letter *e* had been correctly formed, either the letter *e* or *f* would receive credit, but not both. Sequence was restored with the letter *g*, which received credit.

Word Fluency

Written Expression Word Fluency measures written word fluency. Item 2 is administered to examinees in Grades 1–6 and Item 10 is administered to examinees in Grades 7–16. To score the items, follow these three steps:

1. To determine the acceptable responses, refer to the following:

    ■ An acceptable response includes any response that can be categorized as *round*. For example, *tire, donut, sun, clock,* and *globe* are acceptable responses.

    ■ Acceptable responses must be distinct items, not slight variations of an acceptable response. For example, *baseball, basketball,* and *volleyball* are distinct items and each is an acceptable response.

    ■ Different descriptions of the same object count as variations and are not considered acceptable responses. For example, *big ball, red ball,* and *round ball* would count as only one acceptable response (*big ball*).

2. After determining the acceptable responses, refer to the following to award points:

  ■ Score 2 points for a multi-syllable response (e.g., *circle, donut, cupcake, snowball, hockey puck, saucer,* and *apple*).

  ■ Score 1 point for a single-syllable response (e.g., *tire, sun, clock,* and *globe*).

3. The Word Fluency score (for Item 2 or Item 10) is the total number of points earned by the acceptable responses. Record the score in the space provided on the record form. Convert the Word Fluency score to a quartile-based score using Table B.6 (grade-based) or E.6 (age-based). Record the quartile in the space labeled Quartile on the record form and add it to the other item scores in the subtest to calculate the Written Expression total raw score. For further evaluative information, use the Word Fluency quartile as a supplemental score and transfer it to the Supplemental Score Conversion Worksheet and the Summary Report.

Sentences

Score each item 2, 1, or 0 points, depending on the quality of the response. Do not score the responses for punctuation errors that are not listed. Examples and explanations of scored responses for each item follow. These do not represent all of the possible responses. If you need to score a response that is not included as an example, determine the appropriate score by choosing the most comparable example.

Items 3–6 and 11–13:

2 points: Score 2 points for a response that is well-written, maintains the meaning of the original sentences, follows specific item directions, and contains *none* of the following error types:

  ■ missing capitalization of a proper noun or the first word of a sentence

  ■ missing punctuation at the end of a sentence

  ■ incorrect spelling of any word

For Items 5 and 6, or 11–13, a cause and effect relationship must be stated or implied to maintain sentence meaning and receive a score of 2 points.

1 point: Score 1 point for a response that includes *no more than one of each* error type listed under the 2-point response (e.g., one spelling error, one punctuation error, and one capitalization error). Score 1 point for a response that makes minor alterations to the meaning of the sentence. Information may be omitted in a 1-point response providing it does not change the meaning of the original sentences. Score 1 point for a run-on sentence, in the absence of other errors. For Items 3–6, score 1 point for a response that uses the word *and* to join the sentences.

0 points: Score 0 points for a response that is a sentence fragment (does not include both subject and verb) or significantly alters the meaning of the multiple sentences. Score 0 points for a response that includes *more than one* capitalization or spelling error. For Items 11–13, score 0 points for a response that uses the word *and* to join all of the sentences.

Item 3 | The frog is green. The frog jumps.

2 points:

The green frog jumps. • The frog that jumps is green.

1 point:

The green frog jumps	missing end punctuation
The frog is green and jumps. • The frog is green and can jump.	grammatically correct but not well-written
The frogs color is green and the frog jumps.	not well-written; the missing apostrophe is not counted as an error

0 points:

That frog is green so he jumps higher.	changes the meaning
The green frog jumps. He jumps high.	multiple sentences
green frogs jump	missing capitalization and end punctuation and changes meaning

Item 4: Mark has a sister named Ann. Ann is six years old.

2 points:

Mark has a sister named Ann who is six years old. • Mark has a six-year-old sister whose name is Ann. • Mark's six-year-old sister is named Ann.

1 point:

mark has a sister named Ann, and she is six years old.	missing capitalization and is not well-written (uses *and* to join the sentences)
Mark has a sister named Ann and she is six years old.	not well-written (uses *and* to join the sentences)

0 points:

Mark has a sister named Ann and is six years old. • Ann's brother is six. • Mark has a sister and she is six years old.	changes the meaning or changes the meaning by omitting information
Mark has a sister named Ann. She is six years old. • Mark has a sister named Ann Ann is six years old. • Mark has a sister named Ann she is six.	multiple sentences
Mark has a sitter named Ann and is six years old • Ann is Marks little sisters name is Ann she is six.	not well-written and has more than one error type

Item 5 or Item 11: The red team won the game. Petra kicked the winning goal.

2 points:

Petra kicked the winning goal for the
red team.　•　Petra kicked the goal that
won the game for the red team.　•　Petra
kicked the winning goal, so the red team
won the game.

1 point:

Peter kicks the winning goal so the red team won because she did.	not well-written and one spelling error
The red team won because Petra kicked a goal.	changes the meaning by omitting information
The red team won the game and Petra was the one that kicked the winning goal.	not well-written
The red team won the game and Petra kicked the winning goal.	uses *and* to join the sentences (for Item 5)

0 points:

The red team won a game so Petra kicked the winning goal.　•　The red team kicked the winning goal.	changes the meaning or changes the meaning by omitting information
Petra kicked the winning goal. She won the game.　•　The red team won the game. Petra kicked the winning goal.	multiple sentences
Petra kicked the winning goal for the red teem winning the game	not well written and contains two errors
petra kicked the wining goal, wich made her team win.	contains two error types and changes the meaning by omitting information
The red team won the game and Petra kicked the winning goal.	uses *and* to join the sentences (for Item 11)

Item 6 or Item 12: Antonio is a fast runner. Antonio is a strong student. Antonio won the Best Athlete award.

2 points:

Antonio is a fast runner and a strong student who won the Best Athlete award.   •   Because Antonio is a fast runner and strong student, he won the Best Athlete award.   •   Antonio, a fast runner and strong student, won the Best Athlete Award.   •   The Best Athlete Award went to Antonio, a fast runner and strong student.   •   Antonio, who is a fast runner and a strong student, won the Best Athlete award.

1 point:

Antonio is a fast runner and a strong student who won the best Athlete award.	missing capitalization
Antonio is a fast runner, a strong student, and won the Best Athlete award.	does not reflect cause and effect
Antonio won Best athlete award for his speed and academic ability.	changes the meaning by omitting information and missing capitalization
Antonio is a fast runner and a strong student and he won the Best Athlete award.	run-on sentence and uses *and* to join the sentences (Item 6)

0 points:

Antonio is a strong, fast runner who won the Best Athlete award. • Because Antonio is a fast runner and a student he won the best athlete award.	significantly changes the meaning by omitting information
Antonio can run fast and is strong. He won the Best Athlete award.	multiple sentences
Antonio is fast and Antonio is strong and he one the Best Athlite award.	not well-written and contains multiple errors
Antonio is a fast runner and a strong student and he won the Best Athlete award.	run-on sentence and uses *and* to join sentences (Item 12)

Item 13: Marci bought a new car. Her old car cost too much to repair. Marci's new car is smaller than her old car.

2 points:

Because Marci's old car cost too much to repair, she bought a smaller new car.	
• Marci bought a new car, which is smaller than her old car, because the old car cost too much to repair.	

1 point:

Because her old car was going to be too expensive to repare, Marci bought a new, smaller car.	one spelling error
Marci bought a new car because her old car was too much to repair, and her new car is smaller than her old car.	not well-written

0 points:

Marci's bought a new larger car as her old car was going to cost too much to repair. • Marci got a new car and it is smaller than her old car that she broke.	significantly alters the meaning
Because her old car was too expensive to repair, Marci bought a new one. It is smaller than the other one.	multiple sentences
Marci bought a new car becaus her old car cost to much to repair, and the new car is smaller.	not well-written and contains two spelling errors
marci bought a new car, her new car is smaller than her old car, she did this because it cost too much to repair her old car.	run-on sentence with one error

Items 7, 8, 14, and 15:

2 points: Score 2 points for a response that is well-written, reflects the essential information in the picture, follows specific item directions, and contains *none* of the following errors:

- ■ missing capitalization of a proper noun, the first word of a sentence, or the personal pronoun *I*

- ■ missing punctuation at the end of a sentence

- ■ two or more spelling errors (not including proper names)

1 point: Score 1 point for a response that includes *no more than one of each* of the errors listed for the 2-point response and does not follow specific item directions. For example, for Item 8 or 14, the word *however* may have been used incorrectly. For Item 15, a response may fail to summarize all of the information in the picture.

0 points: Score 0 points for a response that is a sentence fragment (does not include both subject and verb); does not accurately represent the information in the picture; includes *more than one* capitalization error; or uses the word *and* in response to Item 7.

Item 7: Picture of two girls playing. Combining ideas without using *and*.

2 points:

Kara is jumping rope while Kate puts together a puzzle. • While Alanna jumps rope, Mary works on a puzzle. • Laura enjoys jumping rope everyday, but Megan always wants to do a puzzle. • Nicole is jump roming, while Carli is doing a puzzle.

one spelling error in the last example does not disqualify it from a 2-point score

1 point:

Two girls are playing separately, but only one is jumping rope. • There are two girls playing in the room. • Ann is jumping wale Kate is doing a puzzle.

does not adequately describe the picture because information is omitted

0 points:

I like to jump rope. • She is jumping. • The girls are playing. • The girls are having recess. • Ann is playing with Jan. • They are playing.

omits significant information

Laura likes to jump rope in her purple tennis shoes. Jen likes to do puzzles on the sidewalk.

multiple sentences

One girl is jumping rope, and her friend is doing a puzzle. • That one is jumping and that one is playing.

uses the word *and* to join sentences

The girl skiped the other one pladed with a puzle. • That girl has a roap she is playing jump roap with it. • There are two girls one is doing a puzle also jump roping but their having fun. • Two people, one kid is playing puzzle, the other kid is jumping rope

multiple errors or run-on sentence with errors

Item 8 or Item 14: Jason's Robots. Use of *however*.

Note: To score 2 points, the sentence does not have to contain the name *Jason*. If there is no punctuation around the word *however*, the response should not be given a 2-point score. A comma used in place of a semi-colon does not count as a grammatical error.

2 points:

Jason has two robots, however, one is shiny and one is not. • Jason's yellow robot is taller, however, the gray one is wider.
• Jason prefers to play with the silver robot; however, the gold robot will do his homework.

1 point:

jason's shiny robot is his favorite, however he also likes his dirty one.	one capitalization error
However you look at it, Jason has two robots.	uses the word *however* but does not compare the two robots
Jason likes his old robot; however the new robot is a shiny robot.	not well-written

0 points:

I like the gold robot best; however, Jason likes the gray one best. • However one is dirty, the other one is clean. • However the robots are not the same.	does not adequately describe the picture.
One robot is tall. One robot is silver.	multiple sentences
The gold robot is shiny and the other one is dirty. • One of them are small. • There is a boy with two robots but one is different than the other one. • The boy is watching the robetes. • I like that robot altho this one is shinny. • Jason likes to show off his two robots.	does not use the word *however*
One of jason's robots is shiny but however one is not. • Two robots are standing with their owner however, he made them very diffrent. • There were two and however they have the same hands • However Jasons two robots have hands, feet, arms, eys, mouth, and a body.	not well-written and has one or more errors

Item 15: Music Warehouse

Note: To score 2 points, the response must summarize, in order, all of the information presented in the bar graph.

2 points:

The Music Warehouse sold more CDs than tapes in January; however, it sold more tapes than CDs in February due to the Tape Clearance sale.   •   February tape sales at the Music Warehouse were significantly higher than January because they were on sale, but CD sales showed the opposite trend.

1 point:

The Music Warehouse sold more CDs than tapes in january; however, it sold more tapes than CDs in February due to the Tape Clearance sale.	one capitalization error
Even though tape sales increased 4-fold from January, February CD sales fell from 300 to 200.	missing information alters the meaning of the graph

0 points:

People would rather have CDs than tapes unless the tapes are on sale. • The red lines mean that more people bought tapes when they were on sale. • In January, the people only bought few tapes; but in February the people bought more.	does not adequately summarize all of the information in the graph
The sale took place in February. Shoppers bought more tapes that month than CDs.	multiple sentences

Paragraph

The paragraph can be scored analytically using the scoring rubric on the record form or by following the guidelines for holistic scoring. To illustrate the evaluative information gained from each scoring procedure, the following section includes a description of the scoring criteria and provides sample responses that have been scored using the scoring rubric and holistic scoring. The sample responses were selected from the standardization sample to represent a variety of scores and score combinations. Each response includes an excerpt from the record form that displays the scores and a description of the reasoning that guided scoring. The scoring rubric has three evaluation categories: Mechanics, Organization, and Vocabulary.

Mechanics Subtotal

To determine the Mechanics subtotal, evaluate if the paragraph includes at least *seven words*. If there are six or fewer words, do *not* count spelling and punctuation errors; record 0 points in the spaces provided for the Spelling Errors Quartile (A) and the Punctuation Errors Quartile (B). If the paragraph contains at least seven words, refer to the following to count the number of spelling and punctuation errors.

A. Spelling Errors

- Incorrect use of a homonym (e.g., *there books*)
- If a word is misspelled in more than one way, count each misspelling as an error. If the same word is misspelled the same way, count the error only once, even if it occurs multiple times.
- Do not count incorrect spelling of proper names.

After counting the spelling errors, convert the number of errors to a quartile-based score using Table B.8 (grade-based) or E.8 (age-based) and record it in the space provided on the record form.

B. Punctuation Errors

- Missing capitalization of a proper noun, the first word of a sentence, or the personal pronoun *I*
- Missing or incorrect punctuation at the end of a sentence
- Missing apostrophe in the possessive (e.g., *Mikes chair*)
- Using an apostrophe in the plural form (e.g., *lots of thing's, new chair's*)
- Improper use of commas in the following cases:
    - Missing commas between items in a series
    - Missing commas in dates or addresses

If the same type of punctuation or capitalization error occurs more than once, count the error only once. For example, if the paragraph does not have end punctuation in any of the sentences, score one punctuation error. The exception is for comma errors. Count each instance of an omitted comma. After counting punctuation errors, convert the number of errors to a quartile-based score using Table B.9 (grade-based) or E.9 (age-based), and record it in the space provided on the record form.

C. Multiple Spellings

- **1 point:** Paragraph contains no multiple spellings for the same word.
- **0 points:** Paragraph contains multiple spellings for the same word.

The **Mechanics subtotal score** is the sum of the spelling and punctuation quartiles and the multiple spellings score. The maximum score is 9.

Organization Subtotal

To determine the Organization subtotal, assess the sentence structure, number of sentences, use of linking expressions, use of examples to illustrate or expand ideas, and the unity and logical order of the paragraph.

A. Sentence Structure: Determine if the paragraph contains complete sentences.

- **2 points:** Every sentence is a complete sentence.

- **1 point:** The majority of sentences are complete sentences rather than fragments or run-ons.

- **0 points:** The majority of sentences are fragments or run-on sentences.

B. Paragraph has at least two sentences: Count the number of identifiable sentences.

- **2 points:** Paragraph has three or more complete sentences that are not run-on sentences.

- **1 point:** Paragraph has at least two complete sentences. If a sentence is a fragment or run-on sentence, do not count it as a complete sentence.

- **0 points:** Paragraph has only one sentence or all of the sentences are fragments or run-on sentences.

C. Paragraph uses linking expressions: Determine if the paragraph uses linking expressions appropriately. Linking expressions include, but are not limited to, *and, because, also, instead, yet, but,* and *so.*

- **2 points:** Paragraph contains five or more linking expressions. At least three of the expressions must be a word other than the word *and.* If four of the five linking expressions are the word *and,* score 1 point.

- **1 point:** Paragraph contains three or four linking expressions. At least one of the expressions must be a word other than the word *and.*

- **0 points:** Paragraph contains two or fewer linking expressions, or if the only linking expression is the word *and.*

D. Paragraph has examples: Determine if the ideas are expanded or developed by the use of examples to illustrate one of the statements in the paragraph.

- **2 points:** Paragraph contains four or more examples.

- **1 point:** Paragraph contains two or three examples.

- **0 points:** Paragraph contains only one or no examples.

E. Paragraph is unified: Determine if the paragraph has any off-topic information.

- **1 point:** Paragraph does not contain any off-topic information.

- **0 points:** Paragraph contains any off-topic information.

F. The sentences follow in a logical order: Determine if the sentences in each paragraph follow a sequential or logical order.

- **1 point:** Sentences follow a sequential or logical order and the information is not contradictory. Score 1 point if the paragraph contains off-topic information but still follows a logical sequence.

- **0 points:** Sentences are not in sequential or logical order. Score 0 points if the information in the paragraph is contradictory.

The **Organization subtotal score** is the sum of the points earned in the six elements. The maximum score is 10.

Vocabulary Subtotal

To determine the Vocabulary subtotal, evaluate the word variety and style of the paragraph.

A. Words are varied: Determine the overall quality of the vocabulary. Begin by reading the paragraph to determine if the examinee used a variety of words. Are the words simplistic, general, and nonspecific? Look for redundancy, use of synonyms, and use of specific and sophisticated words. Do not penalize the examinee for spelling errors when assessing vocabulary because spelling errors are scored in Mechanics.

- **3 points:** Vocabulary is rich, expressive, mature, and the choice of words gives the paragraph depth and interest. *This score should be reserved for exceptional writing only.*

- **2 points:** Vocabulary is slightly above average and contains some vivid expressions. This type of writing has mixed specific and nonspecific words as well as some redundancy, but demonstrates more creativity than ordinary writing.

- **1 point:** Vocabulary is ordinary and average. There is some redundancy, yet some specific words are used.

- **0 points:** Vocabulary is predominately nonspecific, immature, redundant, and simplistic.

B. Any unusual expressions that capture interest: Determine if the writing is poor, ordinary, or average with little spark and few unusual adjectives or phrases or if the examinee used any unusual expression that captured your interest and added creativity to the paragraph.

- **2 points:** Paragraph contains two or more unusual expressions or word combinations that added creativity to the paragraph.

- **1 point:** Paragraph contains at least one unusual expression or word combination.

- **0 points:** Paragraph does not contain any unusual expressions or interesting words.

The **Vocabulary subtotal score** is the sum of the points earned in the two elements. The maximum score is 5.

Word Count

Word Count is an optional supplemental score that can be calculated for the paragraph. To calculate the Word Count total raw score, count the number of words written by the examinee. Do not include the words of the prompt in the score. Acronyms (e.g., P.E.) count as a single word. Transfer the Word Count total raw score to the Supplemental Score Conversion Worksheet and convert it to a quartile using Table B.7 (grade-based) or Table E.7 (age-based). Transfer the quartile to the Summary Report.

Using Holistic Scoring

The paragraph can also be scored using a holistic scoring system that is similar to the holistic scoring on the WIAT. Due to the wide variation in responses, the holistic scoring criteria were designed to be very general. To understand holistic scoring, refer to the holistic scoring criteria and the following sample responses. Paragraphs can be scored 0, 1, 2, 3, 4, 5, or 6 points. A paragraph that demonstrates a basic response to the prompt is probably enough to earn a low score; to achieve a higher score, the paragraph must include appropriate details that provide the reader with a fuller, richer knowledge of the examinee's opinions or ideas. Do not penalize if the paragraph contains incorrect spelling, punctuation, and mechanics. Refer to the following holistic scoring criteria for specific score information.

Written Expression
Paragraph

Holistic Scoring Criteria for Paragraphs

Score	Response
6 points	Well written and presents **clear, organized, and developed descriptions** of the topic. The ideas and details are **clarified and related through the use of effective transitions,** resulting in an overall sense of the subject. Effectiveness is enhanced through the use of vivid imagery.
5 points	Presents a **substantial amount of descriptive and varied detail** of the topic. The ideas and details are **clarified with several descriptions or through elaboration.** Features are related to each other or to the whole. Organization is weak but several ideas are clarified with added details, or organization is clear but the ideas are less well developed.
4 points	Generally well written and contains a **moderate amount of description** of the topic. The ideas or activities are related to each other or to the main idea. **Mentions a few activities** that the examinee enjoys and **adds clarifying descriptive details to each** activity. **Mentions several activities** but **clarifies only a few** of the activities **with several added details.** Organized around a **single activity** that the examinee enjoys **with a moderate amount of description** about the activity.
3 points	Contains a **limited amount of description** of the topic. The ideas or activities are related to each other or to the main idea. **Mentions a few activities** that the examinee enjoys and **clarifies many** of the activities **through additional descriptive details.** **Mentions several activities that are related to each other or to the whole,** some of which are **clarified through an additional detail.**
2 points	Contains a **minimal amount of description** of the topic with a **few activities** that the examinee enjoys and **clarifies through additional descriptive details of at least one of the activities.** **Mentions a single activity** and provides **a few descriptive details** about the activity.
1 point	Indicates that the examinee attempted to respond to the prompt with a coherent **listing of one or more general activities** (e.g., *play games, play outside*). There is **no attempt to further clarify with additional descriptive details.**
0 points	Demonstrates no relationship to the prompt.

A

Sample Responses

9. My favorite game is _in the hovs My mom game is baskball._

Paragraph

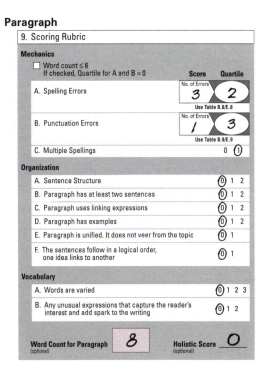

Mechanics Subtotal
max = 9

6

Organization Subtotal
max = 10

0

Vocabulary Subtotal
max = 5

0

max = 40

Grades 3–6
Total Raw Score

Grade 3: Bobby

Bobby veers off topic immediately. However, he produces the minimum number of words, so all of the scores for Mechanics can be calculated. The paragraph consists of a single phrase that is only vaguely coherent in presentation, and does not meet minimum standards for either the analytical or holistic scoring criteria.

9. On a rainy day, I like _to play with my ~~pu~~_
puppy.

Paragraph

9. Scoring Rubric

Mechanics

☑ Word count ≤ 6
If checked, Quartile for A and B = 0

	Score	Quartile
A. Spelling Errors (No. of Errors)	O	O
Use Table B.8/E.8		
B. Punctuation Errors (No. of Errors)	O	O
Use Table B.9/E.9		
C. Multiple Spellings	0 1	

Organization

A. Sentence Structure	⓪ 1 2
B. Paragraph has at least two sentences	⓪ 1 2
C. Paragraph uses linking expressions	⓪ 1 2
D. Paragraph has examples	⓪ 1 2
E. Paragraph is unified. It does not veer from the topic	⓪ 1
F. The sentences follow in a logical order, one idea links to another	⓪ 1

Vocabulary

A. Words are varied	⓪ 1 2 3
B. Any unusual expressions that capture the reader's interest and add spark to the writing	⓪ 1 2

Word Count for Paragraph (optional) **5**

Holistic Score (optional) **1**

Mechanics Subtotal
max = 9

1

Organization Subtotal
max = 10

O

Vocabulary Subtotal
max = 5

O

max = 40

**Grades 3–6
Total Raw Score**

Grade 3: Doug

This paragraph presents a single coherent idea with no additional development, and it receives a holistic score of 1 point. Compare this paragraph to the previous writing by Bobby which received a score of 0 points. The difference between these two (other than the inclusion of off-topic information in Bobby's response), is the level of coherence that makes Doug's paragraph a more acceptable response for a score of 1 point. Doug's paragraph represents the minimal level of information required for a holistic score of 1 point; significant additional detail is still necessary to elevate the holistic score to 2 points.

9. My favorite game is _bowing. My favorite food is pizza. My favorite show is rugrats. My favorite insterment is the drums. My favorite is a Cok-a cola. My favorite baseball team is the Cardinal's._

Paragraph

9. Scoring Rubric			
Mechanics			
☐ Word count ≤ 6			
If checked, Quartile for A and B = 0		Score	Quartile
A. Spelling Errors		No. of Errors **2**	**3**
		Use Table B.8/E.8	
B. Punctuation Errors		No. of Errors **3**	**2**
		Use Table B.9/E.9	
C. Multiple Spellings		0	①
Organization			
A. Sentence Structure		0 1	②
B. Paragraph has at least two sentences		0 1	②
C. Paragraph uses linking expressions		⓪ 1 2	
D. Paragraph has examples		⓪ 1 2	
E. Paragraph is unified. It does not veer from the topic		⓪ 1	
F. The sentences follow in a logical order, one idea links to another		⓪ 1	
Vocabulary			
A. Words are varied		0 ① 2 3	
B. Any unusual expressions that capture the reader's interest and add spark to the writing		⓪ 1 2	
Word Count for Paragraph (optional)	**30**	**Holistic Score** (optional)	**1**

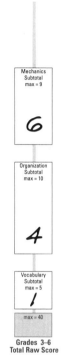

Mechanics Subtotal max = 9

6

Organization Subtotal max = 10

4

Vocabulary Subtotal max = 5

1

max = 40

Grades 3–6
Total Raw Score

Grade 4: Shane

After the completion of the initial sentence, this paragraph veers off-topic and becomes a fragmented list of other favorites. There is no use of linking expressions, no use of examples, and the paragraph contains off-topic information. It cannot be determined if the sentences follow a logical order because the entire paragraph is in list format. The wording is repetitive and simplistic and there are no unusual expressions. The response does not include a description of his favorite game; therefore, the holistic score is 1 point.

A

9. On a rainy day, I like ̲I̲ ̲l̲i̲k̲e̲ ̲t̲o̲ ̲p̲l̲a̲y̲ ̲~~b̲o̲r̲e̲d̲~~ ̲g̲a̲m̲e̲s̲.̲
   ̲I̲ ̲l̲i̲k̲e̲ ̲t̲o̲ ̲t̲a̲k̲ ̲o̲n̲ ̲t̲h̲e̲ ̲p̲h̲o̲n̲e̲.̲ ̲I̲ ̲l̲i̲k̲e̲ ̲t̲o̲ ̲c̲l̲e̲a̲n̲.̲
   ̲I̲ ̲l̲i̲k̲e̲ ̲t̲o̲ ̲p̲l̲a̲y̲ ̲c̲a̲r̲s̲ ̲w̲i̲t̲h̲ ̲m̲y̲ ̲b̲r̲o̲t̲h̲e̲r̲.̲ ̲I̲ ̲l̲i̲k̲e̲ ̲t̲o̲
   ̲t̲a̲k̲e̲ ̲n̲a̲p̲s̲.̲

(above "bord" is written in small letters above "bored")

Paragraph

9. Scoring Rubric		

Mechanics

☐ Word count ≤ 6
If checked, Quartile for A and B = 0 — **Score** — **Quartile**

	No. of Errors	
A. Spelling Errors	2	3
	Use Table B.8/E.8	
B. Punctuation Errors	0	4
	Use Table B.9/E.9	
C. Multiple Spellings	0	(1)

Organization

A. Sentence Structure	0 1 (2)
B. Paragraph has at least two sentences	0 1 (2)
C. Paragraph uses linking expressions	(0) 1 2
D. Paragraph has examples	(0) 1 2
E. Paragraph is unified. It does not veer from the topic	0 (1)
F. The sentences follow in a logical order, one idea links to another	(0) 1

Vocabulary

A. Words are varied	(0) 1 2 3
B. Any unusual expressions that capture the reader's interest and add spark to the writing	(0) 1 2

Word Count for Paragraph (optional)	30	Holistic Score (optional) ___1___

Mechanics
Subtotal
max = 9

8

Organization
Subtotal
max = 10

5

Vocabulary
Subtotal
max = 5

0

max = 40

Grades 3–6
Total Raw Score

Grade 3: June

June's paragraph is a list of things she likes to do on a rainy day. It is a simple, coherent list. Because no additional descriptive details are developed, this passage receives a holistic score of 1 point. However, because there are relatively few spelling and punctuation errors, June earns 8 of the possible 9 points for Mechanics.

A

9. On a rainy day, I like *to play outside. First First I get on my coat. Next I go outside. Then I jump around in the rain. Last, I go inside to get warm.*

Paragraph

9. Scoring Rubric

Mechanics

☐ Word count ≤ 6
If checked, Quartile for A and B = 0

	Score	Quartile
A. Spelling Errors	No. of Errors **O**	**④**
	Use Table B.8/E.8	
B. Punctuation Errors	No. of Errors **O**	**④**
	Use Table B.9/E.9	
C. Multiple Spellings	0	①

Organization

A. Sentence Structure	0	1	②
B. Paragraph has at least two sentences	0	1	②
C. Paragraph uses linking expressions	0	①	2
D. Paragraph has examples	⓪	1	2
E. Paragraph is unified. It does not veer from the topic	0	①	
F. The sentences follow in a logical order, one idea links to another	0	①	

Vocabulary

A. Words are varied	⓪	1	2	3
B. Any unusual expressions that capture the reader's interest and add spark to the writing	⓪	1	2	

Word Count for Paragraph (optional) **27**

Holistic Score (optional) **2**

Mechanics Subtotal max = 9

9

Organization Subtotal max = 10

7

Vocabulary Subtotal max = 5

O

max = 40

**Grades 3–6
Total Raw Score**

Grade 4: Sharon

This paragraph contains no spelling or punctuation errors, resulting in full credit for the Mechanics subtotal score. The linking expressions *first, next, then,* and *last,* contribute to the order of the paragraph by providing some continuity and sequence to the ideas. Sharon's paragraph has an example of playing outside in the sentence, *Then I jump around in the rain,* but is not sufficient to earn credit. Wording is limited and no unusual expressions are used. Had Sharon included more examples and provided greater detail, her holistic score would have been higher.

A

9. My favorite game is

> My favorite game is dodgeball. Dodgeball is for fast reflexed and good athlete people. Dodgeball is a wonderful sport. Dodgeball can keep you in shape. Dodgeball is very fun. Dodgeball is sometimes scary or even nerve wracking.

Paragraph

9. Scoring Rubric

Mechanics

☐ Word count ≤ 6
If checked, Quartile for A and B = 0

	Score	Quartile
A. Spelling Errors (No. of Errors: 1)	Use Table B.8/E.8	3
B. Punctuation Errors (No. of Errors: 1)	Use Table B.9/E.9	3
C. Multiple Spellings	0	①

Organization

	Score		
A. Sentence Structure	0	1	②
B. Paragraph has at least two sentences	0	1	②
C. Paragraph uses linking expressions	⓪	1	2
D. Paragraph has examples	⓪	1	2
E. Paragraph is unified. It does not veer from the topic	0	①	
F. The sentences follow in a logical order, one idea links to another	0	⓪	

Vocabulary

	Score			
A. Words are varied	0	①	2	3
B. Any unusual expressions that capture the reader's interest and add spark to the writing	0	①	2	

Word Count for Paragraph (optional): 33

Holistic Score (optional): 2

Mechanics Subtotal
max = 9

7

Organization Subtotal
max = 10

6

Vocabulary Subtotal
max = 5

2

max = 40

Grades 3–6
Total Raw Score

Grade 6: Tony

Compared to the previous example, the lack of linking expressions in this paragraph is apparent, and the passage seems fragmented and choppy. Without linking expressions, it is difficult to assess whether or not the paragraph has examples, because there may or may not be an implicit connection between the two sentences *Dodgeball is a wonderful sport* and *Dodgeball can keep you in shape*. The repetitive wording resulted in a score of 1 point for word variance; however, the unusual description of dodgeball as *scary or even nerve wracking*, received a score of 1 point for unusual expressions. A holistic score of 2 points reflects the lack of development of any of the details provided.

9. My favorite game is *volleyball. I like volleyball because I take classes from my gym teacher. Also because I think I am good at it. Volleyball is very easy for everyone. I think that everyone should give it a try.*

Paragraph

9. Scoring Rubric

Mechanics

☐ Word count ≤ 6
If checked, Quartile for A and B = 0

	Score	Quartile
A. Spelling Errors	No. of Errors **0**	**4**
		Use Table B.8/E.8
B. Punctuation Errors	No. of Errors **0**	**4**
		Use Table B.9/E.9
C. Multiple Spellings	0	①

Organization

A. Sentence Structure	0 ① 2
B. Paragraph has at least two sentences	0 1 ②
C. Paragraph uses linking expressions	0 ① 2
D. Paragraph has examples	0 ① 2
E. Paragraph is unified. It does not veer from the topic	0 ①
F. The sentences follow in a logical order, one idea links to another	0 ①

Vocabulary

A. Words are varied	0 ① 2 3
B. Any unusual expressions that capture the reader's interest and add spark to the writing	⓪ 1 2

Word Count for Paragraph (optional) **36**   **Holistic Score** (optional) **2**

Mechanics Subtotal max = 9 **9**

Organization Subtotal max = 10 **7**

Vocabulary Subtotal max = 5 **1**

max = 40

Grades 3–6 Total Raw Score

Grade 5: Sarah

In this paragraph, only some of the sentences are complete, resulting in partial credit for sentence structure. Word usage is repetitive and has little variation. Sarah presents volleyball as her favorite game and briefly mentions *where* she gets volleyball lessons (from the gym teacher), *why* she likes the game (because she is good at it), and her overall opinion about the game. The lack of detailed description contributes to the holistic score of 2 points.

9. My favorite game is _minopile. Minople is my favorite game. Minopile is just fun. ~~AA AA~~ I have minopile. We ~~po play~~ evay wicks. It is fun to play with. But I ~~nev~~ nevar win I ~~awqe awqe~~ awae 7uss I got minopile for crissm's I dot cewr if, I 7owers are win. I ~~coma~~ coma in sak't plac the uthar day._

Paragraph

9. Scoring Rubric

Mechanics

☐ Word count ≤ 6
If checked, Quartile for A and B = 0

	Score	Quartile
A. Spelling Errors	No. of Errors **13**	**O**
	Use Table B.8/E.8	
B. Punctuation Errors	No. of Errors **3**	**2**
	Use Table B.9/E.9	
C. Multiple Spellings	⓪ 1	

Organization

A. Sentence Structure	0 ① 2	
B. Paragraph has at least two sentences	0 1 ②	
C. Paragraph uses linking expressions	⓪ 1 2	
D. Paragraph has examples	0 1 ②	
E. Paragraph is unified. It does not veer from the topic	0 ①	
F. The sentences follow in a logical order, one idea links to another	0 ①	

Vocabulary

A. Words are varied	0 ① 2 3	
B. Any unusual expressions that capture the reader's interest and add spark to the writing	⓪ 1 2	

Word Count for Paragraph (optional) **51**   **Holistic Score** (optional) **2**

Mechanics Subtotal max = 9 — **2**

Organization Subtotal max = 10 — **7**

Vocabulary Subtotal max = 5 — **1**

max = 40

Grades 3–6 Total Raw Score

Grade 3: Marcus

Though this paragraph appears to provide more information than the previous paragraph (written by Sarah), it is repetitive and choppy and ultimately condenses to approximately the same number of original ideas. The spelling error of Monopoly is not counted because it is a proper name; however, it does affect the multiple spelling score since it is spelled in more than one way. Because the paragraph does not use complete sentences consistently, it does not earn full credit for sentence structure. No credit is given for linking expressions for the isolated use of the word *but*. Examples explain why the student enjoys the game. Though misspelled, the words used by the student display a basic level of variety, earning Marcus a score of 1 point.

9. My favorite game is *chines ob checkers checkers, because I always win t agents agenst agenst everyone. I have a Lucky color. It is blue. My favorite color is blue. Thats why my t why I alwe always win with blue, I love the color bla blue.*

Paragraph

9. Scoring Rubric			
Mechanics			
☐ Word count ≤ 6 If checked, Quartile for A and B = 0		**Score**	**Quartile**
A. Spelling Errors	No. of Errors **1**	**3**	
	Use Table B.8/E.8		
B. Punctuation Errors	No. of Errors **2**	**2**	
	Use Table B.9/E.9		
C. Multiple Spellings		0 (1)	
Organization			
A. Sentence Structure		0 1 (2)	
B. Paragraph has at least two sentences		0 1 (2)	
C. Paragraph uses linking expressions		(0) 1 2	
D. Paragraph has examples		0 (1) 2	
E. Paragraph is unified. It does not veer from the topic		0 (1)	
F. The sentences follow in a logical order, one idea links to another		0 (1)	
Vocabulary			
A. Words are varied		0 (1) 2 3	
B. Any unusual expressions that capture the reader's interest and add spark to the writing		(0) 1 2	
Word Count for Paragraph (optional) **33**		**Holistic Score** (optional) **3**	

Mechanics Subtotal max = 9

6

Organization Subtotal max = 10

7

Vocabulary Subtotal max = 5

1

max = 40

Grades 3–6 Total Raw Score

Grade 3: Darren

Darren writes about his favorite game, tells why it is his favorite (because he always wins), why he always wins (because he chooses blue), and why he chooses blue (because it is his favorite color). The ideas are loosely organized, but this paragraph represents the minimum amount of information required for a holistic score of 3 points.

9. My favorite game is _Telephone. On this game everything get mixed up. This is how you play. Gather up a bunch of people and sit in a circle. One person tells another person something and they have to get all the way to the last person. When the last person gets the telephone call they tell us what it is. It's real fun and goofy. This game makes everybody laugh._

Paragraph

9. Scoring Rubric		
Mechanics		
☐ Word count ≤ 6 If checked, Quartile for A and B = 0	**Score**	**Quartile**
A. Spelling Errors	*No. of Errors* 1	3
	Use Table B.8/E.8	
B. Punctuation Errors	*No. of Errors* 0	4
	Use Table B.9/E.9	
C. Multiple Spellings	0	①
Organization		
A. Sentence Structure	0 1	②
B. Paragraph has at least two sentences	0 1	②
C. Paragraph uses linking expressions	⓪ 1	2
D. Paragraph has examples	0 1	②
E. Paragraph is unified. It does not veer from the topic	0	①
F. The sentences follow in a logical order, one idea links to another	0	①
Vocabulary		
A. Words are varied	0 ① 2 3	
B. Any unusual expressions that capture the reader's interest and add spark to the writing	⓪ 1 2	

| Word Count for Paragraph (optional) | **66** | Holistic Score (optional) | **4** |

Mechanics Subtotal max = 9	**8**
Organization Subtotal max = 10	**8**
Vocabulary Subtotal max = 5	**1**
max = 40	

Grades 3–6
Total Raw Score

Grade 4: Katie

A moderate amount of description of the game Telephone (*This is how you play*), including reasons why it is enjoyable (*It's real fun and goofy*), earns this paragraph a holistic score of 4 points. Clarification of some of the critical details (e.g., *they have to get all the way to the last person*), and inclusion of why Katie chose this as her favorite game could have enhanced the holistic score. She only used *and* for her linking expressions, which affects the cohesiveness of the paragraph, and little word variance was demonstrated.

9. My favorite game is _Super smash Brothers is my favorite_
game because it has a lot of action. My
sister and I like to play it in are free
time. My favorit Charicter is Link.
My sisters favorit is jigglepuff. When
my mom Chatches us playing it She doesnt
alow us to play. The reson I like it is
because I like it's slow mosion. My
sister plays it more than I do. My aunt aunt
Wactches my sister play it. My sister likes
it more than me. When I play it I cant
stop.

Paragraph

9. Scoring Rubric

Mechanics

☐ Word count ≤ 6
If checked, Quartile for A and B = 0

	Score	Quartile
A. Spelling Errors	No. of Errors **8**	**0**
	Use Table B.8/E.8	
B. Punctuation Errors	No. of Errors **4**	**1**
	Use Table B.9/E.9	
C. Multiple Spellings	⓪ 1	

Organization

A. Sentence Structure	0 1 ②
B. Paragraph has at least two sentences	0 1 ②
C. Paragraph uses linking expressions	0 ① 2
D. Paragraph has examples	0 1 ②
E. Paragraph is unified. It does not veer from the topic	0 ①
F. The sentences follow in a logical order, one idea links to another	0 ①

Vocabulary

A. Words are varied	0 ① 2 3
B. Any unusual expressions that capture the reader's interest and add spark to the writing	⓪ 1 2

Word Count for Paragraph (optional) **90**   **Holistic Score** (optional) **4**

Mechanics
Subtotal
max = 9

1

Organization
Subtotal
max = 10

9

Vocabulary
Subtotal
max = 5

1

max = 40

Grades 3–6
Total Raw Score

Grade 3: Michael

This paragraph received a holistic score of 4 points because it is coherent, somewhat organized, and provides a moderate amount of description. Improvement in organization to enhance the flow of ideas in the passage would have reduced the fragmentation and would have increased the holistic score to 5 points.

9. My favorite game is _the exciting sport of basketball._
I like to play it with my friend, my family,
and even by myself. I love the intensity
I feel when I am losing. I also love the
excitement I feel when I win. I tik like
deffense better than offense, however, I am
a offensive than deffensive player. I like
the challenge of getting rebounds. I really like
playing when it is raining outside. It gives
me more of a challenge and keeps me cool.
I love basketball.

Paragraph

9. Scoring Rubric

Mechanics

☐ Word count ≤ 6
If checked, Quartile for A and B = 0

	No. of Errors	Score	Quartile
A. Spelling Errors	1	3	Use Table B.8/E.8
B. Punctuation Errors	0	4	Use Table B.9/E.9
C. Multiple Spellings		0	①

Organization

A. Sentence Structure	0 1 ②	
B. Paragraph has at least two sentences	0 1 ②	
C. Paragraph uses linking expressions	0 ① 2	
D. Paragraph has examples	0 1 ②	
E. Paragraph is unified. It does not veer from the topic	0 ①	
F. The sentences follow in a logical order, one idea links to another	0 ①	

Vocabulary

A. Words are varied	0 1 ② 3	
B. Any unusual expressions that capture the reader's interest and add spark to the writing	⓪ 1 2	

Word Count for Paragraph (optional): **83**

Holistic Score (optional): **4**

Mechanics Subtotal max = 9: **8**

Organization Subtotal max = 10: **9**

Vocabulary Subtotal max = 5: **2**

max = 40

Grades 3–6 Total Raw Score

Grade 6: Jason

Only one spelling error is recorded for the recurrent misspelling of the word *deffense/deffensive.* Jason's emotions were intensely conveyed with a detailed description, earning a holistic score of 4 points; however, the passage could have earned a score of 5 points if even one reason had been provided for his many likes and loves of the sport. Jason uses a variety of words, but his paragraph lacks adequate detail and description.

9. On a rainy day, I like _to play board games. You ~~can~~ do not know how much fun board games are. I could sit there for hours: playing scrable. Anther good game is ~~mop memon~~ monoply, I like being the car. The car helps me because It reminds me of my go cart. It also helps me because I always race down the borad and ~~Tet~~ beat every body else. My brother gets mad at me cause I brag. ~~Which~~ Wich brings me to another game Yatez. I'm really not that good at ~~Tet~~ it but I still like playing it cause you get to roll dice. Rolling dice make me think of las vegas and all the craps tables. Those are all fun games to play on a rainy day._

Paragraph

9. Scoring Rubric

Mechanics

☐ Word count ≤ 6
If checked, Quartile for A and B = 0

	Score	Quartile
A. Spelling Errors	No. of Errors **6**	**0**
	Use Table B.8/E.8	
B. Punctuation Errors	No. of Errors **4**	**1**
	Use Table B.9/E.9	
C. Multiple Spellings	**0** 1	

Organization

A. Sentence Structure	0 **1** 2	
B. Paragraph has at least two sentences	0 1 **2**	
C. Paragraph uses linking expressions	0 1 **2**	
D. Paragraph has examples	0 1 **2**	
E. Paragraph is unified. It does not veer from the topic	0 **1**	
F. The sentences follow in a logical order, one idea links to another	0 **1**	

Vocabulary

A. Words are varied	0 1 **2** 3	
B. Any unusual expressions that capture the reader's interest and add spark to the writing	0 1 **2**	

Word Count for Paragraph (optional) **119**   **Holistic Score** (optional) **5**

Mechanics Subtotal max = 9

1

Organization Subtotal max = 10

9

Vocabulary Subtotal max = 5

4

max = 40

Grades 3–6
Total Raw Score

Grade 6: Ricky

Not all the sentences in this passage are complete (*Wich brings me to another game . . .*), so Ricky did not earn full credit on sentence structure. Just as in the previous paragraph (Jason), Ricky conveys an enthusiasm for (in this case) board games; however, a significant improvement over the previous paragraph is the inclusion of reasons (e.g., *The car helps me because It reminds me of my go cart*). The paragraph provides one thing he likes to do on a rainy day (play board games) and then supplies examples of the board games, as well as examples of what is good about the game (*Rolling dice make me think of las vegas*). This comment also constituted an unusual expression thus contributing to a score of 2 points. The presentation of ideas was loosely organized; however, Ricky used development of ideas and details, earning the paragraph a holistic score of 5 points.

9. My favorite game is Twisted Metal III because you can team up with a friend and destroy the other monsters or people. My favorite player is a monster named Minian. Eeach player has a special weapon, Minions special is about five following missles and a freeze ball. There are other weapons you can pi.A pick up too. Some of them are, Rain missles, Homing missles, Fire missles, and power missles. My favorite missles are Homing missles because they follow you. You can also travel to other countries and fight. Like Hollywood, Tokyo, Egept and england, but thoes are only some of the places.

Paragraph

9. Scoring Rubric		
Mechanics		
☐ Word count ≤ 6 If checked, Quartile for A and B = 0	**Score**	**Quartile**
A. Spelling Errors	No. of Errors **4** Use Table B.8/E.8	**1**
B. Punctuation Errors	No. of Errors **2** Use Table B.9/E.9	**2**
C. Multiple Spellings	**⓪** 1	
Organization		
A. Sentence Structure	0 ① 2	
B. Paragraph has at least two sentences	0 1 ②	
C. Paragraph uses linking expressions	0 1 ②	
D. Paragraph has examples	0 1 ②	
E. Paragraph is unified. It does not veer from the topic	0 ①	
F. The sentences follow in a logical order, one idea links to another	0 ①	
Vocabulary		
A. Words are varied	0 1 ② 3	
B. Any unusual expressions that capture the reader's interest and add spark to the writing	⓪ 1 2	
Word Count for Paragraph (optional)	**98**	
Holistic Score (optional)	**5**	

Mechanics Subtotal max = 9 — **3**

Organization Subtotal max = 10 — **9**

Vocabulary Subtotal max = 5 — **2**

max = 40

Grades 3–6
Total Raw Score

Grade 5: Lee

This paragraph received a holistic score of 5 points for a fairly well-organized passage with substantial descriptive detail. Had Lee provided additional clarifying detail, such as an explanation of what type of game it was, and/or provided some reasons why Twisted Metal is the favored game, the holistic score would have increased to 6 points. Lee's paragraph includes several mechanical errors, and the sentence structure is weak, but the amount of information included in the paragraph is noteworthy.

9. My favorite game is *Monpoly. I like the pices and the money. We play it alot because it is our familys favorite game. When we play I like to win money and buy properti. When we play Mom makes toptaca with wip cream. I always have a good time except when my brother cheats. When I win I congratulate the losers and do my victory dance. That is my favorite game and some reasons why I like Monopoly.*

Paragraph

9. Scoring Rubric			
Mechanics			
☐ Word count ≤ 6 If checked, Quartile for A and B = 0		**Score**	**Quartile**
A. Spelling Errors	No. of Errors	7	O
		Use Table B.8/E.8	
B. Punctuation Errors	No. of Errors	1	3
		Use Table B.9/E.9	
C. Multiple Spellings		0	①
Organization			
A. Sentence Structure			0 1 ②
B. Paragraph has at least two sentences			0 1 ②
C. Paragraph uses linking expressions			0 1 ②
D. Paragraph has examples			0 1 ②
E. Paragraph is unified. It does not veer from the topic			0 ①
F. The sentences follow in a logical order, one idea links to another			0 ①
Vocabulary			
A. Words are varied			0 ① 2 3
B. Any unusual expressions that capture the reader's interest and add spark to the writing			0 ① 2

Word Count for Paragraph (optional)	74	Holistic Score (optional)	5

Mechanics Subtotal max = 9 — **4**

Organization Subtotal max = 10 — **10**

Vocabulary Subtotal max = 5 — **2**

max = 40

Grades 3–6 Total Raw Score

Grade 5: Jordan

This paragraph provides a substantial amount of descriptive detail about Monopoly in the form of related ideas presented in a loosely organized format. Jordan moves alternately between specific statements describing what he likes about the game (*the pices and the money*) and more general statements about his family and the events surrounding their playing. The description of his winning tradition (the victory dance) is vivid and constitutes an unusual expression.

9. My favorite game is _fencing. I enjoy fencing because you have to be very athletic. Another thing I injoy is that this sport is not about brut force. My parents are both fencers so that really helps me to practice. There are different types of fencing for sport; some of the different fencing types are, Saber, and epiee. Fencing for sport is much different than using sowrds for war. For one thing the sowrds are different. the f The fencing sowrds have rubber tips on the end and are longer and skinnier than normal sowrds. Also you have to keep a stance and if you don't the judges will disquallify you. Points are scored by lunging forward at your oppoment and hitting the chest and stomach area. In short fencing is a very fun sport._

Paragraph

9. Scoring Rubric		
Mechanics		
☐ Word count ≤ 6 If checked, Quartile for A and B = 0	**Score**	**Quartile**
A. Spelling Errors	No. of Errors **5**	**0**
	Use Table B.8/E.8	
B. Punctuation Errors	No. of Errors **0**	**4**
	Use Table B.9/E.9	
C. Multiple Spellings		(0) 1
Organization		
A. Sentence Structure		0 1 (2)
B. Paragraph has at least two sentences		0 1 (2)
C. Paragraph uses linking expressions		0 1 (2)
D. Paragraph has examples		0 1 (2)
E. Paragraph is unified. It does not veer from the topic		0 (1)
F. The sentences follow in a logical order, one idea links to another		0 (1)
Vocabulary		
A. Words are varied		0 1 (2) 3
B. Any unusual expressions that capture the reader's interest and add spark to the writing		0 (1) 2
Word Count for Paragraph (optional)	**129**	**Holistic Score** (optional) **6**

Mechanics Subtotal max = 9

4

Organization Subtotal max = 10

10

Vocabulary Subtotal max = 5

3

max = 40

Grades 3–6 Total Raw Score

Grade 5: Scott

Although lacking in the area of mechanics, this paragraph is well developed and well organized, and includes an unusual expression (*Lunging forward at your opponent*). Scott includes considerable detail with both general and specific statements.

Essay

The essay can be scored using the scoring rubric on the record form or by following the guidelines for holistic scoring. To illustrate the evaluative information gained from each scoring procedure, the following section includes a description of the scoring rules and provides sample responses that have been scored using the scoring rubric and holistic scoring. The sample responses were selected from the standardization sample to represent a variety of scores and score combinations. Each response includes an excerpt from the record form that displays the scores and a description of the reasoning that guided scoring. The scoring rubric has four evaluation categories: Mechanics, Organization, Theme Development, and Vocabulary.

Mechanics Subtotal

To determine the Mechanics subtotal, first count the words in the essay. The essay should contain at least *24 words*. If there are 23 or fewer words, do *not* count spelling and punctuation errors; record 0 points in the space provided for the Spelling Errors Quartile (A) and the Punctuation Errors Quartile (B). If the essay contains at least 24 words, refer to the following to count the number of spelling and punctuation errors.

A. Spelling Errors

- Incorrect use of a homonym (e.g., *there books*)

- If a word is misspelled in more than one way, count each misspelling as an error. If the same word is misspelled the same way, count the error only once, even if it occurs multiple times.

- Do not count incorrect spelling of proper names, commonly used abbreviations (e.g., *Mrs.*), or symbols.

After counting the spelling errors, convert the number of errors to a quartile-based score using Table B.11 (grade-based) or E.11 (age-based) and record it in the space provided on the record form.

B. Punctuation Errors

- Missing capitalization of a proper noun, the first word of a sentence, or the personal pronoun *I*

- Missing capitalization of academic or religious titles (e.g., *Professor Adams*); titles of rank, honor, or respect (e.g., *Dear Editor*); formal government bodies or agencies (e.g., *Texas State Senate*); or for *College, University,* or *High School* when used as part of a proper noun (e.g., *Washington College*)

- Missing capitalization for titles of books, magazines, or other published works

- Missing or incorrect punctuation at the end of a sentence

- Missing apostrophe in the possessive (e.g., *Mikes chair*)

- Using an apostrophe in the plural form (e.g., *lots of thing's; new chair's*)

- Improper use of commas in the following cases:

  - Missing commas between items in a series

  - Missing commas in dates, addresses, or after a greeting or closing in a letter

  - Missing commas before conjunctions, including *and, but, or, not, yet* when they join independent clauses

  - Missing commas that should separate expressions that introduce (e.g., *Finally, I would like . . .*) or interrupt (e.g., *We would be better without uniforms, unless you enjoy looking alike, because . . .*) the sentence

If the same type of punctuation or capitalization error occurs more than once, count the error only once. For example, if the essay does not have end punctuation in any of the sentences, score one punctuation error. The exception is for comma errors. Count each instance of an omitted comma. After counting the punctuation errors, convert the number of errors to a quartile using Table B.12 (grade-based) or E.12 (age-based) and record it in the space provided on the record form.

C. Multiple Spellings

- **1 point:** Essay contains no multiple spellings for the same word.

- **0 points:** Essay contains multiple spellings for the same word.

The **Mechanics subtotal score** is the sum of the spelling and punctuation quartiles and the multiple spelling score. The maximum score is 9.

Organization Subtotal

To determine the Organization subtotal, assess the sentence structure, use of topic sentences, correct sequencing of ideas, use of linking expressions, adherence to the requirement of a letter to the editor, inclusion of introductory and concluding sentences, and the examinee's ability to use organization to persuade.

A. Sentence Structure: Determine if the essay contains complete sentences.

- **4 points:** Every sentence is a complete sentence.

- **3 points:** Essay contains no more than one fragment or run-on sentence. If the essay is very brief (five sentences or fewer), do *not* give a 3-point score if there is one fragment or run-on sentence; score 2 points.

- **2 points:** Majority of the sentences are complete.

- **1 point:** Essay contains several fragments or run-on sentences and some complete sentences. If the essay contains more fragments and run-on sentences than complete sentences, or if there are as many fragments or run-on sentences as there are complete sentences, score 1 point.

- **0 points:** Majority of the sentences are fragments or run-on sentences.

B. Topic Sentence: Determine the number of paragraphs in the essay, and the number of paragraphs that have a topic sentence. A paragraph must contain at least two sentences. Do not consider a single sentence a paragraph, regardless of indentation. Each paragraph should contain a topic sentence. The topic sentence identifies the main idea and is usually the first sentence in a paragraph, but sometimes the topic sentence is at the end of the paragraph as a summary sentence.

- **2 points:** Every paragraph contains a topic sentence.

- **1 point:** Majority of the paragraphs contain a topic sentence. Score 1 point if the essay consists of only a single paragraph and it contains a topic sentence.

- **0 points:** None of the paragraphs contain a topic sentence.

C. Sequencing: Determine if the sentences in each paragraph follow a logical order.

- **3 points:** Sentences in each paragraph follow a logical order. Score 3 points if the essay has at least two paragraphs and the sentences follow a logical order.

- **2 points:** Sentences follow a logical order in half or more of the paragraphs. If the essay contains three paragraphs, at least two of the paragraphs must have sentences that follow a logical order.

- **1 point:** Sentences follow a logical order in less than half of the paragraphs. Score 1 point if the essay contains only one paragraph and the sentences follow a logical order, or if the essay contains only two paragraphs and only one of the paragraphs has a logical order of sentences.

- **0 points:** Sentences in every paragraph fail to follow a logical order.

D. Essay contains linking words or phrases: Determine if the essay used linking words or phrases to appropriately relate ideas to each other and to improve the transitions between paragraphs.

- **3 points:** Essay uses linking words and phrases to develop structure. Ideas can be organized to identify the pros and cons of an issue, to indicate a switch in direction, or to identify cause and effect. Examples of effective linking words or phrases include: *moreover, on the other hand, therefore, as a result,* and *conversely.*

- **2 points:** Essay correctly uses less complex linking words or phrases such as *although, whenever, as soon as, since, unless, first, last, more importantly, finally,* and *in conclusion.* The relationship between paragraphs is evident when more complex linking words or phrases are employed.

- **1 point:** Essay uses primarily simple linking words such as *but, between, if, because, then,* and *next.* Paragraphs utilizing simple linking words may read smoothly within paragraphs, but demonstrate poor transitions between paragraphs.

- **0 points:** Essay does not use linking words or the use was limited to the words *and, or, so,* and *also.* Paragraphs without linking words sound choppy and overly simplistic.

E. Essay is presented as a letter to the editor: Determine if the examinee followed the instructions to write a letter to the editor by including an opening greeting such as: *Dear Editor, To Whom It May Concern,* or another appropriate greeting.

- **2 points:** Essay appears as a letter with an opening greeting to an editor.

- **1 point:** Essay does not contain an opening greeting, but does mention the editor or a reference to the newspaper or it includes an appropriate closing. For example, *Please consider my opinion and publish this letter,* or *Sincerely yours,* (followed by the examinee's name).

- **0 points:** Essay does not use an opening greeting and does not mention the editor or being published in a newspaper.

F. Essay has introductory sentence or paragraph: Determine if the examinee introduces the topic of the essay in either an introductory sentence or a group of sentences that form an introductory paragraph. For example, *I feel that the requirement of gym class is unnecessary for several reasons,* introduces the examinee's position and launches the essay.

- **1 point:** Essay contains an introductory statement in the form of a sentence or paragraph.

- **0 points:** Essay does not contain an introductory statement.

G. Essay has a concluding sentence or paragraph: Determine if the essay has a concluding statement, which can appear as a sentence or an entire paragraph. A concluding sentence or paragraph should bring closure to the essay and reaffirm the examinee's argument. Concluding sentences or paragraphs are often introduced with transitional phrases such as: *in conclusion, in summary, finally,* and *lastly.*

- **1 point:** Essay has a conclusion in the form of a concluding sentence or paragraph.

- **0 points:** Essay does not contain a concluding sentence or paragraph.

H. Essay uses organization to persuade: Determine if the examinee uses organization and structure as a rhetorical device. Good writing uses organization to help build an argument by identifying pros and cons, discussing both sides of an issue, or by evaluating possible solutions to a problem. Some possible organizational structures are:

- The essay is set up in the form of a proposed solution(s) to a problem(s). For example, requiring uniforms may be offered as a solution to gang-related problems within a school; out-of-shape teens may be shown to benefit from mandatory physical education classes; or daylight saving time may be presented as a solution to certain economic problems. These problems and solutions may then be organized, for example, with the first paragraph introducing the problem(s), the subsequent paragraphs discussing the solution(s), and the final paragraph enabling the examinee to draw a conclusion or make a recommendation about how the stated problem(s) should be resolved.

- The essay is organized so that the first paragraph introduces the issue (e.g., *Should university students be provided free tuition by the state?*) and the examinee's position. Each of the subsequent paragraphs offers a different supporting argument, followed by a summary of the argument and a restating of the examinee's position in a concluding paragraph.

- The essay is organized so that the introductory paragraph introduces the issue, subsequent paragraphs discuss various positions regarding the issue, and, in the summary paragraph, the examinee states his or her position based on the arguments presented.

The previous examples demonstrate three types of acceptable organizational styles that examinees may use successfully to persuade the reader. Examinees may use other acceptable styles to organize the essay.

- **1 point:** Essay contains an organizational style that helps the examinee influence or persuade the reader.

- **0 points:** Essay does not contain a discernable organizational style. If the essay contains only one paragraph, score 0 points.

The **Organization subtotal score** is the sum of points earned in these eight elements. The maximum score is 17.

Theme Development Subtotal

Theme Development is evaluated by determining if the essay includes the required three supports, evidence to back up any supporting argument, on-topic information, and any counter arguments. The essay cannot be limited to merely answering a question.

A. Essay contains 3 supports for the position: Determine if the essay includes three supports or reasons for the examinee's position. Do not evaluate the supporting statement on the quality or the validity of the argument. To receive credit, the supporting statements should be on topic.

- **2 points:** Essay contains three supports for the position.

- **1 point:** Essay contains one or two supports for the position.

- **0 points:** Essay does not contain support for the position.

B. Essay contains evidence to back up the supporting argument: Determine if the essay includes evidence or examples that lend credibility to the supporting arguments. These can take the form of reliable facts or statistics, quotes from authorities, or compelling personal experience. To determine if the examinee utilizes evidence to support his or her position, consider the following question: *Tell me how you know?* If the question can be answered using the information provided in the essay, the examinee has provided adequate evidence for the position.

- **2 points:** Essay contains at least three statements of supporting evidence. Each argument does not require matching supporting evidence. For example, one of the required arguments could have two supporting statements.

- **1 point:** Essay contains one or two statements that provide support.

- **0 points:** Essay does not contain any supporting evidence or examples to back up the examinee's reasons for a particular position.

C. Essay contains only on-topic information or ideas: Determine if the essay focuses only on the topic and does not include irrelevant sentences that distract from the argument.

- **1 point:** All of the sentences are on topic and relevant to the argument.

- **0 points:** Essay contains any off-topic information or arguments.

D. Essay is not merely answering a question: Determine if the essay is an obvious response to a question. For example, when the examinee begins the letter with *Yes, I think PE should be required,* it is clear to the reader that a question has been posed and the examinee is merely responding.

- **1 point:** Essay is a persuasive argument for a position rather than an answer to a question.

- **0 points:** Examinee is responding to a question rather than declaring a position and supporting it with evidence.

E. Essay contains counter arguments: Determine if the examinee uses counter arguments to challenge a position or argument. To receive credit, the counter argument must be on topic.

- **2 points:** Essay contains one or more counter arguments that are on topic.

- **0 points:** Essay does not contain counter arguments.

The **Theme Development subtotal score** is the sum of points earned in these five elements. The maximum score is 8.

Vocabulary Subtotal

Vocabulary is evaluated by determining if the examinee's words are specific and varied, and if any unusual expressions were employed to capture the reader's interest and add spark to the writing.

A. Words are specific: Evaluate the vocabulary of the essay by determining the use of specific versus nonspecific words. When specific words are used, the examinee's message is clear and concise. Nonspecific writing can include ambiguous pronouns, the use of vague words or phrases, or over-generalization.

- **2 points:** Vocabulary is predominantly specific and descriptive of the examinee's ideas. *This score should be reserved for exceptional writing only.*

- **1 point:** Vocabulary is a mixture of specific and non-descriptive words.

- **0 points:** Vocabulary is vague and non-descriptive.

B. Words are varied: Determine the variety of the vocabulary by looking at the examinee's range of words. Good writing avoids redundancy, uses appropriate synonyms, and employs a sophisticated vocabulary.

- **3 points:** Vocabulary is rich, expressive, mature, and the choice of words gives the essay depth and interest. *This score should be reserved for exceptional writing only.*

- **2 points:** Vocabulary is above average and contains a few vivid expressions. This type of writing uses a mixture of specific words and some redundancy, but has more creative spark than ordinary writing.

- **1 point:** Vocabulary is ordinary and average. The essay contains some redundancy, yet a few specific words clarify meaning.

- **0 points:** The vocabulary is predominantly immature, redundant, and simplistic.

C. Any unusual expressions that capture the reader's interest: Determine if the examinee includes unusual or vivid words and phrases to capture the reader's interest and add spark to the writing.

- **2 points:** Essay contains two or more unusual expressions or word combinations that added appeal to the writing.

- **1 point:** Essay contains at least one unusual expression or word combination.

- **0 points:** Essay did not contain any unusual expressions or interesting words.

The **Vocabulary subtotal score** is the sum of points earned in these three elements. The maximum score is 7.

Word Count

Word Count is an optional supplemental score that can be calculated for the essay. To calculate the Word Count total raw score, count the number of words written by the examinee. Acronyms count as a single word. Transfer the Word Count total raw score to the Supplemental Score Conversion Worksheet and convert it to a quartile using Table B.10 (grade-based) or Table E.10 (age-based). Transfer the quartile to the Summary Report.

Using Holistic Scoring

The essay can also be scored using a holistic scoring system that is similar to the holistic scoring on the WIAT. Due to the wide variation in responses, the holistic scoring criteria were designed to be very general. To understand holistic scoring, refer to the holistic scoring criteria and the following sample responses. Essays can be scored 0, 1, 2, 3, 4, 5, or 6 points. An essay that demonstrates a basic response to the prompt is probably enough to earn a low score; however, to achieve a higher score, the essay must include appropriate details that provide the reader with a fuller, richer knowledge of the examinee's opinions or ideas. Do not penalize if the essay contains incorrect spelling, punctuation, and mechanics. Refer to the following holistic scoring criteria for specific score information.

Holistic Scoring Criteria for Essays

Score	Response
6 points	**Clearly states or implies a position** and supports it with a **substantial amount of evidence,** so that the essay presents a **cogent, persuasive argument** in favor of the position.
	Well-organized, fluent, vivid, and interesting. The essay shows a strong sense of audience and purpose and uses language effectively and efficiently to influence the reader.
	Does not contain illogical or irrelevant arguments, redundancy, or a verbal assault.
5 points	**States or implies a position** and supports it with a **substantial amount of evidence.**
	Although only **three supports are required,** the essay **may provide additional reasons.**
	Expands on each support or reason with **many clarifying details. The details are well developed and support the position.** Usually a paragraph will be dedicated to each reason and the surrounding details.
	Message is on topic, logical, well stated, and organized.
4 points	**States or implies a position** and supports it with **no fewer than three reasons,** and provides **clarifying detail for at least three of the reasons.** The detail is developed, with generally two or three sentences written for each reason.
	On topic and logical, and has few language problems but may have minor problems with unity or organization.
3 points	**States or implies a position** and supports it with **at least two reasons,** and provides **some clarifying detail** for at least two of the reasons.
	Provides **three or more specific reasons, but clarifies only one** of the reasons.
	Clarifying **details are generally one or two sentences** in length.
	On topic and logical, but may include language problems or poor organization.
2 points	**States or implies a position** and supports it with **at least one reason that is somewhat clarified by details.**
	Provides **several nonspecific or undeveloped reasons.**
	Provides a **few reasons, but only one reason is clarified** with additional detail.
	Provides a **number of reasons, some of which may be illogical, vague, redundant, or have language problems.**
1 point	**States or implies a position** and supports it with **enough details to determine that the response is on topic.**
	Contains **a persuasive tone, but no reasons** for a position **or only a vague, or illogical reason.**
	Contains **extraneous information** or **considerable repetition.**
	Organization, logic, or language control problems interfere with meaning and may confuse the reader.
0 points	Contains no relationship to the prompt. Attempt to persuade the reader is not noticeable.

A

Dear Editor,
    I think people should choose if they want to take P.P. but if they do they dress out and bring all things they must have to play in the gym. Also, I think they should bring a doctors excused if they have been absent for particular day or date. I think all students should be able to dress out unless they have a doctors excuse or note from mom or dad or gaurdian.

Grade 10: David

After stating his position, David's essay veers off topic. He discusses the procedure for reporting absences and dressing for gym class. This digression impacts both the Theme Development subtotal score and the holistic score. The holistic score also is significantly impacted by a failure to develop the essay topic.

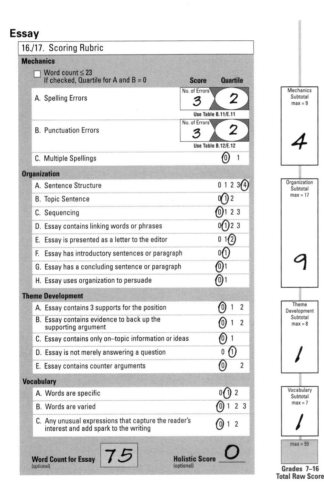

Essay

16./17. Scoring Rubric

Mechanics

☐ Word count ≤ 23
If checked, Quartile for A and B = 0

	Score	Quartile
A. Spelling Errors (No. of Errors)	3	2
Use Table B.11/E.11		
B. Punctuation Errors (No. of Errors)	3	2
Use Table B.12/E.12		
C. Multiple Spellings	⓪ 1	

Mechanics Subtotal max = 9: **4**

Organization

	Score
A. Sentence Structure	0 1 2 3 ④
B. Topic Sentence	0 ① 2
C. Sequencing	⓪ 1 2 3
D. Essay contains linking words or phrases	0 ① 2 3
E. Essay is presented as a letter to the editor	0 1 ②
F. Essay has introductory sentences or paragraph	0 ①
G. Essay has a concluding sentence or paragraph	⓪ 1
H. Essay uses organization to persuade	⓪ 1

Organization Subtotal max = 17: **9**

Theme Development

	Score
A. Essay contains 3 supports for the position	⓪ 1 2
B. Essay contains evidence to back up the supporting argument	⓪ 1 2
C. Essay contains only on–topic information or ideas	⓪ 1
D. Essay is not merely answering a question	0 ①
E. Essay contains counter arguments	⓪ 2

Theme Development Subtotal max = 8: **1**

Vocabulary

	Score
A. Words are specific	0 ① 2
B. Words are varied	⓪ 1 2 3
C. Any unusual expressions that capture the reader's interest and add spark to the writing	⓪ 1 2

Vocabulary Subtotal max = 7: **1**

max = 55

Word Count for Essay (optional): **75**

Holistic Score (optional): **0**

Grades 7–16 Total Raw Score

I am for gym because it's fun, and it's good for your body, and you get to do sports.

Essay

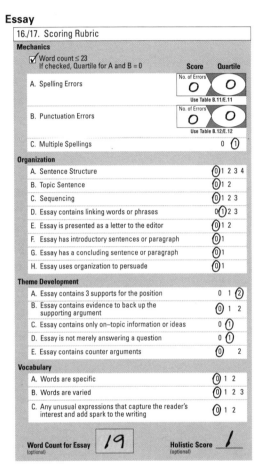

Grade 7: Laurie

Laurie wrote one sentence, providing only the minimum of information required for this category. This essay is similar to the next essay (written by Barry) in terms of the information provided. Because the essay contains fewer than 23 words, the quartile-based score for spelling errors and punctuation errors is 0 points, regardless of whether or not errors are present in the essay.

Dear Mr. Editor,

I think you should let us wear whatever we want to wear
because we have to wear the same thing over and over
day one last day; just let us wear what we want to for
five days only; let us just wear what we want for 5
days only and we'll wear uniforms rest of the year,

Sincerly,
B.

Essay

16./17. Scoring Rubric		
Mechanics		
☐ Word count ≤ 23	Score	Quartile
If checked, Quartile for A and B = 0		
A. Spelling Errors (No. of Errors)	1	3
Use Table B.11/E.11		
B. Punctuation Errors (No. of Errors)	0	4
Use Table B.12/E.12		
C. Multiple Spellings	0	1
Organization		
A. Sentence Structure	0 1 2 3 4	
B. Topic Sentence	0 1 2	
C. Sequencing	0 1 2 3	
D. Essay contains linking words or phrases	0 1 2 3	
E. Essay is presented as a letter to the editor	0 1 2	
F. Essay has introductory sentences or paragraph	0 1	
G. Essay has a concluding sentence or paragraph	0 1	
H. Essay uses organization to persuade	0 1	
Theme Development		
A. Essay contains 3 supports for the position	0 1 2	
B. Essay contains evidence to back up the supporting argument	0 1 2	
C. Essay contains only on–topic information or ideas	0 1	
D. Essay is not merely answering a question	0 1	
E. Essay contains counter arguments	0 2	
Vocabulary		
A. Words are specific	0 1 2	
B. Words are varied	0 1 2 3	
C. Any unusual expressions that capture the reader's interest and add spark to the writing	0 1 2	

Word Count for Essay (optional) 63

Holistic Score (optional) 1

Mechanics Subtotal max = 9 → 8

Organization Subtotal max = 17 → 4

Theme Development Subtotal max = 8 → 3

Vocabulary Subtotal max = 7 → 1

max = 55

Grades 7–16 Total Raw Score

Grade 7: Barry

This essay consists of a single run-on sentence, the topic sentence of the essay. Sequencing receives a score of 0 points due to problems with logic and the vagueness of the position. For example, Barry states that having a free choice on school clothes would be sufficient for only five days out of the year. This statement does not seem to support the position. The one-sentence structure of the essay also makes it impossible to evaluate Barry's use of an introductory sentence or paragraph (since there was no body of work to introduce). Similarly, use of a concluding paragraph and use of organization to persuade cannot be assessed. Barry supplies only one reason for the position against uniforms (i.e. *we have to wear the same thing over and over day one last day*) and no additional evidence to back up the supporting argument. This essay requires a more compelling argument, more detail, better organization, and much more development of ideas in order to increase the holistic score.

Dear Editor,

I think that P.E. should not be Required but made into an alictive class! No one should be forced to dress down and have other's make jokes about their phycal ablity. I think that if they do make it Required you should have it boy with boy and girls with girls. AnyHow that's just my opean

Thanx for your time

M.E.

Essay

16./17. Scoring Rubric		
Mechanics		
☐ Word count ≤ 23 / If checked, Quartile for A and B = 0	**Score**	**Quartile**
A. Spelling Errors	No. of Errors **5**	**1** / Use Table B.11/E.11
B. Punctuation Errors	No. of Errors **4**	**1** / Use Table B.12/E.12
C. Multiple Spellings	0 ①	
Organization		
A. Sentence Structure	0 1 2 3 ④	
B. Topic Sentence	0 ① 2	
C. Sequencing	0 ① 2 3	
D. Essay contains linking words or phrases	0 ① 2 3	
E. Essay is presented as a letter to the editor	0 1 ②	
F. Essay has introductory sentences or paragraph	0 ①	
G. Essay has a concluding sentence or paragraph	⓪ 1	
H. Essay uses organization to persuade	⓪ 1	
Theme Development		
A. Essay contains 3 supports for the position	0 ① 2	
B. Essay contains evidence to back up the supporting argument	⓪ 1 2	
C. Essay contains only on-topic information or ideas	0 ①	
D. Essay is not merely answering a question	⓪ 1	
E. Essay contains counter arguments	⓪ 2	
Vocabulary		
A. Words are specific	0 ① 2	
B. Words are varied	0 ① 2 3	
C. Any unusual expressions that capture the reader's interest and add spark to the writing	⓪ 1 2	
Word Count for Essay (optional) **64**	**Holistic Score** (optional) **1**	

Mechanics Subtotal max = 9 → **3**

Organization Subtotal max = 17 → **10**

Theme Development Subtotal max = 8 → **2**

Vocabulary Subtotal max = 7 → **2**

max = 55

Grades 7–16 Total Raw Score

Grade 9: Melanie

This essay consists of Melanie's position (*against* PE) and one supporting argument (i.e., people should not be exposed to ridicule). She provides additional information in the form of a suggestion to separate the boys from the girls, but gives no explanation how this information ties into the topic. Melanie supplies no evidence to support any of her statements. One poorly developed supporting argument earns this essay a holistic score of 1 point. In addition, several spelling and punctuation errors are reflected in the low Mechanics subtotal score.

A

Dear Mr. Editor,

　　My name is J.B., and I would like to report that I agree with a required physical education class. The class encourages students to keep their bodies in a fit and healthy condition. It also helps them discipline themselves into doing something hard. Another reason is it gives kids minds a rest and lets them exsert some of their excess energy. Finally, I personally enjoy the competition involved in the games played during physical education. I like P.E., and I hope it stay a required class.

Grade 8: JB

This essay, though short, is a well-organized list of ideas or supports for the position. No additional information is supplied in the form of examples, reasons, or evidence and this impacted the holistic score and the Theme Development subtotal score. This level of thought and organization presents information that, if developed into a complete essay, could be an appropriate introductory paragraph.

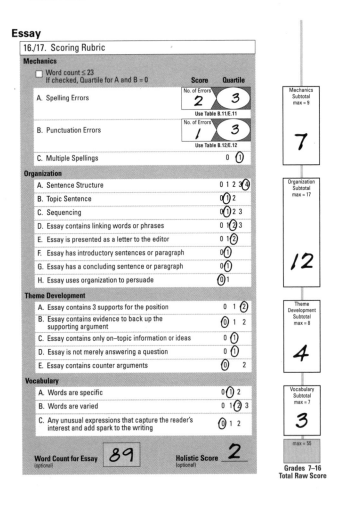

Essay

16./17. Scoring Rubric

Mechanics

☐ Word count ≤ 23
If checked, Quartile for A and B = 0

	Score	Quartile
A. Spelling Errors (No. of Errors)	**2**	**3**
Use Table B.11/E.11		
B. Punctuation Errors (No. of Errors)	**1**	**3**
Use Table B.12/E.12		
C. Multiple Spellings	0 ①	

Mechanics Subtotal max = 9 → **7**

Organization

A. Sentence Structure	0 1 2 3 ④
B. Topic Sentence	0 ① 2
C. Sequencing	0 ① 2 3
D. Essay contains linking words or phrases	0 1 ② 3
E. Essay is presented as a letter to the editor	0 1 ②
F. Essay has introductory sentences or paragraph	0 ①
G. Essay has a concluding sentence or paragraph	0 ①
H. Essay uses organization to persuade	⓪ 1

Organization Subtotal max = 17 → **12**

Theme Development

A. Essay contains 3 supports for the position	0 1 ②
B. Essay contains evidence to back up the supporting argument	⓪ 1 2
C. Essay contains only on–topic information or ideas	0 ①
D. Essay is not merely answering a question	0 ①
E. Essay contains counter arguments	⓪ 2

Theme Development Subtotal max = 8 → **4**

Vocabulary

A. Words are specific	0 ① 2
B. Words are varied	0 1 ② 3
C. Any unusual expressions that capture the reader's interest and add spark to the writing	⓪ 1 2

Vocabulary Subtotal max = 7 → **3**

max = 55

Grades 7–16 Total Raw Score

Word Count for Essay (optional) **89**

Holistic Score (optional) **2**

Dear Editor,

I am writing this letter to you ton the topic whether P.E. is a must for us kids.

I Believe it is because other than lunch break in some schools your sitting in a desk. Why deprive children of exercise? Isn't it a fact that one part of being a healthy person is plenty of exercise? What if the students live in a dangerous area where they can't go for a walk? All these I say because if we aliminate Physical Education and gym at just one school it would not be a showing an example to all children. They would simply see. that it's okay to sit in a desk at school, it must be okay to sit on a couch at home. I hope I have changed your opinion if you did not agree with me before read this.

Yours truly,
N. C.

Essay

16./17. Scoring Rubric

Mechanics

☐ Word count ≤ 23
If checked, Quartile for A and B = 0

	Score	Quartile
	No. of Errors	
A. Spelling Errors	3	② Use Table B.11/E.11
	No. of Errors	
B. Punctuation Errors	1	③ Use Table B.12/E.12
C. Multiple Spellings	0	①

Organization

A. Sentence Structure	0 1 2 3 ④
B. Topic Sentence	0 ① 2
C. Sequencing	0 ① 2 3
D. Essay contains linking words or phrases	0 ① 2 3
E. Essay is presented as a letter to the editor	0 1 ②
F. Essay has introductory sentences or paragraph	0 ①
G. Essay has a concluding sentence or paragraph	⓪ 1
H. Essay uses organization to persuade	⓪ 1

Theme Development

A. Essay contains 3 supports for the position	0 ① 2
B. Essay contains evidence to back up the supporting argument	0 ① 2
C. Essay contains only on–topic information or ideas	0 ①
D. Essay is not merely answering a question	0 ①
E. Essay contains counter arguments	⓪ 2

Vocabulary

A. Words are specific	0 ① 2
B. Words are varied	0 ① 2 3
C. Any unusual expressions that capture the reader's interest and add spark to the writing	0 ① 2

Word Count for Essay (optional) **147**

Holistic Score (optional) **2**

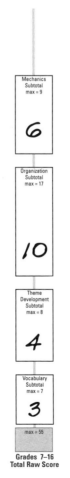

Mechanics
Subtotal
max = 9

6

Organization
Subtotal
max = 17

10

Theme
Development
Subtotal
max = 8

4

Vocabulary
Subtotal
max = 7

3

max = 55

Grades 7–16
Total Raw Score

Grade 7: Nathaniel

Nathaniel states his position (*for* mandatory PE) and continues by providing one complex support for the position (i.e., there may be no other opportunity for a student to get exercise). If more than one support had been presented and expanded upon, the holistic score would have been increased to 3 points.

A

Dear Eiditor

I think that DC schools should have children wear uniforms because, kids be talking about each other clothes, shoes, etc. There wouldn't be a problem if kids wear uniforms, but kids just don't seem to like to wear uniforms. I think kids will look better in uniforms because if they were uniforms, they will look like young men and women. The principal at my school tells kids to tuck in their shirts because, they don't look right with them out.

Sometimes, the teachers will tell girls do not wear jeans in the classroom. They only have to wear a top, shirt, and stalking caps. When the weather is cold outside, we had to dress according to the weather.

Your student,

J.W.

Grade 7: Jamal

Jamal's essay presents only two supports for the position (*for* uniforms): (1) kids talk about each other's clothes, and (2) kids will look better in uniforms. This essay is somewhat simplistic in presentation and includes off-topic information that distracts from the focus of the essay (*The principal at my school tells kids to tuck in their shirts*). The holistic score of 2 points reflects an essay that lacks evidence, development, and descriptive detail, and that has some problems with logic and language.

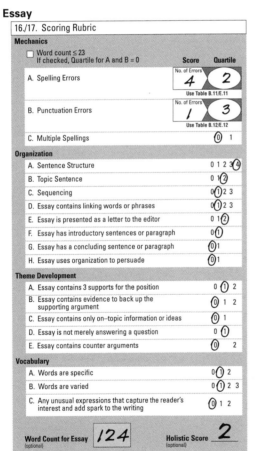

Essay

16./17. Scoring Rubric

Mechanics

☐ Word count ≤ 23
If checked, Quartile for A and B = 0 · Score · Quartile

A. Spelling Errors	No. of Errors **4**	**2**
	Use Table B.11/E.11	
B. Punctuation Errors	No. of Errors **1**	**3**
	Use Table B.12/E.12	
C. Multiple Spellings	⓪ 1	

Organization

A. Sentence Structure	0 1 2 3 ④
B. Topic Sentence	0 1 ②
C. Sequencing	0 ① 2 3
D. Essay contains linking words or phrases	0 ① 2 3
E. Essay is presented as a letter to the editor	0 1 ②
F. Essay has introductory sentences or paragraph	0 ①
G. Essay has a concluding sentence or paragraph	⓪ 1
H. Essay uses organization to persuade	⓪ 1

Theme Development

A. Essay contains 3 supports for the position	0 ① 2
B. Essay contains evidence to back up the supporting argument	⓪ 1 2
C. Essay contains only on–topic information or ideas	⓪ 1
D. Essay is not merely answering a question	0 ①
E. Essay contains counter arguments	⓪ 2

Vocabulary

A. Words are specific	0 ① 2
B. Words are varied	0 ① 2 3
C. Any unusual expressions that capture the reader's interest and add spark to the writing	⓪ 1 2

Word Count for Essay (optional) **124**   **Holistic Score** (optional) **2**

Mechanics Subtotal max = 9

5

Organization Subtotal max = 17

11

Theme Development Subtotal max = 8

2

Vocabulary Subtotal max = 7

2

max = 55

Grades 7–16 Total Raw Score

I think that uniforms should be worn in school. But I also think they should not. Why? Why do I think uniforms should be worn is because you should be in uniforms to represent your school well. And your school would have an good repotation. Why? I think uniforms should not be worn is because kids get tired of wearing uniforms. Especially after going to an elementary school. then going to an middle school with uniforms.

They could atleast have an Free Dress Day every Friday for the students. Also school spirit day. Fun Days or any sport or fun activities on certain days. So that the students will do more fun things & class work more often.

Essay

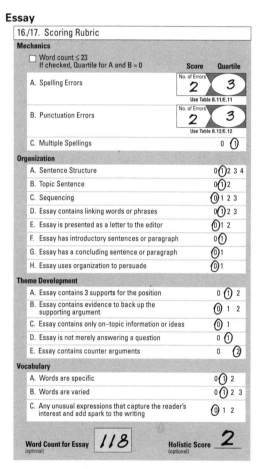

Grade 8: Audrey

This essay is an example of indecisiveness in choosing between opposing positions. Audrey fails to take a definitive stance regarding uniforms and awkwardly straddles the two positions. Poor sentence structure (*And your school would have an good repotation*) is coupled with confusing, off-topic suggestions (*They could at least have an Free Dress Day every Friday*). She attempts little development of detail, and presents only one supporting statement for each position, resulting in a holistic score of 2 points. At the same time, her spelling is moderately strong.

Dear editor of school paper,
I don't think that we should have to wear school uniforms because I don't think it would be very cool to see everybody wearing the same thing day after day. I think that it would be kind of boring. Everybody would be wearing the same kind of clothes, same colors 5 days out of the week and it would be boring or not fun to wear a dress or skirts for 5 days in a row and also having everybody look just like you and everybody else. Could you imagin everybody wearing the same thing everyday and everybody looking a like. I couldn't. Another reason why I think that we shouldn't have to wear uniforms is because somebody might get teased because they look stupid in it or it doesn't fit right, or it rips, or they just don't like it. If I had to go out and have a conversation on who would wear uniforms and who wouldn't, I bet you that majordy of the people or students would say no to uniforms. Personally, I think that they are okay, as long as you don't have to wear them every single day so tht everybody can tease or just sit there and stare at you and tell you how stupid you look in the clothes.

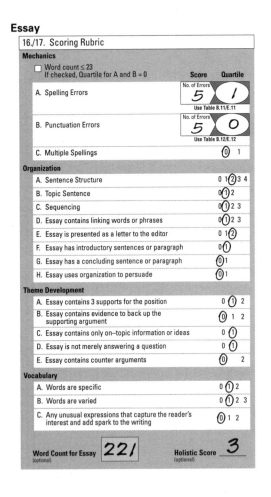

Essay

16./17. Scoring Rubric

Mechanics

☐ Word count ≤ 23
If checked, Quartile for A and B = 0

	Score	Quartile
A. Spelling Errors	No. of Errors 5 / 1	
	Use Table B.11/E.11	
B. Punctuation Errors	No. of Errors 5 / 0	
	Use Table B.12/E.12	
C. Multiple Spellings	0	1

Mechanics Subtotal max = 9 — **1**

Organization

A. Sentence Structure	0 1 2 3 4
B. Topic Sentence	0 1 2
C. Sequencing	0 1 2 3
D. Essay contains linking words or phrases	0 1 2 3
E. Essay is presented as a letter to the editor	0 1 2
F. Essay has introductory sentences or paragraph	0 1
G. Essay has a concluding sentence or paragraph	0 1
H. Essay uses organization to persuade	0 1

Organization Subtotal max = 17 — **8**

Theme Development

A. Essay contains 3 supports for the position	0 1 2
B. Essay contains evidence to back up the supporting argument	0 1 2
C. Essay contains only on–topic information or ideas	0 1
D. Essay is not merely answering a question	0 1
E. Essay contains counter arguments	0 2

Theme Development Subtotal max = 8 — **3**

Vocabulary

A. Words are specific	0 1 2
B. Words are varied	0 1 2 3
C. Any unusual expressions that capture the reader's interest and add spark to the writing	0 1 2

Vocabulary Subtotal max = 7 — **2**

Word Count for Essay (optional) **221**   **Holistic Score** (optional) **3**

max = 55

Grades 7–16
Total Raw Score

Grade 7: Janet

Two sentences in this essay are run-ons (those that begin *Everybody would be wearing . . .* and *Personally, I think . . .*), which impacts the Sentence Structure score. Janet relies very little on the use of linking words as an attempt at organization. Similarly, for a concluding sentence, she fails to reaffirm the position (*against* uniforms) in a final summary statement, and instead introduces a new position of tolerance for uniforms (*Personally, I think that they* [uniforms] *are okay*). Only two supports were stated: (1) it would be boring if everyone dressed alike, and (2) someone might get teased. The holistic score of 3 points reflects an essay that presents two supports and briefly develops each of them in a loosely organized format.

Dear Editor,

I am writing to you because I want to state my opinion about physical education in school. I don't think students should be required to take physical education because some students are not very athletic. For those who aren't athletic, they are forced into taking a gym class to fulfill requirements. Another reason is that some students are unable to participate in this class. Because they are required to take the class, they're conditions may get worse. Also, some parents don't like they're children to play sports or participate in the classes. Please publish this so that my opinion is heard. Thank You. R.L.

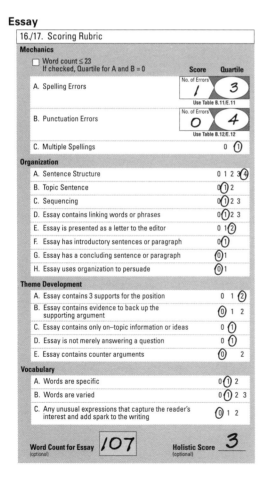

Essay

16./17. Scoring Rubric		Score	Quartile
Mechanics			
☐ Word count ≤ 23 — If checked, Quartile for A and B = 0			
A. Spelling Errors	No. of Errors *1* — Use Table B.11/E.11		**3**
B. Punctuation Errors	No. of Errors *0* — Use Table B.12/E.12		**4**
C. Multiple Spellings		0	①
Organization			
A. Sentence Structure		0 1 2 3 ④	
B. Topic Sentence		0 ① 2	
C. Sequencing		0 ① 2 3	
D. Essay contains linking words or phrases		0 ① 2 3	
E. Essay is presented as a letter to the editor		0 1 ②	
F. Essay has introductory sentences or paragraph		0 ①	
G. Essay has a concluding sentence or paragraph		⓪ 1	
H. Essay uses organization to persuade		⓪ 1	
Theme Development			
A. Essay contains 3 supports for the position		0 1 ②	
B. Essay contains evidence to back up the supporting argument		⓪ 1 2	
C. Essay contains only on-topic information or ideas		0 ①	
D. Essay is not merely answering a question		0 ①	
E. Essay contains counter arguments		⓪ 2	
Vocabulary			
A. Words are specific		0 ① 2	
B. Words are varied		0 ① 2 3	
C. Any unusual expressions that capture the reader's interest and add spark to the writing		⓪ 1 2	

| Word Count for Essay (optional) | **107** | Holistic Score (optional) | **3** |

Mechanics Subtotal max = 9 — **8**

Organization Subtotal max = 17 — **10**

Theme Development Subtotal max = 8 — **4**

Vocabulary Subtotal max = 7 — **2**

max = 55

Grades 7–16 Total Raw Score

Grade 9: Randy

This essay provides a position (*against* PE) and three supports: (1) some students are not athletic, (2) some students cannot participate, and (3) some parents don't want their children to participate. Two of the supports receive minimal expansion. The use of linking words is limited (*because, also, another reason*). The topic and introductory sentences overlap, but there is no concluding sentence or paragraph and no evidence is used to back up any of the supporting arguments. Due to the minimal expansion on arguments, the essay earns a holistic score of 3 points.

Dear Mr. Editor,

I believe physical education classes should be taken in school. You will find that there are many advantages when students persue this class.

First of all, I would like to say that students might want to participate. There is, no reason why this wouldn't be fun or enjoyable, either.

Second, the students need to stay in shape. Some students come home every day and watch T.V. This is not a healthy way of life. By participating in physical education this will get the students more active.

One last reason for physical education is because the student may want to persue an activity or sport later on in life. By taking "P.E." he/she will be more familiar with it and become better.

As you can see, physical education is very important, especially during the early years of your life. I'm sure the students would agree with me completely.

K.

Written Expression
Essay

A

Essay

16./17. Scoring Rubric		
Mechanics		

☐ Word count ≤ 23
If checked, Quartile for A and B = 0

	Score	**Quartile**
A. Spelling Errors	No. of Errors **1**	**3**
	Use Table B.11/E.11	
B. Punctuation Errors	No. of Errors **2**	**3**
	Use Table B.12/E.12	
C. Multiple Spellings	0	①

Organization

A. Sentence Structure	0 1 2 3 ④
B. Topic Sentence	0 1 ②
C. Sequencing	0 1 2 ③
D. Essay contains linking words or phrases	0 1 ② 3
E. Essay is presented as a letter to the editor	0 1 ②
F. Essay has introductory sentences or paragraph	0 ①
G. Essay has a concluding sentence or paragraph	0 ①
H. Essay uses organization to persuade	0 ①

Theme Development

A. Essay contains 3 supports for the position	0 1 ②
B. Essay contains evidence to back up the supporting argument	⓪ 1 2
C. Essay contains only on–topic information or ideas	0 ①
D. Essay is not merely answering a question	0 ①
E. Essay contains counter arguments	⓪ 2

Vocabulary

A. Words are specific	0 ① 2
B. Words are varied	0 1 ② 3
C. Any unusual expressions that capture the reader's interest and add spark to the writing	⓪ 1 2

Word Count for Essay (optional) **152**

Holistic Score (optional) **4**

Mechanics Subtotal max = 9 — **7**

Organization Subtotal max = 17 — **16**

Theme Development Subtotal max = 8 — **4**

Vocabulary Subtotal max = 7 — **3**

max = 55

Grades 7–16 Total Raw Score

Grade 8: Kareem

This essay states (or implies) the position (*for* PE), then presents three supports for the position. All of the supports are expanded upon and developed with additional clarifying detail. For example, *Some students come home everyday and watch TV.* However, no evidence is used to back up the supports. An example of evidence for the second paragraph might have included the following statement: "I never used to exercise, but since I started PE, I feel more active, so I know it will work for others." In short, evidence would be any information that can be added to the statements presented in the essay that would validate them as more than just opinion. The number of supports leads to a higher holistic score than Randy's essay, but the lack of evidence limits the score to 4 points.

Dear School Paper Editor,
I believe that school uniforms are not necessary. Teens need
the ability to express themselves through their clothing. It
could get expensive for parents and could give a dullness
to classrooms.
Everyteen needs to beable to express themselves. Some do it
through the clothes they wear. Many have their own style and
are happy with it.
Furthermore, parents would still have to buy regular clothes
along with one uniform per school day in a week. This could
get very costly.
In adition, most classroom would have all the same colors
giving it a dull, boring look. Students would get board and
not look around to wake themselves up during class.
All together, I believe students should be able to express
themselves the way they want to through the clothing they
wear. It would hold down the cost for parents and keep the
classrooms alive.
Thank you,
D. S.

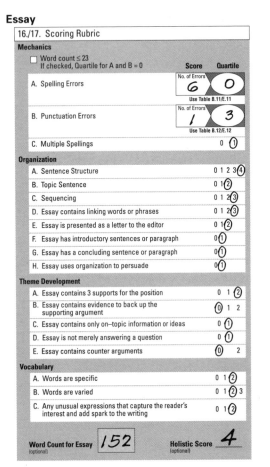

Essay

16./17. Scoring Rubric			
Mechanics		Score	Quartile
☐ Word count ≤ 23 If checked, Quartile for A and B = 0			
A. Spelling Errors (No. of Errors) Use Table B.11/E.11		6	0
B. Punctuation Errors (No. of Errors) Use Table B.12/E.12		1	3
C. Multiple Spellings		0	①
Organization			
A. Sentence Structure		0 1 2 3 ④	
B. Topic Sentence		0 1 ②	
C. Sequencing		0 1 2 ③	
D. Essay contains linking words or phrases		0 1 2 ③	
E. Essay is presented as a letter to the editor		0 1 ②	
F. Essay has introductory sentences or paragraph		0 ①	
G. Essay has a concluding sentence or paragraph		0 ①	
H. Essay uses organization to persuade		0 ①	
Theme Development			
A. Essay contains 3 supports for the position		0 1 ②	
B. Essay contains evidence to back up the supporting argument		⓪ 1 2	
C. Essay contains only on–topic information or ideas		0 ①	
D. Essay is not merely answering a question		0 ①	
E. Essay contains counter arguments		⓪ 2	
Vocabulary			
A. Words are specific		0 1 ②	
B. Words are varied		0 1 ② 3	
C. Any unusual expressions that capture the reader's interest and add spark to the writing		0 1 ②	

Word Count for Essay (optional) **152**   Holistic Score (optional) **4**

Mechanics Subtotal max = 9 **4**

Organization Subtotal max = 17 **17**

Theme Development Subtotal max = 8 **4**

Vocabulary Subtotal max = 7 **6**

max = 55

Grades 7–16 Total Raw Score

Grade 11: Danetra

Danetra's essay demonstrates an appropriately worded concluding paragraph. This well-written essay could have earned a holistic score of 5 points if she had strengthened her argument with examples and additional detail. Note that *everyteen* and *beable* count as spelling errors.

Dear School Editor,

    I do not believe school uniforms should be enforced in our school. Students have a right to wear what please them, and not what "looks better"

    First of all, clothing is a form of expression kids express themselves through their clothing style. Taking this away, is just as bad as taking away one's own personality.

    Also, uniforms cost money for the students, and the school. If the school uses it's money all on uniform in order to appear more civilized, the students suffer. The money should be primarily used to directly benefit students education, (i.e. on supplies, books etc).

    Lastly, as a student myself, I can say that no students would willingly appreciate wearing ugly uniforms on their own, and you want happy students don't you?

    Thank you for your time and I hope I've helped you open your eyes

           Sincerley,
           J.S.

Essay

16./17. Scoring Rubric

Mechanics

☐ Word count ≤ 23
If checked, Quartile for A and B = 0

	Score	Quartile
A. Spelling Errors (No. of Errors)	3	②
Use Table B.11/E.11		
B. Punctuation Errors (No. of Errors)	7	⓪
Use Table B.12/E.12		
C. Multiple Spellings	0	①

Mechanics Subtotal max = 9 → **3**

Organization

A. Sentence Structure	0 1 2 3 ④
B. Topic Sentence	0 1 ②
C. Sequencing	0 1 2 ③
D. Essay contains linking words or phrases	0 1 ② 3
E. Essay is presented as a letter to the editor	0 1 ②
F. Essay has introductory sentences or paragraph	0 ①
G. Essay has a concluding sentence or paragraph	⓪ 1
H. Essay uses organization to persuade	0 ①

Organization Subtotal max = 17 → **15**

Theme Development

A. Essay contains 3 supports for the position	0 1 ②
B. Essay contains evidence to back up the supporting argument	⓪ 1 2
C. Essay contains only on–topic information or ideas	0 ①
D. Essay is not merely answering a question	0 ①
E. Essay contains counter arguments	⓪ 2

Theme Development Subtotal max = 8 → **4**

Vocabulary

A. Words are specific	0 1 ②
B. Words are varied	0 1 ② 3
C. Any unusual expressions that capture the reader's interest and add spark to the writing	⓪ 1 2

Vocabulary Subtotal max = 7 → **4**

Word Count for Essay (optional) **146**

Holistic Score (optional) **4**

max = 55

Grades 7–16 Total Raw Score

Grade 9: Jill

This essay demonstrates an effective use of linking expressions to streamline an argument. Three supports are presented; however, no evidence is provided to back them up. To determine if the examinee utilizes evidence to support his or her position, consider the following question: *Tell me how you know?* If the question can be answered using the information provided in the essay, the examinee has provided adequate evidence for the position. For example, Jill states that, *Taking this* [form of expression] *away, is just as bad as taking away one's own personality,* but provides the reader with no additional evidence (such as a personal or indirect experience) that explains how she knows this information. It is possible to expand on a support for an argument without providing evidence for it, as Jill did in the third paragraph. The holistic score of 4 points indicates that although the essay is minimally developed, it is adequately organized.

A

Dear school Editor,

School uniforms are becoming more and more of a conflict. You have probly recieved numerous previous letters, but I have to say, I do detest wearing them. For so many years, it's difficult to stay updated in the real world. Sure you see the new styles on t.v. or in magazines, but then you go back to seeing everyone dressed the same way. That's like legal brain damage! Plus even if you do marraculously happen to be fashionably "in" getting your parents to buy whatever you need to not look like a hippy, is next to impossible. Uniforms wear designed to lower budgets on clothing, so when you ask "oh mom/dad, can I get this," the answer is usually no. Wearing uniforms could also put a damper on a kid's education. For example, say this kid is a bit poor, and his parents cant afford anything but a shirt, pants and shorts. If the child's shirt got dirty or torn to where he couldn't wear it then he couldn't go to school. In result, the kid would miss school untill his shirt was cleaned or he had the money to buy a new one.

Sincerly,

R.

Essay

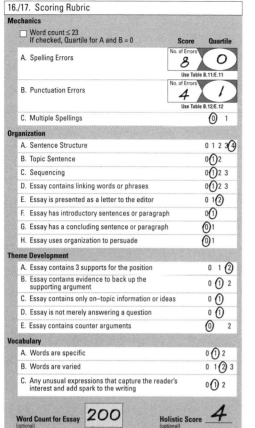

16./17. Scoring Rubric

Mechanics

☐ Word count ≤ 23
If checked, Quartile for A and B = 0

	Score	Quartile
A. Spelling Errors	No. of Errors **8**	⓪
	Use Table B.11/E.11	
B. Punctuation Errors	No. of Errors **4**	①
	Use Table B.12/E.12	
C. Multiple Spellings		⓪ 1

Organization

A. Sentence Structure	0 1 2 3 ④
B. Topic Sentence	0 ① 2
C. Sequencing	0 ① 2 3
D. Essay contains linking words or phrases	0 ① 2 3
E. Essay is presented as a letter to the editor	0 1 ②
F. Essay has introductory sentences or paragraph	0 ①
G. Essay has a concluding sentence or paragraph	⓪ 1
H. Essay uses organization to persuade	⓪ 1

Theme Development

A. Essay contains 3 supports for the position	0 1 ②
B. Essay contains evidence to back up the supporting argument	0 ① 2
C. Essay contains only on–topic information or ideas	0 ①
D. Essay is not merely answering a question	0 ①
E. Essay contains counter arguments	⓪ 2

Vocabulary

A. Words are specific	0 ① 2
B. Words are varied	0 1 ② 3
C. Any unusual expressions that capture the reader's interest and add spark to the writing	0 ① 2

Word Count for Essay (optional) **200**   **Holistic Score** (optional) **4**

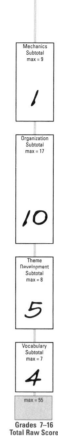

Mechanics
Subtotal
max = 9

1

Organization
Subtotal
max = 17

10

Theme
Development
Subtotal
max = 8

5

Vocabulary
Subtotal
max = 7

4

max = 55

**Grades 7–16
Total Raw Score**

Grade 7: Anna

The scores for topic sentence, sequencing, and use of organization to persuade are all impacted by the "one-paragraph" rule present for each of these items. The linking expressions used in the essay are limited to *plus, so, if,* and *for example,* which did little to impact the flow or transition of the essay. No summarizing paragraph concludes the essay, resulting in a score of 0 points for concluding paragraph. Although three supports are provided, evidence to back up the supports is minimal; in fact only one example is provided (*for example, say this kid is a bit poor . . .*). No counter arguments are provided. The words used are ordinary and nonspecific, earning a score of 1 point for specificity; however, the variety of words used earns a higher score of 2 points. Anna earns a score for unusual expressions for *legal brain damage.* The holistic score reflects the moderate amount of support and evidence presented.

A

Dear Editor,

I strongly believe that physical education or gym class must be taken in school. These help over-all health of students, keep their self-esteem up, and start good habits of exercising for the future leaders of America.

Having a P.E. or gym class help students to be physically fit. Studies prove that 80% f all kids who have the choice to not take P.E. classes, and take it, are not getting enough physical activity to keep their metabolism, et cetera in check. These students could be at risk for all types of disease because their bodies are not fighting off the predators.

When students are able to work out, et cetera in a gym class, they have a higher self-esteem. Some kids are a bit chunky and have a bad self-image, but if they can run some, or have that physical activity, then they aren't as likely to have that bad self-image. P.E. classes also give students a chance to be exposed to sports and may find something they are good at and enjoy, and this always helps kids feel good about themselves.

Exercising at a young age starts a good foundation for the future. 55% of adults do not get near enough exercise and starting anything at a young age will institute that for the future. Having P.E. classes gets....(J. did not finish — she had much more to write)

Grade 11: Judy

Judy presents a well-written essay that earns a holistic score of 5 points for presenting multiple arguments. The essay is very scientifically presented—a fact that indirectly contributes to the essay not receiving a full holistic score. Though apparently accurate, the essay lacks personality and is not presented in a vivid or persuasive tone. The lack of a conclusion (due to lack of time) did not impact the holistic score.

Essay

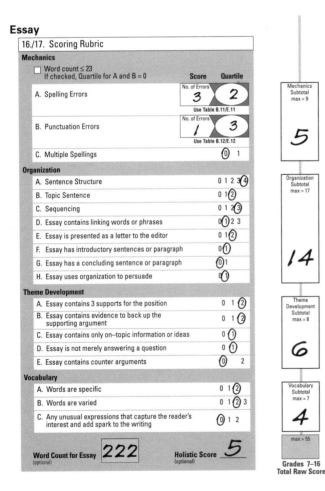

16./17. Scoring Rubric

Mechanics

	Score	Quartile
Word count ≤ 23 — If checked, Quartile for A and B = 0		
A. Spelling Errors (No. of Errors)	3	2 — Use Table B.11/E.11
B. Punctuation Errors (No. of Errors)	1	3 — Use Table B.12/E.12
C. Multiple Spellings	(0) 1	

Mechanics Subtotal max = 9 → **5**

Organization

A. Sentence Structure	0 1 2 3 (4)
B. Topic Sentence	0 1 (2)
C. Sequencing	0 1 2 (3)
D. Essay contains linking words or phrases	0 (1) 2 3
E. Essay is presented as a letter to the editor	0 1 (2)
F. Essay has introductory sentences or paragraph	0 (1)
G. Essay has a concluding sentence or paragraph	(0) 1
H. Essay uses organization to persuade	0 (1)

Organization Subtotal max = 17 → **14**

Theme Development

A. Essay contains 3 supports for the position	0 1 (2)
B. Essay contains evidence to back up the supporting argument	0 1 (2)
C. Essay contains only on–topic information or ideas	0 (1)
D. Essay is not merely answering a question	0 (1)
E. Essay contains counter arguments	(0) 2

Theme Development Subtotal max = 8 → **6**

Vocabulary

A. Words are specific	0 1 (2)
B. Words are varied	0 1 (2) 3
C. Any unusual expressions that capture the reader's interest and add spark to the writing	(0) 1 2

Vocabulary Subtotal max = 7 → **4**

Word Count for Essay (optional): **222**   Holistic Score (optional): **5**

max = 55

Grades 7–16 Total Raw Score

Dear Editor,

Physical Education (PE) or gym classes should definitely be taken in school. Young people need to know the importance of being physically fit. If school doesn't help jump start a young person's thoughts of the importance of PE, where else would he or she receive the knowledge? PE helps a person develop the skill of working together with peers and with an "adult or boss". Team sports such as basketball, baseball, soccer, etc. help children realize the importance of working and cooperating with each other. This is a skill that is used throughout the remaining years of school and can usually be very useful to his or her earn career. When a young person is "forced" to exercise everyday for an hour, he or she is not as lethargic or bovine as he or she would be if he or she sat in a desk all day at school, ate lunch, went home for an after school snack, did homework, ate dinner, and finally went to bed. This is important for health reasons. A third reason for the support of PE or gym classes in school is that a person doesn't feel so bored and trapped at school. The person is able to talk an hour out of the day to talk to friends and run around. It's fun!

Sincerely,
S.

Written Expression
Essay

Essay

16./17. Scoring Rubric

Mechanics

☐ Word count ≤ 23
If checked, Quartile for A and B = 0

	Score	Quartile
A. Spelling Errors	No. of Errors **2**	**3**
	Use Table B.11/E.11	
B. Punctuation Errors	No. of Errors **3**	**2**
	Use Table B.12/E.12	
C. Multiple Spellings	⓪ 1	

Organization

A. Sentence Structure	0 1 2 3 ④
B. Topic Sentence	0 ① 2
C. Sequencing	0 ① 2 3
D. Essay contains linking words or phrases	0 1 ② 3
E. Essay is presented as a letter to the editor	0 1 ②
F. Essay has introductory sentences or paragraph	0 ①
G. Essay has a concluding sentence or paragraph	⓪ 1
H. Essay uses organization to persuade	⓪ 1

Theme Development

A. Essay contains 3 supports for the position	0 1 ②
B. Essay contains evidence to back up the supporting argument	0 1 ②
C. Essay contains only on–topic information or ideas	0 ①
D. Essay is not merely answering a question	0 ①
E. Essay contains counter arguments	⓪ 2

Vocabulary

A. Words are specific	0 1 ②
B. Words are varied	0 1 ② 3
C. Any unusual expressions that capture the reader's interest and add spark to the writing	⓪ 1 2

Word Count for Essay (optional) | **222**

Holistic Score (optional) | **5**

Mechanics Subtotal max = 9 — **5**

Organization Subtotal max = 17 — **11**

Theme Development Subtotal max = 8 — **6**

Vocabulary Subtotal max = 7 — **4**

max = 55

Grades 7–16 Total Raw Score

Grade 11: Seth

Although presented as a single paragraph, this essay meets all the criteria for a holistic score of 5 points. The position is stated and evidence is provided to support it (*Team sports such as basketball, baseball, soccer, etc. help children realize the importance of working and cooperating with each other*). A clearer organization of the ideas (e.g., using terms such as *first, second, most importantly*), with a strong conclusion and separate paragraphs, would have easily enhanced this essay to a holistic score of 6 points.

Dear Editor,

Recently, many students have argued wether the school uniforms required is a good idea or a bad idea. This is why I want to present my important opinion. I think it is a good idea for uniforms to be required. Being equal, represent a school, and uniforms being cheaper are my reason for my opinion

To begin with, being considered equal is an important thing we should respect. While I lived in Madero, Tamps., I experienced being treated the same as all of the students, since I wore a uniform. In that school the social status of ~~race~~ or race didn't matter during the school days. Many kids think that somebody is the best friend just because he is dressed up in the coolest Polo shirt and baggy pants, wich is wrong. With the uniforms, that opinion will be forgotten and every will cositer each other equal.

Secondly, the students could represent an independent school. In my school, the colors blue ~~shirts~~ and golden yellow are color symbols that represent my school. For that reason we are dressed in blue shirts and kuki pants. I'm sure that other school would be honored student would wear uniforms colored the same colors that represent that school.

Last but not least, the uniforms will be easier to buy being low priced. Have you experienced an incredible cost for some blue jeans. The cost of the uniforms will be priced lower that those regular blue jeans. I've learned this fact since two brothers and I go to the same school. This is hard for my mom since she has to spent alot on clothes. But now she doesn't worry about how much the uniforms cost, since they are cheap.

This topic should be shared for everyone so the could present their opinion. My strong opion that agress with wearing uniforms should be tought of.

Sincerely

M.S.

A

Essay

16./17. Scoring Rubric

Mechanics

☐ Word count ≤ 23
If checked, Quartile for A and B = 0

		Score	Quartile
A. Spelling Errors	No. of Errors	14	0
	Use Table B.11/E.11		
B. Punctuation Errors	No. of Errors	4	1
	Use Table B.12/E.12		
C. Multiple Spellings		⓪ 1	

Organization

A. Sentence Structure	0 1 2 3 ④
B. Topic Sentence	0 1 ②
C. Sequencing	0 1 2 ③
D. Essay contains linking words or phrases	0 1 2 ③
E. Essay is presented as a letter to the editor	0 1 ②
F. Essay has introductory sentences or paragraph	0 ①
G. Essay has a concluding sentence or paragraph	0 ①
H. Essay uses organization to persuade	0 ①

Theme Development

A. Essay contains 3 supports for the position	0 1 ②
B. Essay contains evidence to back up the supporting argument	0 1 ②
C. Essay contains only on–topic information or ideas	0 ①
D. Essay is not merely answering a question	0 ①
E. Essay contains counter arguments	⓪ 2

Vocabulary

A. Words are specific	0 1 ②
B. Words are varied	0 1 2 ③
C. Any unusual expressions that capture the reader's interest and add spark to the writing	0 ① 2

| Word Count for Essay (optional) | 311 | Holistic Score (optional) | 6 |

Mechanics
Subtotal
max = 9

1

Organization
Subtotal
max = 17

17

Theme
Development
Subtotal
max = 8

6

Vocabulary
Subtotal
max = 7

6

max = 55

Grades 7–16
Total Raw Score

Grade 7: Marla

Marla's awkward wording, though infrequent, interferes with meaning in some places (*Being equal, represent a school . . .* and *Secondly, the students could represent an independent school*). However, this does not impact the high holistic score or perfect Organization subtotal score.

Dear Editor,

I am writing to voice my opinion on whether or not gym classes must be taken in school. I personally feel that physical education classes are a vital part of developing students.

First of all, it seems that with the new computer age, students have began to shy away from physical activity at home. Therefore, I feel that this class could be used to compensate for the absence at home. These classes will also help to maintain overall wellness in the students. For example, exercise increases your heart rate, therefore strenghting you heart, as well as other body systems. This will also help to burn calories, and tone muscle. Last, I feel that physical education classes will teach students the importance of exercise and a proper diet. If they can be taught correct lifestyles in class then hopefully they will take it home with them. With the increase in heart related deaths, the key to a decline in these untimely deaths is preventive care during the early years.

Contrary to many people's beliefs, I feel that physical education classes play an essential role in students wellbeing. Therefore, I feel that these classes should be mandated.

Written Expression
Essay

Essay

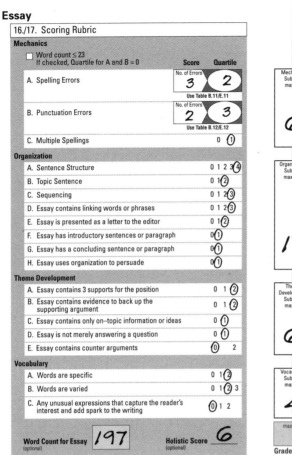

16./17. Scoring Rubric		
Mechanics		
☐ Word count ≤ 23 — If checked, Quartile for A and B = 0	**Score**	**Quartile**
A. Spelling Errors	No. of Errors **3** — Use Table B.11/E.11	**2**
B. Punctuation Errors	No. of Errors **2** — Use Table B.12/E.12	**3**
C. Multiple Spellings	0 ①	
Organization		
A. Sentence Structure	0 1 2 3 ④	
B. Topic Sentence	0 1 ②	
C. Sequencing	0 1 2 ③	
D. Essay contains linking words or phrases	0 1 2 ③	
E. Essay is presented as a letter to the editor	0 1 ②	
F. Essay has introductory sentences or paragraph	0 ①	
G. Essay has a concluding sentence or paragraph	0 ①	
H. Essay uses organization to persuade	0 ①	
Theme Development		
A. Essay contains 3 supports for the position	0 1 ②	
B. Essay contains evidence to back up the supporting argument	0 1 ②	
C. Essay contains only on–topic information or ideas	0 ①	
D. Essay is not merely answering a question	0 ①	
E. Essay contains counter arguments	⓪ 2	
Vocabulary		
A. Words are specific	0 1 ②	
B. Words are varied	0 1 ② 3	
C. Any unusual expressions that capture the reader's interest and add spark to the writing	⓪ 1 2	

Word Count for Essay (optional) **197**

Holistic Score (optional) **6**

Mechanics Subtotal max = 9 **6**

Organization Subtotal max = 17 **17**

Theme Development Subtotal max = 8 **6**

Vocabulary Subtotal max = 7 **4**

max = 55

Grades 7–16 Total Raw Score

Grade 10: Gloria

This is a well-written, well-developed persuasive essay. Gloria's position is supported and includes detailed examples.

Appendix A.3.
Oral Expression

Sentence Repetition

Sentence Repetition is administered to Grades PreK–3. Credit for the unadministered items is *not* awarded to examinees in Grades 4–16. Score 1 point if a sentence is repeated without error; score 0 points if any error occurs in the repetition.

Word Fluency

Oral Expression Word Fluency has two tasks, Word Fluency A (Item 10) and Word Fluency B (Item 13). To calculate the Word Fluency score, add the scores for Word Fluency A and Word Fluency B. Refer to the following section for scoring information.

Word Fluency A

1. Score 1 point for any response that can be categorized as an animal. For example, *insects, fish, birds, snakes, dog, tigers,* and *dinosaurs* are scored 1 point each.

2. Score 1 point each for different types of the same animal, but not for slight variations. For example, *chicken, rooster,* and *bird* are scored 1 point each, and *collie, terrier,* and *poodle* are scored 1 point each because they are different types of the same animal. *Big dog, little dog,* and *spotted dog* receive only 1 point total because all three are slight variations of *dog.*

3. To calculate the total score, add the number of points earned by each response.

Word Fluency B

1. Score 1 point for any response that describes a method of moving that includes a verb. For example, *walking, jogging, flying a plane,* and *riding a horse* are scored 1 point each. Do not score 1 point for the word *go* (e.g., *go in a car, go fast, go backwards*).

2. Score 1 point for each different type of movement based on the verb used. For example, *fly a plane* and *ride in a plane* receive 1 point each because they are two different types of movement. The responses *drive a car, drive a truck,* and *drive a boat* receive 1 point for all three because they are slight variations of *drive.* Variations of an adverb should not be scored separately. For example, *run fast, run slow, run carefully* are scored 1 point total because all three are slight variations of the verb *run.*

3. To calculate the total score, add the number of points earned by each response.

A Visual Passage Retell

To score the Visual Passage Retell responses, use the scoring rubric on the record form and the following guidelines. To calculate the Visual Passage Retell Subtotal, add the scores for Item 11 and Item 12. The sample responses for Item 11 (*The Roller Coaster*) and Item 12 (*The Race*) were selected from the standardization sample to represent a variety of scores and score combinations. Each response includes an excerpt from the record form that displays the scores and a description of the reasoning that guided scoring. The scoring rubric lists the required story elements; generally, use the following scoring criteria to determine evidence and elaboration of a story element.

- **2 points:** Response shows evidence of the specific story element, with considerable elaboration. When this degree of elaboration is given, the examiner can visualize what is occurring in the story without benefit of the pictures. This level is rated *Skilled* on the record form.

- **1 point:** Response shows evidence of the specific story element, with a small degree of elaboration.

- **0 points:** Response shows no evidence of the specific story element.

- Some creative examinees may elaborate differently. If the elaboration makes sense with the pictures, do not penalize for creativity.

Score responses according to the following elements.

A. Main Idea: Determine if the response includes or infers the main idea of the story.

- The main idea for *The Roller Coaster* is that two boys invite a third to go on a ride. He is reluctant to go. The two boys get sick because of the ride, but the third boy has fun. Score 2 points if the main idea is stated with elaboration. Score 1 point when the main idea is included but with little or no elaboration (e.g., *The boys decided to go on a ride, but that boy did not want to go. But, he had a good time. Then they got off and he wanted to go again, but the others didn't.*)

- The main idea for *The Race* is that two girls enter a race. At first, one girl is ahead, but by the end of the race the other girl wins. Both girls show good sportsmanship by shaking hands. Score 2 points for an elaborated response and 1 point for a response with little or no elaboration (e.g., *The girls enter a race and that one is way ahead. Then something happens and the other one passes her and wins. Then they shake hands.*)

B. Details: Determine if the response includes details. Details provide more than a brief description of the plot. If there is no elaboration, the story sounds like a general listing of events depicted in the individual pictures.

- A 2-point or elaborated response might include a physical description of the characters or setting, dialogue between the characters, or an explanation of the motivation or thinking of a character.

- A 1-point response might include any one of the preceding features but has little or no elaboration (e.g., *When the boys went to the fair, they decided to ride on the roller coaster, but John didn't want to go. After he had fun on the ride, he wanted to go again, but the other two boys got sick.*)

C. Names/Labels Characters: Determine if characters are named. To receive 2 points for elaboration, all of the main characters should be named. If only one character is named, score 1 point.

- In *The Roller Coaster* there are three main characters.

- In *The Race* there are two main characters and one minor character, but only the main characters must be named to receive 2 points.

D. Setting: Determine if the response includes a setting. The setting is the location in which a story takes place. An elaborated setting might include a description of the surroundings, a time when the story occurred, or a proper name for the location of the story.

- The setting for *The Roller Coaster* might be an amusement park, fair, carnival, or other place where rides would be available. A 2-point elaborated setting might be *The first day of summer vacation,* or *The boys went to Six Flags for the day.* A 1-point response might be *the fair,* or *the amusement park.*

- A setting for *The Race* that would earn 1 point would include the high school track or a track meet. A 2-point elaborated setting might be *The Central High School track meet* or *The Race for a Cure.*

E. Plot: Determine if the response includes a logical series of events that tell a story. It should have a beginning, a middle, and an ending. A 1-point response for plot will be a description of the action in the pictures. A 2-point elaborated plot will include some or all of the following: character motivation, description of past events not included in the pictures, and dialogue.

- To score 2 points for *The Roller Coaster,* the response *must* include the detail that the boy who did *not* want to go on the ride was the only one who had fun (and wanted to go again). A 1-point response would include one or the other detail (the boy did not want to go *or* he was the only one who had fun).

- To score 2 points for *The Race,* the response *must* include the unexpected turn of events when the girl wearing the number 05 is winning the beginning of the race, but falls behind and actually loses the race in the end. A 1-point response would fail to include the unexpected turn of events.

F. Sequencing: Determine if the examinee tells the story using the correct sequence. Some examinees will elaborate on the pictures by adding actions or explanations for what might happen beyond what is depicted in the pictures, but the sequence of events remains unchanged. Other examinees may include events that occurred either before or after those illustrated.

- In both *The Roller Coaster* and *The Race,* to receive 2 points for elaboration, the examinee should clearly identify the sequence of events (i.e., by using terms like *first, then, next, finally*); make reference to cause and effect (e.g., *When Susan realized that she was winning the race, she stopped pushing herself so hard.*); or include additional information that helps clarify the actions of the characters (e.g., *Peter decided to go on the ride after the boys started calling him "Chicken"*). A 1-point response would tell the events in the correct order, but would not elaborate.

G. Conclusion: Determine if the response summarizes or states an outcome or conclusion. A conclusion can bring the story to an end, but it may also explain what the story was really all about.

- To score 1 point for *The Roller Coaster,* the response should state that when they got off the ride, two boys were sick and the other boy was smiling. To score 2 points, the response should specify that the boy who originally did not want to go on the ride ended up having the best time of all, while the other two boys got sick.

- To score 1 point for *The Race,* the response should state that the girls shook hands. To score 2 points, the response should specify that even though number 05 did not win, she was still able to shake hands and demonstrate her sportsmanship.

H. Prediction: Determine if the response predicts what will happen next in the story. Most examinees end the story by describing the final picture. Other examinees expand the conclusion by commenting on either a general or a specific event that *might* happen as a result of the experience. A prediction is not included in the pictures.

■ For *The Roller Coaster*, a prediction might be that after they got off of the roller coaster, the third boy talked the other two into riding again. A more general 1-point prediction might be that the third boy developed a real love of roller coasters. Score 2 points for exceptional responses that expand upon either a specific or general prediction (e.g., *The boys learned a valuable lesson that day that they never forgot. Joe learned that it was okay to try new things, and Matt and Sean learned to not call other people names because it might come back to them*).

■ For *The Race*, a 1-point prediction might be that the girls shook hands and then they became good friends. A 2-point response might be, *As Susan was shaking Heather's hand, she was already plotting how she could win in a rematch. The very next day she began practicing for next year's race.*

I. Comparing: Determine if the examinee compares the story to his or her own experiences, or to another story.

■ A 2-point response provides greater detail and specifies how the two experiences are similar (e.g., *After Chip got off the roller coaster, he realized it was a lot of fun. That's how I learned how to ride roller coasters. My dad went with me the first time though, and I learned that there was nothing to be scared of*).

■ A 1-point response cites the comparison (e.g., *This story is like something that happened to me one time*).

Sample Responses

Item 11. The Roller Coaster

---

11. The Roller Coaster

Is going to do that. Is going to go and fall over like this. It's going straight and it's going around.

11. Scoring Rubric	No Evidence	Evidence	Skilled	
A. Explains what the story is about (**main idea**)	⓪	1	2	
B. States **details** about the pictures	⓪	1	2	
C. Labels characters (**names**)	⓪	1	2	
D. Describes or tells where story occurs (**setting**)	⓪	1	2	
E. Tells what happens or what is happening (**plot**)	⓪	1	2	
F. Relates a logical order of events (**sequencing**)	⓪	1	2	
G. Summarizes and/or states a final outcome (**conclusion**)	⓪	1	2	Item 11 Score
H. **Predicts** what might happen next	⓪	1	2	max = 18
I. **Compares** story to own experiences or to another story	⓪	1	2	**O**

Grade Kindergarten: Derek

Derek's response received a score of 0 points on all items because the narrative lacks all of the required story elements. Derek responded to the pictured events, but he was unable to generate a story.

---

11. The Roller Coaster

The boys were talking. They went on the roller coaster. They got sick on the roller coaster.

11. Scoring Rubric	No Evidence	Evidence	Skilled	
A. Explains what the story is about (**main idea**)	⓪	1	2	
B. States **details** about the pictures	⓪	1	2	
C. Labels characters (**names**)	⓪	1	2	
D. Describes or tells where story occurs (**setting**)	⓪	1	2	
E. Tells what happens or what is happening (**plot**)	⓪	1	2	
F. Relates a logical order of events (**sequencing**)	0	①	2	Item 11 Score
G. Summarizes and/or states a final outcome (**conclusion**)	⓪	1	2	
H. **Predicts** what might happen next	⓪	1	2	max = 18
I. **Compares** story to own experiences or to another story	⓪	1	2	**1**

Grade Kindergarten: Maria

Maria provided a simplistic description of the pictures, but did not weave the description into a story. Main Idea was scored 0 points because the response did not include the major theme of the story. Because details were not included, 0 points were awarded for all of the other story elements except Sequencing, which met the minimum requirement and was scored 1 point.

A

11. The Roller Coaster

One day they went to the fair and rode on a ride and they got out and they went home.

11. Scoring Rubric	No Evidence	Evidence	Skilled	
A. Explains what the story is about (**main idea**)	⓪	1	2	
B. States **details** about the pictures	⓪	1	2	
C. Labels characters (**names**)	⓪	1	2	
D. Describes or tells where story occurs (**setting**)	0	①	2	
E. Tells what happens or what is happening (**plot**)	⓪	1	2	
F. Relates a logical order of events (**sequencing**)	⓪	1	2	
G. Summarizes and/or states a final outcome (**conclusion**)	⓪	1	2	**Item 11 Score**
H. **Predicts** what might happen next	0	①	2	max = 18
I. **Compares** story to own experiences or to another story	⓪	1	2	**2**

Grade 5: Jake (student with learning disabilities)

The response did not demonstrate any of the story elements except Setting, which was described as *the fair*. Predicts was scored 1 point because the response included *they went home*. All other story elements were scored 0 points.

11. The Roller Coaster

Jack had friends who was laughing at him. He put him on a roller coaster. Jack was laughing at them. He asked if they wanted to get another ride. It would not be a roller coaster, it might be a bumping car. Jack bumped them off the bumping car. They won't get on another thing like a bumping car or a roller coaster.

11. Scoring Rubric	No Evidence	Evidence	Skilled	
A. Explains what the story is about (**main idea**)	⓪	1	2	
B. States **details** about the pictures	⓪	1	2	
C. Labels characters (**names**)	0	①	2	
D. Describes or tells where story occurs (**setting**)	⓪	1	2	
E. Tells what happens or what is happening (**plot**)	⓪	1	2	
F. Relates a logical order of events (**sequencing**)	0	①	2	
G. Summarizes and/or states a final outcome (**conclusion**)	⓪	1	2	**Item 11 Score**
H. **Predicts** what might happen next	0	1	②	max = 18
I. **Compares** story to own experiences or to another story	⓪	1	2	**4**

Kindergarten: Kevin

Kevin's response contained only brief details about the pictures; therefore, Main Idea, Details, Setting, Plot, Conclusion, and Compares were scored 0 points. However, Names/Labels Characters was scored 1 point because one character was given a name. Sequencing was scored 1 point to indicate that all pictures were represented with minimal detail. Predicts was scored 2 points because the response provided detail about riding the bumping car.

11. The Roller Coaster

The Roller Coaster was going fast. The three boys wanted to ride it. It went really, really, fast. Everyone could hear the boys yell. One of the boys felt sick and turned green. Only one boy wanted to ride it again. That would be me. I love roller coasters and I never get sick.

11. Scoring Rubric

	No Evidence	Evidence	Skilled	
A. Explains what the story is about (**main idea**)	(0)	1	2	
B. States **details** about the pictures	0	(1)	2	
C. Labels characters (**names**)	(0)	1	2	
D. Describes or tells where story occurs (**setting**)	(0)	1	2	
E. Tells what happens or is happening (**plot**)	(0)	1	2	
F. Relates a logical order of events (**sequencing**)	0	(1)	2	
G. Summarizes and/or states a final outcome (**conclusion**)	0	(1)	2	Item 11 Score
H. **Predicts** what might happen next	(0)	1	2	max = 18
I. **Compares** story to own experiences or to another story	0	1	(2)	5

Grade 1: Roberto

Details was scored 1 point because Roberto said the roller coaster was going *fast*. Other details are missing, as is Main Idea, which was scored 0 points. Because the sequence of events matches the pictures and the response included a conclusion (*Only one boy wanted to ride it again*), Sequencing and Conclusion were each scored 1 point. Compares was scored 2 points because Roberto compares his feelings about roller coasters to the story.

11. The Roller Coaster

One boy went to the fair and he saw his friends. He asked them if they wanted to get on the roller coaster, and he said yes, they did. So they got on the roller coaster, and the two boys were having fun, but the one that was there first didn't look like he was having too much fun, and then when they went upside down, the two boys didn't look like they were having fun anymore, and the boy who didn't look like he was having fun-now he was having fun and at the end the two boys who got on and were having fun at first, I think they got sick. But if that was me I wouldn't have got sick.

11. Scoring Rubric

	No Evidence	Evidence	Skilled	
A. Explains what the story is about (**main idea**)	0	(1)	2	
B. States **details** about the pictures	(0)	1	2	
C. Labels characters (**names**)	(0)	1	2	
D. Describes or tells where story occurs (**setting**)	0	(1)	2	
E. Tells what happens or is happening (**plot**)	0	(1)	2	
F. Relates a logical order of events (**sequencing**)	0	(1)	2	
G. Summarizes and/or states a final outcome (**conclusion**)	0	(1)	2	Item 11 Score
H. **Predicts** what might happen next	(0)	1	2	max = 18
I. **Compares** story to own experiences or to another story	0	(1)	2	6

Grade 2: Mario

Main Idea was scored 1 point because all of the major points were mentioned, but there was no elaboration. Details was scored 0 points because the story sounds like a list of events with no elaboration. Names/Labels Characters was scored 0 points because none of the characters were given names. Setting, Plot, Sequencing and Conclusion were scored 1 point each because the response meets the minimum requirements, but there is no elaboration. Predicts was scored 0 points. Compares was scored 1 point because of the statement, *But if that was me, I wouldn't have got sick.*

A

11. The Roller Coaster

One day 3 boys went walking to an amusement park, then they saw a sign that said "World's Biggest Roller Coaster." One of the boys said, "Let's go." Another one said, "I don't know." The third boy said, "Ha, ha, you're a 'fraidy-cat!" The second boy said, "No, I'm not." So they went on. The first two who laughed, they started to get scared. But the other boy began to yell out for fun. But the other two were sick, the first boy said, "Let's go on it again." But the other two were too sick and went home and never went to an amusement park again.

11. Scoring Rubric

	No Evidence	Evidence	Skilled
A. Explains what the story is about (**main idea**)	0	1	②
B. States **details** about the pictures	0	1	②
C. Labels characters (**names**)	⓪	1	2
D. Describes or tells where story occurs (**setting**)	0	①	2
E. Tells what happens or what is happening (**plot**)	0	1	②
F. Relates a logical order of events (**sequencing**)	0	①	2
G. Summarizes and/or states a final outcome (**conclusion**)	0	①	2
H. **Predicts** what might happen next	0	①	2
I. **Compares** story to own experiences or to another story	⓪	1	2

Item 11 Score

max = 18

10

Grade 1: Caroline

The response is descriptive and uses dialogue; therefore, Main Idea, Details, and Plot were each scored 2 points for elaboration. Setting was scored 1 point for *Amusement Park*. Prediction was scored 1 point for the brief statement *the two boys went home and never went to an amusement park again*. The response moves beyond a mere description of the pictured events to a story with enough visual information that it could stand alone without the pictures.

11. The Roller Coaster

Three best friends named Jim, Ryan and Kyle decided to be tough and show off in front of their girl friends, so they could brag that they went on the World's Biggest Roller Coaster. They bought tickets and made their way to the coaster. They got on to the coaster and Kyle started having second thoughts while the other two boys were laughing and having fun. As they were approaching the first loop on the coaster Kyle began to have fun while Ryan and Jim held on for dear life. After the ride ended, Kyle asked Jim and Ryan what was wrong and they said that they were sick. Kyle was the only boy that got to brag about his World's Biggest Roller Coaster experience.

11. Scoring Rubric

	No Evidence	Evidence	Skilled
A. Explains what the story is about (**main idea**)	0	1	②
B. States **details** about the pictures	0	1	②
C. Labels characters (**names**)	0	1	②
D. Describes or tells where story occurs (**setting**)	0	①	2
E. Tells what happens or what is happening (**plot**)	0	1	②
F. Relates a logical order of events (**sequencing**)	0	1	②
G. Summarizes and/or states a final outcome (**conclusion**)	0	①	2
H. **Predicts** what might happen next	⓪	1	2
I. **Compares** story to own experiences or to another story	⓪	1	2

Item 11 Score

max = 18

12

Grade 9: Josh

Josh included considerable elaboration in several story elements. The passage is vivid and includes detailed descriptions. For example, Main Idea was elaborated with the phrases, Ryan and Jim *held on for dear life* and Kyle *got to brag* about the ride. Details was elaborated with the statements that indicated the boys were *three best friends*, they *made their way to the coaster*, and Kyle *started having second thoughts*. Names/Label Characters was scored a 2 because all three of the boys were given names. Plot was elaborated when Josh demonstrated motivation: the boys *decided to be tough and show off in front of their girl friends*. Sequencing was elaborated with the phrase *Kyle asked Jim and Ryan what was wrong*.

11. The Roller Coaster

Two brothers, Tom and Lee, and their friend Kid, went to see the new roller coaster. It was the world's biggest roller coaster. They urged Kid to ride it, but he was doubtful. He didn't like roller coaster, he was afraid of them. He had never ridden on one before, though. They urged him so much he didn't want them to feel bad, and also didn't want them to know he was afraid of roller coaster because they might think he was a chicken. So he went on the roller coaster with them. As the roller coaster was moving up the first lift hill, he regretted his decision. But, the only thing Tom and Lee were thinking was how much fun this was going to be. Well, during the roller coaster, Kid started to like it after the first drop. He saw the big loop coming, and as they went around it, he jumped up in joy, and the other two clung for their lives. After the roller coaster, Tom and Lee were sick and ready to go home. But Kid wanted to ride the roller coaster again. Tom and Lee just ignored him and walked away.

Grade 7: Heather

Heather's response included description and character motivation (e.g., Kid was *doubtful* and was *afraid* of roller coasters; He didn't want to be called *chicken* but at first *regretted his decision* to go on the roller coaster; The other two *clung for their lives*.) Main Idea, Details, Names/Labels Characters, Plot, Sequencing, and Conclusion were scored 2 points. However, because no reference was made to the location of the events, Setting was scored 0 points.

11. Scoring Rubric	No Evidence	Evidence	Skilled	
A. Explains what the story is about (**main idea**)	0	1	(2)	
B. States **details** about the pictures	0	1	(2)	
C. Labels characters (**names**)	0	1	(2)	
D. Describes or tells where story occurs (**setting**)	(0)	1	2	
E. Tells what happens or what is happening (**plot**)	0	1	(2)	
F. Relates a logical order of events (**sequencing**)	0	1	(2)	Item 11 Score
G. Summarizes and/or states a final outcome (**conclusion**)	0	1	(2)	max = 18
H. **Predicts** what might happen next	(0)	1	2	**/2**
I. **Compares** story to own experiences or to another story	(0)	1	2	

11. The Roller Coaster

Henry, Fred and Enrique were at the fair. Henry and Fred saw a sign to the world's biggest roller coaster. They said come on but Enrique had never gone on a roller coaster before. For him this was a big step. Henry and Fred got in the front seat. Enrique sat behind them. Henry and Fred joked about how they had been on roller coasters hundreds of times, while Enrique worried and fretted and chewed his fingernails. The roller coaster started and creaked and they were on their way through loops, turns and up and down hills, every way imaginable. Henry and Fred sat in front screaming and gripping the bar tightly as their knuckles turned white Enrique let go entirely and laughed the whole way. As they got off the ride Henry and Fred made a beeline for the nearest bathroom while Enrique said, "Can we do that again?"

Grade 10: Luke

Luke's response elaborated on every picture. It was a *big step* for Enrique to go on a roller coaster, because he had never been on one before. Enrique *worried and fretted and chewed his fingernails.* Henry and Fred were *screaming and gripping the bar tightly as their knuckles turned white,* and *made a beeline for the nearest bathroom while Enrique said, "Can we do that again?"* Setting was scored 1 point because the passage does not elaborate beyond a *fair*. Although no reference was made to Predicts or Compares, the response is exceptional.

11. Scoring Rubric	No Evidence	Evidence	Skilled	
A. Explains what the story is about (**main idea**)	0	1	(2)	
B. States **details** about the pictures	0	1	(2)	
C. Labels characters (**names**)	0	1	(2)	
D. Describes or tells where story occurs (**setting**)	0	(1)	2	
E. Tells what happens or what is happening (**plot**)	0	1	(2)	
F. Relates a logical order of events (**sequencing**)	0	1	(2)	Item 11 Score
G. Summarizes and/or states a final outcome (**conclusion**)	0	1	(2)	max = 18
H. **Predicts** what might happen next	(0)	1	2	**/3**
I. **Compares** story to own experiences or to another story	(0)	1	2	

Item 12. The Race

12. The Race

She had come. She wanted to sign up to be in the race. And she signed up then she won the race.

12. Scoring Rubric	No Evidence	Evidence	Skilled	
A. Explains what the story is about (**main idea**)	0	1	2	
B. States **details** about the pictures	0	1	2	
C. Labels characters (**names**)	0	1	2	
D. Describes or tells where story occurs (**setting**)	0	1	2	
E. Tells what happens or what is happening (**plot**)	0	1	2	
F. Relates a logical order of events (**sequencing**)	0	1	2	
G. Summarizes and/or states a final outcome (**conclusion**)	0	1	2	Item 12 Score
H. **Predicts** what might happen next	0	1	2	max = 18
I. **Compares** story to own experiences or to another story	0	1	2	1

Grade 5: James (student with Expressive Language Disorder)

No elaboration or details were presented in the response. Setting was scored 1 point because the character was in *the race*.

12. The Race

The girl signed up. #14 won. When the race was done they both shook hands!

12. Scoring Rubric	No Evidence	Evidence	Skilled	
A. Explains what the story is about (**main idea**)	0	1	2	
B. States **details** about the pictures	0	1	2	
C. Labels characters (**names**)	0	1	2	
D. Describes or tells where story occurs (**setting**)	0	1	2	
E. Tells what happens or what is happening (**plot**)	0	1	2	
F. Relates a logical order of events (**sequencing**)	0	1	2	
G. Summarizes and/or states a final outcome (**conclusion**)	0	1	2	Item 12 Score
H. **Predicts** what might happen next	0	1	2	max = 18
I. **Compares** story to own experiences or to another story	0	1	2	3

Grade 3: Jay

Jay's response is a good example of how an examinee can receive 1 point for Sequencing, but not for Main Idea or Plot. Sequencing was scored 1 point because the pictures are represented in order. However, Plot was scored 0 points because Jay did not state that the girl who was ahead initially ended up losing the race. Main Idea was scored 0 points because there was not a clear description of the action in the pictures.

Grade 10: Brian

Brian's response was brief and was scored only 1 point each for Main Idea, Setting, and Conclusion. Plot was scored 0 points because Brian did not state that the girl who was ahead initially ended up losing the race.

12. The Race

One day, a girl decided to sign up for a race. She was in the race, but she lost. And she congratulated the winner of the race.

12. Scoring Rubric	No Evidence	Evidence	Skilled	
A. Explains what the story is about (**main idea**)	0	(1)	2	
B. States **details** about the pictures	(0)	1	2	
C. Labels characters (**names**)	(0)	1	2	
D. Describes or tells where story occurs (**setting**)	0	(1)	2	
E. Tells what happens or what is happening (**plot**)	(0)	1	2	
F. Relates a logical order of events (**sequencing**)	(0)	1	2	**Item 12 Score**
G. Summarizes and/or states a final outcome (**conclusion**)	0	(1)	2	
H. **Predicts** what might happen next	(0)	1	2	max = 18
I. **Compares** story to own experiences or to another story	(0)	1	2	**3**

Grade 8: Delia

Delia provided a good example of minimal details that are clearly stated. There was no elaboration on any story element and no prediction or comparison was made.

12. The Race

"It's race day and I have to go sign up," said Helen. The race started and Helen was ahead, but very quickly the girl with red hair started to pull ahead and took the lead and ended up winning. Helen congratulated her though, shaking her hand after she got the trophy.

12. Scoring Rubric	No Evidence	Evidence	Skilled	
A. Explains what the story is about (**main idea**)	0	(1)	2	
B. States **details** about the pictures	0	(1)	2	
C. Labels characters (**names**)	0	(1)	2	
D. Describes or tells where story occurs (**setting**)	0	(1)	2	
E. Tells what happens or what is happening (**plot**)	0	(1)	2	
F. Relates a logical order of events (**sequencing**)	0	(1)	2	**Item 12 Score**
G. Summarizes and/or states a final outcome (**conclusion**)	0	(1)	2	
H. **Predicts** what might happen next	(0)	1	2	max = 18
I. **Compares** story to own experiences or to another story	(0)	1	2	**7**

12. The Race

Michelle decided to sign up for the big race that her school was holding. After the gun went off to start the race Michelle was in the lead with Teresa trailing behind. Towards the end of the race Teresa caught up and was ahead of Michelle by two meters. Teresa won the race. After the race Michelle went up to Teresa and gave her the winner trophy. Shook her hand and said good job.

12. Scoring Rubric

	No Evidence	Evidence	Skilled	
A. Explains what the story is about (**main idea**)	0	①	2	
B. States **details** about the pictures	0	①	2	
C. Labels characters (**names**)	0	1	②	
D. Describes or tells where story occurs (**setting**)	0	①	2	
E. Tells what happens or what is happening (**plot**)	0	①	2	
F. Relates a logical order of events (**sequencing**)	0	①	2	
G. Summarizes and/or states a final outcome (**conclusion**)	0	①	2	Item 12 Score
H. **Predicts** what might happen next	⓪	1	2	max = 18
I. **Compares** story to own experiences or to another story	⓪	1	2	**8**

Grade 9: Lakisha

Lakisha's response contains minimal details except for Names/Labels Characters, as both girls were named. Otherwise, there were enough details to receive 1 point on every other story element, except Predicts and Compares, which were scored 0 points.

12. The Race

There's a girl named Jenny and she wanted to sign up for the big race, and so she did. When she was racing, she saw another girl named Stephanie. Stephanie was running slow behind her. Then Jenny ran out of breath and Stephanie caught up. And, she won the race. Once the race was over they both shook hands and Stephanie got the trophy. They went home.

12. Scoring Rubric

	No Evidence	Evidence	Skilled	
A. Explains what the story is about (**main idea**)	0	①	2	
B. States **details** about the pictures	0	①	2	
C. Labels characters (**names**)	0	1	②	
D. Describes or tells where story occurs (**setting**)	0	①	2	
E. Tells what happens or what is happening (**plot**)	0	①	2	
F. Relates a logical order of events (**sequencing**)	0	①	2	
G. Summarizes and/or states a final outcome (**conclusion**)	0	①	2	Item 12 Score
H. **Predicts** what might happen next	0	①	2	max = 18
I. **Compares** story to own experiences or to another story	⓪	1	2	**9**

Grade 7: Josie

Josie's only instance of elaboration in the response was Names/Labels Characters. Predicts was scored 1 point because Josie included *They went home.* Going home is not depicted in the pictures.

Grade 10: Barbara

In Barbara's response, Main Idea was elaborated when Barbara stated that Jill had to *stay on her toes* which made *me feel really upset because I practiced probably harder*. Details was also elaborated because of the details conveying emotion: at times Jill was *excited, upset,* or *glad*. Plot was elaborated with the details about how Jill was *ahead for most of the trip* but the other girl *made it past,* but Jill congratulated her and knew that *I had more of a chance of doing it again than she did.* Other story elements, such as Sequencing and Conclusion, were not elaborated.

---

12. The Race

Jill was excited to start the big race. She was even telling the guy behind the counter how much she worked up to this and that she was really looking forward to winning. As they started to go, she was ahead for most of the trip. Number 14 was catching up really quickly though, so she had to stay on her toes. Come toward the end, Number 14 made it past which made me feel really upset because I practiced probably harder than she had. But near the end, I congratulated her and felt glad that she won, knowing that I had more of a chance of doing it again than she did.

12. Scoring Rubric	No Evidence	Evidence	Skilled	
A. Explains what the story is about (**main idea**)	0	1	②	
B. States **details** about the pictures	0	1	②	
C. Labels characters (**names**)	0	①	2	
D. Describes or tells where story occurs (**setting**)	0	①	2	
E. Tells what happens or what is happening (**plot**)	0	1	②	
F. Relates a logical order of events (**sequencing**)	0	①	2	
G. Summarizes and/or states a final outcome (**conclusion**)	0	①	2	**Item 12 Score**
H. **Predicts** what might happen next	⓪	1	2	max = 18
I. **Compares** story to own experiences or to another story	⓪	1	2	**10**

A

12. The Race

This is a story about Sue. One Monday afternoon, Sue saw a sign up booth for a big race. A 100-meter dash. She decided she thought she was a good runner, so she signed up. The race was going to be held on Saturday. She practiced every day and ran from 25 meters to 50 meters, to 100 meters. She felt confident, she decided to relax before the big day. When it did arrive, she decided to run in place for a while. She twisted her ankle, but still was ahead of Carol. But then her ankle started hurting again. She dropped in behind and Carol won the race. She didn't care that much, as long as she had fun.

12. Scoring Rubric	No Evidence	Evidence	Skilled	
A. Explains what the story is about (**main idea**)	0	1	②	
B. States **details** about the pictures	0	1	②	
C. Labels characters (**names**)	0	1	②	
D. Describes or tells where story occurs (**setting**)	0	1	②	
E. Tells what happens or what is happening (**plot**)	0	1	②	
F. Relates a logical order of events (**sequencing**)	0	1	②	
G. Summarizes and/or states a final outcome (**conclusion**)	0	①	2	**Item 12 Score**
H. **Predicts** what might happen next	⓪	1	2	max = 18
I. **Compares** story to own experiences or to another story	⓪	1	2	*13*

Grade 11: Clay

Elaboration is evident throughout Clay's response. The type of race was specific (it was a *100-meter dash* and was *held on Saturday*). Sue *twisted her ankle*, which made her fall behind. Emotion was conveyed when Clay stated that Sue lost the race but *didn't care that much.*

12. The Race

Susie had trained all year for the big race. Finally in May it was time for signups. She and five other girls signed up to run. Susie had worked and trained so hard she really wanted to win. The day of the big race came and Susie crouched at the starting line with the five other girls. She crossed her fingers and held her breath. The starter's pistol went off. The six girls raced down the track. Susie was in front until the very last second of the race until Emily, the girl in the lane next to her, won the race. Susie was sad that she hadn't won but she was happy for Emily because she had worked hard too. So, the next year, Susie worked and trained even harder, and won the race.

12. Scoring Rubric	No Evidence	Evidence	Skilled	
A. Explains what the story is about (**main idea**)	0	1	②	
B. States **details** about the pictures	0	1	②	
C. Labels characters (**names**)	0	1	②	
D. Describes or tells where story occurs (**setting**)	0	1	②	
E. Tells what happens or what is happening (**plot**)	0	1	②	
F. Relates a logical order of events (**sequencing**)	0	1	②	
G. Summarizes and/or states a final outcome (**conclusion**)	0	①	2	**Item 12 Score**
H. **Predicts** what might happen next	0	1	②	max = 18
I. **Compares** story to own experiences or to another story	⓪	1	2	*15*

Grade 10: Daryl

Daryl's response provides another demonstration of how the story can be elaborated. Susie had *trained all year* (Details). The race is in *May* (Setting). She *crossed her fingers and held her breath.* A starting pistol went off. Susie was *sad* for herself, but *happy for Emily because she had worked hard too.* Susie *trained even harder, and won the race.*

Giving Directions

To score the Giving Directions responses, use the scoring rubric on the record form and the following guidelines. To calculate the Giving Directions subtotal, add the scores for Item 14 and Item 15. The sample responses for Item 14 (*Vending Machine*) and Item 15 (*Peanut Butter and Jelly*) were selected from the standardization sample to represent a variety of scores and score combinations. Each response includes an excerpt from the record form that displays the scores and a description of the reasoning that guided scoring. The scoring rubric lists the required steps or references; generally, use the following scoring criteria to determine evidence and elaboration of a reference.

- **2 points:** Response specifically explains the step in such a way that the listener could perform the action without the benefit of a picture or a demonstration.

- **1 point:** Response includes enough general information that someone could follow the step or understand the information if they had the benefit of a picture or a demonstration.

- **0 points:** Response omits the specific reference.

- The examinee should not be penalized for using a different term for the same object or action (e.g., using the word *money* instead of *coin*). Some creative examinees may elaborate differently. If the elaboration makes sense with the pictures, do not penalize for creativity.

Item 14. Vending Machine

Score response according to the following.

A. Reference includes the words *vending machine* or *snack machine*

- **2 points:** Examinee uses the term *vending machine, candy machine, snack machine,* or a similar, appropriate term.

- **1 point:** Examinee uses the word *machine.*

- **0 points:** No reference is made to a machine (e.g., *Put your money in there*).

B. Reference made to putting money in machine

- **2 points:** A specific reference to money or to the slot in the machine is made (e.g., *Put a quarter in the machine,* or *Put your money in the slot on the front of the machine*).

- **1 point:** A general reference to inserting money in the machine is mentioned (e.g., *Put your money in the machine*).

- **0 points:** No reference is made of inserting money.

C. Reference made to selecting a snack

- **2 points:** A specific reference to selecting a snack is made (e.g., *Now you have to choose what kind of candy you want. If you want a Snickers bar you should press the button on the machine underneath the Snickers bar*).

- **1 point:** A general reference to selecting a snack is mentioned (e.g., *Put your money into the machine and choose the candy you want*).

- **0 points:** No reference is made to selecting a snack.

D. Reference made to opening bottom of machine

- **2 points:** A specific reference to the process of opening the bottom door is elaborated upon (e.g., *To grab the candy you need to lift the lid at the bottom of the machine. Sometimes these lids are hard to open because they get stuck. Your candy bar will be inside the compartment*).

- **1 point:** A general reference to opening the bottom door of the machine is mentioned (e.g., *Lift the door and you will see the candy bar lying there*).

- **0 points:** No reference is made to opening the bottom door of the machine.

E. Reference made to getting snack

- **2 points:** A specific reference to the process of removing the snack is elaborated upon (e.g., *Reach into the compartment with your hand to pick up the snack from the machine*).

  1 point: A general reference to removing the snack is mentioned (e.g., *Take the candy from the bottom of the machine*).

- **0 points:** No reference is made to removing the snack.

F. Reference made to eating snack

- **2 points:** A specific reference to opening or eating the snack is elaborated upon (e.g., *Open the candy wrapper and take a bite. "Mmmm, it's good."*).

- **1 point:** A general reference to opening or eating the snack is mentioned (e.g., *Take the candy out of the machine and eat it*).

- **0 points:** No reference is made to opening or eating the snack.

Sample Responses

Item 14. Vending Machine

14. Vending Machine

First you take out your money, however much it costs, which is fifty cents. You put it in the coin holder, then you pick out what you want. So you press the button and it will fall down and you open up the lid underneath the candy. And you take out your candy bar. Open it up and eat it.

Grade 7: Nathan

Although Nathan never mentioned the word *machine*, the instructions are adequate, but not elaborate.

14. Scoring Rubric	No Evidence	Evidence	Skilled	
A. Response includes the words *vending machine* or *snack machine*	(0)	1	2	
B. Reference made to putting money in machine	0	(1)	2	
C. Reference made to selecting a snack	0	(1)	2	
D. Reference made to opening bottom door of machine	0	(1)	2	**Item 14 Score**
E. Reference made to getting snack	0	(1)	2	max = 12
F. Reference made to eating snack	0	(1)	2	**5**

14. Vending Machine

He put 50 cents in the machine, then he picked out what kind of candy he wanted, then opened the door and got it out and opened his candy and ate it.

Grade 4: Jeffrey

Jeffrey's response demonstrates how the minimum scoring criteria can be met, but the details are not elaborated.

14. Scoring Rubric	No Evidence	Evidence	Skilled	
A. Response includes the words *vending machine* or *snack machine*	0	(1)	2	
B. Reference made to putting money in machine	0	(1)	2	
C. Reference made to selecting a snack	0	(1)	2	
D. Reference made to opening bottom door of machine	0	(1)	2	**Item 14 Score**
E. Reference made to getting snack	0	(1)	2	max = 12
F. Reference made to eating snack	0	(1)	2	**6**

14. Vending Machine

Put 50 cents in the vending machine. Push the number. Open and get out whatever you picked. Then you open it and eat it.

14. Scoring Rubric	No Evidence	Evidence	Skilled	
A. Response includes the words *vending machine* or *snack machine*	0	1	②	
B. Reference made to putting money in machine	0	①	2	
C. Reference made to selecting a snack	0	①	2	**Item 14 Score**
D. Reference made to opening bottom door of machine	0	①	2	
E. Reference made to getting snack	0	①	2	max = 12
F. Reference made to eating snack	0	①	2	**7**

Grade 3: Cyrus

Cyrus's response contains only one instance of elaboration with the specific mention of a *vending machine*. Otherwise, the response meets the minimal scoring criteria.

14. Vending Machine

The boy put in 50 cents in the hole there where the money goes in for snacks... in the snack machine. Then he pushed the button so he could get a crunch bar. Then he opened the thing where they get the snack. Then he got it. Then he started to scarf it down.

14. Scoring Rubric	No Evidence	Evidence	Skilled	
A. Response includes the words *vending machine* or *snack machine*	0	1	②	
B. Reference made to putting money in machine	0	①	2	
C. Reference made to selecting a snack	0	1	②	**Item 14 Score**
D. Reference made to opening bottom door of machine	0	①	2	
E. Reference made to getting snack	0	①	2	max = 12
F. Reference made to eating snack	0	①	2	**8**

Grade 2: Kevin

Kevin's response includes only two instances of elaboration: specific mention of a *snack machine* and the reference to selecting a snack (*he could get a crunch bar*). Otherwise, the response demonstrates how an examinee can meet minimal scoring criteria while using vague language. For example, *he opened the thing*, and *Then he got it. Then he started to scarf it down.*

14. Vending Machine

First, drop two quarters in the slot provided. Then, pick out which candy bar you want, and when you've made up your mind, press the little red button under that candy bar. You will hear a loud thud, and that would be your candy bar. Open the door by the handle, reach in, and get your candy bar. Enjoy.

14. Scoring Rubric	No Evidence	Evidence	Skilled	
A. Response includes the words *vending machine* or *snack machine*	(0)	1	2	
B. Reference made to putting money in machine	0	1	(2)	
C. Reference made to selecting a snack	0	1	(2)	**Item 14 Score**
D. Reference made to opening bottom door of machine	0	1	(2)	
E. Reference made to getting snack	0	1	(2)	max = 12
F. Reference made to eating snack	0	(1)	2	**9**

Grade 7: Kendra

Kendra's response is elaborate. For example, the instructions state to *drop two quarters in the slot provided*, and *when you've made up your mind, press the little red button*. There is no reference to the machine, and the reference to eating the snack was scored 1 point because Kendra said *Enjoy*.

14. Vending Machine

Put the right amount of change into the slot of the vending machine. Then choose the item you want. Third, you open the door to grab your selection. Then you reach in with your other hand and take out your selection. And finally you unwrap the food and eat it.

14. Scoring Rubric	No Evidence	Evidence	Skilled	
A. Response includes the words *vending machine* or *snack machine*	0	1	(2)	
B. Reference made to putting money in machine	0	(1)	2	
C. Reference made to selecting a snack	0	(1)	2	**Item 14 Score**
D. Reference made to opening bottom door of machine	0	(1)	2	
E. Reference made to getting snack	0	1	(2)	max = 12
F. Reference made to eating snack	0	1	(2)	**9**

Grade 7: Julie Ann

Julie Ann's response was scored 2 points for elaboration because of specific mention to *the vending machine*. Other evidence of elaboration includes reference to getting a snack because Julie Ann gave instructions to *reach in with your other hand and take out your selection*. Reference to eating the snack was scored 2 points because Julie Ann mentioned unwrapping the food before eating it.

14. Vending Machine

When you want to get a snack from a vending machine you must first get 50 cents—two quarters and put them in the coin slot. Next, push the button for the snack you want. To get your snack, push open the black door and reach in and grab the snack. Sometimes the door doesn't open very far, so don't get your arm stuck! Tear open the bag and enjoy the great food.

14. Scoring Rubric	No Evidence	Evidence	Skilled	
A. Response includes the words *vending machine* or *snack machine*	0	1	(2)	
B. Reference made to putting money in machine	0	1	(2)	
C. Reference made to selecting a snack	0	(1)	2	**Item 14 Score**
D. Reference made to opening bottom door of machine	0	1	(2)	max = 12
E. Reference made to getting snack	0	1	(2)	11
F. Reference made to eating snack	0	1	(2)	

Grade 8: Patrick

Patrick's response was scored 2 points for elaboration on putting money in the machine (*you must first get 50 cents—two quarters and put them in the coin slot);* opening the bottom of machine (*Sometimes the door doesn't open very far, so don't get your arm stuck!*); and eating the snack (*Tear open the bag and enjoy the great food*).

14. Vending Machine

First of you all you need to see what you want and see what it costs. It costs 50 cents, so drop two quarters, one by one, in the slot of the vending machine. You push the button for the one you want and the circle things turn until the candy falls down. You see the little slot where the candy comes out, you open the slot with one hand and hold it up while you reach in with your other hand and take the candy out. You open the candy and then you eat it until you're satisfied.

14. Scoring Rubric	No Evidence	Evidence	Skilled	
A. Response includes the words *vending machine* or *snack machine*	0	1	②	
B. Reference made to putting money in machine	0	1	②	
C. Reference made to selecting a snack	0	1	②	**Item 14**
D. Reference made to opening bottom door of machine	0	1	②	**Score**
E. Reference made to getting snack	0	1	②	max = 12
F. Reference made to eating snack	0	1	②	**12**

Grade 7: Stephanie

Stephanie's response demonstrates elaboration in all references. For example, specific reference is made to a *vending machine* and to eating the candy *until you're satisfied*. This response was scored the maximum number of points.

A

Item 15. Peanut Butter and Jelly

Score response according to the following.

A. Reference made to getting bread

- ■ **2 points:** Additional information about getting the bread is included (e.g., *First you take two pieces of bread out of the package and set them on the counter. Then you close the bread package back up*).

- ■ **1 point:** A general reference is made to getting the bread (e.g., *First you need some bread*).

- ■ **0 points:** No reference to bread is made.

B. Reference made to getting peanut butter

- ■ **2 points:** Additional information about getting the peanut butter is included (e.g., *You get the peanut butter out of the cabinet and a butter knife out of the drawer. Then, you twist open the lid on the jar of peanut butter*).

- ■ **1 point:** A general reference is made to getting the peanut butter (e.g., *Then you take out the peanut butter*).

- ■ **0 points:** No reference to peanut butter is made.

C. Reference made to spreading or putting peanut butter on bread

- ■ **2 points:** Additional information about spreading or putting the peanut butter on the bread is included (e.g., *Take a knife and dip it into the jar of peanut butter and scoop some peanut butter out. Spread it evenly on only one slice of bread*).

- ■ **1 point:** A general reference is made to spreading or putting the peanut butter on the bread (e.g., *Spread the peanut butter on one piece of bread*).

- ■ **0 points:** No reference to spreading or putting the peanut butter on the bread is made.

D. Reference made to getting jelly

- ■ **2 points:** Additional information about getting jelly is included (e.g., *You go to the refrigerator and get a jar of grape jelly*).

- ■ **1 point:** A general reference is made to getting the jelly (e.g., *You get the bread. You get the peanut butter and jelly*).

- ■ **0 points:** No reference to jelly is made.

E. Reference made to spreading or putting jelly on bread

- ■ **2 points:** Additional information about spreading or putting jelly on the bread is included (e.g., *You open the jar of jelly. Take a knife or spoon and get some jelly on it and spread it on the other slice of bread. Close the jar of jelly and put it back in the refrigerator*).

- ■ **1 point:** A general reference is made to spreading or putting jelly on the bread (e.g., *Spread some jelly on the piece of bread*).

- ■ **0 points:** No reference to spreading or putting jelly on the bread is made.

F. Reference made to a completed peanut butter and jelly sandwich

■ **2 points:** Additional or specific information about a complete sandwich is included (e.g., *Put the slice of bread with jelly right on top of the slice with peanut butter face down. Now you have a peanut butter and jelly sandwich. Then you can go sit down and eat your sandwich. Don't forget your glass of milk*).

■ **1 point:** A general reference is made to a complete sandwich. The word *sandwich* is not required, but there must be an obvious reference of a final form of the sandwich (e.g., *Put the two pieces together and eat them*, or *Now, cut it in half and eat*).

■ **0 points:** No reference to a complete sandwich is made.

Sample Responses

Item 15. Peanut Butter and Jelly

15. Peanut Butter and Jelly

First you get slice of bread, then you put slice of peanut butter then slice of jelly, put the bread on top, then you eat it.

15. Scoring Rubric	No Evidence	Evidence	Skilled	
A. Reference made to getting bread	0	(1)	2	
B. Reference made to getting peanut butter	(0)	1	2	
C. Reference made to spreading or putting peanut butter on bread	0	(1)	2	**Item 15 Subtotal Raw Score**
D. Reference made to getting jelly	(0)	1	2	
E. Reference made to spreading or putting jelly on bread	0	(1)	2	max = 12
F. Reference made to a completed peanut butter and jelly sandwich	0	(1)	2	**4**

Kindergarten: Cal

Cal's response refers only to getting bread. Spreading peanut butter or jelly is not mentioned, but Cal clearly refers to putting a *slice* of peanut butter and jelly on the bread, and the reference to putting peanut butter and jelly was scored 1 point.

15. Peanut Butter and Jelly

First you need to get the bread and the peanut butter. Then you put some peanut butter on the bread. Then you put them together and then you eat it.

15. Scoring Rubric	No Evidence	Evidence	Skilled	
A. Reference made to getting bread	0	(1)	2	
B. Reference made to getting peanut butter	0	(1)	2	
C. Reference made to spreading or putting peanut butter on bread	0	(1)	2	**Item 15 Subtotal Raw Score**
D. Reference made to getting jelly	(0)	1	2	
E. Reference made to spreading or putting jelly on bread	(0)	1	2	max = 12
F. Reference made to a completed peanut butter and jelly sandwich	0	(1)	2	**4**

Grade 2: Sean

Sean's response says *get the bread and the peanut butter* and *put some peanut butter on the bread*, but does not refer to jelly. Therefore, the references to getting jelly and spreading or putting jelly on bread were scored 0 points.

Grade 4: Emily

Emily's response meets the minimal scoring criteria; however, there is no mention of a completed sandwich, only *you eat it*.

15. Peanut Butter and Jelly

First get bread, then get peanut butter and jelly. Then put peanut butter on bread then put the jelly and then you eat it.

15. Scoring Rubric	No Evidence	Evidence	Skilled	
A. Reference made to getting bread	0	(1)	2	
B. Reference made to getting peanut butter	0	(1)	2	
C. Reference made to spreading or putting peanut butter on bread	0	(1)	2	**Item 15**
D. Reference made to getting jelly	0	(1)	2	**Subtotal Raw Score**
E. Reference made to spreading or putting jelly on bread	0	(1)	2	max = 12
F. Reference made to a completed peanut butter and jelly sandwich	(0)	1	2	**5**

Grade 2: Gerard

Gerard's response is simple and contains no elaboration. There is no mention of where to get ingredients, opening jars, which type of knife to use, or how to spread the ingredients.

15. Peanut Butter and Jelly

You get out the stuff, which would be peanut butter, bread, and jelly. Then you would spread the peanut butter on, then the jelly on the bread. Then you would put the two together and put it in a bag and then when you want, you would eat it.

15. Scoring Rubric	No Evidence	Evidence	Skilled	
A. Reference made to getting bread	0	(1)	2	
B. Reference made to getting peanut butter	0	(1)	2	
C. Reference made to spreading or putting peanut butter on bread	0	(1)	2	**Item 15**
D. Reference made to getting jelly	0	(1)	2	**Subtotal Raw Score**
E. Reference made to spreading or putting jelly on bread	0	(1)	2	max = 12
F. Reference made to a completed peanut butter and jelly sandwich	0	(1)	2	**6**

15. Peanut Butter and Jelly

The ingredients you will need are: 2 slices of bread, peanut butter, jelly. The tools you will need are a spreading knife, a paper plate, or a plastic bag if you want to take it with you. First, take one piece of bread, and spread peanut butter over the top of it with your spreading knife. Spread it equally throughout your slice of bread. Then take your second piece of bread, put peanut butter on the top of that piece. After that, put jelly on top of the peanut butter. Put both toppings facing each other and press the pieces together.

15. Scoring Rubric	No Evidence	Evidence	Skilled	
A. Reference made to getting bread	0	①	2	
B. Reference made to getting peanut butter	0	①	2	
C. Reference made to spreading or putting peanut butter on bread	0	1	②	**Item 15** **Subtotal** **Raw Score**
D. Reference made to getting jelly	0	①	2	
E. Reference made to spreading or putting jelly on bread	0	①	2	max = 12
F. Reference made to a completed peanut butter and jelly sandwich	0	①	2	**7**

Grade 5: Kimberle

Kimberle's response meets the minimal criteria for all of the references. Only the reference to spreading or putting peanut butter on bread was scored 2 points because Kimberle stated a specific utensil, a *spreading knife*, and gives specific instructions: *Spread it equally throughout your slice of bread.*

15. Peanut Butter and Jelly

First step: you take out the bread, a knife, peanut butter, jelly and a plate. You take two pieces of bread. Lay it on the plate and then you take... oh, first you open up the peanut butter and open up the jelly. You take some jelly out. You spread it on a piece of bread. Wipe off the jelly on the jar and then you take some peanut butter with a knife. And then, you put that on the bread. Then you put the peanut butter piece of bread on the jelly piece of bread. And then you eat it. Then you wrap up the bread. Then you put the lids back on the peanut butter and jelly. Then you put them back in the refrigerator. Put the bread in the refrigerator and you're done.

15. Scoring Rubric	No Evidence	Evidence	Skilled	
A. Reference made to getting bread	0	①	2	
B. Reference made to getting peanut butter	0	1	②	
C. Reference made to spreading or putting peanut butter on bread	0	①	2	**Item 15 Subtotal Raw Score**
D. Reference made to getting jelly	0	1	②	
E. Reference made to spreading or putting jelly on bread	0	1	②	max = 12
F. Reference made to a completed peanut butter and jelly sandwich	0	①	2	**9**

Grade 7: Stacey

Stacey's response provides a good example of how some references are elaborated, but other references are brief. The reference to getting bread was scored 1 point because Stacey stated *take out the bread*. The references to getting peanut butter and getting jelly were scored 2 points because initially the peanut butter and jelly were taken out, and then Stacey gave instructions to *open up the peanut butter and open up the jelly*. The reference to spreading or putting jelly on bread was scored 2 points because Stacey's instructions stated *You spread it on a piece of bread. Wipe off the jelly on the jar*. Similar references were not given for peanut butter; instead, Stacy said *you take some peanut butter with a knife. And then, you put that on the bread*.

A

15. Peanut Butter and Jelly

> To make a peanut butter and jelly sandwich you
> must first get out bread and the peanut butter
> and jelly out of the pantry. Open the peanut butter
> and spread it over one slice of bread with a
> knife. Do the same with the jelly. Put the slices
> of bread together and eat it. Clean up your mess.

15. Scoring Rubric	No Evidence	Evidence	Skilled	
A. Reference made to getting bread	0	1	②	
B. Reference made to getting peanut butter	0	1	②	
C. Reference made to spreading or putting peanut butter on bread	0	①	2	**Item 15 Subtotal Raw Score**
D. Reference made to getting jelly	0	1	②	
E. Reference made to spreading or putting jelly on bread	0	①	2	max = 12
F. Reference made to a completed peanut butter and jelly sandwich	0	①	2	**9**

Grade 8: Gilbert

Gilbert's response demonstrates how using one reference to a specific detail resulted in a score of 2 points for three references: the reference to get the bread, peanut butter, and jelly *out of the pantry*. Because a specific place is mentioned, the reference to each ingredient was scored 2 points.

15. Peanut Butter and Jelly

> First take 2 slices of bread out of the
> bag of bread. Then get a knife, a jar of
> peanut butter, and a jar of jelly. Take
> the lid off the jar of peanut butter and
> put some peanut butter on the knife. Wipe
> the peanut butter around one slice of
> bread, then take the lid off the jar of
> jelly. Put some jelly on knife and wipe it
> on other slice of bread. Both slices of
> bread should be covered in either
> peanut butter or jelly. Lastly take the
> peanut butter side of the bread and
> put it face down on the jelly side of
> bread. Take knife and cut sandwich in
> half. Put sandwich on plate and enjoy.

15. Scoring Rubric	No Evidence	Evidence	Skilled	
A. Reference made to getting bread	0	1	②	
B. Reference made to getting peanut butter	0	1	②	
C. Reference made to spreading or putting peanut butter on bread	0	1	②	**Item 15 Subtotal Raw Score**
D. Reference made to getting jelly	0	1	②	
E. Reference made to spreading or putting jelly on bread	0	1	②	max = 12
F. Reference made to a completed peanut butter and jelly sandwich	0	1	②	**12**

Grade 6: Anthony

Anthony's response provides an example of elaboration of each reference. Clear references are given for taking the bread out of the bag, taking the lid off of the jars, covering the bread with the ingredients, cutting the sandwich in half, and putting it on a plate.

Grade-Based Conversion Tables

Table B.1. Total Raw Score Conversion to Weighted Raw Score for Reading Comprehension

B

Total Raw Score	Grade 1 (Items 1–27)	Grade 2 (Items 10–44)	Grade 3 (Items 20–54)	Grade 4 (Items 34–69)	Grade 5 (Items 55–85)	Grade 6 (Items 59–93)	Grade 7 (Items 75–107)	Grade 8 (Items 75–114)	Grades 9–12 (Items 94–127)	Total Raw Score
0	0	21	29	46	63	63	102	94	101	0
1	7	29	38	49	67	66	104	95	103	1
2	14	33	46	52	71	69	106	96	105	2
3	20	37	54	55	74	72	108	97	107	3
4	25	41	57	58	78	75	109	98	109	4
5	29	45	60	61	81	79	110	99	110	5
6	33	48	63	64	85	83	111	100	111	6
7	36	50	66	67	88	87	112	102	112	7
8	39	51	68	70	92	90	113	103	113	8
9	41	52	69	72	94	92	114	105	114	9
10	44	53	70	74	96	94	115	106	115	10
11	46	54	71	76	98	97	116	108	116	11
12	48	55	72	78	100	98	117	109	117	12
13	51	58	73	80	102	100	118	110	118	13
14	53	59	74	82	104	102	119	111	119	14
15	55	65	75	84	106	104	120	112	120	15
16	57	67	76	85	108	105	122	113	121	16
17	59	68	77	87	110	107	123	114	123	17
18	61	71	78	88	112	108	125	115	124	18
19	63	72	79	90	113	110	126	116	125	19
20	65	74	80	91	114	111	127	117	127	20
21	67	75	81	92	116	112	128	118	128	21
22	69	77	82	94	117	113	129	119	129	22
23	72	78	83	95	119	115	130	120	131	23
24	74	79	84	96	120	116	131	121	133	24
25	76	81	85	98	121	117	133	122	136	25
26	78	82	86	99	123	118	134	123	138	26
27	81	83	88	100	124	120	135	124	139	27
28	83	84	89	102	126	121	136	125	140	28
29	85	85	90	105	127	122	137	127	141	29
30	88	88	91	108	128	123	138	128	143	30
31	91	89	93	110	129	125	139	129	144	31
32	94	91	94	112	131	126	140	130	146	32
33	97	92	95	115	132	127	142	131	147	33
34	100	94	98	117	134	128	144	132	153	34
35	103	96	101	119	135	130	153	134	154	35
36	107	97	107	120	136	131	154	135	160	36
37	111	105	115	122	138	133	161	136	163	37
38	115	106	120	123	140	135	162	137	173	38
39	120	112	122	124	142	138	165	138	186	39
40	125	114	123	126	143	140	175	139	197	40
41	132	116	125	127	146	142	181	140	199	41
42	136	117	126	129	149	144	186	141	202	42
43	139	119	128	130	153	151	187	143	204	43
44	140	121	130	132	157	161	195	149	205	44
45		122	131	134	161	162	196	157	207	45
46		124	133	135	167	168	197	162	209	46
47		126	135	136	173	180	200	163	210	47
48		128	137	138	179	186	201	179	211	48
49		130	139	140	185	193	202	185	213	49
50		132	141	142	191	195	203	187	215	50
51		134	144	145	193	199	204	196	217	51
52		137	146	148	195	200	205	197	218	52
53		138	150	152	197	201	206	198	219	53
54		140	153	156	199	202	207	201	220	54
55		141	159	160		203	208	202	221	55
56		145	164	166		204	209	203	222	56
57		149	169	172		205		204	223	57
58		151	174	178		206		205	224	58
59		152	179	184		207		206	225	59
60		158	185	190		208		208	226	60
61								209		61
62								210		62
63								211		63
64								212		64
65								213		65
66								214		66
67								215		67
68								216		68

Table B.2. Grade-Based Standard Score to Quartile Score Conversion for Reading Comprehension

Quartile Score	Standard Score
1	0–90
2	91–100
3	101–110
4	≥111

Table B.3. Grade-Based Raw Score to Quartile Score Conversion for Target Words: Fall, Winter, Spring, and High School

Fall

Quartile Score	Grade 1	2	3	4	5	6	7	8
1	0–7	0–21	0–23	0–23	0–14	0–22	0–22	0–34
2	8–10	22–23	24	24	15	23	23–24	35
3	11–13	24					25	36
4	14–25	25	25	25	16	24	26	37

Winter

Quartile Score	Grade 1	2	3	4	5	6	7	8
1	0–9	0–22	0–23	0–23	0–14	0–22	0–22	0–34
2	10–11	23	24	24	15	23	23–24	35
3	12–13	24					25	36
4	14–25	25	25	25	16	24	26	37

Spring

Quartile Score	Grade 1	2	3	4	5	6	7	8
1	0–11	0–22	0–23	0–24	0–14	0–22	0–23	0–34
2	12	23–24	24		15	23	24	35
3	13						25	36
4	14–25	25	25	25	16	24	26	37

High School

Quartile Score	Grade 9	10	11	12
1	0–20	0–20	0–20	0–21
2	21	21	21	
3				
4	22	22	22	22

Note. If the reverse rule was applied during administration of Reading Comprehension, do not convert the grade-based raw score to a quartile score.

Table B.4. Grade-Based Raw Score to Quartile Score Conversion for Reading Speed: Fall, Winter, Spring, and High School

Fall

Quartile Score	Grade							
	1	2	3	4	5	6	7	8
1	>185	>337	>314	>280	>385	>410	>441	>525
2	117–185	244–337	246–314	215–280	289–385	318–410	352–441	439–525
3	62–116	172–243	180–245	176–214	227–288	251–317	296–351	355–438
4	0–61	0–171	0–179	0–175	0–226	0–250	0–295	0–354

Winter

Quartile Score	Grade							
	1	2	3	4	5	6	7	8
1	>183	>324	>307	>260	>360	>397	>440	>506
2	116–183	243–324	233–307	200–260	282–360	307–397	346–440	415–506
3	62–115	170–242	176–232	163–199	221–281	244–306	287–345	343–414
4	0–61	0–169	0–175	0–162	0–220	0–243	0–286	0–342

Spring

Quartile Score	Grade							
	1	2	3	4	5	6	7	8
1	>180	>310	>300	>239	>335	>384	>438	>487
2	115–180	241–310	219–300	184–239	274–335	296–384	340–438	391–487
3	62–114	168–240	171–218	150–183	214–273	236–295	278–339	331–390
4	0–61	0–167	0–170	0–149	0–213	0–235	0–277	0–330

High School

Quartile Score	Grade			
	9	10	11	12
1	>571	>558	>541	>504
2	478–571	467–558	426–541	387–504
3	391–477	389–466	348–425	332–386
4	0–390	0–388	0–347	0–331

Note. If the reverse rule was applied during administration of Reading Comprehension, do not convert the grade-based raw score to a quartile score.

Table B.5. Grade-Based Raw Score to Decile Score Conversion for Alphabet Writing: Fall, Winter, and Spring

Fall			Winter			Spring		
	Grade			Grade			Grade	
Decile Score	PreK (Age 5)	K	Decile Score	PreK (Age 5)	K	Decile Score	PreK (Age 5)	K
10			10			10		
20			20			20		0
30			30			30		
40			40		0	40		
50			50			50		1
60		0	60		1	60	0	
70		1	70	0		70		2
80	0		80	1	2	80	1	3
90	1	2	90	2	3	90	2	4
100	2–25	3–25	100	3–25	4–25	100	3–25	5–25

Table B.6. Grade-Based Raw Score to Quartile Score Conversion for Written Expression Word Fluency: Fall, Winter, Spring, and High School

Fall

Quartile Score	Grade							
	1	2	3	4	5	6	7	8
0	0	0	0–1	0–1	0–1	0–2	0–3	0–3
1	1	1–3	2–6	2–6	2–7	3–8	4–10	4–10
2	2–3	4–5	7	7–8	8–10	9–10	11–13	11–13
3	4–5	6	8–10	9–10	11–12	11–12	14–15	14–16
4	≥6	≥7	≥11	≥11	≥13	≥13	≥16	≥17

Winter

Quartile Score	Grade							
	1	2	3	4	5	6	7	8
0	0	0–1	0–1	0–1	0–2	0–2	0–3	0–3
1	1–2	2–4	2–6	2–7	3–8	3–9	4–10	4–11
2	3–4	5–6	7–8	8–9	9–10	10–11	11–13	12–14
3	5–6	7	9–10	10–11	11–12	12–14	14–16	15–16
4	≥7	≥8	≥11	≥12	≥13	≥15	≥17	≥17

Spring

Quartile Score	Grade							
	1	2	3	4	5	6	7	8
0	0	0–1	0–1	0–1	0–2	0–3	0–3	0–3
1	1–3	2–5	2–6	2–7	3–8	4–9	4–10	4–11
2	4–5	6–7	7–8	8–10	9–10	10–12	11–13	12–14
3	6	8	9–10	11	11–12	13–15	14–16	15–16
4	≥7	≥9	≥11	≥12	≥13	≥16	≥17	≥17

High School

Quartile Score	Grade			
	9	10	11	12
0	0–3	0–4	0–4	0–5
1	4–12	5–12	5–12	6–12
2	13–15	13–15	13–15	13–15
3	16–18	16–18	16–19	16–19
4	≥19	≥19	≥20	≥20

Note. These are modified quartile-based scores in which the score of 0 represents the bottom 5% of the raw score distribution; the score of 1 represents the bottom 5%–25% of the raw score distribution.

Table B.7. Grade-Based Raw Score to Quartile Score Conversion for Paragraph Word Count: Fall, Winter, and Spring

Fall

Quartile Score	Grade			
	3	4	5	6
1	0–19	0–28	0–31	0–37
2	20–29	29–40	32–45	38–50
3	30–43	41–52	46–57	51–64
4	≥44	≥53	≥58	≥65

Winter

Quartile Score	Grade			
	3	4	5	6
1	0–21	0–30	0–32	0–40
2	22–33	31–42	33–46	41–51
3	34–47	43–54	47–61	52–66
4	≥48	≥55	≥62	≥67

Spring

Quartile Score	Grade			
	3	4	5	6
1	0–23	0–31	0–34	0–42
2	24–36	32–44	35–48	43–51
3	37–50	45–56	49–66	52–67
4	≥51	≥57	≥67	≥68

Table B.8. Grade-Based Raw Score to Quartile Score Conversion for Paragraph Spelling Errors

Quartile Score	Raw Score
0	≥5
1	4
2	3
3	1–2
4	0

Note. These are modified quartile-based scores in which the score of 4 represents zero errors; the score of 3 represents the remaining errors within the 4th quartile.

Table B.9. Grade-Based Raw Score to Quartile Score Conversion for Paragraph Punctuation Errors

Quartile Score	Raw Score
0	≥5
1	4
2	2–3
3	1
4	0

Note. These are modified quartile-based scores in which the score of 4 represents zero errors; the score of 3 represents the remaining errors within the 4th quartile.

Table B.10. Grade-Based Raw Score to Quartile Score Conversion for Essay Word Count: Fall, Winter, Spring, and High School

	Fall			Winter			Spring	
Quartile Score	**Grade**		**Quartile Score**	**Grade**		**Quartile Score**	**Grade**	
	7	**8**		**7**	**8**		**7**	**8**
1	0–42	0–56	1	0–49	0–61	1	0–55	0–65
2	43–63	57–75	2	50–66	62–80	2	56–69	66–85
3	64–84	76–105	3	67–91	81–107	3	70–97	86–109
4	≥85	≥106	4	≥92	≥108	4	≥98	≥110

High School

Quartile Score	Grade			
	9	**10**	**11**	**12**
1	0–65	0–73	0–79	0–83
2	66–88	74–105	80–107	84–110
3	89–118	106–139	108–144	111–148
4	≥119	≥140	≥145	≥149

Table B.11. Grade-Based Raw Score to Quartile Score Conversion for Essay Spelling Errors

Quartile Score	Raw Score
0	≥6
1	5
2	3–4
3	1–2
4	0

Note. These are modified quartile-based scores in which the score of 4 represents zero errors; the score of 3 represents the remaining errors within the 4th quartile.

Table B.12. Grade-Based Raw Score to Quartile Score Conversion for Essay Punctuation Errors

Quartile Score	Raw Score
0	≥5
1	4
2	3
3	1–2
4	0

Note. These are modified quartile-based scores in which the score of 4 represents zero errors; the score of 3 represents the remaining errors within the 4th quartile.

Table B.13. Grade-Based Raw Score to Conversion Score for Oral Expression Word Fluency:
Fall, Winter, Spring, and High School

Fall

Conversion Score	PreK (Age 5)	K	1	2	3	4	5	6	7	8
					Grade					
0	0	0	0	0–3	0–3	0–4	0–5	0–6	0–7	0–7
2	1–9	1–9	1–13	4–15	4–17	5–19	6–19	7–20	8–22	8–23
4	10–12	10–13	14–17	16–19	18–21	20–23	20–24	21–25	23–27	24–28
6	13–15	14–17	18–21	20–23	22–25	24–27	25–28	26–29	28–31	29–33
8	≥16	≥18	≥22	≥24	≥26	≥28	≥29	≥30	≥32	≥34

Winter

Conversion Score	PreK (Age 5)	K	1	2	3	4	5	6	7	8
					Grade					
0	0	0	0–2	0–3	0–4	0–5	0–5	0–6	0–7	0–7
2	1–9	1–10	3–14	4–16	5–18	6–19	6–19	7–21	8–22	8–24
4	10–12	11–14	15–18	17–20	19–21	20–24	20–25	22–26	23–27	25–29
6	13–15	15–18	19–21	21–24	22–25	25–27	26–28	27–30	28–32	30–33
8	≥16	≥19	≥22	≥25	≥26	≥28	≥29	≥31	≥33	≥34

Spring

Conversion Score	PreK (Age 5)	K	1	2	3	4	5	6	7	8
					Grade					
0	0	0	0–3	0–3	0–4	0–5	0–5	0–6	0–7	0–7
2	1–9	1–10	4–14	4–16	5–18	6–19	6–20	7–21	8–23	8–24
4	10–12	11–14	15–18	17–20	19–21	20–24	21–25	22–26	24–28	25–29
6	13–15	15–19	19–21	21–24	22–25	25–27	26–28	27–30	29–32	30–34
8	≥16	≥20	≥22	≥25	≥26	≥28	≥29	≥31	≥33	≥35

High School

Conversion Score	9	10	11	12
	Grade			
0	0–10	0–14	0–14	0–14
2	11–26	15–26	15–27	15–27
4	27–30	27–31	28–31	28–31
6	31–34	32–36	32–36	32–37
8	≥35	≥37	≥37	≥38

Note. These are modified quartile-based scores in which the score of 0 represents the bottom 5% of the raw score distribution; the score of 2 represents the bottom 5%–25% of the raw score distribution.

Grade-Based Normative Tables

C.1. Subtest Standard Scores

Table C.1. Grade-Based Subtest Standard Scores: Fall

Grade: PreK (Age 5)

Standard Score	Word Reading	Numerical Operations	Reading Comprehension	Spelling	Pseudoword Decoding	Math Reasoning	Written Expression	Listening Comprehension	Oral Expression	Standard Score
40										40
41										41
42										42
43										43
44										44
45										45
46										46
47										47
48										48
49										49
50										50
51										51
52										52
53										53
54										54
55										55
56								0		56
57										57
58										58
59									0	59
60								1		60
61									1	61
62										62
63										63
64								2	2	64
65										65
66									3	66
67										67
68								3	4	68
69										69
70										70
71						0			5	71
72								4		72
73						1			6	73
74										74
75						2			7	75
76								5		76
77	0					3			8	77
78										78
79	1								9	79
80						4		6		80
81	2								10	81
82										82
83	3					5			11	83
84								7		84
85	4								12	85
86						6				86
87	5								13	87
88								8		88
89	6					7			14	89
90	7									90
91									15	91
92	8					8		9		92
93	9								16	93
94										94
95	10					9			17	95
96	11							10		96
97	12								18	97
98	13									98
99						10		11	19	99
100	14								20	100

Table C.1. Grade-Based Subtest Standard Scores: Fall

Grade: PreK (Age 5) (continued)

Standard Score	Word Reading	Numerical Operations	Reading Comprehension	Spelling	Pseudoword Decoding	Math Reasoning	Written Expression	Listening Comprehension	Oral Expression	Standard Score
101	15									101
102	16					11		12	21	102
103	17									103
104	18								22	104
105	19					12		13		105
106	20								23	106
107	21									107
108	22					13		14	24	108
109	23									109
110	24–25								25	110
111	26							15		111
112	27–28					14			26	112
113	29									113
114	30–31								27	114
115	32					15		16		115
116	33									116
117	34								28	117
118	35					16				118
119	36							17	29	119
120	37–38									120
121	39					17			30	121
122	40							18		122
123	41								31	123
124	42					18				124
125	43							19	32	125
126	44									126
127						19			33	127
128	45							20		128
129	46								34	129
130						20				130
131	47							21	35	131
132	48									132
133	49					21			36	133
134								22		134
135	50								37	135
136	51					22				136
137	52								38	137
138	53							23		138
139	54					23			39	139
140	55									140
141	56								40	141
142	57					24		24		142
143	58								41	143
144	59									144
145	60					25		25	42	145
146	61									146
147	62								43	147
148	63					26		26		148
149	64								44	149
150	65					27				150
151	66							27	45	151
152	67					28				152
153	68								46	153
154	69					29		28		154
155	70								47	155
156	71					30		29		156
157	72					31			48	157
158	73					32				158
159	74					33		30	49	159
160	75–131					34–67		31–41	50–77	160

Table C.1. Grade-Based Subtest Standard Scores: Winter

Grade: PreK (Age 5)

Standard Score	Word Reading	Numerical Operations	Reading Comprehension	Spelling	Pseudoword Decoding	Math Reasoning	Written Expression	Listening Comprehension	Oral Expression	Standard Score
40										40
41										41
42										42
43										43
44										44
45										45
46										46
47										47
48										48
49										49
50										50
51										51
52										52
53										53
54										54
55										55
56								0		56
57										57
58										58
59									0	59
60								1		60
61									1	61
62										62
63										63
64								2	2	64
65										65
66									3	66
67								3		67
68									4	68
69										69
70						0				70
71								4	5	71
72						1				72
73									6	73
74						2		5		74
75									7	75
76	0					3				76
77									8	77
78	1							6		78
79						4			9	79
80	2									80
81									10	81
82	3					5		7		82
83									11	83
84	4									84
85						6			12	85
86	5							8	13	86
87										87
88	6					7				88
89	7								14	89
90								9		90
91	8								15	91
92	9					8				92
93									16	93
94	10							10		94
95	11					9			17	95
96	12									96
97	13								18	97
98								11		98
99	14					10			19	99
100	15								20	100

Table C.1. Grade-Based Subtest Standard Scores: Winter

Grade: PreK (Age 5) (continued)

Standard Score	Word Reading	Numerical Operations	Reading Comprehension	Spelling	Pseudoword Decoding	Math Reasoning	Written Expression	Listening Comprehension	Oral Expression	Standard Score
101	16							12		101
102	17–18					11			21	102
103	19									103
104	20							13	22	104
105	21					12				105
106	22								23	106
107	23						14			107
108	24–25					13			24	108
109	26									109
110	27–28								25	110
111	29							15		111
112	30–31					14			26	112
113	32									113
114	33								27	114
115	34–35					15		16		115
116	36									116
117	37					16			28	117
118	38									118
119	39							17	29	119
120	40					17				120
121	41								30	121
122	42						18			122
123	43					18			31	123
124	44									124
125	45							19	32	125
126	46					19			33	126
127										127
128	47							20	34	128
129	48					20				129
130	49								35	130
131	50							21		131
132	51					21			36	132
133	52									133
134	53							22	37	134
135	54					22				135
136	55								38	136
137	56									137
138	57					23		23	39	138
139	58									139
140	59								40	140
141	60					24				141
142	61							24	41	142
143	62									143
144	63					25			42	144
145	64							25		145
146	65								43	146
147	66					26				147
148	67							26	44	148
149	68					27				149
150	69								45	150
151	70					28		27		151
152	71								46	152
153	72					29				153
154	73							28	47	154
155	74					30				155
156	75–76							29	48	156
157	77–78					31				157
158	79–80					32			49	158
159	81–82					33		30		159
160	83–131					34–67		31–41	50–77	160

Table C.1. Grade-Based Subtest Standard Scores: Spring

Grade: PreK (Age 5)

Standard Score	Word Reading	Numerical Operations	Reading Comprehension	Spelling	Pseudoword Decoding	Math Reasoning	Written Expression	Listening Comprehension	Oral Expression	Standard Score
40										40
41										41
42										42
43										43
44										44
45										45
46										46
47										47
48										48
49										49
50										50
51										51
52										52
53										53
54										54
55										55
56								0		56
57										57
58									0	58
59										59
60								1	1	60
61										61
62										62
63									2	63
64								2		64
65									3	65
66								3		66
67									4	67
68						0				68
69								4		69
70									5	70
71						1				71
72								5	6	72
73						2				73
74									7	74
75	0					3				75
76								6	8	76
77	1									77
78						4			9	78
79	2									79
80								7	10	80
81	3					5				81
82									11	82
83	4									83
84						6		8	12	84
85	5								13	85
86										86
87	6					7				87
88	7							9	14	88
89										89
90	8								15	90
91	9					8				91
92								10	16	92
93	10									93
94	11					9			17	94
95	12									95
96	13							11	18	96
97	14									97
98	15					10			19	98
99	16							12	20	99
100	17–18									100

Table C.1. Grade-Based Subtest Standard Scores: Spring

Grade: PreK (Age 5) (continued)

Standard Score	Word Reading	Numerical Operations	Reading Comprehension	Spelling	Pseudoword Decoding	Math Reasoning	Written Expression	Listening Comprehension	Oral Expression	Standard Score
					Subtest Total Raw Scores					
101	19					11			21	101
102	20							13		102
103	21–22								22	103
104	23					12				104
105	24–25								23	105
106	26							14		106
107	27–28					13			24	107
108	29									108
109	30–31								25	109
110	32							15		110
111	33					14			26	111
112	34–35									112
113	36								27	113
114	37					15		16		114
115	38									115
116	39					16			28	116
117	40									117
118	41							17	29	118
119	42					17				119
120	43								30	120
121	44							18		121
122	45					18			31	122
123	46									123
124	47							19	32	124
125	48					19			33	125
126	49									126
127	50							20	34	127
128	51					20				128
129	52–53								35	129
130	54							21		130
131	55					21			36	131
132	56									132
133	57							22	37	133
134	58					22				134
135	59								38	135
136	60									136
137	61					23		23	39	137
138	62									138
139	63								40	139
140	64					24				140
141	65							24	41	141
142	66									142
143	67					25			42	143
144	68							25		144
145	69								43	145
146	70					26				146
147	71							26	44	147
148	72					27				148
149	73								45	149
150	74					28		27		150
151	75								46	151
152	76					29				152
153	77							28	47	153
154	78					30				154
155	79							29	48	155
156	80					31				156
157	81					32			49	157
158	82					33		30		158
159	83					34		31	50	159
160	84–131					35–67		32–41	51–77	160

Table C.1. Grade-Based Subtest Standard Scores: Fall

Grade: K

Standard Score	Word Reading	Numerical Operations	Reading Comprehension	Spelling	Pseudoword Decoding	Math Reasoning	Written Expression	Listening Comprehension	Oral Expression	Standard Score
				Subtest Total Raw Scores						
40										40
41										41
42										42
43										43
44										44
45										45
46										46
47										47
48										48
49										49
50										50
51										51
52										52
53										53
54										54
55								0		55
56										56
57									0	57
58								1		58
59									1	59
60										60
61						2				61
62									2	62
63					0					63
64									3	64
65		0						3		65
66						1			4	66
67										67
68								4	5	68
69						2				69
70										70
71		1							6	71
72						3		5		72
73									7	73
74	0									74
75	1					4		6	8	75
76	2									76
77	3	2							9	77
78	4					5				78
79	5			0				7	10	79
80	6–7									80
81	8					6			11	81
82	9									82
83	10	3						8	12	83
84	11					7				84
85	12			1					13	85
86	13							9		86
87	14					8			14	87
88	15	4								88
89	16								15	89
90	17			2		9		10		90
91	18–19								16	91
92	20									92
93	21					10			17	93
94	22	5						11		94
95	23			3					18	95
96	24					11				96
97	25–26							12	19	97
98	27–28									98
99	29–30			4		12			20	99
100	31–32	6						13		100

Table C.1. Grade-Based Subtest Standard Scores: Fall

Grade: K (*continued*)

Standard Score	Word Reading	Numerical Operations	Reading Comprehension	Spelling	Pseudoword Decoding	Math Reasoning	Written Expression	Listening Comprehension	Oral Expression	Standard Score
					Subtest Total Raw Scores					
101									21	101
102	33					13				102
103				5					22	103
104	34							14	23	104
105						14				105
106	35	7							24	106
107	36			6				15	25	107
108	37					15				108
109	38								26	109
110	39								27	110
111	40	8		7		16		16		111
112	41								28	112
113	42–43								29	113
114	44					17		17		114
115	45			8					30	115
116	46									116
117	47	9				18			31	117
118	48							18		118
119	49			9					32	119
120	50					19				120
121	51								33	121
122	52			10				19		122
123	53	10				20			34	123
124	54–55									124
125	56							20	35	125
126	57			11		21				126
127	58								36	127
128	59									128
129	60	11		12		22		21	37	129
130	61									130
131	62								38	131
132	63			13		23		22		132
133	64								39	133
134	65								40	134
135	66–67			14		24				135
136	68	12						23	41	136
137	69									137
138	70			15		25			42	138
139	71									139
140	72							24	43	140
141	73			16		26				141
142	74	13							44	142
143	75							25		143
144	76			17		27			45	144
145	77								46	145
146	78–79			18				26		146
147	80					28			47	147
148	81			19						148
149	82	14				29		27	48	149
150	83			20						150
151	84					30			49	151
152	85			21				28		152
153	86					31			50	153
154	87			22				29		154
155	88	15				32			51	155
156	89			23		33				156
157	90–91					34		30	52	157
158	92	16		24		35		31		158
159	93			25–26		36			53	159
160	94–131	17–54		27–53		37–67		32–41	54–77	160

Table C.1. Grade-Based Subtest Standard Scores: Winter

Grade: K

Standard Score	Word Reading	Numerical Operations	Reading Comprehension	Spelling	Pseudoword Decoding	Math Reasoning	Written Expression	Listening Comprehension	Oral Expression	Standard Score
										Subtest Total Raw Scores
40										40
41										41
42										42
43										43
44										44
45										45
46										46
47										47
48										48
49										49
50										50
51										51
52										52
53										53
54								0		54
55										55
56		0								56
57								1	0	57
58										58
59									1	59
60						0		2		60
61										61
62									2	62
63		1				1				63
64								3	3	64
65	0									65
66	1					2			4	66
67	2							4		67
68	3								5	68
69	4	2				3				69
70									6	70
71	5							5		71
72	6–7					4			7	72
73	8									73
74	9							6	8	74
75				0		5				75
76	10	3							9	76
77	11					6				77
78	12							7	10	78
79	13–14			1						79
80						7			11	80
81	15									81
82	16	4						8	12	82
83	17					8				83
84	18–19			2					13	84
85	20							9		85
86	21					9			14	86
87	22									87
88	23	5		3					15	88
89	24					10		10		89
90									16	90
91	25–26									91
92	27			4		11			17	92
93	28							11		93
94	29–30								18	94
95	31	6				12				95
96	32			5					19	96
97	33									97
98						13			20	98
99	34							13		99
100				6					21	100

Table C.1. Grade-Based Subtest Standard Scores: Winter

Grade: K (continued)

Standard Score	Word Reading	Numerical Operations	Reading Comprehension	Spelling	Pseudoword Decoding	Math Reasoning	Written Expression	Listening Comprehension	Oral Expression	Standard Score
					Subtest Total Raw Scores					
101	35	7				14				101
102	36							14	22	102
103	37								23	103
104	38			7		15				104
105	39							15	24	105
106	40								25	106
107	41					16				107
108	42–43	8		8					26	108
109	44							16	27	109
110						17				110
111	45								28	111
112	46			9				17	29	112
113	47					18				113
114	48	9							30	114
115	49			10						115
116	50					19		18	31	116
117	51									117
118	52								32	118
119	53			11						119
120	54	10				20		19	33	120
121	55									121
122	56								34	122
123	57			12		21		20		123
124	58								35	124
125	59									125
126	60	11		13		22		21	36	126
127	61									127
128	62								37	128
129	63					23				129
130	64			14				22	38	130
131	65									131
132	66					24			39	132
133	67	12						23		133
134	68			15					40	134
135	69					25				135
136	70								41	136
137	71			16				24		137
138	72					26			42	138
139	73	13								139
140	74			17				25	43	140
141	75					27				141
142	76								44	142
143	77			18						143
144	78					28		26	45	144
145	79								46	145
146	80	14		19		29				146
147	81							27	47	147
148	82			20						148
149	83					30			48	149
150	84			21				28		150
151	85					31			49	151
152	86	15		22				29		152
153	87					32			50	153
154	88			23		33				154
155	89							30	51	155
156	90			24		34				156
157	91	16				35		31	52	157
158	92			25		36				158
159	93	17		26		37		32	53	159
160	94–131	18–54		27–53		38–67		33–41	54–77	160

Grade K | Spring

Table C.1. Grade-Based Subtest Standard Scores: Spring

Grade: K

Standard Score	Word Reading	Numerical Operations	Reading Comprehension	Spelling	Pseudoword Decoding	Math Reasoning	Written Expression	Listening Comprehension	Oral Expression	Standard Score
40										40
41										41
42										42
43										43
44										44
45										45
46										46
47		0								47
48										48
49										49
50										50
51										51
52										52
53								0		53
54		1								54
55										55
56	0							1		56
57	1					0			0	57
58	2									58
59	3							2	1	59
60	4					1				60
61		2							2	61
62	5							3		62
63	6					2			3	63
64	7									64
65	8					3			4	65
66	9							4		66
67									5	67
68	10	3				4				68
69								5	6	69
70	11–12									70
71	13–14			0		5			7	71
72										72
73	15			1		6		6	8	73
74	16									74
75	17	4							9	75
76	18					7		7		76
77	19			2					10	77
78	20									78
79	21					8			11	79
80	22							8		80
81	23			3		9			12	81
82	24	5								82
83								9	13	83
84	25					10				84
85	26			4					14	85
86	27									86
87	28					11		10	15	87
88	29									88
89	30	6		5					16	89
90	31					12				90
91	32							11	17	91
92	33									92
93	34			6		13			18	93
94								12		94
95	35								19	95
96	36	7				14				96
97	37			7				13	20	97
98	38									98
99	39					15			21	99
100	40			8				14		100

Table C.1. Grade-Based Subtest Standard Scores: Spring

Grade: K (*continued*)

Standard Score	Word Reading	Numerical Operations	Reading Comprehension	Spelling	Pseudoword Decoding	Math Reasoning	Written Expression	Listening Comprehension	Oral Expression	Standard Score
101	41								22	101
102	42					16			23	102
103	43							15		103
104	44	8		9					24	104
105						17			25	105
106	45									106
107	46							16	26	107
108	47			10					27	108
109	48					18				109
110	49	9						17	28	110
111	50								29	111
112	51			11		19				112
113	52							18	30	113
114	53									114
115	54								31	115
116		10		12		20				116
117	55							19	32	117
118	56									118
119	57					21			33	119
120	58			13				20		120
121	59								34	121
122	60	11				22				122
123	61							21	35	123
124	62									124
125	63			14		23			36	125
126	64									126
127								22	37	127
128	65									128
129	66	12		15		24			38	129
130	67							23		130
131	68								39	131
132	69					25				132
133	70			16				24	40	133
134	71									134
135	72					26			41	135
136	73	13		17						136
137	74							25	42	137
138						27				138
139	75								43	139
140	76			18						140
141	77					28		26	44	141
142	78	14								142
143	79			19		29			45	143
144	80							27		144
145	81								46	145
146	82			20		30				146
147	83							28	47	147
148	84			21		31				148
149		15							48	149
150	85			22		32		29		150
151	86								49	151
152	87			23		33		30		152
153	88								50	153
154	89			24		34				154
155	90	16				35		31	51	155
156	91			25						156
157	92					36		32	52	157
158	93	17		26		37				158
159	94			27		38		33	53	159
160	95–131	18–54		28–53		39–67		34–41	54–77	160

C

Table C.1. Grade-Based Subtest Standard Scores: Fall

Grade: 1

Standard Score	Word Reading	Numerical Operations	Reading Comprehension[a]	Spelling	Pseudoword Decoding	Math Reasoning	Written Expression	Listening Comprehension	Oral Expression	Standard Score
40										40
41										41
42										42
43										43
44										44
45		0								45
46	0									46
47	1					0				47
48	2									48
49	3									49
50	4	1				1		0		50
51	5								0	51
52	6									52
53	7					2		1	1	53
54	8								2	54
55	9	2								55
56	10					3		2	3	56
57	11									57
58	12									58
59	13					4		3	4	59
60	14	3								60
61	15							4	5	61
62	16		0–2			5				62
63	17		3–4						6	63
64	18		5–9					5		64
65	19	4	10–11	0		6			7	65
66	20		12–16							66
67	21		17–18	1		7		6	8	67
68	22		19–22							68
69	23		23	2		8	0		9	69
70	24	5	24–26					7		70
71	25		27	3		9			10	71
72	26		28–30							72
73	27		31					8	11	73
74	28		32–34	4		10				74
75	29		35				1		12	75
76	30	6	36–37					9		76
77	31		38	5		11			13	77
78	32		39							78
79	33		40					10	14	79
80	34		41–42	6		12				80
81	35		43				2		15	81
82	36	7	44					11		82
83	37		45	7	0	13			16	83
84	38		46							84
85	39		47			14		12	17	85
86	40		48–49		1					86
87	41		50	8		15	3		18	87
88	42	8	51							88
89	43		52		2			13	19	89
90	44		53–54	9		16				90
91	45		55						20	91
92	46		56		3	17	4	14		92
93	47		57–58	10					21	93
94	48		59		4					94
95		9	60			18		15	22	95
96	49		61–62	11	5					96
97			63		6	19			23	97
98	50		64				5	16		98
99			65–66	12					24	99
100	51–52		67		7	20				100

[a] Based on weighted raw scores.

Table C.1. Grade-Based Subtest Standard Scores: Fall

Grade: 1 (continued)

Standard Score	Word Reading	Numerical Operations	Reading Comprehension[a]	Spelling	Pseudoword Decoding	Math Reasoning	Written Expression	Listening Comprehension	Oral Expression	Standard Score
			Subtest Total Raw Scores							
101	53–54	10	68		8			17	25	101
102	55–56		69–70	13	9					102
103	57		71–72			21	6		26	103
104	58		73		10			18		104
105	59		74–75	14	11				27	105
106	60		76			22				106
107	61		77		12			19	28	107
108	62	11	78–79	15	13	23	7			108
109	63		80–81		14				29	109
110	64		82	16	15			20		110
111	65		83–84		16	24			30	111
112	66		85–86		17–18		8			112
113	67		87	17	19–20			21	31	113
114	68		88–89		21–22	25				114
115	69	12	90–92	18	23				32	115
116	70		93		24–25	26		22		116
117	71		94–95		26		9		33	117
118	72		96–98	19	27					118
119	73		99		28	27		23	34	119
120	74		100–101	20	29–30					120
121	75	13	102–105		31–32	28	10		35	121
122	76		106–109	21	33					122
123	77		110–113		34			24	36	123
124	78		114–117		35	29			37	124
125	79		118	22	36		11			125
126	80		119–122		37	30		25	38	126
127	81		123–128	23	38					127
128	82	14	129–134		39	31			39	128
129	83		135–137	24	40		12			129
130	84		138		41			26	40	130
131	85		139		42	32				131
132	86		140	25	43				41	132
133	87				44	33	13			133
134	88			26	45			27	42	134
135	89	15				34				135
136	90				46				43	136
137	91			27		35	14	28		137
138	92				47				44	138
139	93					36				139
140	94			28	48				45	140
141	95				49	37	15	29		141
142	96	16							46	142
143	97			29	50	38				143
144	98				51			30	47	144
145	99			30	52	39	16			145
146	100				53				48	146
147	101			31		40		31		147
148	102				54	41			49	148
149	103	17					17			149
150	104			32	55	42		32	50	150
151	105									151
152	106			33		43			51	152
153	107						18	33		153
154	108			34		44			52	154
155	109	18								155
156	110			35		45		34	53	156
157	111						19			157
158	112	19		36		46		35	54	158
159	113			37						159
160	114–131	20–54		38–53		47–67	20–35	36–41	55–77	160

[a] Based on weighted raw scores.

Grade 1 | Winter

Table C.1. Grade-Based Subtest Standard Scores: Winter

Grade: 1

Standard Score	Word Reading	Numerical Operations	Reading Comprehension[a]	Spelling	Pseudoword Decoding	Math Reasoning	Written Expression	Listening Comprehension	Oral Expression	Standard Score
40										40
41										41
42										42
43	0	0								43
44	1–2									44
45	3–4	1				0				45
46	5									46
47	6									47
48	7					1				48
49	8							0		49
50	9	2								50
51	10					2			0	51
52	11							1		52
53	12								1	53
54	13					3			2	54
55	14	3						2		55
56	15								3	56
57	16					4				57
58	17							3		58
59	18								4	59
60	19	4	0–3			5		4	5	60
61	20		4–9							61
62	21		10–11	0		6			6	62
63	22		12–16					5		63
64	23		17–18	1					7	64
65	24	5	19–22	2		7				65
66	25		23–26					6	8	66
67	26		27	3		8				67
68	27		28–30						9	68
69	28		31			9	0	7		69
70	29		32–34	4					10	70
71	30	6	35			10			11	71
72	31		36–37	5				8		72
73	32		38–39						12	73
74	33		40			11	1			74
75	34		41–42	6				9	13	75
76	35		43			12				76
77	36	7	44	7					14	77
78	37		45					10		78
79	38		46–47			13	2		15	79
80	39		48–49							80
81	40		50	8	0	14		11	16	81
82	41		51							82
83	42	8	52			15		12	17	83
84	43		53–54	9	1					84
85	44		55			16	3		18	85
86	45		56							86
87	46		57–58	10	2	17		13	19	87
88	47		59							88
89	48		60						20	89
90		9	61–62	11	3	18	4	14	21	90
91	49		63							91
92	50		64		4				22	92
93	51		65–66	12		19		15		93
94	52		67		5				23	94
95	53–54		68		6					95
96	55	10	69–70	13		20	5	16	24	96
97	56		71–72							97
98	57		73		7				25	98
99	58		74–75	14	8	21		17		99
100	59		76		9		6		26	100

[a] Based on weighted raw scores.

Table C.1. Grade-Based Subtest Standard Scores: Winter
Grade: 1 (*continued*)

Standard Score	Word Reading	Numerical Operations	Reading Comprehension[a]	Spelling	Pseudoword Decoding	Math Reasoning	Written Expression	Listening Comprehension	Oral Expression	Standard Score
			Subtest Total Raw Scores							
101	60		77							101
102	61	11	78–79	15	10	22		18	27	102
103	62		80							103
104	63		81		11	23	7		28	104
105	64		82	16	12			19		105
106	65		83–84		13				29	106
107	66		85–86		14	24				107
108	67		87	17	15		8	20	30	108
109	68	12	88–89		16					109
110	69		90–92		17–18	25			31	110
111	70		93	18	19–20			21		111
112	71		94–95		21–22	26			32	112
113	72		96–98		23		9			113
114	73		99	19	24–25			22	33	114
115	74		100–101		26	27				115
116	75	13	102–104	20	27–28				34	116
117	76		105		29	28		23		117
118	77		106–109		30		10		35	118
119	78		110–112	21	31–32					119
120	79		113		33	29			36	120
121	80		114–117		34			24		121
122	81		118	22	35	30	11		37	122
123	82	14	119–122		36					123
124	83		123–128		37	31		25	38	124
125	84		129–134	23	38					125
126	85		135–137		39		12		39	126
127	86		138	24	40	32				127
128	87		139		41			26	40	128
129	88	15	140		42	33				129
130	89			25	43		13		41	130
131	90					34				131
132	91			26	44			27	42	132
133	92				45	35				133
134	93						14		43	134
135	94				46	36		28		135
136	95			27	47				44	136
137	96	16								137
138	97				48	37	15		45	138
139	98			28	49			29		139
140	99					38			46	140
141	100				50					141
142	101			29	51	39	16	30	47	142
143	102									143
144	103	17		30	52	40			48	144
145	104				53			31		145
146	105			31		41	17		49	146
147	106				54					147
148	107					42		32	50	148
149	108			32	55					149
150	109	18				43	18		51	150
151	110			33				33		151
152	111					44			52	152
153	112			34						153
154	113	19				45	19	34	53	154
155	114–115			35						155
156	116–117					46			54	156
157	118–119			36			20	35		157
158	120–121	20		37		47			55	158
159	122–123	21		38		48	21	36	56	159
160	124–131	22–54		39–53		49–67	22–35	37–41	57–77	160

[a] Based on weighted raw scores.

Table C.1. Grade-Based Subtest Standard Scores: Spring

Grade: 1

Standard Score	Subtest Total Raw Scores									Standard Score
	Word Reading	Numerical Operations	Reading Comprehension[a]	Spelling	Pseudoword Decoding	Math Reasoning	Written Expression	Listening Comprehension	Oral Expression	
40	0–4	0–1								40
41	5									41
42	6									42
43	7					0				43
44	8									44
45	9	2								45
46	10					1				46
47	11							0		47
48	12									48
49	13					2				49
50	14	3						1		50
51	15								0	51
52	16					3				52
53	17							2	1	53
54	18					4			2	54
55	19	4								55
56	20							3	3	56
57	21		0–3			5				57
58	22		4–9						4	58
59	23		10–11	0		6		4	5	59
60	24	5	12–17	1						60
61	25		18–22	2				5	6	61
62	26		23–26			7				62
63	27		27	3					7	63
64	28		28–31			8		6	8	64
65	29	6	32–34	4						65
66	30		35			9			9	66
67	31		36–37	5				7		67
68	32		38–39			10	0		10	68
69	33		40	6					11	69
70	34		41–42			11		8		70
71	35		43–44	7					12	71
72	36	7	45			12	1			72
73	37		46–47					9	13	73
74	38		48–49	8		13				74
75	39		50						14	75
76	40		51–52			14		10	15	76
77	41	8	53	9			2			77
78	42		54			15			16	78
79	43		55–56		0			11		79
80	44		57	10		16			17	80
81	45		58					12		81
82	46		59–60		1	17	3		18	82
83	47		61	11						83
84	48	9	62						19	84
85	49		63–64		2	18		13		85
86	50–51		65	12					20	86
87	52		66		3		4		21	87
88	53		67–68			19		14		88
89	54		69–70	13	4				22	89
90	55	10	71							90
91	56		72		5	20		15	23	91
92	57		73							92
93	58		74–75	14	6		5		24	93
94	59		76			21		16		94
95	60		77		7				25	95
96	61	11	78–79	15	8					96
97	62		80			22	6	17	26	97
98	63		81		9					98
99			82						27	99
100	64		83–84	16	10	23	7	18		100

[a] Based on weighted raw scores.

Table C.1. Grade-Based Subtest Standard Scores: Spring

Grade: 1 (*continued*)

Standard Score	Word Reading	Numerical Operations	Reading Comprehension[a]	Spelling	Pseudoword Decoding	Math Reasoning	Written Expression	Listening Comprehension	Oral Expression	Standard Score
			Subtest Total Raw Scores							
101	65–66		85–86						28	101
102	67	12	87		11			19		102
103	68		88–89	17	12	24			29	103
104	69		90–92		13–14		8			104
105	70		93		15	25		20	30	105
106	71		94–95	18	16					106
107	72		96–98		17–18				31	107
108	73		99		19–20	26		21		108
109	74		100–101	19	21		9		32	109
110	75	13	102		22–23	27				110
111	76		103–104		24–25			22	33	111
112	77		105	20	26					112
113	78		106–108		27–28	28			34	113
114	79		109		29		10	23		114
115	80		110–112	21	30	29			35	115
116	81		113		31–32					116
117	82	14	114–117		33	30			36	117
118	83		118		34		11	24		118
119	84		119–122	22	35				37	119
120	85		123–128		36	31				120
121	86		129–134		37				38	121
122	87		135–137	23	38		12	25		122
123	88	15	138		39	32			39	123
124	89		139							124
125	90		140	24	40	33			40	125
126	91				41		13	26		126
127	92				42	34			41	127
128	93			25	43					128
129	94					35			42	129
130	95			26	44		14	27		130
131	96	16			45	36			43	131
132	97									132
133	98				46			28	44	133
134	99			27	47	37	15			134
135	100								45	135
136	101				48	38				136
137	102			28	49			29	46	137
138	103	17					16			138
139	104				50	39			47	139
140	105			29	51			30		140
141	106					40			48	141
142	107				52		17			142
143	108			30		41		31	49	143
144	109	18			53					144
145	110			31	54	42			50	145
146	111						18	32		146
147	112			32		43			51	147
148	113				55					148
149	114			33		44		33	52	149
150	115	19					19			150
151	116			34		45			53	151
152	117							34		152
153	118			35		46			54	153
154	119						20			154
155	120	20		36		47		35	55	155
156	121									156
157	122			37		48		36	56	157
158	123	21		38			21			158
159	124			39		49		37	57	159
160	125–131	22–54		40–53		50–67	22–35	38–41	58–77	160

[a] Based on weighted raw scores.

Table C.1. Grade-Based Subtest Standard Scores: Fall
Grade: 2

Standard Score	Word Reading	Numerical Operations	Reading Comprehension[a]	Spelling	Pseudoword Decoding	Math Reasoning	Written Expression	Listening Comprehension	Oral Expression	Standard Score
40	0–8	0–1				0				40
41	9	2				1				41
42	10					2				42
43	11					3				43
44	12					4				44
45	13	3				5				45
46	14							0		46
47	15					6				47
48	16							1	0	48
49	17		0–2			7			1	49
50	18	4	3–4							50
51	19		5–9			8		2	2	51
52	20		10–11							52
53	21		12–16			9		3	3	53
54	22		17–18	0						54
55	23	5	19–22						4	55
56	24		23	1		10		4		56
57	25		24–26						5	57
58	26		27	2		11			6	58
59	27		28–30					5		59
60	28	6	31	3		12			7	60
61	29		32–34					6		61
62	30–31		35–36	4					8	62
63	32			5		13			9	63
64	33		37–38					7		64
65	34	7	39	6		14			10	65
66	35		40						11	66
67	36–37		41–42	7	0		8			67
68	38		43–47			15			12	68
69	39		48–49	8						69
70	40	8	50			16		9	13	70
71	41		51	9					14	71
72	42–43		52				1	10		72
73	44		53	10		17			15	73
74	45		54		0					74
75	46		55–57	11		18		11	16	75
76	47–48	9	58						17	76
77	49		59–62	12	1		2			77
78	50		63–66			19		12	18	78
79	51		67		2					79
80	52		68	13					19	80
81	53–54		69–70		3	20		13	20	81
82	55	10	71	14			3			82
83	56		72–73		4	21			21	83
84	57		74					14		84
85	58–59		75	15	5				22	85
86	60		76			22				86
87	61		77		6		4	15	23	87
88	62	11	78	16	7					88
89	63		79–80		8	23			24	89
90	64–65		81					16	25	90
91	66			17	9					91
92	67		82		10	24	5		26	92
93	68		83		11			17		93
94	69		84	18	12				27	94
95	70	12	85–86		13	25				95
96	71		87		14–15		6	18	28	96
97	72		88	19	16	26				97
98	73–74		89–90		17–18				29	98
99	75–76		91		19–21		7	19		99
100	77		92	20	22–23	27			30	100

[a] Based on weighted raw scores.

Table C.1. Grade-Based Subtest Standard Scores: Fall

Grade: 2 (continued)

Standard Score	Subtest Total Raw Scores									Standard Score
	Word Reading	Numerical Operations	Reading Comprehension[a]	Spelling	Pseudoword Decoding	Math Reasoning	Written Expression	Listening Comprehension	Oral Expression	
101			93		24–25			20		101
102	78	13	94		26–27				31	102
103	79		95	21	28	28	8			103
104	80		96		29–30			21	32	104
105	81				31	29				105
106	82		97–101	22	32		9		33	106
107	83		102–105		33			22		107
108	84	14	106–109		34	30			34	108
109	85		110–113	23	35					109
110	86		114–115		36			23	35	110
111	87		116		37	31	10			111
112	88		117–118		38				36	112
113	89		119–120	24		32		24		113
114	90	15	121		39				37	114
115	91–92		122–123							115
116	93		124–125	25	40	33	11	25	38	116
117	94		126–127							117
118	95		128–129		41				39	118
119	96		130–131			34				119
120	97	16	132–133	26	42		12	26	40	120
121	98		134–136		43	35				121
122	99		137		44				41	122
123	100		138–139	27	45		13			123
124	101		140		46	36		27	42	124
125	102		141–143							125
126	103	17	144–147	28	47	37			43	126
127	104		148–150				14			127
128	105		151		48			28		128
129	106		152–155			38			44	129
130	107		156–158	29	49					130
131	108–109					39	15		45	131
132	110	18			50			29		132
133	111			30		40			46	133
134	112				51					134
135	113						16	30	47	135
136	114			31	52	41				136
137	115								48	137
138	116	19				42		31		138
139	117			32	53		17		49	139
140	118					43				140
141	119								50	141
142	120			33	54	44		32		142
143	121	20					18		51	143
144	122					45				144
145	123			34				33	52	145
146	124				55	46				146
147	125–126						19		53	147
148	127	21		35		47		34		148
149	128								54	149
150	129			36		48				150
151	130					49	20	35	55	151
152	131	22								152
153				37		50		36	56	153
154						51				154
155				38			21		57	155
156		23				52		37		156
157				39		53			58	157
158		24		40		54	22	38		158
159						55			59	159
160		25–54		41–53		56–67	23–39	39–41	60–77	160

[a] Based on weighted raw scores.

Table C.1. Grade-Based Subtest Standard Scores: Winter

Grade: 2

Standard Score	Word Reading	Numerical Operations	Reading Comprehension[a]	Spelling	Pseudoword Decoding	Math Reasoning	Written Expression	Listening Comprehension	Oral Expression	Standard Score
					Subtest Total Raw Scores					
40	0–8	0–1				0				40
41	9–10	2				1–2				41
42	11–12					3–4				42
43	13–14									43
44	15–16					5				44
45	17–18	3						0		45
46	19–20		0–2			6			0	46
47	21		3–4					1	1	47
48	22		5–10			7				48
49	23		11–16						2	49
50	24	4	17–18			8		2		50
51	25		19–22						3	51
52	26		23	0		9		3		52
53	27		24–26						4	53
54	28		27	1						54
55	29	5	28–30			10		4	5	55
56	30–31		31	2					6	56
57	32		32–34			11				57
58	33		35–36	3				5	7	58
59	34	6				12				59
60	35		37–38	4				6	8	60
61	36		39			13				61
62	37		40	5					9	62
63	38		41–42	6		14		7		63
64	39	7	43–47						10	64
65	40		48–49	7			0		11	65
66	41		50			15		8		66
67	42–43		51	8					12	67
68	44		52					9		68
69	45	8		9		16			13	69
70	46		53				1		14	70
71	47		54	10		17		10		71
72	48		55–56						15	72
73	49		57–58	11		18		11		73
74	50	9	59–60		0				16	74
75	51		61–62	12			2		17	75
76	52		63–66			19		12		76
77	53–54		67	13	1				18	77
78	55		68			20				78
79	56	10	69–70	14	2			13	19	79
80	57		71			21	3		20	80
81	58		72–73		3					81
82	59		74	15				14	21	82
83	60		75		4	22				83
84	61	11	76	16	5				22	84
85	62		77			23	4	15		85
86	63		78		6				23	86
87	64–65		79–80	17	7					87
88	66		81		8	24		16	24	88
89	67			18					25	89
90	68	12	82		9		5			90
91	69		83		10	25		17	26	91
92	70		84	19	11					92
93	71				12	26			27	93
94	72		85–86		13		6	18		94
95	73	13	87–88	20	14				28	95
96	74		89		15	27				96
97	75–76		90		16		7	19	29	97
98	77		91	21	17–18					98
99			92–93		19–21	28		20	30	99
100	78		94		22–23					100

[a] Based on weighted raw scores.

Table C.1. Grade-Based Subtest Standard Scores: Winter
Grade: 2 (continued)

Standard Score	Word Reading	Numerical Operations	Reading Comprehension[a]	Spelling	Pseudoword Decoding	Math Reasoning	Written Expression	Listening Comprehension	Oral Expression	Standard Score
			Subtest Total Raw Scores							
101	79	14	95	22	24–25	29	8		31	101
102	80		96		26–27			21		102
103	81		97–101		28				32	103
104	82		102–106	23	29–30	30	9		33	104
105	83		107–109		31			22		105
106	84	15	110–113		32				34	106
107	85		114–115	24	33	31				107
108	86		116		34		10	23	35	108
109	87				35					109
110	88		117–118	25	36	32			36	110
111	89		119–120		37			24		111
112	90	16	121		38	33	11		37	112
113	91–92		122–123							113
114	93		124–125	26	39			25	38	114
115	94		126–127		40	34				115
116	95		128–129				12		39	116
117	96	17	130	27	41					117
118	97		131			35		26	40	118
119	98		132–133		42					119
120	99		134–136	28	43		13		41	120
121	100		137			36				121
122	101		138–139		44			27	42	122
123	102	18	140	29	45	37	14			123
124	103		141		46				43	124
125	104		142–143					28		125
126	105		144–147	30	47	38				126
127	106		148–150				15		44	127
128	107		151		48					128
129	108	19	152–155	31		39		29	45	129
130	109		156–158		49		16			130
131	110					40			46	131
132	111			32	50					132
133	112					41		30	47	133
134	113	20			51		17			134
135	114			33		42			48	135
136	115				52			31		136
137	116						18		49	137
138	117			34		43				138
139	118	21			53				50	139
140	119			35		44	19	32		140
141	120								51	141
142	121			36	54	45				142
143	122							33	52	143
144	123	22				46	20			144
145	124			37					53	145
146	125–126				55	47		34		146
147	127			38			21		54	147
148	128	23				48				148
149	129					49		35	55	149
150	130			39			22			150
151	131	24				50			56	151
152				40				36		152
153						51	23		57	153
154		25		41			24			154
155				42		52		37	58	155
156		26		43		53	25			156
157				44			26	38	59	157
158		27		45–46		54			60	158
159		28		47		55	27	39	61	159
160		29–54		48–53		56–67	28–39	40–41	62–77	160

[a] Based on weighted raw scores.

Table C.1. Grade-Based Subtest Standard Scores: Spring

Grade: 2

Standard Score	Word Reading	Numerical Operations	Reading Comprehension[a]	Spelling	Pseudoword Decoding	Math Reasoning	Written Expression	Listening Comprehension	Oral Expression	Standard Score
			Subtest Total Raw Scores							
40	0–21	0–2				0–4				40
41	22									41
42	23					5				42
43	24		0–3							43
44	25	3	4–10			6		0	0	44
45	26		11–16						1	45
46	27		17–18			7		1		46
47	28		19–22						2	47
48	29		23			8				48
49	30	4	24–26					2	3	49
50	31		27	0		9				50
51	32		28–30					3	4	51
52	33		31	1						52
53	34		32–34			10			5	53
54	35	5	35–36	2				4	6	54
55	36					11				55
56	37		37–38	3				5	7	56
57	38		39			12				57
58	39	6	40	4					8	58
59	40		41–44			13		6		59
60	41		45–47	5					9	60
61	42		48–49	6		14		7		61
62	43		50						10	62
63	44	7	51	7	0					63
64	45		52	8		15		8	11	64
65	46									65
66	47		53	9				9	12	66
67	48		54			16			13	67
68	49	8	55	10			1			68
69	50		56			17		10	14	69
70	51		57–58	11						70
71	52		59–60			18		11	15	71
72	53	9	61–62	12						72
73	54		63–66		0	19	2		16	73
74	55		67	13				12	17	74
75	56		68			20				75
76	57	10	69–70	14	1				18	76
77	58		71			21		13		77
78	59		72–73	15	2		3		19	78
79	60		74			22			20	79
80	61	11	75	16	3			14		80
81	62		76			23			21	81
82	63		77	17	4			15		82
83	64		78		5		4		22	83
84	65	12	79	18		24				84
85	66		80		6			16	23	85
86	67		81		7	25			24	86
87	68			19	8		5			87
88	69	13	82		9			17	25	88
89	70		83	20	10	26				89
90	71		84		11				26	90
91	72				12	27	6	18	27	91
92	73		85–86	21						92
93	74	14	87–88		13				28	93
94	75		89		14	28		19		94
95	76		90	22	15		7		29	95
96	77		91		16					96
97	78		92–93		17–18	29		20	30	97
98	79	15	94–95	23	19–21		8			98
99	80		96–98		22–23				31	99
100	81		99–106		24–25	30		21		100

[a] Based on weighted raw scores.

Table C.1. Grade-Based Subtest Standard Scores: Spring

Grade: 2 (continued)

Standard Score	Word Reading	Numerical Operations	Reading Comprehension[a]	Spelling	Pseudoword Decoding	Math Reasoning	Written Expression	Listening Comprehension	Oral Expression	Standard Score
			Subtest Total Raw Scores							
101	82		107–109	24	26–27		9		32	101
102	83		110–112		28				33	102
103	84	16	113		29–30	31		22		103
104	85		114–115	25	31				34	104
105	86		116		32		10			105
106	87				33	32		23	35	106
107	88		117–118	26	34					107
108	89	17	119–120		35	33	11		36	108
109	90		121		36			24		109
110	91		122–123	27	37				37	110
111	92		124–125		38	34				111
112	93		126				12	25	38	112
113	94	18	127	28	39					113
114	95		128–129		40	35			39	114
115	96		130					26		115
116	97		131	29	41		13		40	116
117	98		132–133			36				117
118	99		134–135	30	42				41	118
119	100	19	136		43		14	27		119
120	101		137			37			42	120
121	102		138–139	31	44					121
122	103		140		45		15	28	43	122
123	104		141		46	38				123
124	105	20	142–143	32					44	124
125	106		144–147		47		16			125
126	107		148–150			39		29	45	126
127	108		151	33	48					127
128	109		152–155			40	17		46	128
129	110		156–158		49					129
130	111	21		34		41		30	47	130
131	112				50		18			131
132	113			35		42			48	132
133	114				51		19	31		133
134	115			36					49	134
135	116	22			52	43				135
136	117						20		50	136
137	118			37		44		32		137
138	119				53				51	138
139	120	23		38		45	21			139
140	121							33	52	140
141	122				54	46				141
142	123			39			22		53	142
143	124					47				143
144	125	24						34	54	144
145	126			40	55	48	23			145
146	127								55	146
147	128			41		49		35		147
148	129	25					24		56	148
149	130			42		50				149
150	131							36	57	150
151				43		51	25			151
152		26							58	152
153				44		52		37		153
154							26		59	154
155				45		53				155
156		27		46				38	60	156
157						54	27			157
158		28		47		55		39	61	158
159				48		56				159
160		29–54		49–53		57–67	28–39	40–41	62–77	160

[a] Based on weighted raw scores.

Table C.1. Grade-Based Subtest Standard Scores: Fall

Grade: 3

Standard Score	Subtest Total Raw Scores									Standard Score
	Word Reading	Numerical Operations	Reading Comprehension[a]	Spelling	Pseudoword Decoding	Math Reasoning	Written Expression	Listening Comprehension	Oral Expression	
40	0–32	0–2				0–5				40
41	33					6			0–1	41
42	34		0–3							42
43	35		4–10			7		0	2	43
44	36	3	11–17							44
45	37		18–22			8		1	3	45
46	38		23–27							46
47	39		28–30			9		2	4	47
48	40	4	31	0						48
49	41		32–34					3	5	49
50	42		35			10				50
51	43		36	1					6	51
52	44	5	37	2		11		4		52
53	45		38						7	53
54	46		39–40	3		12		5		54
55	47		41–42						8	55
56	48	6	43–44	4					9	56
57	49		45			13		6		57
58			46	5					10	58
59	50		47	6		14		7		59
60	51	7	48–49						11	60
61	52		50	7		15	0	8		61
62	53		51	8					12	62
63			52				1		13	63
64	54		53	9		16		9		64
65		8							14	65
66			54	10		17	2	10		66
67			55						15	67
68			56	11		18	3	11	16	68
69		9	57–58							69
70	55–56		59	12		19		12	17	70
71	57–59		60–62				4		18	71
72	60–61		63–65	13	0	20				72
73	62–63	10	66–67		1		5	13	19	73
74	64–65		68	14	2	21				74
75	66		69–70						20	75
76	67		71	15	3	22	6	14		76
77	68	11	72		4				21	77
78	69		73–74	16	5	23	7			78
79			75		6			15	22	79
80	70		76	17	7	24	8			80
81	71	12	77		8			16	23	81
82	72		78	18	9	25	9			82
83	73		79		10				24	83
84	74		80	19	11	26	10	17		84
85	75	13	81		12				25	85
86	76			20	13	27				86
87	77		82		14		11	18	26	87
88	78		83		15–16					88
89	79	14	84	21	17	28	12		27	89
90	80				18			19	28	90
91	81		85		19–20	29				91
92	82		86–88	22	21		13		29	92
93	83	15	89		22–23	30		20		93
94	84		90	23	24–25		14		30	94
95	85		91		26	31				95
96	86		92		27–28			21	31	96
97	87	16	93–94	24	29		15		32	97
98	88–89		95–97		30–31	32				98
99	90–91		98–106	25	32			22	33	99
100	92–93	17	107–109		33	33	16			100

[a] Based on weighted raw scores.

Table C.1. Grade-Based Subtest Standard Scores: Fall
Grade: 3 (continued)

Standard Score	Word Reading	Numerical Operations	Reading Comprehension[a]	Spelling	Pseudoword Decoding	Math Reasoning	Written Expression	Listening Comprehension	Oral Expression	Standard Score
101			110–113		34			23	34	101
102	94		114–117	26	35		17			102
103		18	118		36	34		24	35	103
104	95		119–120		37		18			104
105			121	27	38	35			36	105
106	96		122		39			25		106
107		19	123	28	40		19		37	107
108	97		124		41	36				108
109	98		125					26	38	109
110	99		126	29	42					110
111	100	20	127		43	37	20		39	111
112	101		128–129	30				27		112
113	102		130			38			40	113
114	103						21			114
115	104	21	131–132	31	45	39			41	115
116	105		133					28		116
117	106		134	32	46	40				117
118	107		135–136				22		42	118
119	108	22	137		47	41		29		119
120	109		138	33					43	120
121			139–140		48	42	23			121
122	110		141	34				30	44	122
123	111	23	142–143		49	43				123
124	112		144–145						45	124
125	113		146–149	35		44	24			125
126	114		150–151		50			31	46	126
127	115	24	152	36		45				127
128	116		153–158		51					128
129	117		159–161			46	25		47	129
130	118		162–166	37				32		130
131	119	25	167–171		52	47			48	131
132	120		172–176	38						132
133	121		177–182			48	26		49	133
134	122		183–185		53			33		134
135	123	26		39		49			50	135
136	124						27			136
137	125				54	50			51	137
138	126			40				34		138
139	127	27				51			52	139
140	128						28			140
141	129			41	55	52		35	53	141
142		28								142
143	130			42		53	29		54	143
144	131									144
145						54		36	55	145
146		29		43			30			146
147						55			56	147
148				44				37		148
149						56	31		57	149
150		30		45						150
151						57			58	151
152				46			32	38		152
153						58			59	153
154		31		47			33			154
155						59		39	60	155
156				48						156
157		32				60	34		61	157
158				49		61		40		158
159		33		50		62	35		62	159
160		34–54		51–53		63–67	36–40	41	63–77	160

[a] Based on weighted raw scores.

Table C.1. Grade-Based Subtest Standard Scores: Winter

Grade: 3

Standard Score	Word Reading	Numerical Operations	Reading Comprehension[a]	Spelling	Pseudoword Decoding	Math Reasoning	Written Expression	Listening Comprehension	Oral Expression	Standard Score
40	0–32	0–2				0–5				40
41	33–34					6			0–1	41
42	35	3	0–3			7			2	42
43	36		4–10					0	3	43
44	37		11–17			8				44
45	38		18–22					1	4	45
46	39	4	23–27			9				46
47	40		28–30					2	5	47
48	41		31	0		10				48
49	42		32–34					3	6	49
50	43	5	35	1		11				50
51	44		36					4	7	51
52	45		37	2		12				52
53	46		38					5	8	53
54	47	6	39–40	3						54
55	48		41–42	4		13			9	55
56	49		43–44					6		56
57			45	5		14			10	57
58	50	7	46					7		58
59	51		47	6		15			11	59
60	52		48–49					8		60
61	53		50	7		16	0		12	61
62		8	51	8					13	62
63	54		52			17	1	9		63
64			53	9					14	64
65				10		18		10		65
66		9	54				2		15	66
67			55–56	11		19		11	16	67
68	55		57–58				3			68
69	56		59–60	12		20		12	17	69
70		10	61–64						18	70
71	57–59		65	13	0	21	4			71
72	60–62		66–68					13	19	72
73	63–64	11	69	14	1	22	5			73
74	65–66		70		2			14	20	74
75	67		71	15		23				75
76	68		72		3		6		21	76
77	69	12	73–74	16	4	24		15		77
78			75		5		7		22	78
79	70		76	17	6	25				79
80	71		77		7		8	16	23	80
81	72	13	78	18	8	26				81
82	73		79		9		9		24	82
83	74		80	19	10			17		83
84	75	14	81		11	27	10		25	84
85	76		82	20	12					85
86	77		83		13	28		18	26	86
87	78		84		14		11			87
88	79	15	85	21	15–16	29			27	88
89	80		86–87		17		12	19	28	89
90	81		88	22	18	30				90
91	82	16			19–20				29	91
92	83		89	23	21	31	13	20		92
93	84		90		22–23				30	93
94	85	17	91–92		24–25		14			94
95	86		93	24	26	32		21	31	95
96	87		94		27–28					96
97	88		95–97	25	29	33	15		32	97
98	89	18	98–102		30–31			22		98
99	90–91		103–109		32				33	99
100	92–93		110–113	26	33	34	16	23		100

[a] Based on weighted raw scores.

Table C.1. Grade-Based Subtest Standard Scores: Winter
Grade: 3 (continued)

Standard Score	Word Reading	Numerical Operations	Reading Comprehension[a]	Spelling	Pseudoword Decoding	Math Reasoning	Written Expression	Listening Comprehension	Oral Expression	Standard Score
			Subtest Total Raw Scores							
101	94	19	114–117		34				34	101
102	95		118		35–36		17		35	102
103			119–120	27	37	35		24		103
104	96		121		38		18		36	104
105		20	122	28	39	36				105
106	97		123					25	37	106
107			124		40		19			107
108	98		125	29	41	37			38	108
109	99	21	126		42			26		109
110	100		127	30		38	20		39	110
111	101		128–129		43					111
112	102		130					27	40	112
113	103	22		31	44	39	21			113
114	104		131						41	114
115	105		132–133	32	45	40				115
116	106		134					28		116
117	107	23	135–136		46	41	22		42	117
118	108		137	33						118
119			138		47	42		29	43	119
120	109		139–140				23			120
121	110	24	141	34	48	43			44	121
122	111		142–143					30		122
123	112		144–145	35	49	44			45	123
124	113		146–148				24			124
125	114	25	149–151			45			46	125
126	115		152	36	50			31		126
127	116		153–156			46				127
128	117		157–161		51		25		47	128
129	118	26	162–166	37		47				129
130	119		167–171					32	48	130
131	120		172–176	38	52	48				131
132	121		177–182				26		49	132
133	122	27	183–185			49				133
134	123			39	53			33	50	134
135	124					50	27			135
136				40					51	136
137	125	28			54	51				137
138	126							34	52	138
139	127			41		52	28			139
140	128								53	140
141	129	29			55	53		35		141
142	130			42			29		54	142
143	131					54				143
144									55	144
145		30		43		55	30	36		145
146									56	146
147				44		56				147
148							31	37	57	148
149		31		45		57				149
150									58	150
151				46		58	32			151
152		32						38	59	152
153				47		59	33			153
154									60	154
155		33		48		60		39		155
156							34		61	156
157		34		49		61				157
158				50				40	62	158
159		35		51		62	35			159
160		36–54		52–53		63–67	36–40	41	63–77	160

[a] Based on weighted raw scores.

Grade 3 | Spring

Table C.1. Grade-Based Subtest Standard Scores: Spring

Grade: 3

Standard Score	Word Reading	Numerical Operations	Reading Comprehension[a]	Spelling	Pseudoword Decoding	Math Reasoning	Written Expression	Listening Comprehension	Oral Expression	Standard Score
40	0–35	0–3				0–6			0–2	40
41	36		0–3			7			3	41
42	37		4–10			8		0		42
43	38	4	11–17						4	43
44	39		18–22			9		1		44
45	40		23–27						5	45
46	41		28–30			10		2		46
47		5	31	0					6	47
48	42		32–34			11		3		48
49	43		35	1					7	49
50	44		36			12		4		50
51	45	6	37	2					8	51
52	46		38			13		5		52
53	47		39–40	3					9	53
54	48		41–42	4		14				54
55	49	7	43–44					6	10	55
56	50		45	5		15				56
57	51		46					7	11	57
58	52		47	6		16				58
59	53	8	48–49					8	12	59
60			50	7		17	0		13	60
61			51	8				9		61
62	54		52			18	1		14	62
63		9	53	9						63
64				10		19		10	15	64
65	55		54				2		16	65
66		10	55–58	11		20		11		66
67			59–60				3		17	67
68	56		61–64	12		21		12	18	68
69		11	65	13						69
70	57–59		66–68		0	22	4	13	19	70
71	60–62		69	14						71
72	63–64		70		1	23	5	14	20	72
73	65–66	12	71	15	2					73
74	67		72			24			21	74
75	68		73	16	3		6	15		75
76	69	13	74		4	25			22	76
77	70		75	17	5		7			77
78	71		76		6	26		16	23	78
79	72	14	77	18	7		8			79
80	73		78		8				24	80
81	74		79	19	9	27	9	17		81
82		15	80–81		10				25	82
83	75		82–83	20	11	28	10			83
84	76		84–85		12			18	26	84
85	77	16	86		13	29				85
86	78		87	21	14		11		27	86
87	79				15–16	30		19		87
88	80	17	88	22	17		12		28	88
89	81				18	31				89
90	82		89	23	19–20			20	29	90
91	83		90		21		13			91
92	84	18	91–92		22–23	32			30	92
93	85		93	24	24–25		14	21		93
94	86		94		26	33			31	94
95	87	19	95–96	25	27–28					95
96	88		97–99		29		15	22	32	96
97	89		100–102		30–31	34				97
98	90–91		103–109	26	32				33	98
99	92–93	20	110–113		33		16	23		99
100	94–95		114–117	27	34	35			34	100

[a] Based on weighted raw scores.

Table C.1. Grade-Based Subtest Standard Scores: Spring

Grade: 3 (continued)

Standard Score	Word Reading	Numerical Operations	Reading Comprehension[a]	Spelling	Pseudoword Decoding	Math Reasoning	Written Expression	Listening Comprehension	Oral Expression	Standard Score
					Subtest Total Raw Scores					
101			118		35–36		17		35	101
102	96		119–120	28	37	36		24		102
103		21	121		38		18		36	103
104	97		122		39					104
105			123	29		37		25	37	105
106	98		124		40		19			106
107		22	125		41	38			38	107
108	99		126	30	42			26		108
109	100		127				20		39	109
110	101		128–129	31	43	39				110
111	102	23	130					27	40	111
112	103				44	40	21			112
113	104		131	32					41	113
114	105		132–133		45					114
115	106	24	134			41		28		115
116	107		135–136	33	46		22		42	116
117	108		137			42				117
118			138		47			29	43	118
119	109	25	139–140	34		43	23			119
120	110		141		48				44	120
121	111		142–143	35		44		30		121
122	112		144–145		49		24		45	122
123	113	26	146–148			45				123
124	114		149–151	36					46	124
125	115		152		50	46		31		125
126	116		153–156				25			126
127	117	27	157–161	37	51	47			47	127
128	118		162–166							128
129	119		167–171			48		32	48	129
130	120		172–176	38	52		26			130
131	121	28	177–182			49			49	131
132	122		183–185	39						132
133	123				53	50	27	33	50	133
134	124			40						134
135		29				51			51	135
136	125				54					136
137	126			41		52	28	34	52	137
138	127									138
139	128	30				53			53	139
140	129			42	55		29	35		140
141	130					54			54	141
142	131									142
143		31		43		55	30		55	143
144								36		144
145				44		56			56	145
146							31			146
147		32		45		57		37	57	147
148										148
149				46		58	32		58	149
150										150
151		33		47		59		38	59	151
152							33			152
153				48		60			60	153
154		34						39		154
155				49			34		61	155
156						61				156
157		35		50				40	62	157
158				51		62	35			158
159		36		52				41	63	159
160		37–54		53		63–67	36–40		64–77	160

[a] Based on weighted raw scores.

Table C.1. Grade-Based Subtest Standard Scores: Fall

Grade: 4

Standard Score	Word Reading	Numerical Operations	Reading Comprehension[a]	Spelling	Pseudoword Decoding	Math Reasoning	Written Expression	Listening Comprehension	Oral Expression	Standard Score
40	0–44	0–3	0–3	0		0–10				40
41	45		4–10					0		41
42	46	4	11–17	1						42
43			18–22			11		1		43
44	47		23–27	2						44
45	48		28–31			12		2		45
46	49	5	32–34	3						46
47	50		35–37			13		3		47
48	51		38	4						48
49	52		39			14		4		49
50	53	6	40	5					0	50
51			41–42			15		5		51
52	54		43	6					1	52
53	55		44			16		6	2	53
54	56	7	45	7						54
55	57		46			17		7	3	55
56	58		47	8			0			56
57	59		48			18		8	4	57
58		8		9						58
59	60		49–50			19	1	9	5	59
60	61		51	10						60
61	62	9	52–54			20			6	61
62	63		55–57	11			2	10	7	62
63	64		58–60			21				63
64	65	10	61–63	12			3	11	8	64
65			64–66			22				65
66	66		67–69	13				12	9	66
67	67	11	70–73			23	4			67
68	68		74–75	14	0			13	10	68
69	69		76			24	5			69
70	70		77	15	1			14	11	70
71	71	12	78			25	6			71
72			79	16	2			15	12	72
73	72		80			26	7			73
74	73	13		17	3				13	74
75	74		81		4	27	8	16		75
76	75			18	5				14	76
77	76		82		6	28	9			77
78	77	14		19	7			17	15	78
79	78		83		8	29				79
80				20	9		10		16	80
81	79	15	84		10	30		18	17	81
82	80			21	11		11			82
83	81		85		12				18	83
84	82	16	86		13	31		19		84
85	83		87	22	14		12		19	85
86	84		88		15–16	32				86
87		17	89	23	17			20	20	87
88	85		90		18	33	13		21	88
89	86				19–20					89
90	87		91	24	21		14	21	22	90
91	88	18			22–23	34				91
92	89		92–93	25	24–25		15		23	92
93	90		94		26			22		93
94		19	95	26	27–28	35			24	94
95	91		96–98		29		16			95
96	92		99–101		30–31	36		23	25	96
97	93		102–107	27	32					97
98	94	20	108–111		33		17		26	98
99	95–96		112–118		34	37		24		99
100	97–98		119	28	35–36		18		27	100

[a] Based on weighted raw scores.

Table C.1. Grade-Based Subtest Standard Scores: Fall

Grade: 4 *(continued)*

Standard Score	Subtest Total Raw Scores									Standard Score
	Word Reading	Numerical Operations	Reading Comprehension[a]	Spelling	Pseudoword Decoding	Math Reasoning	Written Expression	Listening Comprehension	Oral Expression	
101		21	120		37	38				101
102	99		121	29	38		19	25	28	102
103			122		39					103
104	100	22	123			39			29	104
105			124–125	30	40		20	26		105
106	101		126		41	40			30	106
107	102				42					107
108	103	23	127–128	31	43	41	21	27	31	108
109			129		44					109
110	104		130–131	32					32	110
111	105		132–133		45	42	22			111
112	106	24	134	33				28	33	112
113	107		135		46	43				113
114	108			34			23		34	114
115	109		136–137		47			29		115
116		25	138–139			44			35	116
117	110		140–141	35						117
118	111		142–143		48		24	30	36	118
119	112		144–146	36		45				119
120	113	26	147–150		49				37	120
121	114		151–154			46	25	31		121
122	115		155–158	37					38	122
123			159–163		50	47				123
124	116	27	164–169	38					39	124
125	117		170–175				26	32		125
126	118		176–181	39	51	48			40	126
127	119		182–187							127
128	120	28	188–190			49			41	128
129	121			40	52		27	33		129
130									42	130
131	122					50				131
132	123	29		41	53				43	132
133	124					51	28	34		133
134	125			42					44	134
135	126				54					135
136	127	30				52	29		45	136
137	128			43				35		137
138						53			46	138
139	129	31		44	55		30			139
140	130								47	140
141	131					54		36		141
142		32		45			31		48	142
143						55				143
144									49	144
145		33		46		56	32	37		145
146									50	146
147						57				147
148		34		47			33		51	148
149						58		38		149
150				48					52	150
151		35				59	34			151
152				49				39	53	152
153						60				153
154		36		50			35		54	154
155								40		155
156				51		61			55	156
157		37					36			157
158				52		62	37	41	56	158
159		38		53		63				159
160		39–54				64–67	38–40		57–68	160

[a] Based on weighted raw scores.

Table C.1. Grade-Based Subtest Standard Scores: Winter

Grade: 4

Standard Score	Word Reading	Numerical Operations	Reading Comprehension[a]	Spelling	Pseudoword Decoding	Math Reasoning	Written Expression	Listening Comprehension	Oral Expression	Standard Score
40	0–44	0–3	0–3	0		0–10				40
41	45–46	4	4–17	1				0		41
42	47		18–27			11		1		42
43	48	5	28–31	2						43
44	49		32–34			12		2		44
45	50	6	35–37	3						45
46	51		38–39			13		3		46
47	52		40	4						47
48	53		41–42			14		4		48
49		7	43–44	5					0	49
50	54		45			15		5		50
51	55		46–47	6					1	51
52	56		48			16		6	2	52
53	57	8		7						53
54	58		49–50			17		7	3	54
55	59		51	8			0			55
56		9	52–54			18		8	4	56
57	60		55–56	9						57
58	61		57			19	1	9	5	58
59	62		58–60	10						59
60	63	10	61–62			20			6	60
61	64		63	11			2	10	7	61
62	65		64–66			21				62
63		11	67–68	12				11	8	63
64	66		69			22	3			64
65	67		70–73	13	0			12	9	65
66	68	12	74–75			23	4			66
67	69		76	14	1			13	10	67
68			77			24	5			68
69	70	13	78–79	15	2			14	11	69
70			80			25	6			70
71	71			16	3			15	12	71
72	72		81			26				72
73	73–74	14	82	17	4		7		13	73
74	75				5	27		16		74
75	76		83	18			8		14	75
76	77	15	84		6	28				76
77	78		85	19	7		9	17	15	77
78			86		8	29				78
79	79	16	87–88	20	9		10		16	79
80	80		89		10	30		18	17	80
81	81		90	21	11		11			81
82	82	17	91		12	31			18	82
83	83		92–93		13			19		83
84	84		94	22	14	32	12		19	84
85					15–16					85
86	85	18	95	23	17	33		20	20	86
87	86		96		18		13		21	87
88	87		97	24	19–20			21		88
89	88	19	98		21	34	14		22	89
90	89			25	22–23					90
91	90		99–100		24–25			22	23	91
92		20	101	26	26	35	15			92
93	91		102–107		27–28				24	93
94	92		108		29	36	16	23		94
95	93	21	109–111	27	30–31				25	95
96	94		112–113		32					96
97	95		114–116		33	37	17	24	26	97
98	96	22	117–118	28	34					98
99	97		119		35–36	38	18		27	99
100	98		120–121	29	37			25		100

[a] Based on weighted raw scores.

Table C.1. Grade-Based Subtest Standard Scores: Winter

Grade: 4 (continued)

Standard Score	Word Reading	Numerical Operations	Reading Comprehension[a]	Spelling	Pseudoword Decoding	Math Reasoning	Written Expression	Listening Comprehension	Oral Expression	Standard Score
			Subtest Total Raw Scores							
101	99		122		38	39	19		28	101
102	100	23	123	30	39					102
103	101		124–125			40		26	29	103
104			126		40		20			104
105	102	24		31	41	41			30	105
106	103		127		42			27		106
107			128	32	43		21		31	107
108	104		129		44	42				108
109	105	25	130						32	109
110	106		131	33	45	43	22	28		110
111	107		132–133		46				33	111
112	108		134	34		44				112
113		26	135		47		23	29	34	113
114	109			35						114
115	110		136–137			45			35	115
116	111		138–139	36	48		24	30		116
117	112	27	140–141			46			36	117
118	113		142–143		49					118
119			144–146	37		47	25		37	119
120	114		147–150					31		120
121	115	28	151–154	38	50				38	121
122	116		155–158			48	26			122
123	117		159–163					32	39	123
124	118		164–169	39	51	49				124
125	119	29	170–175				27		40	125
126			176–181							126
127	120		182–187	40	52	50		33	41	127
128	121		188–190				28			128
129	122	30		41		51			42	129
130	123				53					130
131	124						29	34	43	131
132				42	54	52				132
133	125	31							44	133
134	126					53	30			134
135	127			43	55			35	45	135
136	128	32								136
137	129			44		54	31		46	137
138	130									138
139						55			47	139
140	131	33		45			32	36		140
141						56			48	141
142										142
143		34		46			33		49	143
144						57		37		144
145							34		50	145
146		35		47		58				146
147									51	147
148				48		59	35	38		148
149		36							52	149
150				49		60				150
151							36	39	53	151
152		37		50		61				152
153							37		54	153
154				51		62		40		154
155		38					38		55	155
156				52		63				156
157		39		53		64	39	41	56	157
158		40				65	40			158
159		41				66–67			57	159
160		42–54							58–68	160

[a] Based on weighted raw scores.

Table C.1. Grade-Based Subtest Standard Scores: Spring

Grade: 4

Standard Score	Word Reading	Numerical Operations	Reading Comprehension[a]	Spelling	Pseudoword Decoding	Math Reasoning	Written Expression	Listening Comprehension	Oral Expression	Standard Score
40	0–48	0–6	0–31	0–1		0–11		0		40
41	49		32–34	2				1		41
42	50		35–37			12				42
43	51	7	38–40	3		13		2		43
44	52		41–42							44
45			43–45	4				3		45
46	53		46–47			14				46
47	54	8	48	5				4		47
48	55		49–50			15			0	48
49	56		51	6				5		49
50	57		52			16			1	50
51	58	9	53–54	7				6	2	51
52			55–56			17				52
53	59		57	8				7	3	53
54	60		58			18	0			54
55	61	10	59–60	9				8	4	55
56	62		61–62			19				56
57	63		63	10			1	9	5	57
58		11	64			20				58
59	64		65–66	11					6	59
60	65		67–68			21	2	10	7	60
61	66	12	69	12						61
62	67		70–71		0	22		11	8	62
63	68		72–73	13			3			63
64	69	13	74–75		1	23		12	9	64
65			76–77	14			4			65
66			78–79		2	24		13	10	66
67	70	14	80	15			5			67
68			81		3	25		14	11	68
69			82	16			6			69
70	71–72		83		4	26		15	12	70
71	73–74	15	84–86	17						71
72	75		87–89		5	27	7	16	13	72
73	76		90–91	18						73
74	77	16	92–93		6	28	8		14	74
75	78		94	19				17		75
76	79				7	29	9		15	76
77	80	17	95	20	8					77
78					9	30	10	18	16	78
79	81		96	21	10				17	79
80	82	18			11	31	11			80
81	83		97		12			19	18	81
82	84			22	13	32				82
83	85	19	98		14		12		19	83
84	86			23	15–16	33		20		84
85			99		17		13		20–21	85
86	87	20	100	24	18–19			21		86
87	88		101		20–21	34			22	87
88	89		102–104	25	22		14			88
89	90	21	105–107		23–24			22		89
90	91		108	26	25–26	35			23	90
91			109		27–28		15		24	91
92	92	22	110–111	27	29	36		23		92
93	93		112–113		30–31		16		25	93
94	94		114		32	37				94
95	95	23	115–116	28	33			24	26	95
96	96		117–118		34	38	17			96
97	97		119	29	35–36					97
98		24	120–121		37	39	18	25	27	98
99	98–99		122–123	30	38					99
100	100–101		124		39	40	19		28	100

[a] Based on weighted raw scores.

Table C.1. Grade-Based Subtest Standard Scores: Spring
Grade: 4 (continued)

Standard Score	Word Reading	Numerical Operations	Reading Comprehension[a]	Spelling	Pseudoword Decoding	Math Reasoning	Written Expression	Listening Comprehension	Oral Expression	Standard Score
101			125					26	29	101
102	102	25	126	31	40	41				102
103					41		20		30	103
104	103		127	32	42	42		27		104
105			128		43				31	105
106	104	26	129		44	43	21			106
107	105			33					32	107
108	106		130		45	44		28		108
109	107		131	34	46		22		33	109
110	108	27	132–133		47	45				110
111			134	35			23	29	34	111
112	109		135			46				112
113	110			36	48				35	113
114	111	28	136–137			47	24	30		114
115	112		138–139						36	115
116	113		140–141	37	49		25			116
117			142			48			37	117
118	114	29	143–144	38				31		118
119	115		145–147		50		26		38	119
120	116		148–151			49				120
121	117		152–155	39			27	32	39	121
122	118	30	156–159		51	50				122
123	119		160–164				28		40	123
124			165–170	40						124
125	120		171–176		52	51	29	33	41	125
126	121	31	177–182	41						126
127	122		183–188		53	52			42	127
128	123		189–190				30			128
129	124			42	54			34	43	129
130		32				53				130
131	125				55		31		44	131
132	126			43		54				132
133	127							35	45	133
134	128	33					32			134
135	129			44		55			46	135
136	130									136
137						56	33		47	137
138	131	34		45				36		138
139							34		48	139
140						57				140
141		35		46					49	141
142						58	35	37		142
143				47					50	143
144		36				59	36			144
145				48					51	145
146						60		38		146
147		37		49			37		52	147
148						61				148
149				50				39	53	149
150		38				62	38			150
151				51					54	151
152						63				152
153		39		52			39	40	55	153
154						64				154
155				53					56	155
156		40				65	40	41		156
157						66			57	157
158		41				67				158
159									58	159
160		42–54							59–68	160

[a] Based on weighted raw scores.

Table C.1. Grade-Based Subtest Standard Scores: Fall

Grade: 5

Standard Score	Subtest Total Raw Scores									Standard Score
	Word Reading	Numerical Operations	Reading Comprehension[a]	Spelling	Pseudoword Decoding	Math Reasoning	Written Expression	Listening Comprehension	Oral Expression	
40	0–49	0–6	0–46	0–2		0–12		0–1		40
41	50		47–49	3				2		41
42	51	7	50			13			0	42
43	52		51–52	4				3		43
44	53		53			14			1	44
45			54	5				4		45
46	54	8	55			15			2	46
47	55		56–57	6				5		47
48	56		58			16			3	48
49	57		59	7				6		49
50	58	9	60			17			4	50
51			61	8				7		51
52	59		62			18			5	52
53	60		63	9			0	8		53
54	61	10	64			19			6	54
55	62		65	10			1	9		55
56	63		66			20			7	56
57		11	67	11						57
58	64		68			21	2	10	8	58
59	65		69	12						59
60	66	12	70			22		11	9	60
61	67			13	0		3			61
62	68		71			23		12	10	62
63		13	72–73	14	1					63
64	69		74–75			24	4	13	11	64
65			76–77	15	2					65
66		14	78–79			25	5	14		66
67	70		80		3					67
68			81	16		26	6	15	12	68
69			82–83		4				13	69
70	71–72	15	84	17		27		16	14	70
71	73–74		85–86		5		7			71
72	75–76		87–89	18		28		17	15	72
73	77	16	90–91		6		8			73
74	78		92–93	19		29			16	74
75	79		94		7		9	18		75
76	80	17	95	20	8	30			17	76
77					9		10			77
78	81		96	21	10	31		19	18	78
79	82	18			11					79
80	83		97		12	32	11			80
81	84			22	13			20		81
82	85	19			14	33			19	82
83	86		98	23	15–16		12		20	83
84					17	34		21	21	84
85	87	20	99	24	18–19		13			85
86	88		100–101		20–21	35			22	86
87	89		102–103	25	22			22		87
88	90	21	104–105		23–24	36	14			88
89	91		106–107	26	25–26					89
90			108–109		27–28	37		23	23–24	90
91	92	22	110–111	27	29		15			91
92	93–94		112		30–31	38			25	92
93	95		113		32		16	24		93
94	96	23	114–115	28	33	39			26	94
95	97–98		116		34					95
96	99		117–118	29	35–36	40	17	25	27	96
97		24	119		37					97
98	100		120–121	30	38	41	18		28	98
99	101–102		122–123		39			26		99
100	103–104	25	124	31	40	42	19		29	100

[a] Based on weighted raw scores.

Table C.1. Grade-Based Subtest Standard Scores: Fall
Grade: 5 (continued)

Standard Score	Word Reading	Numerical Operations	Reading Comprehension[a]	Spelling	Pseudoword Decoding	Math Reasoning	Written Expression	Listening Comprehension	Oral Expression	Standard Score
			Subtest Total Raw Scores							
101			125		41					101
102	105		126	32	42	43	20	27	30	102
103		26	127		43					103
104	106		128	33	44	44	21		31	104
105								28		105
106	107	27	129–130			45			32	106
107	108		131	34	45		22			107
108					46	46		29	33	108
109	109	28	132–133	35	47		23			109
110	110		134			47			34	110
111	111			36			24	30		111
112	112	29	135		48	48			35	112
113			136	37			25			113
114	113		137		49	49			36	114
115	114	30	138–139	38			26	31		115
116	115		140–141			50			37	116
117	116		142	39						117
118		31	143–144		50	51	27	32	38	118
119	117		145–147	40						119
120	118		148–151		51	52	28		39	120
121	119	32	152–155	41						121
122	120		156–159			53	29	33	40	122
123			160–164	42						123
124	121	33	165–170		52	54			41	124
125	122		171–176	43			30			125
126	123		177–182		53	55		34	42	126
127	124	34	183–188	44						127
128			189–192		54	56	31		43	128
129	125		193–194	45						129
130	126	35	195–196		55	57		35	44	130
131	127		197–198	46			32			131
132	128		199			58			45	132
133		36					33			133
134	129			47		59		36	46	134
135	130						34			135
136	131	37				60			47	136
137				48						137
138						61	35		48	138
139		38						37		139
140				49			36		49	140
141						62				141
142		39						38	50	142
143							37			143
144				50		63			51	144
145		40								145
146							38	39	52	146
147						64				147
148		41		51					53	148
149							39			149
150						65		40	54	150
151		42		52						151
152						66	40		55	152
153										153
154		43		53		67		41	56	154
155										155
156									57	156
157		44								157
158									58	158
159										159
160		45–54							59–68	160

[a] Based on weighted raw scores.

Table C.1. Grade-Based Subtest Standard Scores: Winter

Grade: 5

Standard Score	Word Reading	Numerical Operations	Reading Comprehension[a]	Spelling	Pseudoword Decoding	Math Reasoning	Written Expression	Listening Comprehension	Oral Expression	Standard Score
40	0–49	0–6	0–46	0–2		0–12		0–1		40
41	50–51		47–49	3		13		2		41
42	52–53	7	50	4		14		3	0	42
43	54		51–52	5		15				43
44	55		53					4	1	44
45	56	8	54	6		16				45
46	57		55					5	2	46
47	58		56–57	7		17				47
48			58					6	3	48
49	59	9	59–60	8		18				49
50	60		61					7	4	50
51	61		62	9		19				51
52	62	10	63–64				0	8	5	52
53	63		65	10		20				53
54			66				1	9	6	54
55	64	11	67–68	11		21				55
56	65		69						7	56
57	66		70	12		22	2	10		57
58	67	12	71						8	58
59	68		72–73	13		23		11		59
60			74–75				3		9	60
61	69	13	76	14	0	24		12		61
62			77						10	62
63	70		78–79	15	1	25	4	13		63
64		14	80		2				11	64
65	71		81	16		26	5	14		65
66	72		82–83		3					66
67	73–74		84			27	6	15		67
68		15	85–86	17	4				12	68
69	75–76		87–89			28		16	13	69
70	77	16	90	18	5		7		14	70
71	78		91			29		17		71
72			92–93				8		15	72
73	79	17	94	19	6	30				73
74	80		95				9	18	16	74
75	81			20	7	31				75
76	82	18	96		8		10		17	76
77			97	21	9			19		77
78	83				10	32			18	78
79	84	19	98	22	11–12		11	20		79
80	85		99		13	33				80
81	86		100–101	23	14		12			81
82	87	20	102–103		15	34		21	19	82
83			104–105		16		13		20	83
84	88		106–107	24	17	35			21	84
85	89	21	108		18–19			22		85
86	90		109	25	20–21	36	14		22	86
87	91	22	110–111		22					87
88			112	26	23–24	37	15	23		88
89	92		113		25–26					89
90	93–94	23	114	27	27–28	38			23–24	90
91	95		115		29		16	24		91
92			116	28	30–31	39			25	92
93	96	24	117–118		32					93
94	97–98		119	29	33	40	17	25	26	94
95	99		120		34	41				95
96		25		30	35–36		18		27	96
97	100		121		37	42		26		97
98	101		122–123	31	38–39		19		28	98
99	102	26			40	43				99
100	103–104		124–125	32	41		20	27	29	100

[a] Based on weighted raw scores.

Table C.1. Grade-Based Subtest Standard Scores: Winter

Grade: 5 (continued)

Standard Score	Word Reading	Numerical Operations	Reading Comprehension[a]	Spelling	Pseudoword Decoding	Math Reasoning	Written Expression	Listening Comprehension	Oral Expression	Standard Score
101	105		126		42	44				101
102		27		33	43		21		30	102
103	106		127		44	45				103
104			128					28	31	104
105	107	28		34		46	22			105
106	108		129–130		45				32	106
107			131	35	46	47	23	29		107
108	109								33	108
109	110	29	132–133	36	47	48	24			109
110	111		134					30	34	110
111	112			37	48	49				111
112		30	135				25		35	112
113	113		136	38		50				113
114	114		137		49		26	31	36	114
115	115		138–139	39		51				115
116	116	31	140–141						37	116
117			142	40	50	52	27			117
118	117		143–144					32	38	118
119	118	32	145–147	41		53	28			119
120	119		148–151		51				39	120
121	120		152–155				29			121
122		33	156–160	42		54		33	40	122
123	121		161–165							123
124	122		166–170	43	52	55	30		41	124
125	123	34	171–176							125
126	124		177–182	44	53	56		34	42	126
127			183–188				31			127
128	125	35	189–192	45	54	57			43	128
129	126		193–194							129
130	127		195–196	46	55	58	32	35	44	130
131	128	36	197–198							131
132			199			59	33		45	132
133	129			47						133
134	130	37				60	34	36	46	134
135	131									135
136				48		61			47	136
137		38					35			137
138						62			48	138
139				49			36	37		139
140		39							49	140
141						63				141
142							37	38	50	142
143		40		50		64				143
144									51	144
145							38			145
146		41				65		39	52	146
147				51						147
148						66	39		53	148
149		42								149
150						67		40	54	150
151				52			40			151
152		43							55	152
153										153
154				53				41	56	154
155		44								155
156									57	156
157										157
158		45							58	158
159		46								159
160		47–54							59–68	160

[a] Based on weighted raw scores.

Table C.1. Grade-Based Subtest Standard Scores: Spring

Grade: 5

Standard Score	Word Reading	Numerical Operations	Reading Comprehension[a]	Spelling	Pseudoword Decoding	Math Reasoning	Written Expression	Listening Comprehension	Oral Expression	Standard Score
40	0–55	0–6	0–49	0–5		0–15		0–2		40
41	56	7	50			16		3		41
42	57		51–52	6					0	42
43			53			17		4		43
44	58	8	54	7					1	44
45	59		55			18		5		45
46	60		56–57	8					2	46
47	61	9	58			19		6		47
48			59–60	9					3	48
49	62		61–62			20		7		49
50	63	10	63–64	10					4	50
51	64		65–66			21	0	8		51
52	65		67–68	11					5	52
53		11	69–70			22	1	9		53
54	66		71	12					6	54
55	67		72–73			23		10		55
56	68	12	74–75	13			2		7	56
57	69		76			24		11		57
58	70		77	14					8	58
59		13	78			25	3	12		59
60	71		79–80	15	0				9	60
61	72		81			26		13		61
62	73	14	82–83	16	1		4		10	62
63	74		84		2			14		63
64			85–86		3	27	5		11	64
65	75	15	87	17				15		65
66	76		88–89		4	28	6			66
67	77	16	90					16		67
68	78		91	18		29			12	68
69			92		5		7	17	13	69
70	79	17	93			30			14	70
71	80		94	19			8			71
72	81	18	95		6	31		18	15	72
73	82		96–97	20			9			73
74			98–99		7				16	74
75	83	19		21	8	32	10	19		75
76	84		100–101		9				17	76
77	85		102–103	22	10	33	11	20		77
78	86	20	104–105		11–12				18	78
79	87		106–107	23	13	34	12			79
80			108		14			21		80
81	88	21	109		15	35	13			81
82	89		110–111	24	16			22	19	82
83	90	22	112		17	36	14		20	83
84	91			25	18–19				21	84
85			113		20–21	37	15	23		85
86	92	23	114	26	22				22	86
87	93		115		23–24	38				87
88	94		116	27	25–26		16	24		88
89	95	24	117		27–28	39				89
90			118	28	29				23–24	90
91	96		119		30–31	40	17			91
92	97	25	120	29	32	41		25	25	92
93	98				33		18			93
94	99			30	34	42			26	94
95		26	121		35–36		19	26		95
96	100		122	31	37	43			27	96
97	101		123		38–39		20			97
98	102	27		32	40	44		27	28	98
99	103–104		124–125		41		21			99
100	105		126	33	42	45			29	100

[a] Based on weighted raw scores.

Table C.1. Grade-Based Subtest Standard Scores: Spring

Grade: 5 (*continued*)

Standard Score	Word Reading	Numerical Operations	Reading Comprehension[a]	Spelling	Pseudoword Decoding	Math Reasoning	Written Expression	Listening Comprehension	Oral Expression	Standard Score
						Subtest Total Raw Scores				
101		28			43				30	101
102	106		127	34	44	46	22	28		102
103			128						31	103
104	107			35	45	47	23			104
105	108	29	129–130					29	32	105
106			131	36	46	48				106
107	109						24		33	107
108	110		132–133	37	47	49				108
109	111	30	134					30	34	109
110	112			38	48	50	25			110
111			135						35	111
112	113		136	39		51				112
113	114	31	137		49		26	31	36	113
114	115		138–139			52				114
115	116		140–141	40						115
116	117	32	142		50	53	27		37	116
117			143	41				32	38	117
118	118		144–146				28			118
119	119		147–148		51	54			39	119
120	120	33	149–154	42			29			120
121	121		155–157			55		33	40	121
122			158–164	43						122
123	122	34	165–166		52	56	30		41	123
124	123		167–172							124
125	124		173–176	44	53	57		34	42	125
126	125	35	177–183				31			126
127			184–189	45	54	58			43	127
128	126	36	190–194							128
129	127		195–196	46	55	59	32	35	44	129
130	128		197							130
131	129	37	198–199	47		60	33		45	131
132										132
133	130					61	34	36	46	133
134	131	38		48						134
135						62			47	135
136							35			136
137		39				63			48	137
138				49			36	37		138
139						64			49	139
140		40								140
141						65	37	38	50	141
142				50						142
143		41				66			51	143
144							38			144
145						67		39	52	145
146		42		51						146
147							39		53	147
148										148
149		43						40	54	149
150				52			40			150
151									55	151
152		44								152
153				53				41	56	153
154										154
155		45							57	155
156										156
157									58	157
158		46								158
159									59	159
160		47–54							60–68	160

[a] Based on weighted raw scores.

Table C.1. Grade-Based Subtest Standard Scores: Fall

Grade: 6

Standard Score	Word Reading	Numerical Operations	Reading Comprehension[a]	Spelling	Pseudoword Decoding	Math Reasoning	Written Expression	Listening Comprehension	Oral Expression	Standard Score
					Subtest Total Raw Scores					
40	0–63	0–7	0–49	0–6		0–16		0–3		40
41	64		50–52	7		17				41
42	65	8	53–56	8				4	0	42
43			57			18				43
44	66	9	58–60	9				5	1	44
45	67		61			19				45
46			62	10				6	2	46
47	68	10	63			20				47
48	69		64	11				7	3	48
49	70	11	65			21				49
50			66	12			0	8	4	50
51	71		67			22				51
52	72	12	68				1	9	5	52
53			69–70	13		23				53
54	73		71					10	6	54
55		13	72–73	14		24	2			55
56	74		74–76					11	7	56
57			77			25				57
58	75	14	78	15			3	12	8	58
59			79		0	26				59
60	76		80	16				13	9	60
61		15	81–82		1	27	4			61
62	77		83		2			14	10	62
63		16	84	17	3	28	5			63
64	78		85–86					15	11	64
65			87	18	4	29	6			65
66	79	17	88–89					16		66
67			90–91			30				67
68	80		92	19	5		7	17	12	68
69		18	93		6	31			13	69
70	81–82		94	20	7		8		14	70
71	83–84		95			32		18		71
72	85–86	19	96		8		9		15	72
73	87		97	21	9	33				73
74			98–99				10	19	16	74
75	88	20		22	10	34				75
76	89		100–101				11	20	17	76
77	90		102–103		11–12	35				77
78		21	104–106	23	13		12		18	78
79	91		107		14	36		21		79
80	92		108		15		13			80
81		22	109	24	16	37		22		81
82	93		110–111		17–19		14		19	82
83	94		112	25		38			20	83
84	95	23					15	23	21	84
85			113–114	26	20–23	39				85
86	96		115		24		16		22	86
87	97	24		27	25–26	40		24		87
88			116		27–28					88
89	98		117	28	29–30	41	17			89
90	99	25	118		31–32			25	23–24	90
91	100		119	29		42	18			91
92			120		33–34				25	92
93	101	26	121	30	35–36	43	19	26		93
94	102				37				26	94
95	103		122	31	38–39	44	20			95
96	104	27			40			27	27	96
97	105		123	32	41	45	21			97
98	106		124		42				28	98
99	107		125	33	43			28		99
100	108	28	126–127		44	46	22		29	100

[a] Based on weighted raw scores.

Table C.1. Grade-Based Subtest Standard Scores: Fall

Grade: 6 (continued)

Standard Score	Word Reading	Numerical Operations	Reading Comprehension[a]	Spelling	Pseudoword Decoding	Math Reasoning	Written Expression	Listening Comprehension	Oral Expression	Standard Score
					Subtest Total Raw Scores					
101				34	45				30	101
102	109		128			47		29		102
103		29	129	35			23		31	103
104			130		46	48				104
105	110			36	47				32	105
106		30	131			49	24	30		106
107	111		132	37	48				33	107
108			133			50				108
109	112		134	38			25		34	109
110		31	135–136		49	51		31		110
111	113		137	39					35	111
112	114		138			52	26			112
113	115	32	139	40	50				36	113
114	116		140			53	27	32		114
115	117		141							115
116			142	41	51	54			37	116
117	118	33	143				28	33	38	117
118	119		144–146			55				118
119	120		147–148	42	52		29		39	119
120	121	34	149–154			56		34		120
121			155–157	43	53				40	121
122	122		158–164			57	30			122
123	123	35	165–166						41	123
124	124		167–172	44		58	31	35		124
125	125		173–176		54				42	125
126	126	36	177–183	45			32			126
127			184–189			59		36	43	127
128	127		190–194	46	55					128
129	128	37	195–196				33		44	129
130	129		197			60				130
131		38	198–199	47				37	45	131
132	130		200			61	34			132
133	131		201						46	133
134		39	202	48		62	35			134
135			203					38	47	135
136		40	204			63	36			136
137			205						48	137
138			206	49		64				138
139		41	207–208				37	39	49	139
140						65				140
141		42							50	141
142				50			38			142
143						66		40	51	143
144		43								144
145						67	39		52	145
146		44		51						146
147								41	53	147
148							40			148
149		45							54	149
150				52						150
151									55	151
152		46		53						152
153									56	153
154										154
155		47							57	155
156										156
157									58	157
158		48								158
159									59	159
160		49–54							60–68	160

[a] Based on weighted raw scores.

Table C.1. Grade-Based Subtest Standard Scores: Winter

Grade: 6

Standard Score	Subtest Total Raw Scores									Standard Score
	Word Reading	Numerical Operations	Reading Comprehension[a]	Spelling	Pseudoword Decoding	Math Reasoning	Written Expression	Listening Comprehension	Oral Expression	
40	0–63	0–7	0–49	0–6		0–16		0–3		40
41	64	8	50–52	7		17		4		41
42	65		53–56	8		18			0	42
43		9	57					5	1	43
44	66		58–60	9		19				44
45	67		61						2	45
46		10	62	10		20		6		46
47	68		63							47
48	69	11	64	11		21		7	3	48
49	70		65							49
50			66–67	12		22	0	8	4	50
51	71	12	68							51
52	72		69			23	1	9	5	52
53			70	13						53
54	73	13	71			24		10	6	54
55			72–73	14			2			55
56	74		74–76			25		11	7	56
57		14	77							57
58	75		78	15		26	3	12	8	58
59			79		0					59
60	76	15	80	16		27		13	9	60
61			81–82		1		4			61
62	77		83		2	28		14	10	62
63		16	84	17	3		5			63
64	78		85–86			29		15	11	64
65			87	18	4		6			65
66	79	17	88–89			30		16		66
67			90–91							67
68	80		92	19	5	31	7	17	12	68
69		18	93		6				13	69
70	81–82		94	20	7	32	8		14	70
71	83–84		95–96					18		71
72	85–86	19	97		8	33	9		15	72
73	87		98–99	21	9			19		73
74						34	10		16	74
75	88	20	100–101	22	10					75
76	89		102–103			35	11	20	17	76
77	90		104–106		11–12					77
78		21	107	23	13	36	12		18	78
79	91		108		14			21		79
80	92		109		15	37	13			80
81		22	110–111	24	16		14	22		81
82	93		112		17–19	38			19	82
83	94			25			15		20	83
84	95	23	113–114			39		23	21	84
85			115	26	20–23		16			85
86	96		116		24	40			22	86
87	97	24	117	27	25–26			24		87
88			118		27–28	41	17			88
89	98	25	119	28	29–30					89
90	99		120		31–32	42	18	25	23–24	90
91	100		121	29					25	91
92		26	122		33–34	43	19			92
93	101			30	35–36			26	26	93
94	102		123		37	44	20			94
95	103	27	124	31	38–39					95
96	104		125		40	45		27	27	96
97	105		126	32	41		21		28	97
98	106	28	127		42	46				98
99	107–108			33	43		22	28	29	99
100			128	34	44	47			30	100

[a] Based on weighted raw scores.

Table C.1. Grade-Based Subtest Standard Scores: Winter

Grade: 6 (continued)

Standard Score	Word Reading	Numerical Operations	Reading Comprehension[a]	Spelling	Pseudoword Decoding	Math Reasoning	Written Expression	Listening Comprehension	Oral Expression	Standard Score
			Subtest Total Raw Scores							
101	109	29	129		45			29		101
102			130	35		48	23		31	102
103	110	30		36	46					103
104			131			49		30		104
105	111		132	37	47		24		32	105
106	112	31	133			50				106
107			134	38	48				33	107
108	113		135–136			51	25	31		108
109	114	32	137	39					34	109
110	115		138–139		49	52				110
111	116		140	40			26	32	35	111
112	117	33	141			53				112
113	118		142–143		50		27		36	113
114	119		144–146	41		54		33		114
115	120	34	147–152							115
116	121		153–154		51	55	28		37	116
117			155–160	42					38	117
118	122	35	161–164			56		34		118
119	123		165–166	43	52		29		39	119
120	124		167–174			57			40	120
121	125	36	175–180	44	53		30	35		121
122	126		181–185			58				122
123		37	186–189				31		41	123
124	127		190–194	45					42	124
125	128	38	195–196		54	59	32	36		125
126	129		197	46					43	126
127	130		198–199			60				127
128	131	39	200		55		33		44	128
129			201	47		61		37	45	129
130		40	202						46	130
131			203			62	34		47	131
132		41	204	48						132
133			205			63	35	38	48	133
134		42	206							134
135			207–208			64	36		49	135
136				49						136
137		43				65		39	50	137
138							37		51	138
139									51	139
140		44		50		66				140
141							38	40	52	141
142						67				142
143		45								143
144				51			39		53	144
145								41	54	145
146		46								146
147							40		55	147
148				52						148
149		47							56	149
150										150
151				53					57	151
152		48								152
153									58	153
154		49								154
155									59	155
156		50							60	156
157		51							61	157
158									62	158
159		52							63	159
160		53–54							64–68	160

[a] Based on weighted raw scores.

Table C.1. Grade-Based Subtest Standard Scores: Spring
Grade: 6

Standard Score	Subtest Total Raw Scores									Standard Score
	Word Reading	Numerical Operations	Reading Comprehension[a]	Spelling	Pseudoword Decoding	Math Reasoning	Written Expression	Listening Comprehension	Oral Expression	
40	0–63	0–8	0–50	0–6		0–18		0–4		40
41	64	9	51–56	7				5	0	41
42	65		57	8		19			1	42
43			58–60							43
44	66	10	61	9		20			2	44
45	67		62					6		45
46			63	10		21				46
47	68	11	64					7	3	47
48	69		65	11		22				48
49	70		66–67					8	4	49
50		12	68	12		23	0			50
51	71		69					9	5	51
52	72		70			24	1			52
53		13	71	13				10	6	53
54	73		72–73			25				54
55			74–76	14			2	11	7	55
56	74	14	77			26				56
57			78					12	8	57
58	75		79	15		27	3			58
59		15	80		0			13	9	59
60	76		81–82	16	1	28				60
61			83				4	14	10	61
62	77	16	84		2	29				62
63			85–86	17	3		5	15	11	63
64	78		87			30				64
65		17	88–89	18	4		6	16		65
66	79		90–91			31				66
67			92				7	17		67
68	80	18	93	19	5	32			12	68
69			94		6		8		13	69
70	81–82		95–96	20	7	33		18	14	70
71	83–84	19	97				9		15	71
72	85–86		98–99		8	34		19		72
73	87		100–101	21	9		10		16	73
74		20	102–103			35				74
75	88		104	22	10		11	20	17	75
76	89		105–106			36				76
77	90	21	107		11–12		12		18	77
78			108–109	23	13	37		21		78
79	91		110		14		13			79
80	92	22	111		15	38	14	22		80
81			112	24	16					81
82	93		113–114		17–19	39	15		19	82
83	94	23	115	25				23	20–21	83
84	95		116			40	16			84
85			117	26	20–23				22	85
86	96	24	118		24	41	17	24		86
87	97		119–120	27	25–26					87
88		25	121		27–28	42	18			88
89	98		122	28	29–30			25	23–24	89
90	99	26			31–32	43			25	90
91	100		123–124	29			19			91
92			125		33–34	44		26	26	92
93	101	27		30	35–37		20			93
94	102		126			45				94
95	103	28	127	31	38–39			27	27–28	95
96	104				40	46	21			96
97	105–106		128	32	41				29	97
98	107–108	29	129	33	42	47	22	28		98
99	109			34	43				30	99
100	110	30	130	35	44–45	48		29		100

[a] Based on weighted raw scores.

Table C.1. Grade-Based Subtest Standard Scores: Spring

Grade: 6 (*continued*)

Standard Score	Word Reading	Numerical Operations	Reading Comprehension[a]	Spelling	Pseudoword Decoding	Math Reasoning	Written Expression	Listening Comprehension	Oral Expression	Standard Score
					Subtest Total Raw Scores					
101				36			23		31	101
102	111	31	131		46	49		30		102
103	112		132	37						103
104	113		133		47	50	24		32	104
105	114	32	134	38				31		105
106			135–137		48	51			33	106
107	115	33	138–139	39			25			107
108	116–117		140–141			52		32	34	108
109	118		142–143	40	49					109
110	119	34	144–148			53	26		35	110
111	120		149–153					33		111
112	121	35	154–157	41		54	27		36	112
113			158–161		50					113
114	122		162–163	42		55				114
115	123	36	164–170				28	34		115
116	124		171–178	43	51	56			37–38	116
117	125	37	179–183							117
118	126		184–186	44		57	29	35	39–40	118
119	127	38	187–191		52					119
120	128		192–195			58	30			120
121	129	39	196	45	53					121
122	130		197–198			59	31	36	41–42	122
123	131	40	199–200							123
124			201	46		60	32			124
125		41	202		54				43	125
126			203			61		37	44–47	126
127		42	204	47			33			127
128			205		55	62			48	128
129			206				34			129
130		43	207	48		63		38	49	130
131			208							131
132						64	35		50	132
133		44								133
134				49		65	36	39		134
135									51	135
136		45				66				136
137							37		52	137
138				50				40		138
139		46				67				139
140							38		53	140
141									54	141
142		47		51			39	41		142
143									55	143
144										144
145		48					40		56	145
146				52					57	146
147										147
148		49								148
149									58	149
150				53					59	150
151		50								151
152									60	152
153										153
154		51							61	154
155									62	155
156										156
157		52							63	157
158										158
159									64	159
160		53–54							65–68	160

[a] Based on weighted raw scores.

Table C.1. Grade-Based Subtest Standard Scores: Fall

Grade: 7

Standard Score	Word Reading	Numerical Operations	Reading Comprehension[a]	Spelling	Pseudoword Decoding	Math Reasoning	Written Expression	Listening Comprehension	Oral Expression	Standard Score
40	0–69	0–9	0–77	0–8		0–19		0–4	0	40
41		10	78–79	9					5	1	41
42	70		80–81	10		20					42
43	71		82–83						6		43
44		11	84	11		21				2	44
45	72		85–86						7		45
46	73		87	12		22					46
47		12	88–89						8	3	47
48	74		90			23					48
49	75		91	13					9	4	49
50	76	13	92–93			24	0				50
51			94	14					10	5	51
52	77		95			25	1				52
53	78	14	96–97						11	6	53
54			98	15		26					54
55	79		99				2		12	7	55
56	80	15	100–101	16		27					56
57			102–103		0				13	8	57
58	81		104			28	3				58
59	82	16			1				14	9	59
60			105	17		29					60
61	83				2		4		15	10	61
62	84	17	106		3	30					62
63	85		107	18			5		16	11	63
64			108		4	31					64
65	86	18		19			6		17		65
66	87		109			32					66
67					5		7				67
68	88	19	110	20	6	33			18	12	68
69					7–8		8			13	69
70	89		111			34			19	14	70
71	90	20		21	9		9			15	71
72	91		112		10	35					72
73	92			22			10		20	16	73
74		21	113		11	36					74
75	93						11			17	75
76	94		114	23	12	37			21		76
77		22			13		12			18	77
78	95		115	24	14	38			22		78
79	96				15–16		13				79
80		23	116			39	14				80
81	97			25	17–19						81
82	98	24	117		20	40	15		23	19	82
83				26	21					20–21	83
84	99		118		22–24	41	16		24		84
85	100	25	119	27						22	85
86	101				25–26	42	17				86
87		26	120	28	27–28				25		87
88	102		121		29–30	43	18				88
89			122	29	31–32					23–24	89
90	103	27	123–124		33–34	44			26	25	90
91			125	30	35–36		19				91
92	104	28	126		37	45				26	92
93			127	31	38–39		20		27		93
94	105	29	128		40	46					94
95			129	32	41		21			27–28	95
96	106	30	130	33	42	47			28		96
97	107		131–132		43		22			29	97
98	108	31	133	34	44	48			29		98
99	109		134	35	45		23			30	99
100	110	32	135	36		49	24				100

[a] Based on weighted raw scores.

Table C.1. Grade-Based Subtest Standard Scores: Fall

Grade: 7 (continued)

Standard Score	Word Reading	Numerical Operations	Reading Comprehension[a]	Spelling	Pseudoword Decoding	Math Reasoning	Written Expression	Listening Comprehension	Oral Expression	Standard Score
101								30	31	101
102	111–112	33	136	37	46	50	25			102
103										103
104	113		137	38	47	51	26	31	32	104
105	114	34								105
106			138	39	48	52	27		33	106
107	115		139					32		107
108	116–117	35	140–141	40		53			34	108
109	118		142–143		49		28			109
110	119		144–148	41		54		33	35	110
111	120	36	149–153				29			111
112	121		154–157			55			36	112
113			158–161	42	50		30			113
114	122	37	162–163			56		34		114
115	123		164–170	43			31			115
116	124		171–178		51	57			37–38	116
117	125	38	179–183	44				35		117
118	126		184–186			58	32		39–40	118
119	127	39	187–191		52					119
120	128		192–195	45	53	59	33			120
121	129	40	196					36		121
122	130		197–198			60	34		41–42	122
123	131	41	199–200	46						123
124			201			61	35			124
125		42	202		54			37	43	125
126			203	47		62	36		44–47	126
127		43	204							127
128			205		55	63	37		48	128
129		44	206	48				38		129
130			207			64	38		49	130
131			208							131
132		45	209				39		50	132
133				49		65		39		133
134		46					40			134
135									51	135
136						66	41			136
137		47		50				40	52	137
138							42			138
139		48				67				139
140							43		53	140
141				51				41	54	141
142		49					44			142
143									55	143
144		50					45			144
145				52					56	145
146									57	146
147		51					46			147
148				53						148
149		52							58	149
150							47		59	150
151										151
152		53							60	152
153							48			153
154		54							61	154
155									62	155
156							49			156
157									63	157
158										158
159							50		64	159
160							51–55		65–68	160

[a] Based on weighted raw scores.

Table C.1. Grade-Based Subtest Standard Scores: Winter

Grade: 7

Standard Score	Subtest Total Raw Scores									Standard Score
	Word Reading	Numerical Operations	Reading Comprehension[a]	Spelling	Pseudoword Decoding	Math Reasoning	Written Expression	Listening Comprehension	Oral Expression	
40	0–69	0–9	0–77	0–8		0–19		0–4	0	40
41	70	10	78–81	9		20		5	1	41
42	71		82–83	10		21		6		42
43	72		84							43
44	73	11	85–86	11		22		7	2	44
45	74		87							45
46			88–89	12		23		8		46
47	75	12	90						3	47
48	76		91			24		9		48
49			92–93	13					4	49
50	77	13	94			25	0	10		50
51	78		95	14					5	51
52			96–97			26	1	11		52
53	79	14	98	15					6	53
54	80		99			27	2	12		54
55			100–101	16					7	55
56	81	15	102–103			28		13		56
57	82		104		0		3		8	57
58				17		29		14		58
59	83	16			1				9	59
60	84		105			30	4	15		60
61				18	2				10	61
62	85	17	106		3	31	5	16		62
63			107	19					11	63
64	86		108		4	32	6	17		64
65	87	18	109							65
66				20		33	7		12	66
67	88		110		5		8	18	13	67
68		19	111	21	6	34			14	68
69	89				7–8		9	19		69
70			112			35			15	70
71	90–91	20	113	22	9		10			71
72	92				10	36		20	16	72
73	93		114	23			11			73
74	94	21			11	37			17	74
75			115				12	21		75
76	95	22		24	12	38			18	76
77	96		116		13		13	22		77
78				25	14	39	14			78
79	97	23	117		15–16				19	79
80	98			26	17–19	40	15	23	20	80
81		24	118		20					81
82	99		119	27	21	41	16		21	82
83					22–24			24		83
84	100	25	120	28	25	42	17		22	84
85	101		121		26–27					85
86		26	122	29	28–29	43	18	25	23	86
87	102				30				24	87
88	103		123–124	30	31–32	44			25	88
89		27	125		33		19	26		89
90	104		126	31	34	45			26	90
91		28	127		35–36		20			91
92	105		128	32	37	46		27	27	92
93		29	129		38–39		21		28	93
94	106		130	33	40	47				94
95	107	30	131–132		41		22	28	29	95
96	108		133	34	42	48				96
97	109	31	134	35	43		23	29	30	97
98			135		44	49	24			98
99	110	32		36	45					99
100	111		136			50	25	30		100

[a] Based on weighted raw scores.

Table C.1. Grade-Based Subtest Standard Scores: Winter

Grade: 7 (continued)

Standard Score	Word Reading	Numerical Operations	Reading Comprehension[a]	Spelling	Pseudoword Decoding	Math Reasoning	Written Expression	Listening Comprehension	Oral Expression	Standard Score
			Subtest Total Raw Scores							
101	112	33	137	37					31	101
102	113				46	51	26			102
103			138	38				31		103
104	114	34	139		47	52	27		32	104
105			140	39						105
106	115	35	141–142		48	53		32	33	106
107	116		143–148	40			28			107
108	117		149–153			54			34	108
109	118	36	154–156	41	49		29	33		109
110	119		157–161			55			35	110
111	120	37	162				30			111
112	121		163–169	42		56			36	112
113			170–178		50		31	34		113
114	122	38	179–183	43						114
115	123		184–186			57			37	115
116	124	39	187–191	44	51		32	35	38	116
117	125	40	192–195			58				117
118	126		196				33		39–40	118
119	127	41	197	45	52	59				119
120	128		198–200		53		34	36		120
121	129	42	201			60				121
122	130		202	46			35		41–42	122
123	131	43	203							123
124			204			61	36	37	43	124
125		44	205	47	54					125
126			206			62	37		44–47	126
127			207							127
128		45	208	48	55	63	38	38	48	128
129			209							129
130		46				64	39		49	130
131										131
132		47		49			40	39	50	132
133						65				133
134							41			134
135		48							51	135
136				50		66	42	40		136
137									52	137
138		49					43			138
139						67				139
140		50		51			44	41	53	140
141									54	141
142		51					45			142
143									55	143
144		52		52					56	144
145							46			145
146									57	146
147		53		53						147
148							47			148
149									58	149
150		54							59	150
151							48			151
152									60	152
153										153
154							49		61	154
155									62	155
156										156
157							50		63	157
158										158
159							51		64	159
160							52–55		65–68	160

[a] Based on weighted raw scores.

Table C.1. Grade-Based Subtest Standard Scores: Spring

Grade: 7

Standard Score	Subtest Total Raw Scores									Standard Score
	Word Reading	Numerical Operations	Reading Comprehension[a]	Spelling	Pseudoword Decoding	Math Reasoning	Written Expression	Listening Comprehension	Oral Expression	
40	0–72	0–10	0–81	0–9		0–21		0–5	0	40
41	73		82–83			22		6	1	41
42	74		84	10						42
43		11	85–86			23		7		43
44	75		87	11					2	44
45	76		88–89			24		8		45
46		12	90	12					3	46
47	77		91			25		9		47
48	78		92–93	13					4	48
49		13	94			26	0	10		49
50	79		95	14					5	50
51	80		96–97			27	1	11		51
52		14	98	15					6	52
53	81		99			28	2	12		53
54	82		100–101	16					7	54
55		15	102–103			29		13		55
56	83			17	0		3		8	56
57	84		104			30		14		57
58		16		18	1		4		9	58
59			105			31		15		59
60	85			19	2		5		10	60
61		17	106		3	32		16		61
62	86		107				6		11	62
63			108	20	4	33		17		63
64	87	18	109				7		12	64
65			110	21		34	8		13	65
66	88		111		5			18	14	66
67		19	112		6	35	9			67
68	89		113	22	7			19		68
69					8	36	10		15	69
70	90–92	20	114	23						70
71	93		115		9	37	11	20	16	71
72	94				10				17	72
73		21	116	24	11	38	12	21		73
74	95								18	74
75	96	22	117	25	12	39	13	22	19	75
76					13		14			76
77	97		118	26	14	40			20	77
78	98	23			15–16		15	23		78
79			119	27	17–19	41				79
80	99	24			20–21		16		21	80
81			120	28	22–23	42		24		81
82	100	25	121		24–25		17		22	82
83	101		122	29	26–27	43			23	83
84		26			28–29		18	25	24	84
85	102		123	30	30	44			25	85
86	103		124		31		19			86
87		27	125	31	32	45		26	26	87
88	104		126		33		20			88
89	105	28	127	32	34	46			27	89
90			128		35–36		21	27		90
91	106		129	33	37	47			28	91
92	107	29	130		38–39		22			92
93			131–132	34	40	48		28	29	93
94	108	30	133		41		23			94
95	109		134	35	42	49			30	95
96		31	135		43		24	29		96
97	110		136	36	44	50				97
98	111	32	137				25			98
99			138	37	45	51		30		99
100	112–113	33	139				26		31	100

[a] Based on weighted raw scores.

Table C.1. Grade-Based Subtest Standard Scores: Spring
Grade: 7 (continued)

Standard Score	Word Reading	Numerical Operations	Reading Comprehension[a]	Spelling	Pseudoword Decoding	Math Reasoning	Written Expression	Listening Comprehension	Oral Expression	Standard Score
						Subtest Total Raw Scores				
101				38		52				101
102	114	34	140		46		27	31		102
103			141–142	39		53			32	103
104	115	35	143–146		47					104
105			147–152		48	54	28	32	33	105
106	116	36	153–154	40						106
107	117		155–159				29		34	107
108		37	160–162	41	49	55		33		108
109	118		163–168				30		35	109
110	119	38	169–173	42		56				110
111	120		174–182				31		36	111
112	121	39	183–186		50			34		112
113	122	40	187–190	43		57			37	113
114			191–193				32			114
115	123	41	194–196	44	51	58		35	38	115
116	124		197				33			116
117	125	42	198–199	45					39	117
118	126		200–201		52	59	34		40	118
119	127	43	202					36		119
120	128		203	46	53	60	35			120
121	129	44	204						41–42	121
122	130		205				36	37		122
123	131	45	206	47		61			43	123
124			207				37			124
125		46	208		54	62			44–46	125
126			209				38	38	47	126
127		47		48		63				127
128					55		39		48	128
129						64				129
130		48		49			40	39	49	130
131										131
132						65	41		50	132
133		49								133
134				50			42	40		134
135		50				66			51	135
136							43			136
137		51							52	137
138				51		67	44	41		138
139		52							53	139
140							45		54	140
141										141
142		53		52					55	142
143							46			143
144									56	144
145		54							57	145
146				53			47			146
147										147
148									58	148
149							48		59	149
150										150
151									60	151
152							49			152
153									61	153
154									62	154
155							50			155
156									63	156
157							51			157
158									64	158
159										159
160					52–55				65–68	160

[a] Based on weighted raw scores.

Table C.1. Grade-Based Subtest Standard Scores: Fall

Grade: 8

Standard Score	Word Reading	Numerical Operations	Reading Comprehension[a]	Spelling	Pseudoword Decoding	Math Reasoning	Written Expression	Listening Comprehension	Oral Expression	Standard Score
40	0–73	0–10	0–83	0–9		0–22		0–6	0–1	40
41		11	84	10						41
42	74		85–86	11		23		7		42
43			87						2	43
44	75	12	88–89			24		8		44
45	76		90	12					3	45
46			91			25		9		46
47	77	13	92–93	13					4	47
48	78		94			26	0	10		48
49			95	14					5	49
50	79	14	96–97	15		27	1	11		50
51	80		98						6	51
52			99	16		28	2	12		52
53	81	15	100						7	53
54	82		101–102	17		29		13		54
55			103		0		3		8	55
56	83	16		18		30		14		56
57	84		104		1		4		9	57
58				19		31		15		58
59		17	105		2		5		10	59
60	85		106			32		16		60
61			107	20	3		6		11	61
62	86	18	108			33		17		62
63			109	21	4		7		12	63
64	87		110			34	8	18	13	64
65		19	111	22	5				14	65
66	88		112			35	9	19		66
67			113		6–7					67
68	89	20	114	23	8	36	10	20	15	68
69			115		9					69
70	90–92		116	24	10	37	11	21	16	70
71	93–95	21							17	71
72	96		117	25	11	38	12	22		72
73									18	73
74	97	22	118	26	12	39	13			74
75	98				13		14	23	19	75
76			119	27	14	40				76
77	99	23			15–16		15		20	77
78			120	28	17–19	41		24		78
79	100	24			20–21		16			79
80	101		121	29	22–23	42	17		21	80
81		25			24–25			25		81
82	102		122	30	26–27	43	18		22	82
83	103	26	123		28–29		19		23	83
84			124	31	30–31	44		26	24	84
85	104		125		32–33				25	85
86	105	27	126		34	45	20			86
87			127	32	35			27	26	87
88	106	28				46	21			88
89	107		128	33	36				27	89
90		29	129		37	47	22	28		90
91	108		130	34	38–39				28	91
92			131		40	48				92
93	109	30	132	35	41		23	29	29	93
94	110		133		42	49				94
95		31	134	36	43		24		30	95
96	111		135		44	50				96
97	112	32	136	37	45		25	30		97
98			137			51				98
99	113	33	138	38					31	99
100	114–115		139		46	52	26	31		100

[a] Based on weighted raw scores.

Table C.1. Grade-Based Subtest Standard Scores: Fall

Grade: 8 (continued)

Standard Score	Word Reading	Numerical Operations	Reading Comprehension[a]	Spelling	Pseudoword Decoding	Math Reasoning	Written Expression	Listening Comprehension	Oral Expression	Standard Score
			Subtest Total Raw Scores							
101		34		39	47					101
102	116		140			53	27		32	102
103		35	141–142	40	48			32		103
104			143–146			54			33	104
105	117	36	147–152				28			105
106			153–154	41	49			33	34	106
107	118	37	155–159			55	29			107
108			160–162	42					35	108
109	119	38	163–168			56	30			109
110			169–173		50			34	36	110
111	120	39	174–182	43		57	31			111
112	121	40	183–186						37	112
113	122		187–190		51	58		35	38	113
114		41	191–193	44			32			114
115	123		194–196			59			39	115
116	124	42	197	45	52		33	36		116
117	125		198–199			60			40	117
118	126	43	200–201				34			118
119	127		202	46	53	61			41	119
120	128	44	203				35	37	42	120
121	129		204			62				121
122	130	45	205	47			36		43	122
123	131		206			63				123
124		46	207		54		37	38	44–45	124
125			208	48					46	125
126		47	209				38		47	126
127			210		55	64				127
128				49			39	39	48	128
129		48	211							129
130			212			65	40		49	130
131		49		50				40		131
132			213				41		50	132
133			214			66				133
134		50	215				42			134
135			216			67		41	51	135
136		51		51			43			136
137									52	137
138		52					44			138
139									53	139
140							45		54	140
141		53		52						141
142									55	142
143							46			143
144		54							56	144
145									57	145
146				53			47			146
147										147
148									58	148
149							48		59	149
150										150
151									60	151
152							49			152
153									61	153
154									62	154
155							50			155
156									63	156
157							51			157
158									64	158
159										159
160							52–55		65–68	160

[a] Based on weighted raw scores.

Table C.1. Grade-Based Subtest Standard Scores: Winter

Grade: 8

Standard Score	Word Reading	Numerical Operations	Reading Comprehension[a]	Spelling	Pseudoword Decoding	Math Reasoning	Written Expression	Listening Comprehension	Oral Expression	Standard Score
40	0–73	0–10	0–83	0–9		0–22		0–6	0–1	40
41	74	11	84	10						41
42	75		85–86	11		23		7		42
43	76		87			24			2	43
44		12	88–89					8		44
45	77		90	12		25			3	45
46	78		91					9		46
47		13	92–93	13		26			4	47
48	79		94				0	10		48
49	80	14	95	14		27			5	49
50			96–97	15			1	11		50
51	81		98			28			6	51
52	82	15	99	16			2	12		52
53			100	17		29			7	53
54	83		101–102					13		54
55	84	16	103	18	0	30	3		8	55
56								14		56
57	85		104	19	1	31	4		9	57
58		17	105					15		58
59	86				2	32	5		10	59
60			106	20				16		60
61	87	18	107		3	33	6		11	61
62			108	21				17		62
63	88		109		4	34	7		12	63
64	89	19	110				8	18	13	64
65			111	22	5	35			14	65
66	90		112				9	19		66
67	91	20	113	23	6–7	36				67
68	92		114		8		10	20	15	68
69	93		115	24	9	37				69
70	94	21	116		10		11	21	16	70
71	95			25		38			17	71
72	96		117		11		12	22		72
73		22		26		39			18	73
74	97		118		12		13			74
75	98	23		27	13	40	14	23	19	75
76			119		14	41				76
77	99			28	15–16		15		20	77
78		24	120		17–19	42		24		78
79	100			29	20–21		16		21	79
80	101	25	121		22–23	43	17			80
81				30	24–25			25	22	81
82	102	26	122		26–27	44	18			82
83	103		123	31	28–29		19		23	83
84		27	124		30–31	45		26	24	84
85	104		125–126	32	32–33				25	85
86	105	28	127		34	46	20			86
87			128	33	35			27	26	87
88	106	29	129		36	47	21			88
89	107		130	34	37	48			27	89
90	108		131		38–39		22	28		90
91		30	132	35	40	49			28	91
92	109		133		41		23			92
93	110	31	134	36	42	50		29	29	93
94		32	135		43		24			94
95	111		136	37	44	51			30	95
96	112	33	137				25	30		96
97			138	38	45	52				97
98	113	34	139				26		31	98
99	114		140	39		53		31		99
100	115	35	141–142		46		27			100

[a] Based on weighted raw scores.

Table C.1. Grade-Based Subtest Standard Scores: Winter
Grade: 8 (continued)

Standard Score	Word Reading	Numerical Operations	Reading Comprehension[a]	Spelling	Pseudoword Decoding	Math Reasoning	Written Expression	Listening Comprehension	Oral Expression	Standard Score
101	116		143–145		47	54			32	101
102		36	146–152	40				32		102
103	117		153–154		48		28		33	103
104		37	155–159			55	29			104
105		38	160–162	41				33	34	105
106	118				49	56	30			106
107		39	163–172	42					35	107
108	119	40	173–182			57	31		36	108
109			183–185					34		109
110	120	41	186–190	43	50				37	110
111	121		191–193			58	32			111
112		42	194–196		51			35	38	112
113	122		197	44		59	33			113
114		43	198–199						39	114
115	123		200–201	45			34	36	40	115
116	124	44	202		52	60				116
117	125		203				35		41	117
118	126	45	204	46		61				118
119	127		205		53		36	37	42	119
120	128	46	206						43	120
121	129		207–208	47		62	37			121
122	130	47	209						44	122
123	131		210			63	38	38	45	123
124				48	54				46	124
125		48	211				39			125
126			212						47	126
127		49	213	49	55	64		39		127
128			214				40		48	128
129			215							129
130		50	216	50		65	41	40	49	130
131										131
132		51					42		50	132
133						66				133
134								41	51	134
135		52				67	43			135
136				51					52	136
137							44			137
138		53							53	138
139							45			139
140									54	140
141		54		52						141
142							46		55	142
143										143
144							47		56	144
145									57	145
146				53						146
147							48			147
148									58	148
149							49		59	149
150										150
151									60	151
152							50			152
153									61	153
154							51		62	154
155										155
156							52		63	156
157							53			157
158							54		64	158
159							55			159
160									65–68	160

[a] Based on weighted raw scores.

Table C.1. Grade-Based Subtest Standard Scores: Spring

Grade: 8

Standard Score	Word Reading	Numerical Operations	Reading Comprehension[a]	Spelling	Pseudoword Decoding	Math Reasoning	Written Expression	Listening Comprehension	Oral Expression	Standard Score
40	0–75	0–10	0–84	0–9		0–22		0–6	0–1	40
41	76	11	85	10		23		7		41
42	77		86–87	11		24				42
43	78	12	88					8	2	43
44			89–90			25				44
45	79		91	12				9	3	45
46	80	13	92			26				46
47			93–94	13				10	4	47
48	81	14	95			27	0			48
49	82		96	14				11	5	49
50			97	15		28	1			50
51	83	15	98	16				12	6	51
52	84		99	17		29	2			52
53			100					13	7	53
54	85	16	101–102	18		30				54
55			103		0		3	14	8	55
56	86		104	19		31				56
57	87	17	105		1		4	15	9	57
58				20		32				58
59	88		106		2		5	16	10	59
60	89	18	107		3	33				60
61			108	21			6	17	11	61
62	90		109		4	34				62
63	91	19	110				7	18	12	63
64			111	22	5	35	8		13	64
65			112					19	14	65
66	92	20	113	23	6	36	9			66
67	93		114		7			20		67
68	94		115	24	8	37	10		15	68
69		21	116		9			21		69
70	95			25	10	38	11		16	70
71	96	22	117	26	11	39		22	17	71
72							12			72
73	97	23	118	27	12	40			18	73
74	98				13	41	13	23		74
75			119	28	14		14		19	75
76	99	24			15–16	42				76
77			120	29	17–18		15	24	20	77
78	100	25			19–20	43			21	78
79	101		121	30	21–22	44	16			79
80		26			23–24		17	25	22	80
81	102		122	31	25–27	45				81
82	103	27	123		28–29		18		23	82
83			124	32	30–31	46	19	26		83
84	104	28	125–126		32–33				24	84
85	105		127–128	33	34	47			25	85
86		29	129		35	48	20	27		86
87	106		130	34	36				26	87
88	107	30	131		37	49	21			88
89	108		132	35	38–39			28	27	89
90		31	133–134		40–41	50	22–23			90
91	109	32	135	36	42				28	91
92	110		136		43	51	24	29		92
93		33	137	37					29	93
94	111		138		44	52	25			94
95	112	34	139	38				30	30	95
96		35	140		45	53	26			96
97	113		141–142	39					31	97
98	114	36	143–145			54	27	31		98
99	115		146–152		46				32	99
100	116–117	37	153–157	40	47	55	28			100

[a] Based on weighted raw scores.

Table C.1. Grade-Based Subtest Standard Scores: Spring

Grade: 8 (continued)

Standard Score	Word Reading	Numerical Operations	Reading Comprehension[a]	Spelling	Pseudoword Decoding	Math Reasoning	Written Expression	Listening Comprehension	Oral Expression	Standard Score
			Subtest Total Raw Scores							
101		38	158–160				29	32		101
102		39	161–162		48	56			33	102
103				41			30			103
104	118	40	163–172					33	34	104
105			173–184		49	57	31		35	105
106	119	41	185	42					36	106
107			186–190				32			107
108	120	42	191–196			58		34	37	108
109			197	43	50		33			109
110	121	43	198						38	110
111			199–201		51	59	34	35		111
112	122	44	202	44					39	112
113			203				35		40	113
114	123	45	204	45		60		36		114
115	124		205		52		36		41	115
116	125	46	206	46						116
117	126		207–208			61			42	117
118	127	47	209				37	37	43	118
119	128		210	47	53					119
120	129	48	211			62	38		44	120
121	130		212					38	45	121
122	131	49	213				39			122
123			214	48		63			46	123
124			215		54					124
125		50	216				40	39	47	125
126				49		64				126
127					55				48	127
128		51					41			128
129				50		65		40	49	129
130							42			130
131		52							50	131
132						66				132
133							43	41	51	133
134		53								134
135				51		67	44		52	135
136										136
137		54					45		53	137
138										138
139									54	139
140				52			46			140
141									55	141
142							47			142
143									56	143
144							48		57	144
145				53						145
146							49			146
147									58	147
148							50		59	148
149										149
150							51		60	150
151										151
152							52		61	152
153										153
154							53		62	154
155										155
156							54		63	156
157										157
158							55		64	158
159										159
160									65–68	160

Based on weighted raw scores.

Grade 9

Table C.1. Grade-Based Subtest Standard Scores
Grade: 9

Standard Score				Subtest Total Raw Scores						Standard Score
Standard Score	Word Reading	Numerical Operations	Reading Comprehension[a]	Spelling	Pseudoword Decoding	Math Reasoning	Written Expression	Listening Comprehension	Oral Expression	Standard Score
40	0–82	0–11	0–88	0–9		0–24		0–7	0–3	40
41	83–84	12	89	10		25		8		41
42			90	11					4	42
43	85	13	91			26		9		43
44			92	12					5	44
45	86	14	93			27	0	10		45
46			94	13					6	46
47	87		95			28	1	11		47
48		15	96	14					7	48
49	88		97	15		29	2	12		49
50			98	16					8	50
51	89	16	99			30	3	13		51
52			100–101	17					9	52
53	90		102			31	4	14		53
54		17	103	18	0				10	54
55	91		104	19		32	5	15		55
56			105		1				11	56
57	92	18				33	6	16		57
58			106	20	2				12	58
59	93		107	21		34	7	17		59
60	94	19	108		3				13	60
61			109	22		35	8	18		61
62	95		110	23	4				14	62
63			111			36	9	19		63
64	96	20	112	24	5				15	64
65	97		113			37	10	20		65
66			114	25	6				16	66
67	98	21	115		7–8	38	11	21		67
68			116	26	9	39			17	68
69	99	22			10		12	22		69
70			117	27		40			18	70
71	100	23			11	41	13			71
72	101		118	28	12		14	23	19	72
73		24			13	42				73
74	102		119	29	14		15	24	20	74
75		25			15	43	16			75
76	103		120	30	16		17		21	76
77		26			17–19	44	18	25		77
78	104		121	31	20–21	45			22	78
79	105	27			22–23		19			79
80			122	32	24–25	46	20	26	23	80
81	106	28	123		26–27					81
82			124	33	28–31	47	21		24	82
83	107	29	125–126		32–34			27		83
84	108		127–128	34	35–36	48	22		25	84
85		30	129		37					85
86	109		130	35	38	49	23	28	26	86
87		31	131		39					87
88	110		132	36	40	50	24		27	88
89		32	133–134		41			29		89
90	111		135	37	42	51	25		28	90
91	112	33	136		43	52				91
92			137				26	30	29	92
93	113	34	138–139	38	44	53				93
94									30	94
95	114	35	140–141	39	45	54	27	31		95
96		36	142						31	96
97	115		143–145		46					97
98	116	37	146–151	40		55	28	32	32	98
99	117		152–158		47					99
100	118	38	159–161	41			29			100

[a] Based on weighted raw scores.

Table C.1. Grade-Based Subtest Standard Scores

Grade: 9 (continued)

Standard Score	Word Reading	Numerical Operations	Reading Comprehension[a]	Spelling	Pseudoword Decoding	Math Reasoning	Written Expression	Listening Comprehension	Oral Expression	Standard Score
			Subtest Total Raw Scores							
101		39	162		48	56		33	33	101
102		40	163–166				30			102
103	119		167–169	42					34	103
104		41	170–182		49	57				104
105	120		183–185				31	34	35	105
106		42	186–191	43					36	106
107	121		192–196		50	58	32			107
108		43	197						37	108
109	122		198				33	35		109
110	123	44	199–201	44		59			38	110
111			202		51		34			111
112	124	45	203	45				36	39	112
113			204			60	35		40	113
114	125	46	205							114
115	126		206	46	52		36		41	115
116		47	207–208			61		37		116
117	127		209						42	117
118	128	48	210	47			37		43	118
119	129		211		53	62				119
120	130	49	212				38	38	44	120
121	131		213	48					45	121
122		50	214			63	39			122
123			215						46	123
124		51	216	49	54			39		124
125			217			64	40		47	125
126									48	126
127		52	218	50	55					127
128						65	41	40	49	128
129			219	51						129
130		53					42		50	130
131			220			66		41		131
132									51	132
133		54	221	52			43			133
134						67			52	134
135			222	53			44			135
136									53	136
137			223				45			137
138									54	138
139			224							139
140							46		55	140
141										141
142			225				47		56	142
143										143
144			226				48		57	144
145										145
146							49		58	146
147										147
148							50		59	148
149										149
150							51		60	150
151										151
152							52		61	152
153										153
154							53		62	154
155										155
156							54		63	156
157										157
158							55		64	158
159										159
160									65–68	160

[a] Based on weighted raw scores.

Table C.1. Grade-Based Subtest Standard Scores

Grade: 10

Standard Score	Word Reading	Numerical Operations	Reading Comprehension[a]	Spelling	Pseudoword Decoding	Math Reasoning	Written Expression	Listening Comprehension	Oral Expression	Standard Score
40	0–86	0–12	0–90	0–9		0–24		0–8	0–3	40
41		13	91	10		25		9	4	41
42	87		92	11		26			5	42
43		14	93				0	10		43
44	88		94	12		27			6	44
45		15	95	13		28	1	11		45
46	89		96			29			7	46
47			97	14			2	12		47
48	90	16	98	15		30			8	48
49			99				3	13		49
50	91		100–101	16					9	50
51		17	102	17		31	4	14		51
52	92		103						10	52
53			104	18	0	32	5	15		53
54	93	18	105	19					11	54
55			106		1			16		55
56	94			20		33	6		12	56
57			107	21	2	34	7	17		57
58	95	19	108						13	58
59				22	3	35	8	18		59
60	96		109			36			14	60
61		20	110	23	4	37	9	19		61
62	97		111	24					15	62
63		21	112		5	38	10	20		63
64	98		113	25		39			16	64
65			114		6		11	21		65
66	99	22	115	26	7	40			17	66
67			116		8		12	22		67
68	100	23		27	9–10	41			18	68
69			117		11	42	13	23		69
70	101			28	12				19	70
71		24	118		13	43	14	24		71
72	102			29	14		15		20	72
73		25	119		15	44				73
74	103			30	16		16	25	21	74
75		26	120		17–18	45	17			75
76	104			31	19–20				22	76
77		27	121		21–22	46	18	26		77
78	105		122	32	23–24				23	78
79		28	123		25–26	47	19			79
80	106		124	33	27–28		20	27	24	80
81	107	29	125–126		29–31	48				81
82	108		127	34	32–35		21		25	82
83		30	128		36	49		28		83
84	109		129–130	35	37–38		22		26	84
85		31	131–132		39	50				85
86	110		133–134	36	40		23	29	27	86
87		32	135–137		41	51				87
88	111		138	37	42		24		28	88
89		33	139		43	52		30		89
90	112		140	38			25		29	90
91		34	141–142		44	53	26			91
92	113		143					31	30	92
93	114	35	144–145	39	45	54	27			93
94			146					32	31	94
95	115	36		40	46		28			95
96		37	147–151			55			32	96
97	116		152–153		47		29	33		97
98	117	38	154–158	41						98
99	118–119		159–162		48	56			33	99
100	120–121	39	163–166				30			100

[a] Based on weighted raw scores.

Table C.1. Grade-Based Subtest Standard Scores

Grade: 10 (continued)

Standard Score	Word Reading	Numerical Operations	Reading Comprehension[a]	Spelling	Pseudoword Decoding	Math Reasoning	Written Expression	Listening Comprehension	Oral Expression	Standard Score
101		40	167–169	42				34	34	101
102			170–182		49	57	31			102
103	122	41	183–191						35	103
104			192–198	43			32		36	104
105		42	199–200		50	58		35		105
106	123		201				33		37	106
107		43	202							107
108		44	203	44		59	34		38	108
109	124		204		51			36		109
110		45		45					39	110
111	125		205			60	35		40	111
112		46	206							112
113	126		207		52		36	37	41	113
114		47	208	46		61				114
115	127		209						42	115
116	128						37		43	116
117	129	48	210		53	62		38		117
118			211	47					44	118
119	130	49	212			63	38		45	119
120	131									120
121		50	213	48			39	39	46	121
122			214		54	64				122
123		51	215	49					47	123
124			216				40			124
125		52	217					40	48	125
126				50		65				126
127		53	218		55		41		49	127
128				51					50	128
129		54	219			66		41		129
130							42		51	130
131			220							131
132				52		67	43		52	132
133			221							133
134				53			44		53	134
135			222							135
136							45		54	136
137			223							137
138							46		55	138
139			224							139
140							47		56	140
141										141
142			225				48		57	142
143										143
144			226				49		58	144
145										145
146							50		59	146
147										147
148							51		60	148
149										149
150							52		61	150
151										151
152							53		62	152
153										153
154							54		63	154
155										155
156							55		64	156
157										157
158									65	158
159										159
160									66–68	160

[a] Based on weighted raw scores.

Grade 11

Table C.1. Grade-Based Subtest Standard Scores

Grade: 11

Standard Score	Word Reading	Numerical Operations	Reading Comprehension[a]	Spelling	Pseudoword Decoding	Math Reasoning	Written Expression	Listening Comprehension	Oral Expression	Standard Score
			Subtest Total Raw Scores							
40	0–86	0–13	0–94	0–10		0–25		0–10	0–4	40
41	87	14	95	11		26			5	41
42			96				0	11		42
43	88		97	12		27			6	43
44		15	98	13		28	1	12		44
45	89		99			29			7	45
46			100–101	14			2	13		46
47	90	16	102	15		30			8	47
48			103				3	14		48
49	91		104	16					9	49
50		17	105	17		31	4	15		50
51	92		106						10	51
52				18	0	32	5	16		52
53	93	18	107	19					11	53
54			108		1		6	17		54
55	94			20		33			12	55
56			109	21	2	34	7	18		56
57	95	19							13	57
58			110	22	3	35	8	19		58
59	96	20				36			14	59
60			111	23	4		9	20		60
61	97					37			15	61
62		21	112	24	5		10	21		62
63	98		113			38			16	63
64		22	114	25	6	39	11	22		64
65	99		115		7				17	65
66		23	116	26	8	40	12	23		66
67	100				9–10				18	67
68		24	117	27	11	41	13	24		68
69	101		118			42			19	69
70		25		28	12–13		14			70
71	102		119–120		14	43	15	25	20	71
72		26	121–122	29	15–16					72
73	103		123		17	44	16		21	73
74			124	30	18		17	26		74
75	104	27	125–126		19–20	45			22	75
76			127	31	21–22		18			76
77	105	28	128		23–24	46	19	27	23	77
78			129–130	32	25–26					78
79	106	29	131–132		27–28	47	20		24	79
80	107		133–134	33	29–31			28		80
81	108	30	135–137		32–34	48	21		25	81
82			138	34	35–36			29		82
83	109	31	139		37–38	49	22		26	83
84				35	39					84
85	110	32	140		40	50	23	30	27	85
86	111		141	36	41					86
87		33	142		42	51	24		28	87
88	112		143	37	43			31		88
89		34				52	25		29	89
90	113		144	38	44		26			90
91	114	35	145			53		32	30	91
92		36	146		45		27			92
93	115			39		54			31	93
94	116	37	147–148		46		28			94
95			149–151	40				33	32	95
96	117	38	152–153		47	55	29			96
97	118	39	154–162						33	97
98		40	163–182	41	48		30	34		98
99	119–120		183–191	42		56			34	99
100	121–122	41	192–197				31			100

[a] Based on weighted raw scores.

Table C.1. Grade-Based Subtest Standard Scores

Grade: 11 (continued)

Standard Score	Word Reading	Numerical Operations	Reading Comprehension[a]	Spelling	Pseudoword Decoding	Math Reasoning	Written Expression	Listening Comprehension	Oral Expression	Standard Score
101		42	198	43		57			35	101
102		43			49		32	35		102
103	123		199–200	44		58			36	103
104		44	201		50		33			104
105						59			37	105
106	124	45	202	45			34	36	38	106
107			203							107
108	125	46	204		51	60	35		39	108
109			205	46					40	109
110	126	47	206					37		110
111	127		207			61	36		41	111
112		48	208	47	52					112
113	128		209				37		42	113
114		49				62		38		114
115	129	50	210				38		43	115
116			211	48	53	63				116
117	130		212						44	117
118		51					39	39	45	118
119	131	52	213			64				119
120			214	49			40		46	120
121		53	215		54					121
122			216			65			47	122
123			217	50			41	40		123
124		54							48	124
125			218			66	42			125
126				51	55				49	126
127			219					41	50	127
128						67	43			128
129			220	52					51	129
130										130
131			221				44		52	131
132				53					53	132
133			222							133
134							45		54	134
135			223							135
136							46		55	136
137			224							137
138									56	138
139							47			139
140			225				48		57	140
141										141
142			226				49		58	142
143										143
144							50		59	144
145										145
146							51		60	146
147										147
148							52		61	148
149										149
150							53		62	150
151										151
152							54		63	152
153										153
154							55		64	154
155										155
156									65	156
157										157
158									66	158
159										159
160									67–68	160

[a] Based on weighted raw scores.

Table C.1. Grade-Based Subtest Standard Scores

Grade: 12

Standard Score	Word Reading	Numerical Operations	Reading Comprehension[a]	Spelling	Pseudoword Decoding	Math Reasoning	Written Expression	Listening Comprehension	Oral Expression	Standard Score
40	0–89	0–14	0–95	0–11		0–27	0	0–11	0–4	40
41			96	12		28		12	5	41
42	90		97			29	1			42
43		15	98	13				13	6	43
44	91		99	14		30	2			44
45			100					14	7	45
46	92		101–102	15			3			46
47		16	103	16		31		15	8	47
48	93		104				4			48
49			105	17				16	9	49
50	94	17	106	18	0	32	5			50
51						33		17	10	51
52	95	18	107	19	1		6			52
53			108	20		34		18	11	53
54	96				2		7			54
55			109	21		35		19	12	55
56	97	19		22	3	36	8			56
57			110					20	13	57
58	98	20		23	4	37	9			58
59			111					21	14	59
60	99	21	112	24	5	38	10			60
61			113			39		22	15	61
62	100		114	25	6	40	11			62
63		22	115		7			23	16	63
64	101		116	26	8–9	41	12			64
65		23	117		10			24	17	65
66	102		118	27	11	42	13			66
67		24			12				18	67
68	103			28	13	43	14	25		68
69		25			14		15		19	69
70	104		119–120	29	15–16	44		26		70
71	105	26	121–123		17	45	16		20	71
72	106		124–125	30	18		17			72
73	107	27	126–127		19–20	46		27	21	73
74	108		128	31	21		18			74
75		28	129		22–23	47			22	75
76	109		130–131	32	24–26		19	28		76
77		29	132–133		27–28	48			23	77
78	110		134–136	33	29–31		20			78
79		30	137–138		32–34	49		29	24	79
80	111		139	34	35–36		21			80
81		31	140		37–38	50		30	25	81
82	112			35	39		22			82
83		32	141		40	51	23		26	83
84	113		142–143	36	41		24	31		84
85		33			42				27	85
86	114		144	37	43	52	25			86
87	115	34	145						28	87
88			146		44	53	26	32		88
89	116	35		38					29	89
90		36	147		45		27			90
91	117	37	148–153	39		54		33	30	91
92					46		28			92
93	118	38	154–155			55			31	93
94		39	156–160	40	47		29			94
95	119		161–166					34	32	95
96		40	167	41		56	30			96
97	120	41	168–179		48				33	97
98		42	180–185	42		57	31	35		98
99	121		186–197						34	99
100	122–123	43	198–199	43	49	58	32		35	100

[a] Based on weighted raw scores.

Table C.1. Grade-Based Subtest Standard Scores

Grade: 12 (continued)

Standard Score	Word Reading	Numerical Operations	Reading Comprehension[a]	Spelling	Pseudoword Decoding	Math Reasoning	Written Expression	Listening Comprehension	Oral Expression	Standard Score
101			200						36	101
102		44	201–202	44			33	36		102
103	124				50	59			37	103
104		45	203–204				34			104
105				45					38	105
106	125	46				60	35	37	39	106
107			205	46	51				40	107
108	126	47	206			61	36		41	108
109			207						42	109
110	127	48	208	47			37	38		110
111			209		52	62			43	111
112	128			48			38			112
113		49	210						44	113
114	129		211			63	39	39		114
115		50		49	53				45	115
116	130		212			64				116
117			213	50			40		46	117
118	131	51	214							118
119		52	215		54	65	41	40	47	119
120			216	51						120
121		53	217			66	42		48	121
122										122
123			218	52					49	123
124		54			55	67	43	41		124
125			219						50	125
126							44			126
127			220	53					51	127
128							45			128
129			221						52	129
130									53	130
131			222				46			131
132									54	132
133			223				47			133
134									55	134
135			224				48			135
136									56	136
137							49			137
138			225						57	138
139										139
140			226				50		58	140
141										141
142							51		59	142
143										143
144							52		60	144
145										145
146							53		61	146
147										147
148							54		62	148
149										149
150							55		63	150
151										151
152									64	152
153										153
154									65	154
155										155
156									66	156
157										157
158									67	158
159										159
160									68	160

[a] Based on weighted raw scores.

Table C.2. Grade-Based Composite Standard Scores

Standard Score	Sums of Standard Scores					Standard Score
	Reading	Mathematics	Written Language	Oral Language	Total	
40	120–136	80–93	80–100	80–92	360–463	40
41	137–141	94–96	101–102	93–96	464–471	41
42	142–146	97–99	103–104	97–99	472–480	42
43	147–151	100–102	105–106	100–102	481–488	43
44	152–156	103–105	107–108	103–105	489–495	44
45	157–159	106–107	109–110	106–108	496–501	45
46	160–162	108–109	111–112	109–110	502–509	46
47	163–165	110	113	111	510–517	47
48	166–168	111–112	114–115	112–113	518–524	48
49	169–171	113	116	114	525–532	49
50	172–174	114–115	117–118	115–116	533–539	50
51	175–177	116	119	117	540–547	51
52	178–180	117–118	120	118–119	548–554	52
53	181–182	119	121–122	120	555–561	53
54	183–184	120–121	123	121–122	562–568	54
55	185–187	122	124–125	123	569–576	55
56	188–189	123–124	126	124–125	577–584	56
57	190–191	125	127–128	126	585–591	57
58	192–194	126–127	129	127–128	592–599	58
59	195–196	128	130–131	129	600–606	59
60	197–198	129–130	132	130–131	607–613	60
61	199–200	131	133–134	132	614–620	61
62	201–202	132–133	135	133–134	621–627	62
63	203–204	134	136–137	135	628–635	63
64	205–206	135–136	138	136–137	636–642	64
65	207–208	137	139	138–140	643–648	65
66	209–210	138–140	140	141–142	649–654	66
67	211	141	141	143	655–661	67
68	212–213	142	142	144–145	662–669	68
69	214	143–144	143–144	146	670–678	69
70	215–217	145	145–146	147–148	679–685	70
71	218–221	146–147	147	149	686–692	71
72	222–224	148–149	148–149	150–151	693–700	72
73	225–227	150	150–151	152	701–709	73
74	228–231	151–152	152–153	153–154	710–718	74
75	232–235	153–154	154	155–156	719–726	75
76	236–237	155–156	155	157–158	727–736	76
77	238–240	157–158	156–157	159–160	737–745	77
78	241–243	159–160	158–159	161–162	746–755	78
79	244–246	161–162	160–162	163–164	756–764	79
80	247–248	163–164	163–164	165–166	765–773	80
81	249–251	165–166	165–166	167	774–781	81
82	252–255	167–168	167–168	168–169	782–789	82
83	256–258	169–170	169–170	170–171	790–797	83
84	259–261	171–172	171–172	172–173	798–805	84
85	262–264	173–174	173–174	174–175	806–813	85
86	265–267	175–176	175–176	176–177	814–821	86
87	268–270	177–178	177–178	178–179	822–829	87
88	271–274	179–180	179	180–181	830–837	88
89	275–280	181–183	180–181	182–184	838–846	89
90	281	184–185	182–183	185	847–852	90
91	282	186	184–185	186	853–858	91
92	283–284	187–188	186–187	187–188	859–865	92
93	285–287	189	188–189	189	866–871	93
94	288–291	190–191	190–191	190–191	872–879	94
95	292–294	192–193	192–193	192–193	880–886	95
96	295–297	194–195	194–195	194–195	887–892	96
97	298–300	196–197	196	196	893–899	97
98	301–303	198	197–198	197–198	900–905	98
99	304–306	199–200	199–200	199–200	906–912	99
100	307–309	201–202	201–202	201–202	913–918	100

Table C.2. Grade-Based Composite Standard Scores (*continued*)

Standard Score	Sums of Standard Scores					Standard Score
	Reading	Mathematics	Written Language	Oral Language	Total	
101	310–312	203–204	203–204	203	919–924	101
102	313–314	205	205–206	204–205	925–930	102
103	315–316	206–207	207	206–207	931–937	103
104	317–318	208–209	208–209	208–209	938–943	104
105	319–320	210–211	210–211	210	944–949	105
106	321–322	212–213	212–213	211–212	950–955	106
107	323–324	214–215	214	213–214	956–961	107
108	325–326	216–217	215–216	215	962–966	108
109	327–328	218–219	217–218	216–217	967–976	109
110	329–330	220	219	218–219	977–978	110
111	331–332	221	220–221	220	979–984	111
112	333–334	222–223	222	221–222	985–990	112
113	335–336	224	223–224	223	991–995	113
114	337–338	225	225	224–225	996–1001	114
115	339–340	226–227	226–227	226	1002–1006	115
116	341–342	228		227	1007–1012	116
117	343–344	229	228–229	228–229	1013–1018	117
118	345–346	230–232	230–232	230–231	1019–1023	118
119	347–348	233–236	233–234	232–234	1024–1028	119
120	349	237–238	235	235	1029–1034	120
121	350	239	236–237	236	1035–1040	121
122	351	240–241	238	237	1041–1047	122
123	352	242	239–240	238–239	1048–1053	123
124	353–354	243–244	241	240	1054–1060	124
125	355–356	245–246	242–243	241–242	1061–1064	125
126	357–358	247	244	243	1065–1069	126
127	359–360	248	245–246	244–245	1070–1074	127
128	361–362	249	247	246–247	1075–1079	128
129	363–364	250–252	248–249	248–250	1080–1087	129
130	365–366	253	250	251	1088–1097	130
131	367–368	254	251–252	252	1098–1104	131
132	369–370	255	253	253	1105–1112	132
133	371–372	256	254–255	254	1113–1118	133
134	373–374	257	256	255	1119–1126	134
135	375–376	258–259	257–258	256	1127–1132	135
136	377–378	260	259	257	1133–1139	136
137	379–380	261–262	260–261	258–259	1140–1145	137
138	381–382	263	262	260	1146–1152	138
139	383–385	264–265	263–264	261–262	1153–1158	139
140	386	266	265	263	1159–1164	140
141	387	267–268	266–267	264	1165–1170	141
142	388–389	269	268	265	1171–1177	142
143	390–391	270–271	269–270	266–267	1178–1183	143
144	392–393	272	271–272	268	1184–1190	144
145	394–395	273–274	273	269–270	1191–1197	145
146	396–397	275	274	271–272	1198–1204	146
147	398	276–277	275	273–274	1205–1210	147
148	399–400	278	276–277	275	1211–1216	148
149	401–402	279–280	278	276–277	1217–1223	149
150	403–404	281	279	278	1224–1230	150
151	405–406	282–283	280–281	279–280	1231–1236	151
152	407–408	284	282	281	1237–1243	152
153	409–410	285–286	283–284	282–283	1244–1249	153
154	411–412	287	285	284	1250–1256	154
155	413–414	288–289	286–287	285–286	1257–1262	155
156	415–416	290	288	287	1263–1269	156
157	417–418	291–292	289–290	288–289	1270–1275	157
158	419–420	293	291	290	1276–1281	158
159	421–422	294–295	292–293	291–292	1282–1287	159
160	423–480	296–320	294–320	293–320	1288–1440	160

Additional Grade-Based Normative Tables

D

Table D.1. Confidence Interval Magnitudes for the Grade-Based Subtest Standard Scores

						Subtest Standard Scores					
Grade	Confidence Level	Word Reading	Numerical Operations	Reading Comp	Spelling	Pseudoword Decoding	Math Reasoning	Written Expression	Listening Comp	Oral Expression	Confidence Level
PreK	95%	4					9		15	10	95%
(Age 5)	90%	4					8		13	9	90%
K	95%	5	12		9		9		14	10	95%
	90%	4	10		8		8		12	9	90%
1	95%	4	15	9	8	5	9	9	13	10	95%
	90%	4	13	8	7	4	8	7	11	9	90%
2	95%	4	13	9	7	4	9	9	13	10	95%
	90%	4	11	7	6	4	7	7	11	9	90%
3	95%	5	10	8	8	4	8	14	12	12	95%
	90%	4	9	7	7	4	7	12	10	10	90%
4	95%	5	11	8	8	5	9	14	13	12	95%
	90%	4	9	7	7	4	7	12	11	10	90%
5	95%	5	10	7	7	4	7	13	14	13	95%
	90%	4	9	6	6	4	6	11	12	11	90%
6	95%	5	9	9	6	5	7	13	12	13	95%
	90%	5	7	7	5	4	6	11	10	11	90%
7	95%	7	9	6	8	5	8	11	12	11	95%
	90%	6	8	5	7	4	7	9	10	9	90%
8	95%	6	8	7	7	5	8	11	12	11	95%
	90%	5	7	6	6	5	7	9	10	9	90%
9	95%	7	7	8	9	6	9	11	13	11	95%
	90%	6	6	7	7	5	7	9	11	9	90%
10	95%	7	9	7	9	7	9	10	14	12	95%
	90%	6	7	6	8	6	7	9	12	10	90%
11	95%	5	7	9	8	6	7	10	13	12	95%
	90%	4	6	8	7	5	6	9	11	10	90%
12	95%	7	7	9	8	5	8	10	12	12	95%
	90%	6	6	7	7	4	7	9	10	10	90%

Note. Each value is the average of the values obtained separately for the Fall and Spring standardization samples (PreK–8).

Table D.2. Confidence Interval Magnitudes for the Grade-Based Composite Standard Scores

| | | Composite Standard Scores | | | | | |
Grade	Confidence Level	Reading	Mathematics	Written Language	Oral Language	Total	Confidence Level
PreK	95%				9		95%
(Age 5)	90%				8		90%
K	95%		9		9		95%
	90%		7		8		90%
1	95%	4	10	7	9	4	95%
	90%	4	8	6	8	4	90%
2	95%	4	9	7	9	4	95%
	90%	4	7	6	8	4	90%
3	95%	4	7	8	10	4	95%
	90%	4	6	7	8	4	90%
4	95%	4	7	8	10	4	95%
	90%	3	6	7	8	4	90%
5	95%	4	7	8	11	4	95%
	90%	3	6	7	9	4	90%
6	95%	4	6	8	10	4	95%
	90%	3	5	7	9	4	90%
7	95%	4	7	7	10	4	95%
	90%	4	6	6	8	4	90%
8	95%	4	6	7	9	4	95%
	90%	3	5	6	8	3	90%
9	95%	5	6	7	10	4	95%
	90%	4	5	6	8	4	90%
10	95%	4	7	8	11	4	95%
	90%	4	6	7	9	4	90%
11	95%	5	5	7	11	4	95%
	90%	4	4	6	9	4	90%
12	95%	4	6	7	11	4	95%
	90%	4	5	6	9	4	90%

Note. Each value is the average of the values obtained separately for the Fall and Spring standardization samples (PreK–8).

Table D.3. Percentile Ranks, Normal Curve Equivalents, and Stanines Corresponding to the Grade-Based Subtest and Composite Standard Scores

Standard Score	Percentile Rank	Normal Curve Equivalent	Stanine	Standard Score	Percentile Rank	Normal Curve Equivalent	Stanine
160				96	39	44	
159				95	37	43	
158				94	34	42	
157				93	32	40	
156				92	30	39	4
155				91	27	37	
154				90	25	36	
153				89	23	35	
152				88	21	33	
151				87	19	32	
150				86	18	30	
149	>99.9			85	16	29	3
148	99.9			84	14	28	
147	99.9			83	13	26	
146	99.9			82	12	25	
145	99.9			81	10	23	
144	99.8			80	9	22	
143	99.8			79	8	21	
142	99.7			78	7	19	
141	99.7			77	6	18	2
140	99.6			76	5	16	
139	99.5			75	5	15	
138	99			74	4	13	
137	99			73	4	12	
136	99	>99		72	3	11	
135	99	99		71	3	9	
134	99	98		70	2	8	
133	99	96	9	69	2	6	
132	98	95		68	2	5	
131	98	94		67	1	4	
130	98	92		66	1	2	1
129	97	91		65	1	1	
128	97	89		64	1	<1	
127	96	88		63	1		
126	96	87		62	1		
125	95	85		61	0.5		
124	95	84		60	0.4		
123	94	82		59	0.3		
122	93	81		58	0.3		
121	92	79	8	57	0.2		
120	91	78		56	0.2		
119	90	77		55	0.1		
118	88	75		54	0.1		
117	87	74		53	0.1		
116	86	72		52	0.1		
115	84	71		51	<0.1		
114	82	70	7	50			
113	81	68		49			
112	79	67		48			
111	77	65		47			
110	75	64		46			
109	73	63		45			
108	70	61		44			
107	68	60	6	43			
106	66	58		42			
105	63	57		41			
104	61	56		40			
103	58	54					
102	55	53					
101	53	51					
100	50	50					
99	47	49	5				
98	45	47					
97	42	46					

Table D.4. Grade Equivalents Corresponding to the Subtest Total Raw Scores and Weighted Raw Scores

Subtest Total Raw Scores

Grade Equivalents	Word Reading	Numerical Operations	Reading Comprehension[a]	Spelling	Pseudoword Decoding	Math Reasoning	Written Expression	Listening Comprehension	Oral Expression (PreK–3)[b]	Oral Expression (4–12)[c]
PreK5:0	0–4	0		0	0	0–3	0	0–3	0–6	0
PreK5:1	5–9					4–6		4–7	7–13	
PreK5:2	10–14	1				7–10		8–11	14–20	1
PreK5:3				1						
PreK5:4		2			1					2
PreK5:5	15						1	12		
PreK5:6	16	3		2						3
PreK5:7	17–19				2					
PreK5:8	20–22	4				11				4
PreK5:9	23–25			3						
K:0	26–27	5			3		2			5
K:1	28–30									
K:2	31–32	6		4		12		13		6
K:3	33			5	4	13				
K:4	34						3			7
K:5	35–36	7		6		14			21	
K:6	37–38			7	5	15				8
K:7	39–40			8						
K:8	41–43	8		9		16	4	14	22	9
K:9	44–45			10	6	17		15		
1:0	46–48	9	60–62			18			23	10
1:1	49–50		63–65	11		19		16		
1:2	51–53	10	66–68	12	7	20	5	17	24	11
1:3	54–56		69–71	13	8				25	
1:4	57–58		72–74							12
1:5	59–60	11	75–77	14	9	21	6		26	
1:6	61–62		78–79	15	10–11	22				13
1:7	63–65		80–82	16	12	23			27	
1:8	66–68	12	83–84	17	13–14	24	7	18	28	14
1:9	69–70		85–86	18	15–16	25				
2:0	71–73		87–88		17–18				29	15
2:1	74–75		89–90	19	19–20	26				
2:2	76–77	13	91–92	20	21–22	27		19	30	16
2:3				21						
2:4			93			28				17
2:5	78	14	94	22			8	20		
2:6	79		95–96	23	23	29	9		31	18
2:7	80–81		97–98		24–25					
2:8	82–84	15	99–100	24	26	30	10	21	32	19
2:9	85–86		101–102		27–28	31	11			
3:0	87–88	16	103–104		29–30		12–13			20
3:1	89–90		105–107		31–32	32	14–15			
3:2	91–92	17	108	25	33	33	16	22	33	21
3:3		18	109							
3:4			110							22
3:5		19	111–112	26		34		23	34	
3:6	93		113							23
3:7	94		114				17		35	
3:8	95	20	115	27	34	35				24
3:9			116						36	
4:0	96		117			36				25
4:1			118						37	26
4:2	97	21	119	28	35	37	18	24		27
4:3					36	38			38	
4:4		22	120							
4:5	98		121	29	37			25	39	
4:6	99	23	122		38	39				
4:7	100	24	123						40	
4:8	101			30	39	40	19	26		28
4:9									41	
5:0	102		124			41				
5:1									42	
5:2	103	25		31	40	42				29
5:3									43	
5:4						43				
5:5		26		32	41		20	27	44	
5:6	104	27	125			44				
5:7									45	
5:8	105	28	126	33	42	45	21			
5:9	106								46	

Note. For subtests not administered to Grades PreK or K, grade equivalents are extrapolated.

[a] Based on weighted raw scores. Scores below 60 have a grade equivalent of less than Grade 1:0.

[b] Scores are for Grades PreK–3.

[c] Scores are for Grades 4–12.

Table D.4. Grade Equivalents Corresponding to the Subtest Total Raw Scores and Weighted Raw Scores (*continued*)

Subtest Total Raw Scores

Grade Equivalents	Word Reading	Numerical Operations	Reading Comprehension[a]	Spelling	Pseudoword Decoding	Math Reasoning	Written Expression	Listening Comprehension	Oral Expression (PreK–3)[b]	Oral Expression (4–12)[c]
6:0					43					
6:1	107								47	
6:2	108				44	46	22	28		
6:3			127						48	
6:4										
6:5		29	128	34		47			49	30
6:6	109									
6:7			129						50	
6:8	110	30	130	35		48	23	29		
6:9			131						51	
7:0		31	132–133							
7:1			134						52	
7:2		32	135	36	45	49	24	30		
7:3									53	
7:4										
7:5	111		136			50	25		54	31
7:6			137	37						
7:7	112		138			51			55	
7:8	113	33					26			
7:9									56	
8:0			139							
8:1									57	
8:2	114			38	46	52		31		
8:3		34	140						58	
8:4						53				
8:5	115	35	141–143	39			27		59	32
8:6		36	144–148			54				
8:7	116		149–152						60	
8:8		37	153–155	40	47	55	28	32		
8:9			156						61	
9:0	117									
9:1			157						62	
9:2			158							
9:3									63	
9:4	118	38	159	41		56	29	33		33
9:5			160						64	
9:6										
9:7			161						65	
9:8	119									
9:9			162						66	
10:0										
10:1									67	
10:2	120		163							
10:3									68	
10:4		39	164	42	48		30	34		
10:5			165						69	
10:6			166–168							
10:7			169–171							
10:8			172–174						70	
10:9	121	40	175–177							34
11:0			178–180							
11:1			181–183						71	
11:2			184–186							
11:3			187–189							
11:4		41	190–192				31	35	72	
11:5			193–194							
11:6			195							
11:7								36	73	
11:8						57				
11:9	122	42	196							
12:0									74	
12:1			197							
12:2										
12:3									75	
12:4	123	43	198	43	49	58	32			35
12:5								37		
12:6			199						76	
12:7										
12:8	124									
12:9			200	44					77	
>12:9	125–131	44–54	201–233	45–53	50–55	59–67	33–55	38–41		36–68

Note. For subtests not administered to Grades PreK or K, grade equivalents are extrapolated.

[a] Based on weighted raw scores.
[b] Scores are for Grades PreK–3.
[c] Scores are for Grades 4–12.

Age-Based Conversion Tables

Table E.1. Total Raw Score Conversion to Weighted Raw Score for Reading Comprehension

Total Raw Score	Item Set Administered									Total Raw Score
	Grade 1 (Items 1–27)	Grade 2 (Items 10–44)	Grade 3 (Items 20–54)	Grade 4 (Items 34–69)	Grade 5 (Items 55–85)	Grade 6 (Items 59–93)	Grade 7 (Items 75–107)	Grade 8 (Items 75–114)	Grades 9–12 (Items 94–127)	
0	0	21	29	46	63	63	102	94	101	0
1	7	29	38	49	67	66	104	95	103	1
2	14	33	46	52	71	69	106	96	105	2
3	20	37	54	55	74	72	108	97	107	3
4	25	41	57	58	78	75	109	98	109	4
5	29	45	60	61	81	79	110	99	110	5
6	33	48	63	64	85	83	111	100	111	6
7	36	50	66	67	88	87	112	102	112	7
8	39	51	68	70	92	90	113	103	113	8
9	41	52	69	72	94	92	114	105	114	9
10	44	53	70	74	96	94	115	106	115	10
11	46	54	71	76	98	97	116	108	116	11
12	48	55	72	78	100	98	117	109	117	12
13	51	58	73	80	102	100	118	110	118	13
14	53	59	74	82	104	102	119	111	119	14
15	55	65	75	84	106	104	120	112	120	15
16	57	67	76	85	108	105	122	113	121	16
17	59	68	77	87	110	107	123	114	123	17
18	61	71	78	88	112	108	125	115	124	18
19	63	72	79	90	113	110	126	116	125	19
20	65	74	80	91	114	111	127	117	127	20
21	67	75	81	92	116	112	128	118	128	21
22	69	77	82	94	117	113	129	119	129	22
23	72	78	83	95	119	115	130	120	131	23
24	74	79	84	96	120	116	131	121	133	24
25	76	81	85	98	121	117	133	122	136	25
26	78	82	86	99	123	118	134	123	138	26
27	81	83	88	100	124	120	135	124	139	27
28	83	84	89	102	126	121	136	125	140	28
29	85	85	90	105	127	122	137	127	141	29
30	88	88	91	108	128	123	138	128	143	30
31	91	89	93	110	129	125	139	129	144	31
32	94	91	94	112	131	126	140	130	146	32
33	97	92	95	115	132	127	142	131	147	33
34	100	94	98	117	134	128	144	132	153	34
35	103	96	101	119	135	130	153	134	154	35
36	107	97	107	120	136	131	154	135	160	36
37	111	105	115	122	138	133	161	136	163	37
38	115	106	120	123	140	135	162	137	173	38
39	120	112	122	124	142	138	165	138	186	39
40	125	114	123	126	143	140	175	139	197	40
41	132	116	125	127	146	142	181	140	199	41
42	136	117	126	129	149	144	186	141	202	42
43	139	119	128	130	153	151	187	143	204	43
44	140	121	130	132	157	161	195	149	205	44
45		122	131	134	161	162	196	157	207	45
46		124	133	135	167	168	197	162	209	46
47		126	135	136	173	180	200	163	210	47
48		128	137	138	179	186	201	179	211	48
49		130	139	140	185	193	202	185	213	49
50		132	141	142	191	195	203	187	215	50
51		134	144	145	193	199	204	196	217	51
52		137	146	148	195	200	205	197	218	52
53		138	150	152	197	201	206	198	219	53
54		140	153	156	199	202	207	201	220	54
55		141	159	160		203	208	202	221	55
56		145	164	166		204	209	203	222	56
57		149	169	172		205		204	223	57
58		151	174	178		206		205	224	58
59		152	179	184		207		206	225	59
60		158	185	190		208		208	226	60
61								209		61
62								210		62
63								211		63
64								212		64
65								213		65
66								214		66
67								215		67
68								216		68

E

Table E.2. Age-Based Standard Score to Quartile Score Conversion for Reading Comprehension

Quartile Score	Standard Score
1	0–90
2	91–100
3	101–110
4	≥111

Table E.3. Age-Based Raw Score to Quartile Score Conversion for Target Words

	Age			
Quartile Score	14	15	16	17–19
1	0–20	0–20	0–20	0–20
2	21	21	21	21
3				
4	22	22	22	22

Note. Age-based information is provided for examinees administered the Grades 9–12 item set for Reading Comprehension. Scores are for comparison purposes only. The grade-based conversion tables in Appendix B are strongly recommended for reporting purposes. Scores for ages 6–14 in Grades 1–8 are not provided because examinees of the same age but different grades read different sentences.

Table E.4. Age-Based Raw Score to Quartile Score Conversion for Reading Speed

	Age			
Quartile Score	14	15	16	17–19
1	>581	>575	>545	>539
2	472–581	468–575	442–545	426–539
3	394–471	389–467	375–441	350–425
4	0–393	0–388	0–374	0–349

Note. Age-based information is provided for examinees administered the Grades 9–12 item set for Reading Comprehension. Scores are for comparison purposes only. The grade-based conversion tables in Appendix B are strongly recommended for reporting purposes. Scores for ages 6–14 in Grades 1–8 are not provided because examinees of the same age but different grades read different passages.

Table E.5. Age-Based Raw Score to Decile Score Conversion for Alphabet Writing

Decile Score	Age		
	4	5	6
10			
20			
30			
40			0
50			
60		0	1
70			2
80		1	
90	0	2–3	3
100	1–25	4–25	4–25

Table E.6. Age-Based Raw Score to Quartile Score Conversion for Written Expression Word Fluency

Item 2 Quartile Score	Age						
	6	7	8	9	10	11	12
0	0	0	0	0	0	0–1	0–3
1	1	1–3	1–5	1–6	1–7	2–8	4–9
2	2–3	4–5	6–7	7–8	8–9	9–10	10
3	4–5	6	8–9	9–10	10–11	11–13	11–14
4	≥6	≥7	≥10	≥11	≥12	≥14	≥15

Item 10 Quartile Score	Age						
	12	13	14	15	16	17–19	
0	0–4	0–4	0–4	0–4	0–4	0–5	
1	5–10	5–11	5–11	5–12	5–12	6–12	
2	11–13	12–13	12–14	13–15	13–15	13–15	
3	14–16	14–16	15–16	16–18	16–19	16–19	
4	≥17	≥17	≥17	≥19	≥20	≥20	

Note. These are modified quartile-based scores in which the score of 0 represents the bottom 5% of the raw score distribution; the score of 1 represents the bottom 5%–25% of the raw score distribution.

Table E.7. Age-Based Raw Score to Quartile Score Conversion for Paragraph Word Count

Quartile Score	Age					
	8	9	10	11	12	
1	0–19	0–27	0–32	0–36	0–40	
2	20–29	28–41	33–45	37–50	41–51	
3	30–42	42–51	46–59	51–66	52–67	
4	≥43	≥52	≥60	≥67	≥68	

Table E.8. Age-Based Raw Score to Quartile Score Conversion for Paragraph Spelling Errors

Quartile Score	Raw Score
0	≥5
1	4
2	3
3	1–2
4	0

Note. These are modified quartile-based scores in which the score of 4 represents zero errors; the score of 3 represents the remaining errors within the 4th quartile.

Table E.9. Age-Based Raw Score to Quartile Score Conversion for Paragraph Punctuation Errors

Quartile Score	Raw Score
0	≥5
1	4
2	2–3
3	1
4	0

Note. These are modified quartile-based scores in which the score of 4 represents zero errors; the score of 3 represents the remaining errors within the 4th quartile.

Table E.10. Age-Based Raw Score to Quartile Score Conversion for Essay Word Count

Quartile Score	Age					
	12	13	14	15	16	17–19
1	0–51	0–53	0–65	0–66	0–74	0–80
2	52–68	54–71	66–87	67–90	75–106	81–109
3	69–94	72–103	88–115	91–122	107–141	110–145
4	≥95	≥104	≥116	≥123	≥142	≥146

Table E.11. Age-Based Raw Score to Quartile Score Conversion for Essay Spelling Errors

Quartile Score	Raw Score
0	≥6
1	5
2	3–4
3	1–2
4	0

Note. These are modified quartile-based scores in which the score of 4 represents zero errors; the score of 3 represents the remaining errors within the 4th quartile.

Table E.12. Age-Based Raw Score to Quartile Score Conversion for Essay Punctuation Errors

Quartile Score	Raw Score
0	≥5
1	4
2	3
3	1–2
4	0

Note. These are modified quartile-based scores in which the score of 4 represents zero errors; the score of 3 represents the remaining errors within the 4th quartile.

E

Table E.13. Age-Based Raw Score to Conversion Score for Oral Expression Word Fluency

Conversion Score	Age													
	4	5	6	7	8	9	10	11	12	13	14	15	16	17–19
0	0	0	0–2	0–5	0–5	0–5	0–6	0–6	0–6	0–7	0–7	0–11	0–12	0–12
2	1–7	1–9	3–12	6–15	6–17	6–18	7–19	7–21	7–22	8–22	8–24	12–25	13–27	13–27
4	8–10	10–13	13–16	16–18	18–20	19–23	20–25	22–26	23–27	23–27	25–28	26–30	28–31	28–32
6	11–13	14–16	17–20	19–22	21–25	24–27	26–28	27–30	28–31	28–33	29–34	31–35	32–35	33–36
8	≥14	≥17	≥21	≥23	≥26	≥28	≥29	≥31	≥32	≥34	≥35	≥36	≥36	≥37

Note. These are modified quartile-based scores in which the score of 0 represents the bottom 5% of the raw score distribution; the score of 2 represents the bottom 5%–25% of the raw score distribution.

Age-Based
Normative Tables

F.1. Subtest Standard Scores

F.2. Composite Standard Scores

Table F.1. Age-Based Subtest Standard Scores
Ages: 4 years, 0 months, 0 days—4 years, 3 months, 30 days

Standard Score	Word Reading	Numerical Operations	Reading Comprehension	Spelling	Pseudoword Decoding	Math Reasoning	Written Expression	Listening Comprehension	Oral Expression	Standard Score
				Subtest Total Raw Scores						
40										40
41										41
42										42
43										43
44										44
45										45
46										46
47										47
48										48
49										49
50										50
51										51
52										52
53										53
54										54
55										55
56										56
57										57
58										58
59										59
60										60
61										61
62										62
63										63
64										64
65										65
66										66
67										67
68										68
69										69
70						0		0		70
71										71
72									0	72
73								1		73
74									1	74
75										75
76						1		2	2	76
77										77
78									3	78
79								3		79
80									4	80
81						2				81
82								4	5	82
83										83
84	0								6	84
85								5		85
86									7	86
87	1					3				87
88								6	8	88
89	2									89
90									9	90
91	3							7		91
92						4			10	92
93										93
94	4								11	94
95								8		95
96	5					5			12	96
97										97
98	6							9	13	98
99										99
100						6			14	100

F

Table F.1. Age-Based Subtest Standard Scores
Ages: 4 years, 0 months, 0 days—4 years, 3 months, 30 days (*continued*)

Standard Score	Word Reading	Numerical Operations	Reading Comprehension	Spelling	Pseudoword Decoding	Math Reasoning	Written Expression	Listening Comprehension	Oral Expression	Standard Score
101	7							10		101
102									15	102
103	8									103
104						7			16	104
105	9									105
106								11	17	106
107						8				107
108	10								18	108
109								12		109
110	11					9			19	110
111										111
112	12							13	20	112
113	13					10				113
114	14								21	114
115	15									115
116	16					11		14	22	116
117	17									117
118	18					12			23	118
119	19							15		119
120	20								24	120
121	21					13				121
122	22							16	25	122
123	23								26	123
124	24					14				124
125	25							17	27	125
126										126
127	26								28	127
128	27					15		18		128
129	28								29	129
130	29								30	130
131	30					16				131
132	31							19	31	132
133	32					17				133
134	33								32	134
135	34							20		135
136	35					18			33	136
137	36									137
138	37					19		21	34	138
139	38									139
140	39								35	140
141						20		22		141
142	40								36	142
143	41					21			37	143
144	42									144
145	43							23	38	145
146	44					22				146
147	45								39	147
148	46					23		24		148
149	47								40	149
150	48									150
151	49					24		25	41	151
152	50									152
153	51					25			42	153
154	52							26		154
155	53								43	155
156	54					26				156
157	55							27	44	157
158	56					27				158
159	57								45	159
160	58–131					28–67		28–41	46–77	160

Age-Based Normative Tables | **APPENDIX F**

Table F.1. Age-Based Subtest Standard Scores
Ages: 4 years, 4 months, 0 days—4 years, 7 months, 30 days

Standard Score	Word Reading	Numerical Operations	Reading Comprehension	Spelling	Pseudoword Decoding	Math Reasoning	Written Expression	Listening Comprehension	Oral Expression	Standard Score
40										40
41										41
42										42
43										43
44										44
45										45
46										46
47										47
48										48
49										49
50										50
51										51
52										52
53										53
54										54
55										55
56										56
57										57
58										58
59										59
60										60
61										61
62										62
63										63
64										64
65										65
66										66
67										67
68						0		0		68
69									0	69
70										70
71							1		1	71
72										72
73						1			2	73
74								2		74
75									3	75
76										76
77								3	4	77
78						2				78
79									5	79
80								4		80
81									6	81
82	0									82
83						3		5	7	83
84	1									84
85									8	85
86	2							6		86
87									9	87
88	3					4				88
89								7	10	89
90	4									90
91									11	91
92	5					5				92
93								8	12	93
94	6									94
95									13	95
96	7					6		9		96
97									14	97
98	8									98
99								10	15	99
100	9					7				100

Table F.1. Age-Based Subtest Standard Scores

Ages: 4 years, 4 months, 0 days—4 years, 7 months, 30 days (*continued*)

Standard Score	Word Reading	Numerical Operations	Reading Comprehension	Spelling	Pseudoword Decoding	Math Reasoning	Written Expression	Listening Comprehension	Oral Expression	Standard Score
			Subtest Total Raw Scores							
101									16	101
102	10									102
103						8		11	17	103
104	11									104
105									18	105
106	12					9		12		106
107	13								19	107
108	14									108
109	15					10		13	20	109
110	16									110
111	17								21	111
112	18					11				112
113	19							14	22	113
114	20					12				114
115	21								23	115
116	22							15		116
117	23					13			24	117
118	24									118
119	25							16	25	119
120	26					14			26	120
121	27									121
122	28							17	27	122
123	29					15				123
124	30								28	124
125	31							18		125
126	32					16			29	126
127	33								30	127
128	34					17				128
129	35							19	31	129
130	36									130
131	37					18			32	131
132	38							20		132
133	39					19			33	133
134	40									134
135	41							21	34	135
136	42					20				136
137	43								35	137
138	44					21		22		138
139	45								36	139
140	46								37	140
141	47					22				141
142	48							23	38	142
143	49					23				143
144	50								39	144
145	51							24		145
146	52					24			40	146
147	53									147
148	54					25		25	41	148
149	55									149
150	56								42	150
151	57					26		26		151
152	58								43	152
153	59					27				153
154	60							27	44	154
155	61									155
156	62					28			45	156
157	63							28		157
158	64					29			46	158
159	65									159
160	66–131					30–67		29–41	47–77	160

Table F.1. Age-Based Subtest Standard Scores
Ages: 4 years, 8 months, 0 days—4 years, 11 months, 30 days

Standard Score	Word Reading	Numerical Operations	Reading Comprehension	Spelling	Pseudoword Decoding	Math Reasoning	Written Expression	Listening Comprehension	Oral Expression	Standard Score
40										40
41										41
42										42
43										43
44										44
45										45
46										46
47										47
48										48
49										49
50										50
51										51
52										52
53										53
54										54
55										55
56										56
57										57
58										58
59										59
60										60
61										61
62										62
63										63
64										64
65										65
66						0		0	0	66
67										67
68									1	68
69								1		69
70						1			2	70
71										71
72								2	3	72
73										73
74									4	74
75						2		3		75
76									5	76
77										77
78								4	6	78
79						3				79
80	0								7	80
81	1							5		81
82									8	82
83	2									83
84						4		6	9	84
85	3									85
86	4								10	86
87								7		87
88	5					5			11	88
89										89
90	6								12	90
91	7							8		91
92						6			13	92
93	8									93
94								9	14	94
95	9									95
96	10					7			15	96
97								10		97
98	11								16	98
99						8				99
100	12							11	17	100

Table F.1. Age-Based Subtest Standard Scores
Ages: 4 years, 8 months, 0 days—4 years, 11 months, 30 days (*continued*)

Standard Score	Word Reading	Numerical Operations	Reading Comprehension	Spelling	Pseudoword Decoding	Math Reasoning	Written Expression	Listening Comprehension	Oral Expression	Standard Score
101	13									101
102	14					9			18	102
103	15							12		103
104	16								19	104
105	17					10				105
106	18							13	20	106
107	19									107
108	20					11			21	108
109	21									109
110	22					12		14	22	110
111	23									111
112	24								23	112
113	25–26					13		15		113
114	27								24	114
115	28									115
116	29					14		16	25	116
117	30								26	117
118	31					15				118
119	32							17	27	119
120	33									120
121	34					16			28	121
122	35							18		122
123	36					17			29	123
124	37								30	124
125	38									125
126	39–40					18		19	31	126
127	41									127
128	42					19			32	128
129	43							20		129
130	44								33	130
131	45					20				131
132	46							21	34	132
133	47					21				133
134	48								35	134
135	49							22		135
136	50					22			36	136
137	51								37	137
138	52					23				138
139	53							23	38	139
140	54									140
141	55					24			39	141
142	56							24		142
143	57					25			40	143
144	58									144
145	59							25	41	145
146	60					26				146
147	61								42	147
148	62					27		26		148
149	63								43	149
150	64					28				150
151	65							27	44	151
152	66–69									152
153	70–72					29			45	153
154	73–75							28		154
155	76–78					30–31			46	155
156	79–81					32				156
157	82–84					33		29	47–48	157
158	85–87					34		30	49	158
159	88–90					35–36		31	50–51	159
160	91–131					37–67		32–41	52–77	160

Table F.1. Age-Based Subtest Standard Scores

Ages: 5 years, 0 months, 0 days—5 years, 3 months, 30 days

Standard Score	Word Reading	Numerical Operations	Reading Comprehension	Spelling	Pseudoword Decoding	Math Reasoning	Written Expression	Listening Comprehension	Oral Expression	Standard Score
					Subtest Total Raw Scores					
40										40
41										41
42										42
43										43
44										44
45										45
46										46
47										47
48										48
49										49
50										50
51										51
52										52
53										53
54										54
55										55
56										56
57										57
58										58
59										59
60										60
61										61
62										62
63						0		0		63
64									0	64
65										65
66								1	1	66
67										67
68						1			2	68
69		0						2		69
70									3	70
71										71
72						2		3	4	72
73										73
74									5	74
75								4		75
76		1				3			6	76
77	0									77
78								5	7	78
79	1									79
80	2					4			8	80
81	3							6		81
82									9	82
83	4	2				5				83
84	5							7	10	84
85	6			0						85
86									11	86
87	7					6				87
88	8	3						8	12	88
89	9			1						89
90									13	90
91	10					7		9		91
92	11								14	92
93	12	4								93
94	13			2		8		10	15	94
95	14									95
96	15								16	96
97	16									97
98	17	5		3		9		11	17	98
99	18									99
100	19								18	100

Table F.1. Age-Based Subtest Standard Scores

Ages: 5 years, 0 months, 0 days—5 years, 3 months, 30 days (*continued*)

Standard Score	Subtest Total Raw Scores									Standard Score
	Word Reading	Numerical Operations	Reading Comprehension	Spelling	Pseudoword Decoding	Math Reasoning	Written Expression	Listening Comprehension	Oral Expression	
101	20			4		10		12		101
102	21								19	102
103	22									103
104	23	6		5		11		13	20	104
105	24								21	105
106	25					12				106
107	26							14	22	107
108	27			6		13				108
109	28	7							23	109
110	29–30							15		110
111	31			7		14			24	111
112	32									112
113	33–34							16	25	113
114	35	8		8		15				114
115	36								26	115
116	37					16				116
117	38			9				17	27	117
118	39								28	118
119	40					17				119
120	41	9		10				18	29	120
121	42					18				121
122	43								30	122
123	44			11		19		19		123
124	45–46								31	124
125	47	10							32	125
126	48			12		20		20		126
127	49								33	127
128	50					21				128
129	51							21	34	129
130	52	11		13		22				130
131	53								35	131
132	54							22		132
133	55			14		23			36	133
134	56–57								37	134
135	58	12				24		23		135
136	59			15					38	136
137	60					25			39	137
138	61									138
139	62			16				24	40	139
140	63	13				26				140
141	64								41	141
142	65			17		27		25		142
143	66								42	143
144	67									144
145	68–70			18		28		26	43	145
146	71	14								146
147	72–73					29			44	147
148	74			19				27		148
149	75–76					30			45	149
150	77									150
151	78–79	15		20		31		28	46	151
152	80									152
153	81–82					32			47	153
154	83			21		33		29		154
155	84–85					34			48	155
156	86	16						30	49	156
157	87–88			22		35			50	157
158	89							31		158
159	90–91					36			51	159
160	92–131	17–54		23–53		37–67		32–41	52–77	160

Table F.1. Age-Based Subtest Standard Scores

Ages: 5 years, 4 months, 0 days—5 years, 7 months, 30 days

Standard Score	Word Reading	Numerical Operations	Reading Comprehension	Spelling	Pseudoword Decoding	Math Reasoning	Written Expression	Listening Comprehension	Oral Expression	Standard Score
40										40
41										41
42										42
43										43
44										44
45										45
46										46
47										47
48										48
49										49
50										50
51										51
52										52
53										53
54										54
55										55
56										56
57										57
58										58
59										59
60										60
61						0		0	0	61
62										62
63									1	63
64						1				64
65		0				1			2	65
66										66
67								2	3	67
68										68
69						2			4	69
70						3				70
71									5	71
72		1				3				72
73								4	6	73
74										74
75	0								7	75
76	1					4		5		76
77	2								8	77
78	3	2								78
79	4					5		6	9	79
80	5									80
81	6			0					10	81
82	7							7		82
83	8	3				6			11	83
84	9									84
85	10			1					12	85
86	11							8		86
87	12					7			13	87
88	13	4								88
89	14			2				9	14	89
90	15					8				90
91	16								15	91
92	17							10		92
93	18	5		3					16	93
94	19					9				94
95	20							11	17	95
96	21			4						96
97	22					10			18	97
98	23							12		98
99	24	6		5					19	99
100	25–26					11				100

Table F.1. Age-Based Subtest Standard Scores

Ages: 5 years, 4 months, 0 days—5 years, 7 months, 30 days (*continued*)

Standard Score	Word Reading	Numerical Operations	Reading Comprehension	Spelling	Pseudoword Decoding	Math Reasoning	Written Expression	Listening Comprehension	Oral Expression	Standard Score
101	27							13	20	101
102	28			6		12			21	102
103	29–30									103
104	31	7				13		14	22	104
105	32			7						105
106	33–34								23	106
107	35					14		15		107
108	36			8					24	108
109	37	8				15				109
110	38							16	25	110
111	39–40			9		16				111
112	41								26	112
113	42									113
114	43			10		17		17	27	114
115	44	9							28	115
116	45–46					18				116
117	47			11				18	29	117
118	48					19				118
119	49								30	119
120	50	10		12				19		120
121	51					20			31	121
122	52								32	122
123	53			13		21		20		123
124	54								33	124
125	55	11				22				125
126	56–57			14				21	34	126
127	58									127
128	59					23			35	128
129	60			15				22		129
130	61	12				24			36	130
131	62								37	131
132	63			16		25		23		132
133	64								38	133
134	65								39	134
135	66	13		17		26				135
136	67							24	40	136
137	68–69					27				137
138	70			18					41	138
139	71					28		25		139
140	72								42	140
141	73	14		19						141
142	74					29		26	43	142
143	75									143
144	76			20		30			44	144
145	77							27		145
146	78	15				31			45	146
147	79			21						147
148	80							28	46	148
149	81					32				149
150	82			22					47	150
151	83	16				33		29		151
152	84								48	152
153	85			23		34				153
154	86							30	49	154
155	87									155
156	88	17		24		35			50	156
157	89							31		157
158	90					36			51	158
159	91			25						159
160	92–131	18–54		26–53		37–67		32–41	52–77	160

Table F.1. Age-Based Subtest Standard Scores
Ages: 5 years, 8 months, 0 days—5 years, 11 months, 30 days

Standard Score	Word Reading	Numerical Operations	Reading Comprehension	Spelling	Pseudoword Decoding	Math Reasoning	Written Expression	Listening Comprehension	Oral Expression	Standard Score
40										40
41										41
42										42
43										43
44										44
45										45
46										46
47										47
48										48
49										49
50										50
51										51
52										52
53										53
54										54
55										55
56										56
57										57
58									0		58
59						0				0	59
60										60
61		0						1	1	61
62						1				62
63									2	63
64								2		64
65									3	65
66						2			4	66
67								3		67
68		1				3			5	68
69	0									69
70	1							4	6	70
71	2									71
72	3					4			7	72
73	4	2						5		73
74	5								8	74
75	6					5				75
76	7							6	9	76
77	8			0						77
78	9	3				6			10	78
79	10							7		79
80	11								11	80
81	12			1						81
82	13					7			12	82
83	14	4						8		83
84	15			2					13	84
85	16					8				85
86	17							9	14	86
87	18									87
88	19	5		3		9			15	88
89	20–21							10		89
90	22								16	90
91	23			4		10				91
92	24							11	17	92
93	25–26									93
94	27	6		5		11			18	94
95	28							12		95
96	29			6		12			19	96
97	30									97
98	31					13		13	20	98
99	32–33	7		7					21	99
100	34–35									100

Table F.1. Age-Based Subtest Standard Scores
Ages: 5 years, 8 months, 0 days—5 years, 11 months, 30 days (continued)

Standard Score	Subtest Total Raw Scores									Standard Score
	Word Reading	Numerical Operations	Reading Comprehension	Spelling	Pseudoword Decoding	Math Reasoning	Written Expression	Listening Comprehension	Oral Expression	
101	36					14		14	22	101
102	37			8						102
103	38					15			23	103
104	39–40	8						15		104
105	41			9		16			24	105
106	42									106
107	43							16	25	107
108	44			10		17				108
109	45–46								26	109
110	47	9				18		17		110
111	48			11					27	111
112	49					19			28	112
113	50							18		113
114	51			12					29	114
115	52	10				20				115
116	53			13				19	30	116
117	54					21				117
118	55								31	118
119	56–57			14		22		20	32	119
120	58	11								120
121	59								33	121
122	60			15		23		21		122
123	61								34	123
124	62					24				124
125	63	12		16				22	35	125
126	64									126
127	65					25			36	127
128	66			17				23		128
129	67					26			37	129
130	68–69	13							38	130
131	70			18						131
132	71					27		24	39	132
133	72									133
134	73			19		28			40	134
135	74							25	41	135
136	75	14								136
137	76			20		29			42	137
138	77							26		138
139	78					30			43	139
140	79			21						140
141	80	15				31		27	44	141
142	81–82									142
143	83			22					45	143
144	84					32		28		144
145	85								46	145
146	86	16		23		33				146
147	87							29	47	147
148	88					34				148
149	89			24					48	149
150	90	17						30		150
151	91			25		35			49	151
152	92									152
153	93–95			26		36		31	50	153
154	96–99			27						154
155	100–102	18		28		37			51	155
156	103–105	19		29–30		38		32		156
157	106–108			31		39		33	52	157
158	109–111	20		32		40		34	53–54	158
159	112–114	21		33		41–42		35	55	159
160	115–131	22–54		34–53		43–67		36–41	56–77	160

F

Table F.1. Age-Based Subtest Standard Scores

Ages: 6 years, 0 months, 0 days—6 years, 3 months, 30 days

Standard Score	Word Reading	Numerical Operations	Reading Comprehension[a]	Spelling	Pseudoword Decoding	Math Reasoning	Written Expression	Listening Comprehension	Oral Expression	Standard Score
40										40
41										41
42										42
43										43
44										44
45										45
46										46
47										47
48										48
49										49
50										50
51										51
52										52
53										53
54										54
55								0		55
56						0			0	56
57										57
58		0						1	1	58
59						1				59
60									2	60
61								2		61
62						2			3	62
63		1								63
64	0		0–2						4	64
65	1		3–4			3				65
66	2		5–9						5	66
67	3		10–11					4		67
68	4		12–16			4			6	68
69	5–6	2	17–18							69
70	7		19–22			5		5	7	70
71	8		23–26							71
72	9		27						8	72
73	10		28–30	0		6		6		73
74	11	3	31						9	74
75	12		32–34							75
76	13		35	1		7	0	7	10	76
77	14		36–37							77
78	15–16		38						11	78
79	17	4	39			8		8		79
80	18		40	2					12	80
81	19		41–42				1			81
82	20		43			9		9	13	82
83	21		44	3						83
84	22	5	45						14	84
85	23			4		10		10		85
86	24–25		46–47				2		15	86
87	26		48–49			11				87
88	27		50	5				11	16	88
89	28	6	51							89
90	29–30		52		0	12			17	90
91	31		53–54	6	1		3	12		91
92	32		55		2				18	92
93	33–34		56		3	13			19	93
94	35		57–58	7	4			13		94
95	36–37	7	59			14			20	95
96	38		60		5		4			96
97	39		61–62	8	6			14	21	97
98	40–41		63		7	15				98
99	42		64	9	8				22	99
100	43	8	65–66		9	16	5	15		100

[a] Based on weighted raw scores.

F

Table F.1. Age-Based Subtest Standard Scores

Ages: 6 years, 0 months, 0 days—6 years, 3 months, 30 days (*continued*)

Standard Score	Word Reading	Numerical Operations	Reading Comprehension[a]	Spelling	Pseudoword Decoding	Math Reasoning	Written Expression	Listening Comprehension	Oral Expression	Standard Score
			Subtest Total Raw Scores							
101	44		67	10	10				23	101
102	45		68		11					102
103	46–47				12	17		16	24	103
104	48		69–71	11	13					104
105	49		72–73		14	18			25	105
106	50–51	9	74–75				6		26	106
107	52		76	12		19		17		107
108	53		77		15				27	108
109	54		78–79		16					109
110	55	10	80	13	17	20	7	18	28	110
111	56		81		18				29	111
112	57		82		19	21				112
113	58		83–84	14				19	30	113
114	59		85–86		20	22	8			114
115	60		87		21				31	115
116	61	11	88–89	15	22		9	20		116
117	62		90–92		23	23			32	117
118	63		93–94		24					118
119	64–65		95–98	16	25	24		21	33	119
120	66		99		26		10			120
121	67	12	100–101		27	25			34	121
122	68		102–105	17				22		122
123	69		106–109		28		11		35	123
124	70–71		110–112		29	26				124
125	72		113	18	30			23	36	125
126	73	13	114–117		31	27			37	126
127	74		118	19	32		12			127
128	75		119–125		33	28		24	38	128
129	76		126–134		34				39	129
130	77		135–137	20	35		13			130
131	78	14	138		36	29		25	40	131
132	79		139							132
133	80		140	21		30			41	133
134	81		141		37–38			26		134
135	82	15	142		39		14		42	135
136	83		143	22	40	31				136
137	84		144		41			27	43	137
138	85		145	23	42	32	15			138
139	86		146						44	139
140	87	16	147					28	45	140
141	88		148	24	43–44	33				141
142	89		149		45		16		46	142
143	90		150			34		29		143
144	91		151	25					47	144
145	92–93	17	152		46		17			145
146	94		153	26	47	35		30	48	146
147	95–96		154		48					147
148	97		155	27	49	36			49	148
149	98–100	18	156	28	50		18	31		149
150	101		157		51				50	150
151	102–103		158	29	52	37				151
152	104	19	159		53	38	19	32	51	152
153	105–106		160	30	54	39				153
154	107		161		55	39		33	52	154
155	108–109	20	162	31		40			53	155
156	110		163					34		156
157	111–112		164	32		41	20		54	157
158	113	21	165					35	55	158
159	114–115		166	33–34		42			56	159
160	116–131	22–54	167–233	35–53		43–67	21–55	36–41	57–77	160

[a] Based on weighted raw scores.

Table F.1. Age-Based Subtest Standard Scores

Ages: 6 years, 4 months, 0 days—6 years, 7 months, 30 days

Standard Score	Word Reading	Numerical Operations	Reading Comprehension[a]	Spelling	Pseudoword Decoding	Math Reasoning	Written Expression	Listening Comprehension	Oral Expression	Standard Score
40										40
41										41
42										42
43										43
44										44
45										45
46										46
47										47
48										48
49										49
50										50
51										51
52								0		52
53										53
54		0				0			0	54
55								1		55
56						1			1	56
57										57
58	0							2	2	58
59	1	1				2				59
60	2								3	60
61	3		0–2			3		3	4	61
62	4		3–4							62
63	5–6		5–9						5	63
64	7	2	10–11			4		4		64
65	8		12–16						6	65
66	9		17–18			5				66
67	10		19–22					5	7	67
68	11		23–26			6				68
69	12	3	27	0					8	69
70	13		28–30					6		70
71	14		31			7			9	71
72	15–16		32–34	1						72
73	17		35					7	10	73
74	18	4	36–37			8	0			74
75	19		38	2					11	75
76	20–21		39			9		8		76
77	22		40						12	77
78	23		41–42	3						78
79	24–25	5	43			10	1	9	13	79
80	26		44	4						80
81	27		45			11			14	81
82	28		46–47					10		82
83	29		48–49	5					15	83
84	30	6	50			12	2			84
85	31		51	6				11	16	85
86	32–33		52							86
87	34–35		53–54			13			17	87
88	36–37		55	7	0			12		88
89	38		56		1	14	3		18	89
90	39	7	57–58		2				19	90
91	40–41		59	8	3			13		91
92	42		60		4	15			20	92
93	43		61–62	9						93
94	44		63		5	16	4	14	21	94
95	45	8	64	10	6					95
96	46–47		65–66		7				22	96
97	48		67		8	17		15		97
98	49		68	11	9		5		23	98
99	50–51		69–70		10	18				99
100	52		71–72		11			16	24	100

[a] Based on weighted raw scores.

F

Table F.1. Age-Based Subtest Standard Scores

Ages: 6 years, 4 months, 0 days—6 years, 7 months, 30 days (continued)

Standard Score	Subtest Total Raw Scores									Standard Score
	Word Reading	Numerical Operations	Reading Comprehension[a]	Spelling	Pseudoword Decoding	Math Reasoning	Written Expression	Listening Comprehension	Oral Expression	
101	53	9	73	12	12	19				101
102	54		74–75		13				25	102
103	55		76	13	14		6	17	26	103
104	56		77			20				104
105	57	10	78–79		15				27	105
106	58		80	14	16	21		18		106
107	59		81		17		7		28	107
108	60		82		18	22			29	108
109	61		83–84	15	19			19		109
110	62		85–86						30	110
111	63	11	87		20	23	8			111
112	64–65		88–89	16	21			20	31	112
113	66		90–92		22	24				113
114	67		93		23		9		32	114
115	68		94–95	17	24			21		115
116	69	12	96–98		25	25			33	116
117	70–71		99		26					117
118	72		100–101	18	27	26	10	22	34	118
119	73		102–105							119
120	74		106–109	19	28				35	120
121	75	13	110–112		29	27	11	23		121
122	76		113		30				36	122
123	77		114–117	20	31	28				123
124	78		118		32			24	37	124
125	79		119–122		33		12		38	125
126	80	14	123–128	21	34	29				126
127	81–82		129–134		35			25	39	127
128	83		135–137		36	30	13			128
129	84		138	22					40	129
130	85	15	139		37			26	41	130
131	86		140	23	38	31				131
132	87		141		39		14		42	132
133	88		142		40	32		27		133
134	89		143	24	41				43	134
135	90	16	144		42		15			135
136	91		145	25		33		28	44	136
137	92		146		43				45	137
138	93		147		44	34				138
139	94	17	148	26	45		16	29	46	139
140	95		149							140
141	96		150		46	35			47	141
142	97		151	27	47		17	30		142
143	98–99		152		48	36			48	143
144	100	18	153	28	49					144
145	101		154		50			31	49	145
146	102		155		51	37	18			146
147	103		156	29	52				50	147
148	104	19	157		53	38		32		148
149	105		158	30	54		19		51	149
150	106		159		55					150
151	107		160			39		33	52	151
152	108		161	31						152
153	109	20	162			40	20		53	153
154	110		163					34		154
155	111		164	32					54	155
156	112		165			41	21			156
157	113	21	166					35	55	157
158	114		167	33		42				158
159	115		168	34			22		56	159
160	116–131	22–54	169–233	35–53		43–67	23–55	36–41	57–77	160

[a] Based on weighted raw scores.

Table F.1. Age-Based Subtest Standard Scores

Ages: 6 years, 8 months, 0 days—6 years, 11 months, 30 days

Standard Score	Word Reading	Numerical Operations	Reading Comprehension[a]	Spelling	Pseudoword Decoding	Math Reasoning	Written Expression	Listening Comprehension	Oral Expression	Standard Score
40										40
41										41
42										42
43										43
44										44
45										45
46										46
47										47
48										48
49		0						0		49
50						0				50
51									0	51
52						1		1		52
53	0	1							1	53
54	1									54
55	2					2		2	2	55
56	3									56
57	4					3			3	57
58	5–6	2	0–2					3	4	58
59	7		3–4			4				59
60	8		5–9						5	60
61	9		10–11			5	4			61
62	10		12–16						6	62
63	11	3	17–18			6				63
64	12–13		19–22					5	7	64
65	14		23–26	0						65
66	15–16		27			7			8	66
67	17		28–30					6		67
68	18	4	31	1					9	68
69	19		32–34			8				69
70	20–21		35	2				7	10	70
71	22		36–37			9				71
72	23		38				0		11	72
73	24	5	39	3				8		73
74	25–26		40			10			12	74
75	27		41–42	4						75
76	28		43			11		9	13	76
77	29		44				1			77
78	30	6	45–47	5		12			14	78
79	31		48–49					10		79
80	32–33		50	6					15	80
81	34		51			13				81
82	35		52				2	11	16	82
83	36–37		53–54	7		14				83
84	38	7	55						17	84
85	39		56					12		85
86	40–41		57–58	8	0	15			18	86
87	42		59		1		3			87
88	43		60	9	2	16		13	19	88
89	44	8	61–62		3					89
90	45		63	10	4				20	90
91	46–47		64			17		14		91
92	48		65–66		5		4		21	92
93	49		67	11	6	18			22	93
94	50–51		68–70		7			15		94
95	52	9	71		8				23	95
96	53		72	12	9	19	5			96
97	54		73		10			16	24	97
98	55		74–75	13	11	20				98
99	56	10	76		12				25	99
100	57		77		13		6	17		100

[a] Based on weighted raw scores.

Table F.1. Age-Based Subtest Standard Scores

Ages: 6 years, 8 months, 0 days—6 years, 11 months, 30 days (*continued*)

Standard Score	Word Reading	Numerical Operations	Reading Comprehension[a]	Spelling	Pseudoword Decoding	Math Reasoning	Written Expression	Listening Comprehension	Oral Expression	Standard Score
			Subtest Total Raw Scores							
101	58		78–79	14	14	21			26	101
102	59		80		15					102
103	60		81		16	22		18	27	103
104	61–62		82	15	17		7			104
105	63	11	83–84		18				28	105
106	64		85–86		19	23		19	29	106
107	65		87	16						107
108	66		88–89		20	24	8		30	108
109	67		90–92	17	21			20		109
110	68–69	12	93		22	25			31	110
111	70		94		23					111
112	71		95	18	24	26	9	21	32	112
113	72		96–98		25					113
114	73		99	19	26				33	114
115	74–75	13	100–101		27	27		22		115
116	76		102–105				10		34	116
117	77		106–109	20	28	28				117
118	78		110–112		29			23	35	118
119	79		113		30		11			119
120	80	14	114–117	21	31	29			36	120
121	81–82		118		32			24		121
122	83		119–122	22	33	30			37	122
123	84		123–125		34		12		38	123
124	85	15	126–128	23	35			25		124
125	86		129–134		36	31			39	125
126	87		135–137		37		13			126
127	88		138	24		32		26	40	127
128	89		139		38				41	128
129	90		140	25	39		14			129
130	91	16	141		40	33		27	42	130
131	92		142		41					131
132	93		143	26	42	34	15		43	132
133	94		144		43			28		133
134	95	17	145						44	134
135	96		146	27	44	35			45	135
136	97		147		45		16	29		136
137	98–99		148	28	46	36			46	137
138	100		149		47					138
139	101	18	150		48		17	30	47	139
140	102		151	29	49	37				140
141	103		152		50				48	141
142	104		153	30	51	38		31		142
143	105	19	154		52		18		49	143
144	106		155		53					144
145	107		156	31	54	39		32	50	145
146	108		157		55		19			146
147	109		158			40			51	147
148	110	20	159	32				33		148
149	111		160			41	20		52	149
150	112		161							150
151	113		162	33				34	53	151
152	114	21	163	34		42	21			152
153	115		164						54	153
154	116		165	35		43–44		35		154
155	117–119	22	166	36–37		45	22		55	155
156	120–122	23	167	38		46				156
157	123–125		168	39		47	23	36	56	157
158	126–128	24	169–170	40		48	24	37	57	158
159	129–131	25	171–173	41		49	25	38	58–59	159
160		26–54	174–233	42–53		50–67	26–55	39–41	60–77	160

[a] Based on weighted raw scores.

Table F.1. Age-Based Subtest Standard Scores

Ages: 7 years, 0 months, 0 days—7 years, 3 months, 30 days

Standard Score	Word Reading	Numerical Operations	Reading Comprehension[a]	Spelling	Pseudoword Decoding	Math Reasoning	Written Expression	Listening Comprehension	Oral Expression	Standard Score
40										40
41										41
42										42
43										43
44										44
45		0								45
46						0				46
47	0							0		47
48	1	1				1			0	48
49	2									49
50	3					2		1	1	50
51	4									51
52	5					3		2	2	52
53	6–7	2								53
54	8								3	54
55	9					4	3			55
56	10		0–2						4	56
57	11		3–4			5				57
58	12	3	5–9					4	5	58
59	13		10–11			6				59
60	14		12–17	0					6	60
61	15–16		18–22			7		5		61
62	17		23						7	62
63	18	4	24–26	1		8				63
64	19–20		27					6	8	64
65	21		28–31							65
66	22		32–34	2		9			9	66
67	23		35					7		67
68	24–25	5	36			10			10	68
69	26		37–38	3						69
70	27		39			11		8	11	70
71	28		40	4			0			71
72	29		41–42						12	72
73	30	6	43			12		9		73
74	31		44–45	5					13	74
75	32–33		46–47							75
76	34–35		48–49	6		13	1	10	14	76
77	36		50							77
78	37–38	7	51	7		14			15	78
79	39		52–53					11		79
80	40		54	8					16	80
81	41		55–56			15	2			81
82	42		57					12	17	82
83	43	8	58	9		16				83
84	44–45		59–60		0				18	84
85	46		61–62	10	1		3	13	19	85
86	47		63–64		2	17				86
87	48		65–66		3				20	87
88	49	9	67	11	4	18		14		88
89	50		68		5		4		21	89
90	51		69–70	12	6	19				90
91	52–53		71–72		7			15	22	91
92	54		73		8					92
93	55–56	10	74	13	9	20	5		23	93
94	57		75–76		10			16		94
95	58		77	14	11	21			24	95
96	59		78		12					96
97	60		79–80		13	22		17	25	97
98	61	11		15	14		6		26	98
99	62		81							99
100	63		82		15	23		18	27	100

[a] Based on weighted raw scores.

Table F.1. Age-Based Subtest Standard Scores

Ages: 7 years, 0 months, 0 days—7 years, 3 months, 30 days (*continued*)

Standard Score	Word Reading	Numerical Operations	Reading Comprehension[a]	Spelling	Pseudoword Decoding	Math Reasoning	Written Expression	Listening Comprehension	Oral Expression	Standard Score
101	64–65		83	16	16					101
102	66		84–86		17	24	7		28	102
103	67	12	87		18			19		103
104	68		88	17	19				29	104
105	69		89–90		20	25				105
106	70–71		91–92	18	21		8	20	30	106
107	72		93		22	26				107
108	73		94–95	19	23				31	108
109	74	13	96		24	27	9	21	32	109
110	75		97–99		25					110
111	76		100–101	20	26				33	111
112	77		102–104		27	28		22		112
113	78–79		105	21	28		10		34	113
114	80	14	106–109		29	29				114
115	81		110–112		30			23	35	115
116	82		113	22	31					116
117	83		114–116		32	30	11		36	117
118	84		117–118	23	33			24		118
119	85	15	119–120		34	31			37	119
120	86–87		121–122		35		12		38	120
121	88		123–128	24	36	32		25		121
122	89		129–131						39	122
123	90		132–134	25	37	33	13			123
124	91	16	135–137		38			26	40	124
125	92		138		39					125
126	93		139	26	40	34			41	126
127	94		140		41		14	27		127
128	95		141	27	42	35			42	128
129	96	17	142							129
130	97		143		43		15	28	43	130
131	98		144	28	44	36				131
132	99		145		45				44	132
133	100		146	29		37	16	29	45	133
134	101	18	147		46					134
135	102		148		47				46	135
136	103		149	30	48	38	17	30		136
137	104		150		49				47	137
138	105	19	151	31	50	39				138
139	106		152		51		18	31	48	139
140	107		153		52	40				140
141	108		154	32	53				49	141
142	109	20	155		54		19	32	50	142
143	110		156	33	55	41				143
144	111		157						51	144
145	112		158			42		33		145
146	113	21	159	34			20		52	146
147	114		160	35		43				147
148	115		161					34	53	148
149	116–117		162	36		44	21			149
150	118	22	163						54	150
151	119–120		164	37		45		35		151
152	121		165			46	22		55	152
153	122–123	23	166	38						153
154	124		167	39		47	23	36	56	154
155	125–126	24	168							155
156	127		169	40		48	24	37	57	156
157	128–129		170–171	41		49			58	157
158	130	25	172				25	38		158
159	131		173–174	42		50			59	159
160		26–54	175–233	43–53		51–67	26–55	39–41	60–77	160

[a] Based on weighted raw scores.

Table F.1. Age-Based Subtest Standard Scores

Ages: 7 years, 4 months, 0 days—7 years, 7 months, 30 days

Standard Score	Subtest Total Raw Scores									Standard Score
	Word Reading	Numerical Operations	Reading Comprehension[a]	Spelling	Pseudoword Decoding	Math Reasoning	Written Expression	Listening Comprehension	Oral Expression	
40		0								40
41										41
42	0	1				0				42
43	1									43
44	2					1		0		44
45	3								0	45
46	4					2				46
47	5	2						1	1	47
48	6–7					3				48
49	8							2	2	49
50	9					4				50
51	10								3	51
52	11	3				5		3		52
53	12–13		0–2						4	53
54	14		3–4			6				54
55	15–16		5–9					4	5	55
56	17		10–11	0		7				56
57	18	4	12–17						6	57
58	19–20		18–22			8		5		58
59	21		23	1					7	59
60	22		24–26							60
61	23		27	2		9		6	8	61
62	24	5	28–31							62
63	25–26		32–34			10			9	63
64	27		35	3				7		64
65	28		36			11			10	65
66	29		37–38	4						66
67	30	6	39			12		8	11	67
68	31		40							68
69	32–33		41–42	5			0		12	69
70	34		43			13		9		70
71	35		44–47	6					13	71
72	36	7	48–49			14				72
73	37–38		50	7				10	14	73
74	39		51				1			74
75	40		52–53	8		15			15	75
76	41		54					11		76
77	42	8	55–56			16			16	77
78	43		57	9						78
79	44–45		58				2	12	17	79
80	46		59–60	10		17				80
81	47		61–62						18	81
82	48	9	63–64		0	18		13		82
83	49		65–66	11	1		3		19	83
84	50		67		2					84
85	51		68–70	12	3	19		14	20	85
86	52–53		71		4					86
87	54	10	72		5	20	4		21	87
88	55–56		73	13	6			15	22	88
89	57		74		7					89
90	58		75–76	14	8	21			23	90
91	59		77		9		5	16		91
92	60	11	78		10	22			24	92
93	61–62		79–80	15	11					93
94	63				12			17	25	94
95	64		81		13	23	6			95
96	65		82	16	14				26	96
97	66	12	83		15	24		18		97
98	67		84–86	17	16				27	98
99	68–69		87		17	25	7			99
100	70		88	18	18			19	28	100

[a] Based on weighted raw scores.

Table F.1. Age-Based Subtest Standard Scores

Ages: 7 years, 4 months, 0 days—7 years, 7 months, 30 days (*continued*)

Standard Score	Subtest Total Raw Scores									Standard Score
	Word Reading	Numerical Operations	Reading Comprehension[a]	Spelling	Pseudoword Decoding	Math Reasoning	Written Expression	Listening Comprehension	Oral Expression	
101	71		89–90		19	26				101
102	72		91–92	19	20				29	102
103	73	13	93		21	27	8	20		103
104	74–75		94		22				30	104
105	76		95	20	23					105
106	77		96		24	28		21	31	106
107	78–79		97–99	21	25		9		32	107
108	80	14	100–101		26	29				108
109	81		102–104	22	27			22	33	109
110	82		105		28					110
111	83		106–109	23	29	30	10		34	111
112	84		110–112		30			23		112
113	85	15	113		31	31			35	113
114	86–87		114–116	24	32					114
115	88		117–118		33	32	11	24	36	115
116	89		119–120	25	34					116
117	90		121–122		35	33			37	117
118	91		123–125		36		12	25	38	118
119	92	16	126–128	26	37					119
120	93		129–131			34			39	120
121	94		132–134	27	38		13	26		121
122	95		135–137		39	35			40	122
123	96		138		40					123
124	97	17	139	28	41		14	27	41	124
125	98		140		42	36				125
126	99		141	29	43				42	126
127	100		142			37	15	28		127
128	101		143		44				43	128
129	102	18	144	30	45					129
130	103		145		46	38	16	29	44	130
131	104		146	31	47				45	131
132	105		147		48	39				132
133	106	19	148		49		17	30	46	133
134	107		149	32	50	40				134
135	108		150		51				47	135
136	109		151	33	52	41	18	31		136
137	110	20	152		53				48	137
138	111		153		54					138
139	112		154	34	55	42	19	32	49	139
140	113		155						50	140
141	114	21	156	35		43				141
142	115		157				20	33	51	142
143	116		158			44				143
144	117		159	36					52	144
145	118	22	160				21	34		145
146	119		161	37		45			53	146
147	120		162							147
148	121		163			46	22	35	54	148
149	122	23	164	38						149
150	123		165						55	150
151	124		166	39		47	23	36		151
152	125		167						56	152
153	126	24	168							153
154	127		169	40		48	24	37	57	154
155	128		170							155
156	129		171	41		49			58	156
157	130	25	172				25	38		157
158	131		173						59	158
159			174	42		50				159
160		26–54	175–233	43–53		51–67	26–55	39–41	60–77	160

[a] Based on weighted raw scores.

Table F.1. Age-Based Subtest Standard Scores

Ages: 7 years, 8 months, 0 days—7 years, 11 months, 30 days

Standard Score	Word Reading	Numerical Operations	Reading Comprehension[a]	Spelling	Pseudoword Decoding	Math Reasoning	Written Expression	Listening Comprehension	Oral Expression	Standard Score
			Subtest Total Raw Scores							
40		0								40
41	0	1				0				41
42	1									42
43	2–3					1		0	0	43
44	4					2				44
45	5–7	2				3		1	1	45
46	8							2		46
47	9–10					4			2	47
48	11									48
49	12–14	3				5		3	3	49
50	15–16		0–3							50
51	17		4–9			6			4	51
52	18		10–11	0				4		52
53	19–20		12–17			7			5	53
54	21	4	18–22							54
55	22		23	1		8		5	6	55
56	23		24–26							56
57	24		27	2		9			7	57
58	25–26		28–31					6		58
59	27	5	32–34			10			8	59
60	28		35	3						60
61	29		36			11		7	9	61
62	30		37–38	4						62
63	31	6	39			12			10	63
64	32–33		40					8		64
65	34		41–42	5					11	65
66	35		43			13				66
67	36		44–47	6			0	9	12	67
68	37–38	7	48–49			14				68
69	39		50	7					13	69
70	40		51					10		70
71	41		52	8		15	1		14	71
72	42		53							72
73	43	8	54			16		11	15	73
74	44–45		55–56	9						74
75	46		57			17			16	75
76	47		58	10			2	12		76
77	48		59–60			18			17	77
78	49	9	61–62							78
79	50		63–64	11			3	13	18	79
80	51		65–66		0	19				80
81	52–53		67	12	1				19	81
82	54	10	68–70		2	20		14	20	82
83	55–56		71		3		4			83
84	57		72	13	4				21	84
85	58		73		5	21		15		85
86	59		74	14	6				22	86
87	60	11	75–76		7	22	5			87
88	61–62		77	15	8			16	23	88
89	63		78		9					89
90	64		79–80		10	23	6		24	90
91	65			16	11			17		91
92	66	12	81		12	24			25	92
93	67		82	17	13					93
94	68–69		83		14	25	7	18	26	94
95	70		84		15					95
96	71		85–86	18	16	26			27	96
97	72	13	87		17		8	19		97
98	73		88	19	18				28	98
99	74–75		89–90		19	27				99
100	76		91–92		20			20	29	100

[a] Based on weighted raw scores.

F

Table F.1. Age-Based Subtest Standard Scores

Ages: 7 years, 8 months, 0 days—7 years, 11 months, 30 days (*continued*)

Standard Score	Word Reading	Numerical Operations	Reading Comprehension[a]	Spelling	Pseudoword Decoding	Math Reasoning	Written Expression	Listening Comprehension	Oral Expression	Standard Score
101	77		93	20	21	28	9			101
102	78	14	94		22				30	102
103	79		95–96	21	23	29		21		103
104	80		97–98		24–25				31	104
105	81–82		99–101	22	26		10		32	105
106	83	15	102–104		27	30		22		106
107	84		105–106	23	28				33	107
108	85		107–109		29	31				108
109	86		110–113		30		11	23	34	109
110	87		114–115	24	31	32				110
111	88		116		32		12		35	111
112	89	16	117–118	25	33	33		24		112
113	90		119–120		34				36	113
114	91		121–122		35		13		37	114
115	92		123–125	26	36	34		25		115
116	93	17	126		37				38	116
117	94		127–128	27		35	14			117
118	95		129–130		38			26	39	118
119	96		131–132		39					119
120	97		133–134	28	40	36	15		40	120
121	98	18	135–137		41			27		121
122	99		138	29	42	37			41	122
123	100		139		43		16		42	123
124	101		140					28		124
125	102	19	141	30	44	38	17		43	125
126	103		142		45					126
127	104		143	31	46	39		29	44	127
128	105		144–145		47		18			128
129	106	20	146		48	40			45	129
130	107		147	32	49			30	46	130
131	108		148–149			41	19			131
132	109		150	33	50				47	132
133	110	21	151		51			31		133
134	111		152		52	42	20		48	134
135	112		153–154	34	53					135
136	113	22	155		54	43		32	49	136
137	114		156	35	55		21		50	137
138	115		157–158			44				138
139	116		159					33	51	139
140	117	23	160	36			22			140
141	118		161			45			52	141
142	119		162	37			23	34		142
143	120		163			46			53	143
144	121	24	164							144
145	122		165	38			24	35	54	145
146	123		166			47				146
147	124		167	39					55	147
148	125	25	168			48	25	36		148
149	126		169						56	149
150	127		170	40						150
151	128	26	171			49	26	37	57	151
152	129	27	172	41			27–28			152
153	130	28	173			50	29		58	153
154	131		174				30	38		154
155		29	175	42		51–52	31		59	155
156		30	176–178	43		53	32			156
157		31	179–181	44		54	33	39	60	157
158		32	182–184	45		55–56	34–35	40	61	158
159		33	185–187	46–47		57	36	41	62–63	159
160		34–54	188–233	48–53		58–67	37–55		64–77	160

[a] Based on weighted raw scores.

Table F.1. Age-Based Subtest Standard Scores

Ages: 8 years, 0 months, 0 days—8 years, 3 months, 30 days

Standard Score	Word Reading	Numerical Operations	Reading Comprehension[a]	Spelling	Pseudoword Decoding	Math Reasoning	Written Expression	Listening Comprehension	Oral Expression	Standard Score
40		0								40
41	0–2	1				0–1		0		41
42	3–5	2				2		1	0	42
43	6–9					3			1	43
44	10–13					4		2	2	44
45	14–15					5				45
46	16		0–2						3	46
47	17	3	3–4			6		3		47
48	18–19		5–10	0					4	48
49	20		11–17			7				49
50	21		18–22					4	5	50
51	22–23	4	23	1		8				51
52	24		24–27						6	52
53	25–26		28–30	2				5		53
54	27		31			9			7	54
55	28	5	32–34							55
56	29		35	3		10		6	8	56
57	30		36							57
58	31		37	4		11			9	58
59	32		38					7		59
60	33–34	6	39–40			12			10	60
61	35		41–42	5				8		61
62	36		43–44			13			11	62
63	37–38		45–46	6						63
64	39	7	47–48			14		9	12	64
65	40		49				0			65
66	41		50	7		15			13	66
67	42		51					10		67
68	43		52–53	8		16			14	68
69	44	8	54				1			69
70	45							11	15	70
71	46–47		55	9		17				71
72	48		56				2		16	72
73	49	9	57–59	10		18		12		73
74	50		60						17	74
75	51		61–63	11						75
76	52		64–66			19	3	13	18	76
77	53–54		67	12	0					77
78	55	10	68		1	20			19	78
79	56		69–70	13	2		4	14		79
80	57		71		3				20	80
81	58		72–73	14	4	21				81
82	59	11	74		5		5	15	21	82
83	60–61		75		6	22			22	83
84	62		76	15	7					84
85	63		77		8			16	23	85
86	64	12	78		9	23	6			86
87	65		79	16	10				24	87
88	66–67		80		11	24	7	17		88
89	68		81	17	12				25	89
90	69		82		13	25				90
91	70	13		18	14			18	26	91
92	71		83		15	26	8			92
93	72–73		84–85	19	16				27	93
94	74		86		17			19		94
95	75	14	87–88		18	27			28	95
96	76		89	20	19		9			96
97	77		90		20	28		20	29	97
98	78–79		91	21	21					98
99	80		92–94		22	29	10		30	99
100	81	15	95	22	23			21		100

[a] Based on weighted raw scores.

Table F.1. Age-Based Subtest Standard Scores

Ages: 8 years, 0 months, 0 days—8 years, 3 months, 30 days (*continued*)

Standard Score	Word Reading	Numerical Operations	Reading Comprehension[a]	Spelling	Pseudoword Decoding	Math Reasoning	Written Expression	Listening Comprehension	Oral Expression	Standard Score
101	82		96		24				31	101
102	83		97–99		25	30	11			102
103	84		100–105	23	26			22	32	103
104	85	16	106–109		27	31			33	104
105	86–87		110–112	24	28		12			105
106	88		113		29	32		23	34	106
107	89		114–116		30					107
108	90		117–118	25	31	33	13		35	108
109	91	17	119–120		32			24		109
110	92		121	26	33	34	14		36	110
111	93		122		34					111
112	94		123		35		15	25	37	112
113	95	18	124–125	27	36	35			38	113
114	96		126–127		37					114
115	97		128–129	28	38	36	16	26	39	115
116	98		130		39					116
117	99	19	131		40	37			40	117
118	100		132–133	29	41		17	27		118
119	101		134–135		42				41	119
120	102	20	136	30	43	38				120
121	103		137				18	28	42	121
122	104		138–139		44	39				122
123	105		140	31	45		19		43	123
124	106	21	141			40		29		124
125	107		142–143	32	46				44	125
126	108		144		47		20		45	126
127	109		145–147		48	41		30		127
128	110	22	148	33	49		21		46	128
129	111		149–150		50	42				129
130	112		151	34	51			31	47	130
131	113		152–153		52	43	22			131
132	114	23	154–155		53				48	132
133	115		156–157	35	54			32		133
134	116		158		55	44	23		49	134
135	117	24	159						50	135
136	118		160	36		45		33		136
137	119		161				24		51	137
138	120		162	37		46				138
139	121	25	163				25	34	52	139
140	122		164			47				140
141	123		165	38			26		53	141
142	124	26	166					35		142
143	125		167	39		48	27		54	143
144	126		168							144
145	127	27	169			49	28	36	55	145
146	128		170	40						146
147	129	28	171				29		56	147
148	130		172	41		50		37		148
149	131	29	173			51	30		57	149
150			174				31			150
151		30	175–176	42		52		38	58	151
152			177				32			152
153			178–179	43		53	33		59	153
154		31	180			54		39		154
155			181–182	44		55	34		60	155
156		32	183	45				40	61	156
157			184–185			56	35		62	157
158			186	46			36	41		158
159		33	187–188	47		57			63	159
160		34–54	189–233	48–53		58–67	37–55		64–77	160

[a] Based on weighted raw scores.

Table F.1. Age-Based Subtest Standard Scores

Ages: 8 years, 4 months, 0 days—8 years, 7 months, 30 days

Standard Score	Word Reading	Numerical Operations	Reading Comprehension[a]	Spelling	Pseudoword Decoding	Math Reasoning	Written Expression	Listening Comprehension	Oral Expression	Standard Score
40	0–15	0–2				0–3		0–1	0	40
41	16					4		2	1	41
42	17					5			2	42
43	18–19		0–3							43
44	20	3	4–10	0		6		3	3	44
45	21		11–17							45
46	22–23		18–22			7			4	46
47	24		23	1				4		47
48	25–26	4	24–27			8			5	48
49	27		28–30	2						49
50	28		31			9		5	6	50
51	29		32–34							51
52	30	5	35	3		10			7	52
53	31		36					6		53
54	32		37	4		11			8	54
55	33–34		38							55
56	35	6	39–40			12		7	9	56
57	36		41–42	5						57
58	37–38		43–44			13		8	10	58
59	39		45–46	6						59
60	40	7	47–48			14			11	60
61	41		49					9		61
62	42		50	7		15			12	62
63	43		51				0			63
64	44		52	8		16		10	13	64
65	45	8	53							65
66	46–47		54			17	1		14	66
67	48			9				11		67
68	49		55			18			15	68
69	50	9	56	10			2			69
70	51		57–59					12	16	70
71	52		60	11		19				71
72	53–54		61–63				3		17	72
73	55	10	64–66	12		20		13		73
74	56		67						18	74
75	57		68	13	0		4			75
76	58		69–70		1	21		14	19	76
77	59	11	71	14	2				20	77
78	60–61		72–73		3	22	5			78
79	62		74	15	4			15	21	79
80	63		75		5					80
81	64	12	76		6	23	6		22	81
82	65		77	16	7			16		82
83	66–67		78		8	24	7		23	83
84	68		79	17	9					84
85	69	13	80		10	25		17	24	85
86	70		81		11		8			86
87	71		82	18	12	26			25	87
88	72–73				13			18		88
89	74	14	83	19	14				26	89
90	75		84		15		9			90
91	76		85		16	27		19	27	91
92	77		86	20	17	28				92
93	78	15	87–88		18		10		28	93
94	79		89	21	19	29		20		94
95	80		90		20				29	95
96	81–82		91	22	21		11			96
97	83	16	92–94		22	30		21	30	97
98	84		95–96		23		12			98
99	85		97–98	23	24–25	31			31	99
100	86		99–106		26			22		100

[a] Based on weighted raw scores.

Table F.1. Age-Based Subtest Standard Scores

Ages: 8 years, 4 months, 0 days—8 years, 7 months, 30 days (*continued*)

Standard Score	Word Reading	Numerical Operations	Reading Comprehension[a]	Spelling	Pseudoword Decoding	Math Reasoning	Written Expression	Listening Comprehension	Oral Expression	Standard Score
101	87	17	107–109	24	27	32	13		32	101
102	88		110–113		28				33	102
103	89		114–115		29	33	14	23		103
104	90		116	25	30				34	104
105	91	18	117–118		31	34	15			105
106	92		119–120	26	32			24	35	106
107	93		121		33					107
108	94		122		34	35	16		36	108
109	95	19	123	27	35			25	37	109
110	96		124–125		36	36	17			110
111	97		126	28	37				38	111
112	98	20	127		38	37		26		112
113	99		128–129		39		18		39	113
114	100		130	29	40					114
115	101				41	38	19	27	40	115
116	102	21	131–132	30	42					116
117	103		133		43	39			41	117
118	104		134–135				20	28	42	118
119	105	22	136	31	44	40				119
120	106		137		45		21		43	120
121	107		138–139	32				29		121
122	108		140		46	41			44	122
123	109	23	141		47		22			123
124	110		142–143	33	48	42		30	45	124
125	111		144–147		49		23		46	125
126	112	24	148–150	34		43				126
127	113		151		50			31	47	127
128	114		152–155		51		24			128
129	115		156–158	35	52	44			48	129
130	116	25	159		53		25	32		130
131	117		160		54	45			49	131
132	118		161	36	55		26		50	132
133	119	26	162			46		33		133
134	120		163	37					51	134
135	121		164			47	27			135
136	122		165					34	52	136
137	123	27	166	38		48	28			137
138	124		167						53	138
139	125		168	39				35		139
140	126	28	169			49	29		54	140
141	127		170							141
142	128		171	40		50		36	55	142
143	129		172				30			143
144	130	29	173	41		51			56	144
145	131		174				31	37		145
146			175			52			57	146
147		30	176	42						147
148			177				32	38	58	148
149			178	43		53				149
150			179				33		59	150
151		31	180			54		39		151
152			181	44					60	152
153			182			55	34			153
154		32	183	45				40	61	154
155			184			56	35			155
156			185						62	156
157			186	46			36	41		157
158		33	187	47		57			63	158
159			188							159
160		34–54	189–233	48–53		58–67	37–55		64–77	160

[a] Based on weighted raw scores.

Table F.1. Age-Based Subtest Standard Scores

Ages: 8 years, 8 months, 0 days—8 years, 11 months, 30 days

Standard Score	Word Reading	Numerical Operations	Reading Comprehension[a]	Spelling	Pseudoword Decoding	Math Reasoning	Written Expression	Listening Comprehension	Oral Expression	Standard Score
40	0–15	0–2				0–3		0–1	0	40
41	16–17					4–5		2	1–2	41
42	18–19		0–3							42
43	20–21	3	4–10	0		6		3	3	43
44	22–23		11–17			7				44
45	24–26		18–22	1				4	4	45
46	27		23			8				46
47	28–29	4	24–27	2		9			5	47
48	30		28–31					5		48
49	31		32–34			10			6	49
50	32	5	35	3						50
51	33–34		36			11		6	7	51
52	35		37	4						52
53	36		38			12			8	53
54	37–38	6	39–40					7		54
55	39		41–42	5		13			9	55
56	40		43–44							56
57	41		45	6		14		8	10	57
58	42	7	46							58
59	43		47–48			15		9	11	59
60	44		49	7			0			60
61	45		50			16			12	61
62	46–47		51	8				10		62
63	48	8	52				1		13	63
64	49		53–54	9		17				64
65	50							11	14	65
66	51	9	55	10		18	2			66
67	52		56–57						15	67
68	53–54		58–60	11		19		12		68
69	55		61–63				3		16	69
70	56	10	64–66	12		20				70
71	57		67					13	17	71
72	58		68	13			4			72
73	59		69–70		0	21			18	73
74	60–61	11	71–73	14	1		5	14		74
75	62		74		2	22			19	75
76	63		75	15	3				20	76
77	64		76		4		6	15		77
78	65	12	77		5	23			21	78
79	66		78	16	6		7			79
80	67		79		7	24		16	22	80
81	68	13	80	17	8					81
82	69		81		9	25	8		23	82
83	70–71		82		10			17		83
84	72			18	11	26			24	84
85	73	14	83		12					85
86	74–75			19	13		9	18	25	86
87	76		84		14	27				87
88	77		85		15	28			26	88
89	78	15	86	20	16		10	19		89
90	79		87		17	29			27	90
91	80		88	21	18		11			91
92	81		89		19			20	28	92
93	82	16	90	22	20	30				93
94	83		91		21		12		29	94
95	84		92–94		22	31		21		95
96	85		95	23	23		13		30	96
97	86	17	96		24–25	32				97
98	87		97–99	24	26			22	31	98
99	88		100–106		27	33	14			99
100	89		107–109		28				32	100

[a] Based on weighted raw scores.

F

Table F.1. Age-Based Subtest Standard Scores

Ages: 8 years, 8 months, 0 days—8 years, 11 months, 30 days (*continued*)

Standard Score	Word Reading	Numerical Operations	Reading Comprehension[a]	Spelling	Pseudoword Decoding	Math Reasoning	Written Expression	Listening Comprehension	Oral Expression	Standard Score
101	90	18	110–113	25	29	34	15	23	33	101
102	91		114–116		30					102
103	92		117–118	26	31				34	103
104	93	19	119–120		32	35	16	24		104
105	94		121		33				35	105
106	95		122	27	34	36	17			106
107	96	20	123		35			25	36	107
108	97		124	28	36	37			37	108
109	98		125		37		18			109
110	99		126		38			26	38	110
111	100	21	127	29	39	38	19			111
112	101		128–129		40				39	112
113	102		130	30	41	39		27		113
114	103	22	131–132		42		20		40	114
115	104		133	31	43	40				115
116	105		134				21	28	41	116
117	106		135	32	44				42	117
118	107	23	136		45	41				118
119	108		137–139				22	29	43	119
120			140	33	46	42				120
121	109	24	141		47		23		44	121
122	110		142–143	34	48	43		30		122
123	111		144–145		49				45	123
124	112		146–149				24		46	124
125	113	25	150–151	35	50	44		31		125
126	114		152–155		51		25		47	126
127	115		156–158		52	45				127
128	116	26	159	36	53		26	32	48	128
129	117		160–161		54	46				129
130	118		162	37	55				49	130
131	119		163–164			47	27	33	50	131
132		27	165							132
133	120		166	38		48	28		51	133
134	121		167					34		134
135	122	28	168–169	39					52	135
136	123		170			49	29			136
137	124		171–172	40				35	53	137
138	125		173			50				138
139	126	29	174				30		54	139
140	127		175–176	41		51		36		140
141	128		177				31		55	141
142	129	30	178	42		52				142
143	130		179–180					37	56	143
144	131		181	43			32			144
145			182–183			53			57	145
146		31	184				33	38		146
147			185	44		54			58	147
148			186–187							148
149		32	188	45		55	34	39	59	149
150			189–192							150
151			193–195			56	35		60	151
152			196–198	46				40		152
153		33	199–201	47			36		61	153
154			202–204			57				154
155		34	205–207	48				41	62	155
156		35	208–210	49		58–59	37			156
157			211–213	50		60	38		63	157
158		36	214–216	51–52		61	39			158
159		37	217–219	53		62	40		64	159
160		38–54	220–233			63–67	41–55		65–77	160

[a] Based on weighted raw scores.

Table F.1. Age-Based Subtest Standard Scores

Ages: 9 years, 0 months, 0 days—9 years, 3 months, 30 days

Standard Score	Word Reading	Numerical Operations	Reading Comprehension[a]	Spelling	Pseudoword Decoding	Math Reasoning	Written Expression	Listening Comprehension	Oral Expression[b]	Standard Score
					Subtest Total Raw Scores					
40	0–16	0–2				0–4		0–2		40
41	17–20		0–3	0		5–6		3		41
42	21–24	3	4–10			7				42
43	25–28		11–17	1		8				43
44	29–30		18–22					4		44
45	31	4	23–27	2		9				45
46	32		28–30							46
47	33		31			10		5		47
48	34–35		32–34	3					0	48
49	36	5	35–37			11				49
50	37		38	4				6	1	50
51	38–39		39			12				51
52	40	6	40	5					2	52
53	41		41–42			13		7	3	53
54	42		43							54
55	43		44	6		14		8	4	55
56	44	7	45–46							56
57	45		47	7		15			5	57
58	46		48				0	9		58
59	47–48			8		16			6	59
60	49	8	49–50				1			60
61	50		51–52			17		10	7	61
62	51		53	9					8	62
63	52		54			18	2			63
64	53	9	55–56	10				11	9	64
65	54		57–59				3			65
66	55		60	11		19			10	66
67	56	10	61–63					12		67
68	57		64–66	12		20	4		11	68
69	58–59		67–70							69
70	60	11	71	13		21		13	12	70
71	61		72–74		0		5			71
72	62		75	14	1	22			13	72
73	63		76		2			14		73
74	64	12	77	15	3	23	6		14	74
75	65		78		4			15		75
76	66–67		79	16	5	24	7		15	76
77	68		80		6					77
78	69	13		17	7	25		16	16	78
79	70		81		8		8			79
80	71		82		9	26			17	80
81	72–73			18	10		9	17	18	81
82	74	14	83		11					82
83	75		84	19	12	27			19	83
84	76				13		10	18		84
85	77	15	85	20	14	28			20	85
86	78				15					86
87	79		86		16	29	11	19	21	87
88	80		87–88	21	17				22	88
89	81–82	16	89		18	30	12			89
90	83		90	22	19			20	23	90
91	84		91		20	31				91
92	85			23	21–22		13		24	92
93	86	17	92		23			21		93
94	87		93–94		24	32	14		25	94
95	88		95–96	24	25					95
96	89	18	97–98		26	33		22		96
97	90		99–102	25	27		15		26	97
98	91		103–108		28	34				98
99	92		109–112	26	29			23	27	99
100	93	19	113–115		30	35	16			100

[a] Based on weighted raw scores.

[b] For 9-year-old examinees in Grade 3, use Table F.1 for Ages 9:0–9:11 (Grade 3).

Table F.1. Age-Based Subtest Standard Scores

Ages: 9 years, 0 months, 0 days—9 years, 3 months, 30 days (*continued*)

Standard Score	Word Reading	Numerical Operations	Reading Comprehension[a]	Spelling	Pseudoword Decoding	Math Reasoning	Written Expression	Listening Comprehension	Oral Expression[b]	Standard Score
101	94		116–118		31				28	101
102	95		119	27	32		17	24		102
103		20	120		33	36			29	103
104	96		121	28	34					104
105	97		122		35	37	18	25	30	105
106	98		123		36					106
107	99	21	124–125	29	37	38			31	107
108	100		126		38		19	26		108
109	101		127	30	39	39			32	109
110	102	22	128		40		20			110
111	103		129–130		41	40		27	33	111
112				31	42					112
113	104	23	131–133		43	41	21		34	113
114	105		134	32	44			28		114
115	106		135				22		35	115
116	107	24	136		45	42				116
117	108		137	33	46			29	36	117
118	109		138–139		47	43	23			118
119	110	25	140	34	48				37	119
120	111		141–142		49	44	24	30		120
121	112		143	35					38	121
122			144–147		50	45				122
123	113	26	148–150	36	51		25	31	39	123
124	114		151–154			46				124
125	115		155–157		52		26		40	125
126		27	158–160	37	53	47		32		126
127	116		161–163						41	127
128	117		164	38	54		27			128
129	118		165		55	48		33	42	129
130	119	28	166–168	39			28			130
131	120		169–171			49			43	131
132	121		172					34		132
133	122	29	173–175	40		50	29		44	133
134	123		176							134
135	124		177–179	41			30	35	45	135
136	125		180–182			51				136
137		30	183						46	137
138	126		184–186	42		52	31	36		138
139	127		187–189						47	139
140	128	31	190–191	43		53	32			140
141	129		192–193					37	48	141
142	130		194	44						142
143	131		195–196			54	33		49	143
144		32	197					38		144
145			198–199	45		55	34		50	145
146			200							146
147		33	201–202	46		56		39	51	147
148			203				35			148
149			204–205	47		57			52	149
150			206				36	40		150
151		34	207–208	48		58			53	151
152			209							152
153		35	210–211	49		59	37	41	54	153
154			212	50			38			154
155		36	213–214	51		60			55	155
156			215				39			156
157		37	216–217	52		61	40		56	157
158			218	53		62				158
159			219–220				41		57	159
160		38–54	221–233			63–67	42–55		58–77	160

[a] Based on weighted raw scores.

[b] For 9-year-old examinees in Grade 3, use Table F.1 for Ages 9:0–9:11 (Grade 3).

Table F.1. Age-Based Subtest Standard Scores

Ages: 9 years, 4 months, 0 days—9 years, 7 months, 30 days

Standard Score	Word Reading	Numerical Operations	Reading Comprehension[a]	Spelling	Pseudoword Decoding	Math Reasoning	Written Expression	Listening Comprehension	Oral Expression[b]	Standard Score
40	0–30	0–2	0–3	0		0–7		0–3		40
41	31	3	4–10	1		8				41
42	32		11–17			9		4		42
43	33		18–22	2						43
44	34–35	4	23–27			10				44
45	36		28–31					5		45
46	37		32–34	3		11				46
47	38–39	5	35–37							47
48	40		38	4		12		6	0	48
49	41		39							49
50	42	6	40	5		13			1	50
51	43		41–42					7		51
52	44		43			14			2	52
53	45		44	6					3	53
54	46	7	45			15		8		54
55	47–48		46	7			0		4	55
56	49		47			16		9		56
57	50		48	8			1		5	57
58	51	8								58
59	52		49–50	9		17		10	6	59
60	53		51–52				2			60
61	54	9	53–54	10		18			7	61
62	55		55–57				3	11	8	62
63	56		58–60	11		19				63
64	57	10	61–63						9	64
65	58–59		64–66	12		20	4	12		65
66	60		67–70						10	66
67	61	11	71–74	13		21	5			67
68	62		75					13	11	68
69	63		76	14	0	22				69
70	64		77		1		6		12	70
71	65	12	78	15	2	23		14		71
72	66		79		3		7		13	72
73	67		80	16	4	24		15		73
74	68	13			5				14	74
75	69		81	17	6	25	8			75
76	70–71		82		7			16	15	76
77	72				8	26	9			77
78	73	14	83	18	9				16	78
79	74–75				10	27		17		79
80	76		84	19	11		10		17	80
81	77	15			12	28			18	81
82	78		85	20	13		11	18		82
83	79				14	29			19	83
84	80		86		15					84
85	81	16	87	21	16	30	12	19	20	85
86	82		88		17					86
87	83		89	22	18	31	13		21	87
88	84		90		19			20	22	88
89	85	17	91	23	20					89
90	86				21–22	32	14		23	90
91	87		92		23			21		91
92	88	18	93–94	24	24	33			24	92
93	89		95		25		15			93
94	90		96	25	26	34		22	25	94
95	91	19	97–99		27					95
96	92		100–102	26	28	35	16		26	96
97	93		103–108		29			23		97
98	94	20	109–112		30		17		27	98
99	95		113–118	27	31	36				99
100			119		32			24	28	100

[a] Based on weighted raw scores.

[b] For 9-year-old examinees in Grade 3, use Table F.1 for Ages 9:0–9:11 (Grade 3).

Table F.1. Age-Based Subtest Standard Scores
Ages: 9 years, 4 months, 0 days—9 years, 7 months, 30 days (*continued*)

Standard Score	Word Reading	Numerical Operations	Reading Comprehension[a]	Spelling	Pseudoword Decoding	Math Reasoning	Written Expression	Listening Comprehension	Oral Expression[b]	Standard Score
101	96		120	28	33	37	18			101
102	97	21	121		34				29	102
103	98		122		35	38		25		103
104	99		123	29	36		19		30	104
105	100	22	124		37	39				105
106	101		125	30	38		20	26	31	106
107	102		126		39	40				107
108	103	23	127	31	40				32	108
109			128		41	41	21	27		109
110	104		129–130	32	42				33	110
111	105	24	131–133		43		22			111
112	106		134		44	42		28	34	112
113	107			33						113
114	108	25	135		45	43	23		35	114
115			136	34	46			29		115
116	109		137–139		47	44	24		36	116
117	110		140	35	48					117
118	111	26	141–142		49	45		30	37	118
119	112		143	36			25			119
120			144–145		50	46			38	120
121	113	27	146–149		51		26	31		121
122	114		150–154	37		47			39	122
123	115		155–157		52					123
124			158–164	38	53		27	32	40	124
125	116	28	165			48				125
126	117		166–172	39	54		28		41	126
127	118		173–176		55	49		33		127
128	119	29	177–183	40					42	128
129			184–189			50	29			129
130	120		190–191					34	43	130
131	121		192	41			30			131
132	122	30	193			51			44	132
133	123		194	42				35		133
134	124		195			52	31		45	134
135	125	31	196	43						135
136			197			53	32	36	46	136
137	126		198	44						137
138	127		199						47	138
139	128	32	200			54	33	37		139
140	129		201	45					48	140
141	130		202			55	34			141
142	131	33	203	46				38	49	142
143			204			56				143
144			205	47			35		50	144
145			206			57		39		145
146		34	207	48			36		51	146
147			208			58				147
148			209					40	52	148
149		35	210	49		59	37			149
150			211						53	150
151			212	50			38	41		151
152			213			60			54	152
153		36	214	51						153
154			215				39		55	154
155			216	52		61				155
156		37	217				40		56	156
157			218	53		62				157
158			219						57	158
159			220				41			159
160		38–54	221–233			63–67	42–55		58–77	160

[a] Based on weighted raw scores.

[b] For 9-year-old examinees in Grade 3, use Table F.1 for Ages 9:0–9:11 (Grade 3).

Table F.1. Age-Based Subtest Standard Scores

Ages: 9 years, 8 months, 0 days—9 years, 11 months, 30 days

Standard Score	Word Reading	Numerical Operations	Reading Comprehension[a]	Spelling	Pseudoword Decoding	Math Reasoning	Written Expression	Listening Comprehension	Oral Expression[b]	Standard Score
40	0–30	0–2	0–3	0		0–7		0–3		40
41	31–32	3	4–17	1		8–9		4		41
42	33		18–22	2						42
43	34–36	4	23–31			10		5		43
44	37		32–34	3		11				44
45	38–40		35–37			12				45
46	41	5	38	4				6		46
47	42		39–40			13				47
48	43		41–42	5					0	48
49	44	6	43			14		7		49
50	45		44–45						1	50
51	46		46	6		15				51
52	47–48	7	47					8	2	52
53	49		48	7		16			3	53
54	50		49–50				0	9		54
55	51		51	8		17			4	55
56	52	8	52				1			56
57	53		53–54	9				10	5	57
58	54		55–57			18				58
59	55	9	58–59	10			2		6	59
60	56		60			19		11		60
61	57		61–63	11			3		7	61
62	58–59	10	64–65			20			8	62
63	60		66	12				12		63
64	61		67–70			21	4		9	64
65	62	11	71	13						65
66	63		72–74			22	5	13	10	66
67	64		75	14						67
68	65		76–77		0	23			11	68
69	66	12	78	15	1		6	14		69
70	67		79		2	24			12	70
71	68		80	16	3		7	15		71
72	69	13			4	25			13	72
73	70–71		81	17	5					73
74	72		82		6	26	8	16	14	74
75	73	14	83		7					75
76	74–75			18	8	27	9		15	76
77	76		84		9			17		77
78	77	15	85	19	10	28			16	78
79	78				11		10			79
80	79		86–87	20	12	29		18	17	80
81	80		88		13		11		18	81
82	81	16	89		14	30				82
83	82		90	21	15			19	19	83
84	83		91		16	31	12			84
85	84	17	92	22	17				20	85
86	85		93–94		18		13	20		86
87	86		95	23	19	32			21	87
88	87	18			20				22	88
89	88		96		21–22	33	14	21		89
90	89		97	24	23				23	90
91	90	19	98–99		24	34				91
92	91			25	25		15	22	24	92
93	92		100–102		26	35				93
94	93	20	103–107	26	27				25	94
95	94		108		28		16	23	26	95
96	95		109–112	27	29	36				96
97			113–115		30		17		27	97
98	96	21	116–118	28	31	37		24		98
99	97		119		32				28	99
100	98		120		33	38	18			100

[a] Based on weighted raw scores.

[b] For 9-year-old examinees in Grade 3, use Table F.1 for Ages 9:0–9:11 (Grade 3).

Table F.1. Age-Based Subtest Standard Scores

Ages: 9 years, 8 months, 0 days—9 years, 11 months, 30 days (*continued*)

Standard Score	Word Reading	Numerical Operations	Reading Comprehension[a]	Spelling	Pseudoword Decoding	Math Reasoning	Written Expression	Listening Comprehension	Oral Expression[b]	Standard Score
			Subtest Total Raw Scores							
101	99	22	121–122	29	34			25	29	101
102	100		123		35	39	19			102
103	101		124	30	36				30	103
104		23	125		37	40		26		104
105	102		126	31	38		20		31	105
106	103				39	41				106
107	104	24	127	32	40		21	27	32	107
108			128		41					108
109	105		129–130		42	42			33	109
110	106	25	131	33	43		22	28		110
111	107		132–133		44	43			34	111
112	108		134	34			23			112
113			135		45	44		29	35	113
114	109	26		35	46					114
115	110		136–137		47	45	24		36	115
116	111		138–139	36	48			30		116
117	112	27	140–141		49	46	25		37	117
118			142							118
119	113		143	37	50	47		31	38	119
120	114		144–146		51		26			120
121	115	28	147–149	38		48			39	121
122			150–154		52		27	32		122
123	116		155–157	39	53	49			40	123
124	117	29	158–164							124
125	118		165–166	40	54	50	28	33	41	125
126	119		167–172		55					126
127		30	173–176				29		42	127
128	120		177–183	41		51		34		128
129	121		184–189						43	129
130	122	31	190–191	42		52	30			130
131			192					35	44	131
132	123		193	43		53	31			132
133	124		194						45	133
134	125	32	195	44				36		134
135			196			54	32		46	135
136	126		197							136
137	127	33	198	45		55	33	37	47	137
138	128		199							138
139	129		200	46		56			48	139
140	130		201				34	38		140
141	131	34	202	47		57			49	141
142			203				35			142
143			204	48		58		39	50	143
144		35	205							144
145			206			59	36		51	145
146			207	49				40		146
147		36	208				37		52	147
148			209	50		60				148
149			210					41	53	149
150		37	211	51			38			150
151			212			61			54	151
152			213	52			39			152
153			214			62			55	153
154		38	215	53						154
155		39	216			63	40		56	155
156		40	217			64				156
157		41	218			65	41		57	157
158		42	219			66–67				158
159		43	220				42–43		58	159
160		44–54	221–233				44–55		59–77	160

[a] Based on weighted raw scores.

[b] For 9-year-old examinees in Grade 3, use Table F.1 for Ages 9:0–9:11 (Grade 3).

F

Table F.1. Age-Based Subtest Standard Scores
Ages: 9 years, 0 months, 0 days—9 years, 11 months, 30 days (Grade 3)

Standard Score	Oral Expression Subtest Total Raw Score			Standard Score
	Ages 9:0–9:3	Ages 9:4–9:7	Ages 9:8–9:11	
40	0–1	0–2	0–2	40
41	2		3	41
42		3		42
43	3		4	43
44		4		44
45	4		5	45
46		5		46
47	5		6	47
48		6		48
49	6		7	49
50		7		50
51	7		8	51
52		8		52
53	8		9	53
54		9		54
55	9		10	55
56		10		56
57	10		11	57
58		11		58
59	11		12	59
60		12		60
61	12		13	61
62		13		62
63	13		14	63
64		14		64
65	14		15	65
66		15		66
67	15		16	67
68		16		68
69	16		17	69
70		17		70
71	17		18	71
72		18		72
73	18		19	73
74		19	20	74
75	19	20		75
76	20		21	76
77		21		77
78	21		22	78
79		22		79
80	22		23	80
81		23		81
82	23		24	82
83		24		83
84	24		25	84
85		25		85
86	25		26	86
87		26		87
88	26		27	88
89		27		89
90	27		28	90
91		28		91
92	28		29	92
93		29		93
94	29		30	94
95		30		95
96	30		31	96
97		31		97
98	31		32	98
99		32	33	99
100	32	33		100

F

Table F.1. Age-Based Subtest Standard Scores

Ages: 9 years, 0 months, 0 days—9 years, 11 months, 30 days (Grade 3, *continued*)

Standard Score	Oral Expression Subtest Total Raw Score			Standard Score
	Ages 9:0–9:3	Ages 9:4–9:7	Ages 9:8–9:11	
101	33		34	101
102		34		102
103	34		35	103
104		35		104
105	35		36	105
106		36	37	106
107	36	37		107
108	37		38	108
109		38		109
110	38		39	110
111		39		111
112	39		40	112
113		40		113
114	40		41	114
115		41	42	115
116	41	42		116
117	42		43	117
118		43		118
119	43		44	119
120		44		120
121	44		45	121
122		45	46	122
123	45	46		123
124	46		47	124
125		47		125
126	47		48	126
127		48		127
128	48		49	128
129		49	50	129
130	49	50		130
131	50		51	131
132		51		132
133	51		52	133
134		52		134
135	52		53	135
136		53		136
137	53		54	137
138		54		138
139	54		55	139
140		55		140
141	55		56	141
142		56		142
143	56		57	143
144		57		144
145	57		58	145
146		58	59	146
147	58	59		147
148	59		60	148
149		60		149
150	60		61	150
151		61		151
152	61		62	152
153		62		153
154	62		63	154
155		63		155
156	63		64	156
157		64		157
158	64			158
159	65	65	65	159
160	66–77	66–77	66–77	160

Table F.1. Age-Based Subtest Standard Scores

Ages: 10 years, 0 months, 0 days—10 years, 3 months, 30 days

Standard Score	Word Reading	Numerical Operations	Reading Comprehension[a]	Spelling	Pseudoword Decoding	Math Reasoning	Written Expression	Listening Comprehension	Oral Expression	Standard Score
					Subtest Total Raw Scores					
40	0–31	0–3	0–10	0–1		0–8		0–3		40
41	32–35	4	11–27	2		9–10		4		41
42	36–39		28–31			11		5		42
43	40–41		32–37	3		12		6		43
44	42	5	38–39			13				44
45	43		40–42	4						45
46	44		43–44			14		7		46
47	45	6	45–46	5		15			0	47
48	46		47–48							48
49	47			6		16		8	1	49
50	48		49–50							50
51	49–50	7	51–52	7					2	51
52	51		53–54			17	0	9	3	52
53	52		55	8						53
54	53	8	56–57			18	1		4	54
55	54		58	9				10		55
56	55		59–60			19			5	56
57	56	9	61–62	10			2			57
58	57		63			20		11	6	58
59	58		64	11			3			59
60	59–60	10	65–66			21			7	60
61	61		67–68	12				12	8	61
62	62		69				4			62
63	63	11	70	13		22			9	63
64	64		71–73				5	13		64
65	65		74–75	14		23			10	65
66	66	12	76							66
67	67–68		77	15	0	24	6	14	11	67
68	69		78–79		1					68
69	70	13	80	16	2				12	69
70	71		81		3	25	7	15		70
71	72		82	17	4				13	71
72	73				5	26	8			72
73	74	14	83–84	18	6			16	14	73
74	75				7	27				74
75	76		85–86		8		9		15	75
76	77	15	87	19	9	28		17		76
77	78		88–90		10		10		16	77
78	79		91	20	11	29		18		78
79	80	16	92		12				17	79
80	81		93	21	13	30	11		18	80
81	82		94		14			19		81
82	83	17	95	22	15	31	12		19	82
83	84		96		16					83
84	85			23	17	32	13	20	20	84
85	86	18	97		18					85
86	87		98		19	33			21	86
87	88			24	20		14	21	22	87
88	89	19	99		21–22	34				88
89	90		100	25	23				23	89
90	91		101–102		24	35	15	22		90
91	92	20	103–105	26	25				24	91
92	93		106–108		26	36				92
93	94		109–110		27		16	23	25	93
94	95	21	111–112	27	28	37				94
95	96		113–114		29		17		26	95
96	97		115–117	28	30	38		24		96
97	98	22	118–119		31				27	97
98			120		32	39	18			98
99	99		121	29	33			25	28	99
100	100	23	122		34					100

[a] Based on weighted raw scores.

Table F.1. Age-Based Subtest Standard Scores

Ages: 10 years, 0 months, 0 days—10 years, 3 months, 30 days (*continued*)

Standard Score	Word Reading	Numerical Operations	Reading Comprehension[a]	Spelling	Pseudoword Decoding	Math Reasoning	Written Expression	Listening Comprehension	Oral Expression	Standard Score
			Subtest Total Raw Scores							
101	101		123	30	35	40	19		29	101
102	102		124		36			26		102
103	103	24	125	31	37	41	20		30	103
104			126		38					104
105	104		127	32	39	42			31	105
106	105	25	128		40		21	27		106
107	106		129	33	41	43			32	107
108	107		130		42		22			108
109		26	131	34	43	44		28	33	109
110	108		132–133		44					110
111	109		134	35		45	23		34	111
112		27			45			29		112
113	110		135		46	46	24		35	113
114	111		136	36	47					114
115			137–139		48	47		30	36	115
116	112	28	140	37			25			116
117	113		141–142		49				37	117
118	114		143	38	50	48	26	31		118
119	115	29	144–145		51				38	119
120			146–149	39		49				120
121	116		150–154		52		27	32	39	121
122	117		155–157		53	50				122
123	118	30	158–164	40			28		40	123
124			165		54	51		33		124
125	119		166–172	41	55				41	125
126	120	31	173–176			52	29			126
127			177–183	42				34	42	127
128	121		184–189			53	30			128
129	122	32	190–191	43					43	129
130	123		192			54		35		130
131	124		193				31		44	131
132		33	194	44						132
133	125		195			55	32	36	45	133
134	126		196	45						134
135		34	197			56			46	135
136	127		198	46			33	37		136
137	128		199			57			47	137
138		35	200	47			34			138
139	129		201			58		38	48	139
140	130		202							140
141	131		203	48		59	35		49	141
142		36	204					39		142
143			205	49			36		50	143
144			206			60				144
145		37	207	50				40	51	145
146			208			61	37			146
147			209						52	147
148		38	210	51		62	38	41		148
149			211						53	149
150		39	212	52						150
151			213			63	39		54	151
152		40	214	53		64				152
153			215				40		55	153
154		41	216			65				154
155			217			66			56	155
156		42	218				41			156
157			219			67	42		57	157
158		43	220							158
159			221				43		58	159
160		44–54	222–233				44–55		59–77	160

[a] Based on weighted raw scores.

Table F.1. Age-Based Subtest Standard Scores

Ages: 10 years, 4 months, 0 days—10 years, 7 months, 30 days

Standard Score	Subtest Total Raw Scores									Standard Score
	Word Reading	Numerical Operations	Reading Comprehension[a]	Spelling	Pseudoword Decoding	Math Reasoning	Written Expression	Listening Comprehension	Oral Expression	
40	0–41	0–4	0–31	0–2		0–12		0–5		40
41	42		32–37	3		13		6		41
42	43		38–42							42
43	44	5	43–46	4		14				43
44	45		47–48			15		7		44
45	46		49–50	5						45
46	47	6	51			16				46
47	48		52	6				8	0	47
48	49–50		53–54			17				48
49	51	7	55	7					1	49
50	52		56–57					9		50
51	53		58	8		18	0		2	51
52	54	8	59						3	52
53	55		60	9		19	1	10		53
54	56		61–62						4	54
55	57	9	63	10		20				55
56	58		64				2	11	5	56
57	59–60		65	11		21			6	57
58	61	10	66				3		6	58
59	62		67–68	12				12		59
60	63		69			22			7	60
61	64	11	70	13			4		8	61
62	65		71			23		13		62
63	66		72–73	14			5		9	63
64	67–68	12	74–75			24				64
65	69		76–77	15				14	10	65
66	70		78–79		0		6			66
67	71	13	80	16	1	25		15	11	67
68	72		81		2					68
69	73		82	17	3	26	7		12	69
70	74	14	83–84		4					70
71	75		85–87	18	5	27	8	16	13	71
72	76		88–90		6					72
73	77	15	91–92		7	28			14	73
74	78		93	19	8		9	17		74
75	79		94		9	29			15	75
76	80	16	95	20	10		10	18		76
77	81				11	30			16	77
78	82	17	96	21	12					78
79	83				13	31	11	19	17	79
80	84		97	22	14				18	80
81	85	18			15	32	12			81
82	86		98	23	16			20	19	82
83	87				17	33	13			83
84	88	19	99		18				20	84
85	89			24	19	34		21		85
86	90		100		20		14		21	86
87	91	20	101–102	25	21–22	35			22	87
88	92		103–105		23			22		88
89	93		106–107	26	24	36	15		23	89
90	94	21	108		25					90
91	95		109–110	27	26	37		23	24	91
92	96		111–112		27		16			92
93	97	22	113–114	28	28	38			25	93
94	98		115		29		17	24	26	94
95			116–117		30	39				95
96	99	23	118–119	29	31				27	96
97	100		120		32		18	25		97
98	101		121–122	30	33	40			28	98
99		24	123		34		19			99
100	102		124	31	35	41		26	29	100

[a] Based on weighted raw scores.

F

Table F.1. Age-Based Subtest Standard Scores

Ages: 10 years, 4 months, 0 days—10 years, 7 months, 30 days (*continued*)

Standard Score	Word Reading	Numerical Operations	Reading Comprehension[a]	Spelling	Pseudoword Decoding	Math Reasoning	Written Expression	Listening Comprehension	Oral Expression	Standard Score
101	103		125		36					101
102	104	25	126	32	37	42	20		30	102
103					38					103
104	105		127	33	39	43	21	27	31	104
105	106	26	128		40					105
106	107		129	34	41	44			32	106
107			130		42		22	28		107
108	108	27	131	35	43	45			33	108
109	109				44		23			109
110			132–133			46		29	34	110
111	110		134	36	45					111
112	111	28	135		46	47	24		35	112
113				37	47			30		113
114	112		136–137		48	48	25		36	114
115	113	29	138–139	38						115
116	114		140–141		49	49		31	37	116
117	115		142	39	50		26			117
118		30	143		51	50			38	118
119	116		144–146				27	32		119
120	117		147–149	40	52	51			39	120
121	118	31	150–154		53					121
122			155–157	41		52	28	33	40	122
123	119		158–164		54					123
124	120	32	165–166	42	55	53	29		41	124
125			167–172					34		125
126	121		173–176	43		54			42	126
127	122	33	177–183				30			127
128			184–189					35	43	128
129	123		190–191	44		55	31			129
130	124	34	192						44	130
131			193	45		56		36		131
132	125		194				32		45	132
133	126	35	195	46		57				133
134			196				33	37	46	134
135	127		197	47		58				135
136	128	36	198						47	136
137			199			59	34	38		137
138	129		200	48					48	138
139	130	37	201				35			139
140	131		202	49		60		39	49	140
141			203							141
142		38	204	50		61	36		50	142
143			205					40		143
144			206			62	37		51	144
145		39	207	51						145
146			208			63		41	52	146
147			209	52			38			147
148		40	210			64			53	148
149			211	53			39			149
150			212						54	150
151		41	213			65				151
152			214				40		55	152
153			215			66				153
154		42	216				41		56	154
155			217			67				155
156			218				42		57	156
157		43	219							157
158			220				43		58	158
159			221							159
160		44–54	222–233				44–55		59–77	160

[a] Based on weighted raw scores.

Table F.1. Age-Based Subtest Standard Scores

Ages: 10 years, 8 months, 0 days—10 years, 11 months, 30 days

Standard Score	Word Reading	Numerical Operations	Reading Comprehension[a]	Spelling	Pseudoword Decoding	Math Reasoning	Written Expression	Listening Comprehension	Oral Expression	Standard Score
40	0–41	0–4	0–31	0–2		0–12		0–5		40
41	42–43		32–42	3		13		6		41
42	44	5	43–46	4		14				42
43	45–46		47–49			15		7		43
44	47	6	50	5		16				44
45	48		51–52					8		45
46	49		53–54	6		17				46
47	50	7	55						0	47
48	51		56–57	7		18		9		48
49	52		58						1	49
50	53	8	59	8		19	0			50
51	54		60					10	2	51
52	55	9	61–62	9		20	1		3	52
53	56–57		63							53
54	58		64	10		21		11	4	54
55	59	10	65				2			55
56	60–61		66	11					5	56
57	62		67–68			22	3	12		57
58	63	11	69–70	12					6	58
59	64		71			23				59
60	65		72–73	13			4	13	7	60
61	66	12	74–75			24			8	61
62	67		76	14			5			62
63	68		77					14	9	63
64	69	13	78–79	15		25				64
65	70		80		0		6		10	65
66	71		81	16	1	26		15		66
67	72	14	82–83		2		7		11	67
68	73–74		84	17	3	27				68
69	75		85–87		4			16	12	69
70	76	15	88–90	18	5	28	8			70
71	77		91		6				13	71
72	78		92		7	29	9	17		72
73	79	16	93	19	8				14	73
74	80		94		9	30		18		74
75	81	17	95	20	10		10		15	75
76	82		96		11	31				76
77	83			21	12		11	19	16	77
78	84	18	97		13	32				78
79	85		98	22	14				17	79
80	86				15	33	12	20	18	80
81	87	19	99	23	16					81
82	88				17	34	13		19	82
83	89		100–101	24	18–19			21		83
84	90	20	102–103		20	35			20	84
85	91		104–105	25	21		14			85
86	92		106–107		22	36		22	21	86
87	93	21	108	26	23				22	87
88	94		109–110		24	37	15			88
89	95		111–112	27	25			23	23	89
90	96	22	113		26	38	16			90
91	97		114		27				24	91
92	98		115	28	28	39		24	25	92
93		23	116–117		29		17		25	93
94	99		118–119	29	30				26	94
95	100		120		31	40		25		95
96	101	24		30	32		18		27	96
97	102		121–122		33	41				97
98		25	123		34		19	26	28	98
99	103			31	35	42				99
100	104		124–125		36		20		29	100

[a] Based on weighted raw scores.

F

Table F.1. Age-Based Subtest Standard Scores

Ages: 10 years, 8 months, 0 days—10 years, 11 months, 30 days (continued)

Standard Score	Word Reading	Numerical Operations	Reading Comprehension[a]	Spelling	Pseudoword Decoding	Math Reasoning	Written Expression	Listening Comprehension	Oral Expression	Standard Score
101		26	126	32	37	43				101
102	105				38		21	27	30	102
103	106		127	33	39	44			31	103
104	107	27	128		40					104
105			129	34	41	45	22	28	32	105
106	108		130		42					106
107	109		131	35	43	46	23		33	107
108		28			44			29		108
109	110		132–133	36	45	47			34	109
110	111		134				24			110
111		29	135	37	46	48		30	35	111
112	112				47		25			112
113	113		136–137	38	48	49			36	113
114	114	30	138					31		114
115	115		139–140	39	49	50	26		37	115
116		31	141		50					116
117	116		142		51	51	27	32	38	117
118	117		143	40						118
119		32	144–146		52	52			39	119
120	118		147–149	41	53		28	33		120
121			150–154			53			40	121
122	119	33	155–157	42	54		29			122
123	120		158–164		55	54		34	41	123
124			165–166							124
125	121	34	167–172	43			30		42	125
126	122		173–176			55		35		126
127			177–183	44			31		43	127
128	123	35	184–189			56				128
129	124		190–192	45				36	44	129
130			193			57	32			130
131	125	36	194						45	131
132	126		195–196	46		58	33	37		132
133			197						46	133
134	127	37	198	47		59				134
135	128		199				34	38	47	135
136	129		200							136
137		38	201	48		60	35		48	137
138	130		202					39		138
139	131		203	49		61			49	139
140		39	204				36			140
141			205	50		62		40	50	141
142			206				37			142
143		40	207			63			51	143
144			208	51				41		144
145			209			64	38		52	145
146		41	210	52						146
147			211				39		53	147
148			212	53		65				148
149		42	213						54	149
150			214			66	40			150
151			215						55	151
152		43	216			67	41			152
153			217						56	153
154			218				42			154
155		44	219						57	155
156		45	220				43			156
157		46	221						58	157
158		47	222–223				44			158
159		48	224–226				45–46		59	159
160		49–54	227–233				47–55		60–77	160

[a] Based on weighted raw scores.

Table F.1. Age-Based Subtest Standard Scores

Ages: 11 years, 0 months, 0 days—11 years, 3 months, 30 days

Standard Score	Word Reading	Numerical Operations	Reading Comprehension[a]	Spelling	Pseudoword Decoding	Math Reasoning	Written Expression	Listening Comprehension	Oral Expression	Standard Score
40	0–42	0–4	0–37	0–3		0–13		0–6		40
41	43–45	5	38–48			14–15		7		41
42	46		49–50	4		16				42
43	47	6	51	5		17		8		43
44	48		52							44
45	49–50	7	53–54	6						45
46	51		55–56			18		9	0	46
47	52	8	57	7						47
48	53		58–60			19	0		1	48
49	54		61	8				10		49
50	55	9	62			20	1		2	50
51	56		63–64	9					3	51
52	57		65			21		11		52
53	58	10	66	10			2		4	53
54	59–60		67–68			22				54
55	61		69	11			3	12	5	55
56	62	11	70			23				56
57	63		71	12					6	57
58	64		72–73			24	4	13		58
59	65	12	74–75	13					7	59
60	66		76–77			25	5		8	60
61	67–68	13	78	14				14		61
62	69		79–80			26			9	62
63	70		81	15	0		6			63
64	71	14	82		1	27		15	10	64
65	72		83–84	16	2					65
66	73		85–86		3	28	7		11	66
67	74	15	87	17	4			16		67
68	75		88–89		5	29	8		12	68
69	76	16	90	18	6					69
70	77		91–92		7	30		17	13	70
71	78		93	19	8		9			71
72	79–80	17	94		9	31		18	14	72
73	81		95	20	10		10			73
74	82				11	32			15	74
75	83	18	96–97	21	12			19		75
76	84				13	33	11		16	76
77	85		98–99	22	14					77
78	86	19			15	34	12	20	17	78
79	87		100	23	16				18	79
80	88	20	101–102		17		13			80
81	89		103–105		18	35		21	19	81
82	90		106–107	24	19					82
83	91	21	108		20	36	14		20	83
84	92		109	25	21–22			22		84
85	93		110–111		23	37			21	85
86	94	22	112	26	24		15		22	86
87	95				25	38		23		87
88	96		113–114	27	26				23	88
89	97	23	115		27	39	16			89
90	98		116	28	28			24	24	90
91	99		117		29	40	17			91
92	100	24	118		30				25	92
93	101		119	29	31	41		25	26	93
94			120		32		18			94
95	102	25	121	30	33	42			27	95
96	103				34		19	26		96
97	104		122	31	35	43			28	97
98		26	123		36					98
99	105		124	32	37	44	20	27	29	99
100	106	27	125		38					100

[a] Based on weighted raw scores.

Table F.1. Age-Based Subtest Standard Scores

Ages: 11 years, 0 months, 0 days—11 years, 3 months, 30 days (*continued*)

Standard Score	Word Reading	Numerical Operations	Reading Comprehension[a]	Spelling	Pseudoword Decoding	Math Reasoning	Written Expression	Listening Comprehension	Oral Expression	Standard Score
101			126	33	39		21		30	101
102	107		127		40	45				102
103	108	28	128	34	41			28	31	103
104			129		42	46	22			104
105	109		130	35	43				32	105
106	110	29			44	47	23	29		106
107			131						33	107
108	111		132	36	45	48				108
109	112	30	133		46		24	30	34	109
110			134	37	47	49				110
111	113		135		48		25		35	111
112	114	31	136	38		50		31		112
113			137		49				36	113
114	115		138–139	39	50	51	26			114
115		32	140–141						37	115
116	116		142		51	52	27	32		116
117	117		143	40					38	117
118	118	33	144–146		52	53				118
119			147–149	41			28	33	39	119
120	119		150–154		53					120
121	120	34	155–157	42	54	54	29		40	121
122			158–164					34		122
123	121		165–166	43	55	55	30		41	123
124	122	35	167–172							124
125			173–176			56		35	42	125
126	123		177–183	44			31			126
127	124	36	184–189			57			43	127
128			190–191	45			32	36		128
129	125	37	192–194			58			44	129
130	126		195	46						130
131			196				33	37	45	131
132	127	38	197	47		59				132
133	128		198–199				34		46	133
134			200			60		38		134
135	129	39	201	48					47	135
136	130		202			61	35			136
137	131		203	49				39	48	137
138		40	204			62	36			138
139			205						49	139
140			206	50				40		140
141		41	207			63	37		50	141
142			208	51						142
143			209			64	38	41	51	143
144		42	210	52						144
145			211			65	39		52	145
146			212							146
147		43	213	53		66	40		53	147
148			214							148
149			215			67	41		54	149
150		44	216							150
151			217						55	151
152		45	218				42			152
153			219						56	153
154		46	220				43			154
155			221						57	155
156		47	222				44			156
157			223–224				45		58	157
158		48	225							158
159			226–227				46		59	159
160		49–54	228–233				47–55		60–77	160

[a] Based on weighted raw scores.

Table F.1. Age-Based Subtest Standard Scores

Ages: 11 years, 4 months, 0 days—11 years, 7 months, 30 days

Standard Score	Word Reading	Numerical Operations	Reading Comprehension[a]	Spelling	Pseudoword Decoding	Math Reasoning	Written Expression	Listening Comprehension	Oral Expression	Standard Score
40	0–46	0–5	0–49	0–3		0–16		0–7		40
41	47	6	50	4		17		8		41
42	48		51–52	5						42
43	49	7	53–54			18				43
44	50		55–56	6				9		44
45	51	8	57			19				45
46	52		58–60	7					0	46
47	53	9	61			20	0	10		47
48	54		62	8					1	48
49	55		63–64			21	1			49
50	56–57	10	65	9				11	2	50
51	58		66			22			3	51
52	59		67–68	10			2			52
53	60–61	11	69–70			23		12	4	53
54	62		71	11			3			54
55	63		72–73			24			5	55
56	64	12	74–75	12				13		56
57	65		76			25	4		6	57
58	66	13	77	13						58
59	67		78			26	5	14	7	59
60	68		79–80	14					8	60
61	69	14	81			27				61
62	70		82–83	15	0		6	15	9	62
63	71		84		1	28				63
64	72	15	85–86	16	2		7		10	64
65	73–74		87		3	29		16		65
66	75	16	88–89	17	4				11	66
67	76		90		5	30	8			67
68	77		91	18	6			17	12	68
69	78	17	92		7	31	9			69
70	79–80		93	19	8			18	13	70
71	81		94		9	32				71
72	82	18	95	20	10		10		14	72
73	83		96–97		11	33		19		73
74	84		98–99	21	12		11		15	74
75	85	19			13	34				75
76	86		100–101	22	14			20	16	76
77	87	20	102–103		15		12			77
78	88		104–105	23	16	35			17	78
79	89		106–107		17		13	21	18	79
80	90	21	108	24	18–19	36				80
81	91		109		20				19	81
82	92		110–111	25	21	37	14	22		82
83	93	22	112		22				20	83
84	94			26	23	38				84
85	95		113		24		15	23	21	85
86	96	23	114	27	25	39			22	86
87	97		115		26		16			87
88	98		116		27	40		24	23	88
89	99	24	117	28	28					89
90	100		118		29	41	17		24	90
91	101	25	119	29	30			25		91
92	102		120		31	42			25	92
93				30	32		18		26	93
94	103	26	121		33	43		26		94
95	104				34		19		27	95
96		27	122	31	35	44				96
97	105		123		36		20	27	28	97
98	106			32	37					98
99		28	124–125		38	45	21		29	99
100	107		126	33	39					100

[a] Based on weighted raw scores.

Table F.1. Age-Based Subtest Standard Scores

Ages: 11 years, 4 months, 0 days—11 years, 7 months, 30 days (*continued*)

Standard Score	Word Reading	Numerical Operations	Reading Comprehension[a]	Spelling	Pseudoword Decoding	Math Reasoning	Written Expression	Listening Comprehension	Oral Expression	Standard Score
			Subtest Total Raw Scores							
101	108		127		40	46		28	30	101
102		29	128	34	41		22		31	102
103	109		129		42	47				103
104	110		130	35	43		23	29	32	104
105		30			44	48				105
106	111		131	36	45				33	106
107	112	31	132			49	24	30		107
108			133	37	46				34	108
109	113		134		47	50	25			109
110	114	32	135	38	48			31	35	110
111			136			51				111
112	115		137	39	49		26		36	112
113		33	138		50	52				113
114	116		139–140				27	32	37	114
115	117		141	40	51	53				115
116		34	142						38	116
117	118		143	41	52		28	33		117
118			144–146			54			39	118
119	119	35	147–149	42	53		29			119
120	120		150–154		54	55		34	40	120
121			155–157				30			121
122	121	36	158–164	43	55	56			41	122
123	122		165–166					35		123
124		37	167–172	44		57	31		42	124
125	123		173–176							125
126	124		177–183	45		58	32	36	43	126
127		38	184–189							127
128	125		190–194						44	128
129	126		195–196	46		59	33	37		129
130		39	197						45	130
131	127		198–199	47		60	34			131
132	128		200					38	46	132
133	129	40	201			61				133
134			202	48			35		47	134
135	130		203			62		39		135
136	131	41	204	49			36		48	136
137			205							137
138			206			63		40	49	138
139		42	207	50			37			139
140			208			64			50	140
141			209	51			38	41		141
142		43	210			65			51	142
143			211	52			39			143
144			212			66			52	144
145		44	213				40			145
146			214	53		67			53	146
147			215				41			147
148		45	216						54	148
149			217							149
150			218				42		55	150
151		46	219							151
152			220				43		56	152
153			221							153
154		47	222				44		57	154
155			223							155
156			224				45		58	156
157		48	225							157
158			226				46		59	158
159			227							159
160		49–54	228–233				47–55		60–77	160

[a] Based on weighted raw scores.

Table F.1. Age-Based Subtest Standard Scores
Ages: 11 years, 8 months, 0 days—11 years, 11 months, 30 days

Standard Score	Word Reading	Numerical Operations	Reading Comprehension[a]	Spelling	Pseudoword Decoding	Math Reasoning	Written Expression	Listening Comprehension	Oral Expression	Standard Score
40	0–46	0–5	0–49	0–3		0–16		0–7		40
41	47–48	6	50	4–5		17		8		41
42	49	7	51–54			18				42
43	50–51		55–56	6		19		9		43
44	52	8	57							44
45	53		58–61	7		20		10	0	45
46	54	9	62				0			46
47	55		63–64	8		21			1	47
48	56–57		65				1	11		48
49	58	10	66	9		22			2	49
50	59		67–68						3	50
51	60–61		69–70	10		23	2	12		51
52	62	11	71–73						4	52
53	63		74–75	11		24	3			53
54	64		76					13	5	54
55	65	12	77	12		25				55
56	66		78				4		6	56
57	67	13	79–80	13		26		14		57
58	68		81				5		7	58
59	69		82–83	14		27			8	59
60	70	14	84					15		60
61	71		85–86	15	0	28	6		9	61
62	72	15	87		1					62
63	73–74		88–89	16	2	29	7	16	10	63
64	75		90		3					64
65	76	16	91	17	4	30			11	65
66	77		92–93		5		8	17		66
67	78	17	94	18	6	31			12	67
68	79–80		95		7		9			68
69	81		96–97	19	8	32		18	13	69
70	82	18	98		9					70
71	83		99	20	10	33	10		14	71
72	84		100–101		11			19		72
73	85	19	102–103	21	12	34	11		15	73
74	86		104		13					74
75	87	20	105	22	14			20	16	75
76	88		106–107		15	35	12			76
77	89		108	23	16				17	77
78	90	21	109		17	36	13	21	18	78
79	91		110	24	18–19					79
80	92		111		20	37			19	80
81	93	22	112	25	21		14	22		81
82	94				22	38			20	82
83	95		113	26	23		15			83
84	96	23	114		24	39		23	21	84
85	97		115	27	25		16		22	85
86	98		116		26	40				86
87	99	24	117		27			24	23	87
88	100		118	28	28	41	17			88
89	101	25	119		29				24	89
90	102		120	29	30	42		25		90
91					31		18		25	91
92	103	26	121	30	32	43			26	92
93	104				33		19	26		93
94		27	122	31	34	44			27	94
95	105		123		35		20			95
96	106		124	32	36	45		27	28	96
97		28	125		37		21			97
98	107		126	33	38	46			29	98
99	108	29	127		39			28		99
100			128	34	40	47	22		30	100

[a] Based on weighted raw scores.

Table F.1. Age-Based Subtest Standard Scores
Ages: 11 years, 8 months, 0 days—11 years, 11 months, 30 days (*continued*)

Standard Score	Word Reading	Numerical Operations	Reading Comprehension[a]	Spelling	Pseudoword Decoding	Math Reasoning	Written Expression	Listening Comprehension	Oral Expression	Standard Score
			Subtest Total Raw Scores							
101	109		129		41				31	101
102	110	30	130	35	42	48	23	29		102
103					43				32	103
104	111	31	131	36	44	49				104
105	112		132		45		24	30	33	105
106			133	37		50				106
107	113	32	134		46		25		34	107
108	114		135	38	47	51		31		108
109			136		48				35	109
110	115	33	137	39		52	26			110
111	116		138		49				36	111
112			139–140		50	53	27	32		112
113	117	34	141	40					37	113
114	118		142–143		51		28			114
115		35	144–146	41		54		33	38	115
116	119		147–149		52		29			116
117			150–154	42		55			39	117
118	120	36	155–157		53		30	34		118
119			158–163			56			40	119
120	121	37	164–166	43	54					120
121	122		167–172			57	31	35	41	121
122			173–176	44	55					122
123	123	38	177–183			58	32		42	123
124	124		184–189	45				36		124
125			190–194						43	125
126	125	39	195–196			59	33			126
127	126		197	46				37	44	127
128			198–199			60	34			128
129	127	40	200	47					45	129
130			201			61		38		130
131	128	41	202				35		46	131
132	129		203	48		62				132
133			204				36	39	47	133
134	130	42	205	49						134
135	131		206			63			48	135
136			207				37	40		136
137		43	208	50		64			49	137
138			209				38			138
139			210	51		65		41	50	139
140		44	211				39			140
141			212			66			51	141
142		45	213	52			40			142
143			214			67			52	143
144			215	53			41			144
145		46	216						53	145
146			217							146
147			218				42		54	147
148		47	219							148
149			220				43		55	149
150			221							150
151		48	222				44		56	151
152			223							152
153			224				45		57	153
154		49–50	225							154
155		51	226				46		58	155
156		52	227							156
157		53–54	228–229				47		59	157
158			230–232				48			158
159			233				49–50		60	159
160							51–55		61–77	160

[a] Based on weighted raw scores.

Table F.1. Age-Based Subtest Standard Scores

Ages: 12 years, 0 months, 0 days—12 years, 3 months, 30 days

Standard Score	Word Reading	Numerical Operations	Reading Comprehension[a]	Spelling	Pseudoword Decoding	Math Reasoning	Written Expression	Listening Comprehension	Oral Expression	Standard Score
40	0–47	0–6	0–50	0–4		0–17		0–8		40
41	48–50	7	51–52	5		18		9		41
42	51		53–57	6		19				42
43	52	8	58–60			20				43
44	53		61	7				10		44
45	54–55	9	62–63			21			0	45
46	56		64–65	8			0			46
47	57		66–68			22		11	1	47
48	58–59	10	69–70	9			1			48
49	60		71			23			2	49
50	61	11	72–73	10			2	12	3	50
51	62		74–77			24				51
52	63		78	11					4	52
53	64	12	79			25	3	13		53
54	65		80–81	12					5	54
55	66	13	82–83			26	4			55
56	67		84	13				14	6	56
57	68		85–86			27	5			57
58	69–70	14	87	14					7	58
59	71		88–89			28	6	15	8	59
60	72		90	15						60
61	73	15	91		0	29			9	61
62	74		92	16	1		7	16		62
63	75	16	93		2	30			10	63
64	76		94	17	3		8			64
65	77–78		95		4	31		17	11	65
66	79	17	96–97	18	5					66
67	80		98–99		6	32	9	18	12	67
68	81			19	7					68
69	82	18	100–101		8	33	10		13	69
70	83		102–103	20	9			19		70
71	84	19	104–105		10	34			14	71
72	85		106	21	11		11			72
73	86		107		12	35		20	15	73
74	87	20	108	22	13		12			74
75	88		109		14	36			16	75
76	89	21		23	15		13	21		76
77	90		110–111		16	37			17	77
78	91			24	17–18				18	78
79	92	22	112		19–20	38	14	22		79
80	93		113	25	21				19	80
81	94	23	114		22	39				81
82	95			26	23		15	23	20	82
83	96		115		24	40				83
84	97	24	116	27	25		16		21	84
85	98				26	41		24	22	85
86	99	25	117	28	27					86
87	100		118		28	42	17		23	87
88	101		119	29	29			25		88
89	102	26	120		30	43	18		24	89
90	103		121	30	31					90
91	104	27	122		32	44		26	25	91
92					33		19		26	92
93	105		123	31	34					93
94	106	28	124–125		35	45	20	27	27	94
95	107		126	32	36					95
96			127		37	46	21		28	96
97	108	29		33	38					97
98	109		128		39	47	22	28	29	98
99	110		129	34	40					99
100		30	130		41	48			30	100

[a] Based on weighted raw scores.

Table F.1. Age-Based Subtest Standard Scores

Ages: 12 years, 0 months, 0 days—12 years, 3 months, 30 days (*continued*)

Standard Score	Word Reading	Numerical Operations	Reading Comprehension[a]	Spelling	Pseudoword Decoding	Math Reasoning	Written Expression	Listening Comprehension	Oral Expression	Standard Score
					Subtest Total Raw Scores					
101	111			35	42		23	29	31	101
102	112	31	131–132		43	49				102
103			133	36			24		32	103
104	113	32	134		44	50		30		104
105	114		135	37	45		25		33	105
106		33	136		46	51				106
107	115		137	38			26	31	34	107
108					47	52				108
109	116	34	138–139	39	48		27		35	109
110	117		140–141			53		32		110
111			142	40	49				36	111
112	118	35	143		50	54	28			112
113			144–148	41				33	37	113
114	119	36	149–153		51		29			114
115	120		154–157			55			38	115
116			158–161	42	52		30	34		116
117	121	37	162–164			56			39	117
118			165–170	43	53					118
119	122	38	171–178		54	57	31		40	119
120	123		179–183					35		120
121		39	184–186	44	55	58	32		41	121
122	124		187–191							122
123			192–195	45			33	36	42	123
124	125	40	196			59				124
125			197–198				34		43	125
126	126		199–200	46		60		37		126
127		41	201				35		44	127
128	127		202	47		61				128
129	128	42	203					38	45	129
130			204			62	36			130
131	129		205	48					46	131
132		43	206			63	37	39		132
133	130		207	49					47	133
134	131	44	208			64	38			134
135			209					40	48	135
136			210	50		65	39			136
137		45	211						49	137
138			212	51		66		41		138
139			213				40		50	139
140		46	214	52		67				140
141			215				41		51	141
142		47	216							142
143			217	53			42		52	143
144		48	218							144
145			219				43		53	145
146			220							146
147		49	221						54	147
148			222				44			148
149		50	223						55	149
150		51	224				45			150
151			225						56	151
152		52	226				46			152
153		53	227						57	153
154			228				47			154
155		54	229–230						58	155
156			231				48			156
157			232–233				49		59	157
158										158
159							50		60	159
160							51–55		61–77	160

[a] Based on weighted raw scores.

Table F.1. Age-Based Subtest Standard Scores

Ages: 12 years, 4 months, 0 days—12 years, 7 months, 30 days

Standard Score	Word Reading	Numerical Operations	Reading Comprehension[a]	Spelling	Pseudoword Decoding	Math Reasoning	Written Expression	Listening Comprehension	Oral Expression	Standard Score
40	0–51	0–7	0–50	0–5		0–19		0–9		40
41	52		51–57	6		20				41
42	53	8	58–61					10		42
43	54–55		62–63	7		21				43
44	56	9	64–65						0	44
45	57		66–68	8		22	0	11		45
46	58–59		69–70						1	46
47	60	10	71–73	9		23	1			47
48	61		74–77					12	2	48
49	62	11	78	10		24	2		3	49
50	63		79							50
51	64		80–81	11		25		13	4	51
52	65	12	82–83				3			52
53	66		84	12		26			5	53
54	67	13	85–86				4	14		54
55	68		87	13		27			6	55
56	69–70		88–89				5			56
57	71	14	90	14		28		15	7	57
58	72		91				6		8	58
59	73	15	92–93	15		29				59
60	74		94		0			16	9	60
61	75		95	16	1	30	7			61
62	76	16	96–97		2				10	62
63	77–78		98	17	3	31	8	17		63
64	79	17	99		4				11	64
65	80		100–101	18	5	32				65
66	81		102–103		6		9	18	12	66
67	82	18	104	19	7	33				67
68	83		105		8		10		13	68
69	84	19	106	20	9	34		19		69
70	85		107		10				14	70
71	86		108	21	11	35	11			71
72	87	20	109		12			20	15	72
73	88			22	13	36	12			73
74	89	21	110		14				16	74
75	90		111	23	15	37	13	21		75
76	91				16				17	76
77	92	22	112	24	17–18	38			18	77
78	93		113		19–20		14	22		78
79	94	23	114	25	21	39			19	79
80	95				22		15			80
81	96		115	26	23	40		23	20	81
82	97	24	116		24		16			82
83	98			27	25	41			21	83
84	99	25	117		26			24	22	84
85	100		118	28	27	42	17			85
86	101		119		28				23	86
87	102	26	120	29	29	43	18	25		87
88	103		121		30				24	88
89	104	27	122	30	31	44				89
90					32		19	26	25	90
91	105		123–124	31	33	45			26	91
92	106	28	125		34		20			92
93	107		126	32	35	46		27	27	93
94		29	127		36		21			94
95	108			33	37	47			28	95
96	109		128		38		22	28		96
97	110	30	129	34	39	48			29	97
98			130		40					98
99	111	31		35	41	49	23	29	30	99
100	112		131–132		42				31	100

[a] Based on weighted raw scores.

Table F.1. Age-Based Subtest Standard Scores

Ages: 12 years, 4 months, 0 days—12 years, 7 months, 30 days (*continued*)

Standard Score	Word Reading	Numerical Operations	Reading Comprehension[a]	Spelling	Pseudoword Decoding	Math Reasoning	Written Expression	Listening Comprehension	Oral Expression	Standard Score
101		32	133	36	43	50	24			101
102	113		134					30	32	102
103	114	33	135	37	44	51	25			103
104			136		45				33	104
105	115		137	38	46	52	26	31		105
106	116	34							34	106
107			138–139	39	47	53	27			107
108	117	35	140–141		48			32	35	108
109	118		142–143	40		54	28			109
110		36	144–148		49				36	110
111	119		149–153	41	50		29	33		111
112			154–157			55			37	112
113	120	37	158–161		51		30			113
114			162–163	42		56		34	38	114
115	121	38	164–170		52					115
116			171–178	43		57	31		39	116
117	122	39	179–183		53					117
118	123		184–186			58	32	35	40	118
119			187–191	44	54					119
120	124	40	192–195				33		41	120
121			196	45	55	59		36		121
122	125	41	197–198				34		42	122
123			199–200			60				123
124	126	42	201	46			35	37	43	124
125			202			61				125
126	127		203	47					44	126
127		43	204			62	36	38		127
128	128		205						45	128
129		44	206	48		63	37			129
130	129		207					39	46	130
131		45	208	49		64	38			131
132	130		209						47	132
133	131		210			65	39	40		133
134		46	211	50					48	134
135			212			66				135
136		47	213	51			40	41	49	136
137			214			67				137
138		48	215				41		50	138
139			216	52						139
140			217				42		51	140
141		49	218	53						141
142			219				43		52	142
143		50	220							143
144			221						53	144
145		51	222				44			145
146			223						54	146
147			224				45			147
148		52	225						55	148
149			226				46			149
150		53	227						56	150
151			228				47			151
152		54	229						57	152
153			230							153
154			231				48		58	154
155			232							155
156			233				49		59	156
157										157
158							50		60	158
159										159
160							51–55		61–77	160

[a] Based on weighted raw scores.

Table F.1. Age-Based Subtest Standard Scores
Ages: 12 years, 8 months, 0 days—12 years, 11 months, 30 days

Standard Score	Word Reading	Numerical Operations	Reading Comprehension[a]	Spelling	Pseudoword Decoding	Math Reasoning	Written Expression	Listening Comprehension	Oral Expression	Standard Score
			Subtest Total Raw Scores							
40	0–51	0–7	0–50	0–5		0–19		0–9		40
41	52–53	8	51–61	6		20		10		41
42	54–55		62–63	7		21				42
43	56–57	9	64–68							43
44	58–59		69–70	8		22	0	11	0	44
45	60		71–77			23				45
46	61	10	78	9			1		1	46
47	62		79–81			24		12		47
48	63	11	82–83	10			2		2	48
49	64		84			25			3	49
50	65		85–86	11				13		50
51	66	12	87			26	3		4	51
52	67		88–89	12						52
53	68	13	90			27	4	14	5	53
54	69–70		91	13						54
55	71		92–93			28	5		6	55
56	72	14	94	14				15		56
57	73		95			29	6		7	57
58	74	15	96–97	15					8	58
59	75		98		0	30		16		59
60	76		99	16	1		7		9	60
61	77–78	16	100–101		2	31				61
62	79		102	17	3		8	17	10	62
63	80	17	103		4	32				63
64	81		104	18	5				11	64
65	82		105		6	33	9	18		65
66	83	18	106	19	7				12	66
67	84		107		8	34	10			67
68	85	19	108	20	9			19	13	68
69	86		109		10	35				69
70	87			21	11		11		14	70
71	88	20	110		12	36		20		71
72	89		111	22	13		12		15	72
73	90	21			14	37				73
74	91		112	23	15		13	21	16	74
75	92		113		16	38				75
76	93	22	114	24	17–18		14		17	76
77	94				19–20	39		22	18	77
78	95	23	115	25	21					78
79	96		116		22	40	15		19	79
80	97			26	23			23		80
81	98	24	117		24	41	16		20	81
82	99		118	27	25					82
83	100	25	119		26	42	17	24	21	83
84	101			28	27				22	84
85	102	26	120		28	43	18			85
86	103		121	29	29			25	23	86
87	104	27	122		30	44				87
88				30	31		19		24	88
89	105		123–124		32	45		26		89
90	106	28	125	31	33		20		25	90
91	107		126		34	46			26	91
92		29	127	32	35		21	27		92
93	108				36	47			27	93
94			128	33	37		22			94
95	109	30	129		38	48		28	28	95
96	110		130	34	39					96
97		31			40	49	23		29	97
98	111		131–132	35	41			29		98
99	112	32	133		42	50	24		30	99
100			134	36	43				31	100

[a] Based on weighted raw scores.

Table F.1. Age-Based Subtest Standard Scores

Ages: 12 years, 8 months, 0 days—12 years, 11 months, 30 days (*continued*)

Standard Score	Word Reading	Numerical Operations	Reading Comprehension[a]	Spelling	Pseudoword Decoding	Math Reasoning	Written Expression	Listening Comprehension	Oral Expression	Standard Score
			Subtest Total Raw Scores							
101	113	33	135			51	25	30		101
102	114		136	37	44				32	102
103			137		45	52	26			103
104	115	34	138	38	46			31	33	104
105	116		139			53	27			105
106		35	140–141	39	47				34	106
107	117		142–143			54	28	32		107
108	118	36	144–148	40	48				35	108
109			149–153				29		36	109
110	119	37	154–157	41	49	55		33		110
111			158–161		50		30		37	111
112	120	38	162–163			56				112
113			164–170	42	51			34	38	113
114	121	39	171–178			57	31			114
115			179–183	43	52				39	115
116	122		184–186			58	32			116
117	123	40	187–191		53			35	40	117
118			192–195	44			33			118
119	124	41	196		54	59			41	119
120			197–198	45			34	36		120
121	125	42	199–200		55	60			42	121
122			201				35			122
123	126		202	46		61		37	43	123
124		43	203							124
125	127		204	47		62	36		44	125
126		44	205					38		126
127	128		206			63	37		45	127
128		45	207	48						128
129	129		208			64	38	39	46	129
130		46	209	49						130
131	130		210			65	39		47	131
132		47	211					40		132
133	131		212	50		66	40		48	133
134		48	213							134
135			214	51		67	41	41	49	135
136			215							136
137		49	216						50	137
138			217	52			42			138
139		50	218						51	139
140			219	53			43			140
141		51	220						52	141
142			221				44			142
143			222						53	143
144		52	223				45			144
145			224						54	145
146		53								146
147			225				46		55	147
148		54	226							148
149			227				47		56	149
150			228							150
151			229				48		57	151
152			230							152
153			231				49		58	153
154			232							154
155			233				50		59	155
156										156
157							51		60	157
158							52			158
159							53–54		61–62	159
160							55		63–77	160

Based on weighted raw scores.

Table F.1. Age-Based Subtest Standard Scores

Ages: 13 years, 0 months, 0 days—13 years, 3 months, 30 days

Standard Score	Word Reading	Numerical Operations	Reading Comprehension[a]	Spelling	Pseudoword Decoding	Math Reasoning	Written Expression	Listening Comprehension	Oral Expression	Standard Score
40	0–52	0–7	0–57	0–6		0–20		0–9		40
41	53–56	8–9	58–65	7		21		10		41
42	57–58		66–73	8		22				42
43	59		74–79					11		43
44	60	10	80–81	9		23	0		0	44
45	61–62		82–83							45
46	63	11	84	10		24	1	12	1	46
47	64		85–86							47
48	65		87	11		25	2		2	48
49	66	12	88–89					13	3	49
50	67		90	12		26				50
51	68	13	91				3		4	51
52	69		92–93	13		27		14		52
53	70		94				4		5	53
54	71–72	14	95	14		28				54
55	73		96–97				5	15	6	55
56	74	15	98	15		29				56
57	75		99				6		7	57
58	76		100–101	16		30		16	8	58
59	77	16	102–103		0		7			59
60	78		104	17	1	31			9	60
61	79	17			2		8	17		61
62	80		105	18	3	32			10	62
63	81				4		9			63
64	82	18	106	19	5	33		18	11	64
65	83		107		6		10			65
66	84	19	108	20	7	34			12	66
67	85		109		8			19		67
68	86		110	21	9–10	35	11		13	68
69	87	20			11					69
70	88		111	22	12	36	12	20	14	70
71	89	21	112		13					71
72	90		113	23	14	37	13		15	72
73	91		114		15			21		73
74	92	22	115	24	16–17	38			16	74
75	93		116		18		14			75
76	94	23		25	19	39		22	17	76
77	95		117		20		15		18	77
78	96			26	21	40				78
79	97	24	118		22–23		16	23	19	79
80	98			27	24	41				80
81	99	25			25				20	81
82	100		119	28	26	42	17	24		82
83	101		120		27				21	83
84	102	26	121	29	28	43	18		22	84
85	103		122		29			25		85
86	104	27		30	30	44	19		23	86
87			123		31					87
88	105	28	124	31	32	45	20	26	24	88
89	106		125		33					89
90	107		126	32	34	46			25	90
91		29	127		35		21	27	26	91
92	108		128	33	36	47				92
93	109	30	129		37		22		27	93
94			130	34	38	48		28		94
95	110	31	131		39		23		28	95
96	111		132–133	35	40	49				96
97		32	134		41		24	29	29	97
98	112		135	36	42	50				98
99		33	136		43		25		30	99
100	113		137	37		51		30	31	100

[a] Based on weighted raw scores.

F

Table F.1. Age-Based Subtest Standard Scores

Ages: 13 years, 0 months, 0 days—13 years, 3 months, 30 days (*continued*)

Standard Score	Word Reading	Numerical Operations	Reading Comprehension[a]	Spelling	Pseudoword Decoding	Math Reasoning	Written Expression	Listening Comprehension	Oral Expression	Standard Score
101	114	34			44		26		32	101
102			138–139	38		52				102
103	115	35			45		27	31	33	103
104			140	39	46	53				104
105	116	36	141–142				28		34	105
106	117		143–146	40	47	54		32		106
107			147–152		48		29		35	107
108	118	37	153–154	41		55				108
109			155–159		49		30	33	36	109
110	119	38	160–162			56				110
111	120		163–168	42	50		31		37	111
112		39	169–173			57		34		112
113	121		174–182	43	51		32		38	113
114		40	183–186			58				114
115	122		187–190		52		33	35	39	115
116		41	191–193	44		59			40	116
117	123		194–196		53		34			117
118		42	197	45		60		36	41	118
119	124		198–199		54					119
120		43	200–201			61	35		42	120
121	125		202	46	55			37		121
122		44	203			62	36		43	122
123	126		204	47						123
124		45	205			63	37	38	44	124
125	127		206							125
126			207	48		64	38		45	126
127	128	46	208					39		127
128			209	49		65	39		46	128
129	129	47	210							129
130			211			66		40	47	130
131	130	48	212	50			40			131
132	131		213			67			48	132
133		49	214	51			41	41	49	133
134			215							134
135		50	216				42		50	135
136			217	52						136
137		51	218				43		51	137
138			219	53						138
139		52	220						52	139
140			221				44			140
141		53	222						53	141
142			223				45			142
143		54	224						54	143
144							46			144
145			225						55	145
146							47			146
147			226						56	147
148			227							148
149			228				48		57	149
150			229							150
151			230				49		58	151
152			231							152
153			232				50		59	153
154			233							154
155							51		60	155
156							52			156
157							53		61	157
158										158
159							54		62	159
160							55		63–77	160

[a] Based on weighted raw scores.

Ages 13:4–13:7

Table F.1. Age-Based Subtest Standard Scores

Ages: 13 years, 4 months, 0 days—13 years, 7 months, 30 days

Standard Score	Word Reading	Numerical Operations	Reading Comprehension[a]	Spelling	Pseudoword Decoding	Math Reasoning	Written Expression	Listening Comprehension	Oral Expression	Standard Score
				Subtest Total Raw Scores						
40	0–58	0–9	0–81	0–7		0–21		0–10		40
41	59		82–83	8		22				41
42	60		84			23		11		42
43	61–62	10	85–86	9			0			43
44	63		87			24			0	44
45	64	11	88–89	10			1	12		45
46	65		90			25			1	46
47	66		91	11			2			47
48	67	12	92–93			26		13	2	48
49	68		94	12					3	49
50	69	13	95			27	3			50
51	70		96–97	13				14	4	51
52	71–72		98			28	4			52
53	73	14	99	14					5	53
54	74		100–101			29	5	15		54
55	75	15	102	15					6	55
56	76		103			30	6			56
57	77		104	16				16	7	57
58	78	16			0	31	7		8	58
59	79		105	17	1					59
60	80	17			2	32	8	17	9	60
61	81		106	18	3					61
62	82		107		4	33	9		10	62
63	83	18	108	19	5			18		63
64	84		109		6	34	10		11	64
65	85	19	110	20	7					65
66	86				8	35		19	12	66
67	87		111	21	9–10		11			67
68	88	20	112		11	36			13	68
69	89		113	22	12		12	20		69
70	90	21	114		13	37			14	70
71	91		115	23	14		13			71
72	92		116		15	38		21	15	72
73	93	22		24	16–17		14			73
74	94		117		18	39			16	74
75	95	23		25	19			22		75
76	96		118		20	40	15		17	76
77	97			26	21				18	77
78	98	24	119		22–23	41	16	23		78
79	99			27	24				19	79
80	100	25	120		25	42	17			80
81	101			28	26			24	20	81
82	102	26	121		27	43	18			82
83	103		122	29	28				21	83
84	104	27			29	44	19	25	22	84
85			123	30	30					85
86	105	28	124		31	45	20		23	86
87	106		125	31	32			26		87
88	107		126		33	46			24	88
89		29	127	32	34		21			89
90	108		128		35	47		27	25	90
91		30	129	33	36		22		26	91
92	109		130		37	48				92
93		31	131	34	38		23	28	27	93
94	110		132–133		39	49				94
95	111	32	134	35	40		24		28	95
96			135		41	50		29		96
97	112	33	136	36	42		25		29	97
98			137		43	51				98
99	113	34	138	37			26	30	30	99
100	114		139		44	52			31	100

[a] Based on weighted raw scores.

Table F.1. Age-Based Subtest Standard Scores
Ages: 13 years, 4 months, 0 days—13 years, 7 months, 30 days (*continued*)

Standard Score	Word Reading	Numerical Operations	Reading Comprehension[a]	Spelling	Pseudoword Decoding	Math Reasoning	Written Expression	Listening Comprehension	Oral Expression	Standard Score
101		35		38			27		32	101
102	115		140		45	53		31		102
103		36	141–142	39	46		28		33	103
104	116		143–146			54				104
105	117	37	147–152	40	47		29	32	34	105
106			153–154			55				106
107	118	38	155–159	41	48		30		35	107
108			160–162			56		33	36	108
109	119	39	163–168		49		31			109
110	120		169–173	42		57			37	110
111		40	174–182		50		32	34		111
112	121		183–186	43		58			38	112
113		41	187–190		51		33			113
114	122		191–193			59		35	39	114
115		42	194–196	44	52		34		40	115
116	123		197			60				116
117		43	198–199	45	53			36	41	117
118	124		200–201			61	35			118
119		44	202		54				42	119
120	125		203	46		62	36	37		120
121		45	204		55				43	121
122	126		205	47		63	37			122
123		46	206					38	44	123
124	127		207			64	38			124
125		47	208	48					45	125
126	128		209			65	39	39		126
127		48	210	49					46	127
128	129		211			66	40			128
129		49	212					40	47	129
130	130		213	50		67	41			130
131		50	214						48	131
132	131		215	51				41	49	132
133		51	216				42			133
134			217						50	134
135		52	218	52			43			135
136			219						51	136
137		53	220	53			44			137
138			221						52	138
139		54	222				45			139
140			223						53	140
141			224							141
142							46		54	142
143										143
144			225				47		55	144
145										145
146			226				48		56	146
147			227							147
148			228				49		57	148
149			229							149
150			230				50		58	150
151			231							151
152			232				51		59	152
153			233							153
154							52		60	154
155										155
156							53		61	156
157										157
158							54		62	158
159										159
160							55		63–77	160

[a] Based on weighted raw scores.

Table F.1. Age-Based Subtest Standard Scores

Ages: 13 years, 8 months, 0 days—13 years, 11 months, 30 days

Standard Score	Word Reading	Numerical Operations	Reading Comprehension[a]	Spelling	Pseudoword Decoding	Math Reasoning	Written Expression	Listening Comprehension	Oral Expression	Standard Score
40	0–58	0–9	0–81	0–7		0–21		0–10		40
41	59–60		82–84	8		22–23		11		41
42	61–62	10	85–86	9			0			42
43	63		87–88			24		12	0	43
44	64	11	89–90	10		25	1			44
45	65–66		91						1	45
46	67		92	11		26	2	13		46
47	68	12	93						2	47
48	69		94	12		27			3	48
49	70	13	95				3	14		49
50	71–72		96–97	13		28			4	50
51	73		98				4			51
52	74	14	99	14		29		15	5	52
53	75		100–101				5			53
54	76	15	102	15		30			6	54
55	77		103				6	16		55
56	78		104	16		31			7	56
57	79	16			0		7		8	57
58	80		105	17	1	32		17		58
59	81	17			2		8		9	59
60	82		106	18	3	33				60
61	83		107		4		9	18	10	61
62	84	18	108	19	5	34				62
63	85		109		6		10		11	63
64	86	19	110	20	7	35		19		64
65	87				8				12	65
66	88		111	21	9–10	36	11			66
67	89	20	112		11			20	13	67
68	90		113	22	12	37	12			68
69	91	21	114		13				14	69
70	92		115	23	14	38	13	21		70
71	93		116		15				15	71
72	94	22		24	16–17	39	14		16	72
73	95		117		18			22		73
74	96	23		25	19	40				74
75	97		118		20		15		17	75
76	98		119	26	21	41		23	18	76
77	99	24			22–23		16			77
78	100		120	27	24	42			19	78
79	101	25			25		17	24		79
80	102		121	28	26	43				80
81	103	26			27		18		20	81
82	104		122	29	28	44		25	21	82
83		27	123		29		19		22	83
84	105		124	30	30	45				84
85	106	28	125		31		20	26	23	85
86	107		126	31	32	46				86
87			127		33				24	87
88	108	29	128	32	34	47	21	27		88
89			129		35				25	89
90	109	30	130–131	33	36	48	22		26	90
91					37			28		91
92	110	31	132–133	34	38	49	23		27	92
93	111		134		39					93
94		32	135–136	35	40	50	24	29	28	94
95	112		137		41					95
96		33	138	36	42	51	25		29	96
97	113		139		43			30		97
98		34		37		52	26		30	98
99	114		140		44				31	99
100	115	35	141–142	38		53	27	31	32	100

[a] Based on weighted raw scores.

F

Table F.1. Age-Based Subtest Standard Scores
Ages: 13 years, 8 months, 0 days—13 years, 11 months, 30 days (continued)

Standard Score	Subtest Total Raw Scores									Standard Score
	Word Reading	Numerical Operations	Reading Comprehension[a]	Spelling	Pseudoword Decoding	Math Reasoning	Written Expression	Listening Comprehension	Oral Expression	
101			143–146		45					101
102	116	36	147–151	39		54	28		33	102
103			152–153		46					103
104	117	37	154–158	40		55	29	32	34	104
105		38	159–162		47					105
106	118		163–166	41			30		35	106
107	119	39	167–169		48	56		33	36	107
108			170–182				31			108
109	120	40	183–185	42	49	57			37	109
110			186–190				32	34		110
111	121	41	191–193	43	50	58			38	111
112			194–196				33			112
113	122	42	197		51	59		35	39	113
114			198–199	44			34			114
115	123	43	200–201		52	60			40	115
116			202	45				36	41	116
117	124	44	203		53	61	35			117
118			204						42	118
119	125	45	205	46	54	62	36	37		119
120			206						43	120
121	126	46	207	47	55	63	37			121
122			208					38	44	122
123	127	47	209			64	38			123
124			210	48					45	124
125	128	48	211			65	39	39		125
126			212	49					46	126
127	129	49	213			66	40			127
128			214					40	47	128
129	130	50	215	50		67	41			129
130			216						48	130
131	131	51	217	51				41	49	131
132			218				42			132
133		52							50	133
134			219	52			43			134
135		53	220						51	135
136			221	53			44			136
137		54							52	137
138			222				45			138
139			223						53	139
140			224							140
141							46		54	141
142										142
143			225				47		55	143
144										144
145			226				48		56	145
146			227							146
147			228				49		57	147
148			229							148
149			230				50		58	149
150			231							150
151			232				51		59	151
152			233							152
153							52		60	153
154										154
155							53		61	155
156										156
157							54		62	157
158										158
159							55		63	159
160									64–77	160

[a] Based on weighted raw scores.

Table F.1. Age-Based Subtest Standard Scores

Ages: 14 years, 0 months, 0 days—14 years, 11 months, 30 days

Standard Score	Subtest Total Raw Scores									Standard Score
	Word Reading	Numerical Operations	Reading Comprehension[a]	Spelling	Pseudoword Decoding	Math Reasoning	Written Expression	Listening Comprehension	Oral Expression	
40	0–63	0–9	0–84	0–9		0–24		0–12		40
41	64	10	85–87	10		25	0			41
42	65–66		88						0	42
43	67–68	11	89–90	11		26	1	13		43
44	69		91						1	44
45	70		92	12		27	2			45
46	71	12	93					14	2	46
47	72		94	13		28	3		3	47
48	73	13	95							48
49	74		96	14		29	4	15	4	49
50	75–76	14	97							50
51	77		98	15		30			5	51
52	78		99				5	16		52
53	79	15	100–101	16		31			6	53
54	80		102				6			54
55	81	16	103	17		32		17	7	55
56	82		104		0		7		8	56
57	83		105	18	1	33				57
58	84	17			2		8	18	9	58
59	85		106	19	3	34				59
60	86	18	107		4		9		10	60
61	87		108	20	5	35		19		61
62	88		109		6		10		11	62
63	89	19	110	21	7	36				63
64	90		111		8–9		11	20	12	64
65	91	20	112	22	10	37				65
66	92		113		11		12		13	66
67	93	21	114	23	12–13	38		21		67
68	94		115		14		13		14	68
69	95		116	24	15	39				69
70	96	22			16		14	22	15	70
71	97		117	25	17	40				71
72	98	23			18				16	72
73	99		118	26	19–20	41	15	23		73
74	100	24			21				17	74
75	101		119	27	22	42	16		18	75
76	102				23			24		76
77		25	120	28	24	43	17		19	77
78	103				25–26					78
79	104	26	121	29	27	44	18	25		79
80	105				28				20	80
81	106	27	122	30	29	45	19		21	81
82			123		30			26	22	82
83	107	28	124	31	31	46	20			83
84			125–126		32				23	84
85	108		127–128	32	33	47	21	27		85
86		29	129		34				24	86
87	109		130	33	35	48	22			87
88	110	30	131		36			28	25	88
89			132	34	37	49			26	89
90	111	31	133–134		38		23			90
91			135	35	39	50		29	27	91
92	112	32	136		40		24			92
93			137	36	41	51			28	93
94	113	33	138–139		42		25	30		94
95				37		52			29	95
96	114	34	140–141		43		26			96
97	115		142	38		53		31	30	97
98		35	143–145		44		27		31	98
99	116		146–152	39		54			32	99
100		36	153–158		45		28			100

[a] Based on weighted raw scores.

F

Table F.1. Age-Based Subtest Standard Scores

Ages: 14 years, 0 months, 0 days—14 years, 11 months, 30 days (*continued*)

Standard Score	Word Reading	Numerical Operations	Reading Comprehension[a]	Spelling	Pseudoword Decoding	Math Reasoning	Written Expression	Listening Comprehension	Oral Expression	Standard Score
101	117	37	159–161	40		55		32	33	101
102		38	162							102
103	118	39	163–166	41	46		29		34	103
104	119	40	167–172			56		33		104
105			173–184		47		30		35	105
106	120	41	185	42		57			36	106
107			186–191		48		31	34		107
108	121	42	192–196	43		58			37	108
109			197		49		32			109
110	122	43	198		50	59		35	38	110
111			199–201	44			33			111
112	123	44	202		51				39	112
113			203	45		60	34			113
114	124	45	204	52				36	40	114
115			205			61	35		41	115
116	125	46	206	46	53					116
117			207–208			62	36	37	42	117
118	126	47	209	47	54					118
119			210			63	37		43	119
120	127	48	211		55			38		120
121			212	48					44	121
122	128	49	213			64	38			122
123			214	49				39	45	123
124	129	50	215			65	39			124
125			216						46	125
126	130	51	217	50		66	40	40		126
127									47	127
128	131	52	218	51		67	41			128
129								41	48	129
130		53	219				42		49	130
131				52						131
132		54	220						50	132
133				53			43			133
134			221						51	134
135							44			135
136			222						52	136
137							45		53	137
138			223							138
139									54	139
140			224				46			140
141									55	141
142							47			142
143			225						56	143
144							48			144
145			226						57	145
146			227				49			146
147			228						58	147
148			229				50			148
149			230						59	149
150			231				51			150
151			232						60	151
152			233				52			152
153									61	153
154							53			154
155									62	155
156							54			156
157									63	157
158							55			158
159									64	159
160									65–77	160

[a] Based on weighted raw scores.

Table F.1. Age-Based Subtest Standard Scores

Ages: 15 years, 0 months, 0 days—15 years, 11 months, 30 days

	Subtest Total Raw Scores									
Standard Score	Word Reading	Numerical Operations	Reading Comprehension[a]	Spelling	Pseudoword Decoding	Math Reasoning	Written Expression	Listening Comprehension	Oral Expression	Standard Score
40	0–68	0–11	0–88	0–11		0–27	0	0–13	0	40
41	69	12	89–90	12			1			41
42	70		91			28		14	1	42
43	71–72	13	92	13		29	2			43
44	73		93						2	44
45	74		94	14		30	3	15	3	45
46	75	14	95							46
47	76–77		96	15		31	4		4	47
48	78	15	97					16		48
49	79		98	16		32			5	49
50	80		99				5			50
51	81	16	100–101	17		33		17	6	51
52	82		102				6			52
53	83	17	103	18	0	34			7	53
54	84		104		1		7	18	8	54
55	85–86		105	19	2	35				55
56	87	18			3		8		9	56
57	88		106	20	4	36		19		57
58	89	19	107		5		9		10	58
59	90		108	21	6	37				59
60	91				7		10	20	11	60
61	92	20	109	22	8	38				61
62	93		110		9–10		11		12	62
63	94	21	111	23	11	39		21		63
64	95		112		12		12		13	64
65	96		113	24	13–14	40				65
66	97	22	114		15		13	22	14	66
67	98		115	25	16	41				67
68	99	23	116		17		14		15	68
69	100			26	18–19	42		23		69
70			117		20				16	70
71	101	24		27	21–22	43	15			71
72	102		118		23			24	17	72
73		25	119	28	24	44	16		18	73
74	103				25					74
75	104	26	120	29	26	45	17	25	19	75
76					27					76
77	105	27	121	30	28	46	18		20	77
78	106				29			26		78
79		28	122–123	31	30	47	19		21	79
80	107		124		31				22	80
81		29		32	32	48	20	27		81
82	108		125–127		33				23	82
83		30	128	33	34	49	21			83
84	109		129		35			28	24	84
85	110	31	130–131		36	50	22			85
86				34	37				25	86
87	111	32	132–133		38			29	26	87
88			134	35	39	51	23			88
89	112	33	135–136		40				27	89
90			137–138	36	41		24	30		90
91	113	34	139		42				28	91
92			140	37		52	25			92
93	114	35	141		43			31	29	93
94			142–143	38			26			94
95	115	36	144–146		44	53			30	95
96		37	147	39			27		31	96
97	116		148–151					32	32	97
98		38	152–153		45	54	28			98
99	117		154–158	40					33	99
100		39	159–162		46		29	33		100

[a] Based on weighted raw scores.

Table F.1. Age-Based Subtest Standard Scores
Ages: 15 years, 0 months, 0 days—15 years, 11 months, 30 days (continued)

Standard Score	Word Reading	Numerical Operations	Reading Comprehension^a	Spelling	Pseudoword Decoding	Math Reasoning	Written Expression	Listening Comprehension	Oral Expression	Standard Score
101	118		163–166			55			34	101
102	119	40	167–169	41	47					102
103			170–182				30		35	103
104	120	41	183–185			56		34	36	104
105			186–191	42	48		31			105
106	121	42	192–197			57			37	106
107			198		49		32	35		107
108	122	43	199–201	43		58			38	108
109			202		50		33			109
110	123	44	203			59			39	110
111			204	44	51		34	36		111
112	124	45							40	112
113			205	45	52	60	35		41	113
114	125	46	206					37		114
115			207–208		53	61	36		42	115
116	126	47	209	46						116
117					54	62	37		43	117
118	127	48	210	47				38		118
119			211		55	63			44	119
120	128	49	212				38			120
121			213	48				39	45	121
122	129	50	214			64	39			122
123			215	49					46	123
124	130	51	216			65	40	40		124
125			217						47	125
126	131	52		50		66	41			126
127			218					41	48	127
128		53		51		67	42		49	128
129			219							129
130		54							50	130
131			220	52			43			131
132									51	132
133			221	53			44			133
134									52	134
135			222				45		53	135
136										136
137			223				46		54	137
138										138
139			224						55	139
140							47			140
141									56	141
142			225				48			142
143									57	143
144			226				49			144
145			227						58	145
146			228				50			146
147			229						59	147
148			230				51			148
149			231						60	149
150			232				52			150
151			233						61	151
152							53			152
153									62	153
154							54			154
155									63	155
156							55			156
157									64	157
158										158
159									65	159
160									66–77	160

^a Based on weighted raw scores.

Table F.1. Age-Based Subtest Standard Scores

Ages: 16 years, 0 months, 0 days—16 years, 11 months, 30 days

Standard Score	Word Reading	Numerical Operations	Reading Comprehension[a]	Spelling	Pseudoword Decoding	Math Reasoning	Written Expression	Listening Comprehension	Oral Expression	Standard Score
40	0–71	0–12	0–90	0–12		0–27	0	0–14	0–1	40
41	72	13	91–92			28	1	15		41
42	73		93–94	13		29	2		2	42
43	74–75		95						3	43
44	76	14	96	14		30	3	16		44
45	77		97						4	45
46	78–79	15	98	15		31	4			46
47	80		99					17	5	47
48	81		100–101	16		32				48
49	82	16	102				5		6	49
50	83		103	17		33		18		50
51	84	17	104				6		7	51
52	85		105	18		34			8	52
53	86		106		0		7	19		53
54	87	18		19	1	35			9	54
55	88		107		2		8			55
56	89	19	108	20	3	36		20	10	56
57	90				4		9			57
58	91		109	21	5	37			11	58
59	92	20			6		10	21		59
60	93		110	22	7	38			12	60
61	94	21	111		8		11			61
62	95			23	9–10	39		22	13	62
63	96		112		11		12			63
64	97	22	113	24	12	40			14	64
65	98		114		13–14		13	23		65
66	99	23	115	25	15	41			15	66
67	100		116		16		14			67
68	101			26	17	42		24	16	68
69	102	24	117		18–19		15			69
70			118	27	20	43			17	70
71	103	25			21–22		16	25	18	71
72	104		119	28	23	44				72
73	105	26	120		24		17		19	73
74				29	25	45		26		74
75	106	27	121–122		26–27		18		20	75
76	107		123	30	28	46				76
77	108	28	124		29		19		21	77
78			125–126	31	30	47		27	22	78
79	109	29	127		31		20			79
80			128	32	32	48			23	80
81	110	30	129–130		33		21	28		81
82			131–132	33	34	49			24	82
83	111	31	133–134		35		22			83
84			135–137	34	36	50		29	25	84
85	112	32	138		37		23		26	85
86			139	35	38					86
87	113	33			39	51	24	30	27	87
88			140	36	40					88
89	114	34	141–142		41		25		28	89
90			143	37		52		31		90
91	115	35			42				29	91
92			144–145	38			26			92
93	116	36	146		43	53			30	93
94		37		39			27	32	31	94
95	117		147–148		44				32	95
96		38	149–151	40		54	28			96
97	118		152–153					33	33	97
98	119	39	154–162		45		29			98
99			163–166	41		55			34	99
100	120	40	167–182		46		30			100

[a] Based on weighted raw scores.

Table F.1. Age-Based Subtest Standard Scores
Ages: 16 years, 0 months, 0 days—16 years, 11 months, 30 days (continued)

Standard Score	Word Reading	Numerical Operations	Reading Comprehension[a]	Spelling	Pseudoword Decoding	Math Reasoning	Written Expression	Listening Comprehension	Oral Expression	Standard Score
						Subtest Total Raw Scores				
101	121		183–191					34	35	101
102	122	41	192–197	42	47	56	31		36	102
103			198							103
104	123	42	199–200			57	32	35	37	104
105			201	43	48					105
106	124	43				58	33		38	106
107			202		49					107
108	125	44	203	44		59	34	36	39	108
109			204		50					109
110	126	45	205	45			35		40	110
111			206		51	60				111
112	127	46	207				36	37	41	112
113			208	46	52	61				113
114	128	47	209				37		42	114
115				47	53	62		38		115
116	129	48	210				38		43	116
117			211		54	63				117
118	130	49	212	48					44	118
119					55		39	39		119
120	131	50	213	49		64			45	120
121			214				40			121
122		51	215			65		40	46	122
123			216	50			41		47	123
124		52	217			66				124
125							42	41	48	125
126		53	218	51		67				126
127							43		49	127
128		54	219							128
129				52			44		50	129
130			220						51	130
131							45			131
132			221	53					52	132
133							46			133
134			222						53	134
135									54	135
136			223				47			136
137									55	137
138			224				48			138
139									56	139
140							49			140
141			225						57	141
142							50			142
143			226						58	143
144			227				51			144
145			228						59	145
146			229				52			146
147			230						60	147
148			231				53			148
149			232						61	149
150			233				54			150
151									62	151
152							55			152
153									63	153
154										154
155									64	155
156										156
157									65	157
158										158
159									66	159
160									67–77	160

[a] Based on weighted raw scores.

Table F.1. Age-Based Subtest Standard Scores

Ages: 17 years, 0 months, 0 days—19 years, 11 months, 30 days

Standard Score	Word Reading	Numerical Operations	Reading Comprehension[a]	Spelling	Pseudoword Decoding	Math Reasoning	Written Expression	Listening Comprehension	Oral Expression	Standard Score
			Subtest Total Raw Scores							
40	0–74	0–12	0–95	0–12		0–27	0	0–15	0–1	40
41	75	13	96			28	1	16	2	41
42	76		97	13		29	2		3	42
43	77–78		98							43
44	79	14	99	14		30	3	17	4	44
45	80		100							45
46	81	15	101–102	15		31	4		5	46
47	82		103					18		47
48	83		104	16		32			6	48
49	84	16	105				5			49
50	85		106	17	0	33		19	7	50
51	86	17			1		6		8	51
52	87		107	18	2	34				52
53	88		108		3		7		9	53
54	89	18		19	4	35		20		54
55	90		109		5–6		8		10	55
56	91	19		20	7	36				56
57	92		110		8		9	21	11	57
58	93			21	9	37				58
59	94	20	111		10		10		12	59
60	95		112	22	11	38		22		60
61	96	21	113		12		11		13	61
62	97		114	23	13	39				62
63	98		115		14–15		12	23	14	63
64	99	22	116	24	16	40				64
65			117		17		13		15	65
66	100	23		25	18–19	41		24		66
67	101				20		14		16	67
68	102		118	26	21	42				68
69		24			22		15	25	17	69
70	103		119	27	23	43			18	70
71	104	25	120–123		24		16			71
72	105		124	28	25	44		26	19	72
73		26	125–126		26		17			73
74	106		127	29	27	45			20	74
75	107	27	128–129		28		18	27		75
76	108		130	30	29	46			21	76
77		28	131–133		30		19		22	77
78			134–136	31	31	47		28		78
79	109	29	137		32		20		23	79
80			138	32	33	48				80
81	110	30	139–140		34		21		24	81
82				33	35	49		29		82
83	111	31	141		36		22		25	83
84			142	34	37	50			26	84
85	112	32	143		38		23	30		85
86			144	35	39	51			27	86
87	113	33	145		40		24			87
88				36	41	52	25	31	28	88
89	114	34	146		42					89
90			147	37	43	53	26		29	90
91	115	35	148–152					32	30	91
92			153	38	44		27			92
93	116	36	154–155			54			31	93
94	117	37	156–159	39			28		32	94
95			160–166		45	55		33		95
96	118	38	167	40			29		33	96
97			168–179		46					97
98	119	39	180–185	41		56	30		34	98
99	120		186–196					34		99
100		40	197–199	42	47	57	31		35	100

[a] Based on weighted raw scores.

Table F.1. Age-Based Subtest Standard Scores
Ages: 17 years, 0 months, 0 days—19 years, 11 months, 30 days (continued)

Standard Score	Word Reading	Numerical Operations	Reading Comprehension[a]	Spelling	Pseudoword Decoding	Math Reasoning	Written Expression	Listening Comprehension	Oral Expression	Standard Score
101	121	41	200						36	101
102	122		201–202	43			32	35		102
103		42			48	58			37	103
104	123	43	203–204	44			33			104
105					49	59			38	105
106	124	44					34	36		106
107			205	45	50				39	107
108	125	45	206			60	35			108
109			207	46					40	109
110	126	46	208		51	61	36	37		110
111			209						41	111
112	127	47		47	52		37			112
113		48	210			62		38	42	113
114	128		211		53		38			114
115		49		48		63			43	115
116	129		212		54		39		44	116
117		50	213					39		117
118	130	51	214	49	55	64	40		45	118
119			215							119
120	131	52	216			65	41	40	46	120
121			217	50						121
122		53				66	42		47	122
123			218					41		123
124		54		51		67	43		48	124
125			219						49	125
126							44			126
127			220	52					50	127
128							45			128
129			221						51	129
130				53			46			130
131			222						52	131
132							47		53	132
133			223							133
134							48		54	134
135			224							135
136							49		55	136
137										137
138			225				50		56	138
139										139
140			226				51		57	140
141			227							141
142			228				52		58	142
143			229							143
144			230				53		59	144
145			231							145
146			232				54		60	146
147			233							147
148							55		61	148
149										149
150									62	150
151										151
152									63	152
153										153
154									64	154
155										155
156									65	156
157										157
158									66	158
159										159
160									67–77	160

[a] Based on weighted raw scores.

Table F.2. Age-Based Composite Standard Scores

Standard Score	Sums of Standard Scores					Standard Score
	Reading	Mathematics	Written Language	Oral Language	Total	
40	120–136	80–93	80–100	80–92	360–463	40
41	137–141	94–96	101–102	93–96	464–471	41
42	142–146	97–99	103–104	97–99	472–480	42
43	147–151	100–102	105–106	100–102	481–488	43
44	152–156	103–105	107–108	103–105	489–495	44
45	157–159	106–107	109–110	106–108	496–501	45
46	160–162	108–109	111–112	109–110	502–509	46
47	163–165	110	113	111	510–517	47
48	166–168	111–112	114–115	112–113	518–524	48
49	169–171	113	116	114	525–532	49
50	172–174	114–115	117–118	115–116	533–539	50
51	175–177	116	119	117	540–547	51
52	178–180	117–118	120	118–119	548–554	52
53	181–182	119	121–122	120	555–561	53
54	183–184	120–121	123	121–122	562–568	54
55	185–187	122	124–125	123	569–576	55
56	188–189	123–124	126	124–125	577–584	56
57	190–191	125	127–128	126	585–591	57
58	192–194	126–127	129	127–128	592–599	58
59	195–196	128	130–131	129	600–606	59
60	197–198	129–130	132	130–131	607–613	60
61	199–200	131	133–134	132	614–620	61
62	201–202	132–133	135	133–134	621–627	62
63	203–204	134	136–137	135	628–634	63
64	205–206	135–136	138	136–137	635–640	64
65	207–208	137	139	138–140	641–645	65
66	209–210	138–140	140	141–142	646–651	66
67	211–212	141	141	143	652–657	67
68	213–214	142	142	144–145	658–664	68
69	215–216	143–144	143–144	146	665–670	69
70	217–218	145	145–146	147–148	671–680	70
71	219–221	146–147	147	149	681–689	71
72	222–224	148–149	148–149	150–151	690–697	72
73	225–226	150	150–151	152	698–706	73
74	227–229	151–152	152–153	153–154	707–715	74
75	230–231	153–154	154	155–156	716–723	75
76	232–235	155–156	155	157–158	724–732	76
77	236–238	157–158	156–157	159–160	733–740	77
78	239–242	159–160	158–159	161–162	741–748	78
79	243–244	161–162	160–161	163–164	749–756	79
80	245–247	163–164	162–163	165–166	757–765	80
81	248–251	165–166	164–165	167	766–773	81
82	252–255	167–168	166–167	168–172	774–781	82
83	256–258	169–170	168–170	173–174	782–791	83
84	259–261	171–172	171	175	792–800	84
85	262–264	173–174	172–174	176–177	801–808	85
86	265–267	175–176	175–176	178–179	809–817	86
87	268–270	177–179	177–178	180–181	818–825	87
88	271–273	180–181	179–180	182–183	826–832	88
89	274–275	182–183	181–182	184	833–840	89
90	276–278	184	183–184	185–186	841–848	90
91	279–281	185–186	185–186	187–188	849–855	91
92	282–285	187–188	187–188	189–190	856–863	92
93	286–288	189	189	191	864–871	93
94	289–291	190–191	190–191	192–193	872–878	94
95	292–294	192–193	192–193	194	879–885	95
96	295–297	194–195	194–195	195–196	886–893	96
97	298–300	196–197	196–197	197–198	894–901	97
98	301–303	198–199	198–199	199	902–908	98
99	304–306	200–201	200–201	200–201	909–916	99
100	307–309	202–203	202–203	202	917–922	100

F

Table F.2. Age-Based Composite Standard Scores (*continued*)

Standard Score	Sums of Standard Scores					Standard Score
	Reading	Mathematics	Written Language	Oral Language	Total	
101	310–312	204–205	204	203–204	923–928	101
102	313–314	206	205–206	205–206	929–935	102
103	315–316	207	207	207	936–940	103
104	317–318	208	208–209	208–209	941–946	104
105	319–320	209–210	210–211	210	947–952	105
106	321–323	211–212	212–213	211–212	953–957	106
107	324–325	213–214	214	213–214	958–963	107
108	326–327	215–216	215–216	215	964–969	108
109	328	217–219	217–218	216–217	970–975	109
110	329–330		219	218	976–983	110
111	331–332	220	220–221	219–220	984–989	111
112	333–334	221	222	221	990–994	112
113	335–336	222	223–224	222–223	995–999	113
114	337–338	223	225	224–225	1000–1004	114
115	339–340	224–225	226–227	226	1005–1009	115
116	341–342	226		227–228	1010–1014	116
117	343	227–228	228–229	229	1015–1019	117
118	344–345	229–230	230–231	230–231	1020–1024	118
119	346–347	231–235	232–233	232–233	1025–1028	119
120	348	236	234–235	234	1029–1034	120
121	349–350	237	236	235	1035–1040	121
122	351–352	238	237–238	236–237	1041–1047	122
123	353	239–240	239	238	1048–1053	123
124	354–355	241–242	240–241	239–240	1054–1060	124
125	356–357	243–244	242	241	1061–1065	125
126	358–359	245	243	242–243	1066–1069	126
127	360	246	244–245	244	1070–1074	127
128	361–362	247	246	245–246	1075–1079	128
129	363	248	247–248	247	1080–1087	129
130	364–365	249–250	249	248	1088–1097	130
131	366–367	251–252	250	249	1098–1104	131
132	368–369	253–254	251–252	250–251	1105–1112	132
133	370–371	255–256	253	252–253	1113–1118	133
134	372–373	257	254–255	254	1119–1126	134
135	374–375	258–259	256	255–256	1127–1132	135
136	376–377	260	257–258	257	1133–1139	136
137	378–379	261–262	259	258–259	1140–1145	137
138	380–381	263	260	260	1146–1152	138
139	382–383	264–265	261–262	261–262	1153–1158	139
140	384–385	266	263–264	263	1159–1164	140
141	386–387	267–268	265	264–265	1165–1170	141
142	388–389	269	266–267	266	1171–1177	142
143	390–391	270–271	268	267–268	1178–1183	143
144	392–393	272	269–270	269	1184–1190	144
145	394–395	273–274	271–272	270–271	1191–1197	145
146	396–397	275	273	272	1198–1204	146
147	398	276–277	274	273–274	1205–1210	147
148	399–400	278	275	275	1211–1216	148
149	401–402	279–280	276–277	276–277	1217–1223	149
150	403–404	281	278	278	1224–1230	150
151	405–406	282–283	279	279–280	1231–1236	151
152	407–408	284	280–281	281	1237–1243	152
153	409–410	285–286	282	282–283	1244–1249	153
154	411–412	287	283–284	284	1250–1256	154
155	413–414	288–289	285	285–286	1257–1262	155
156	415–416	290	286–287	287	1263–1269	156
157	417–418	291–292	288	288–289	1270–1275	157
158	419–420	293	289–290	290	1276–1281	158
159	421–422	294–295	291	291–292	1282–1287	159
160	423–480	296–320	292–320	293–320	1288–1440	160

F

G Additional Age-Based Normative Tables

G

Table G.1. Confidence Interval Magnitudes for the Age-Based Subtest Standard Scores

						Subtest Standard Scores					
Age	Confidence Level	Word Reading	Numerical Operations	Reading Comp	Spelling	Pseudoword Decoding	Math Reasoning	Written Expression	Listening Comp	Oral Expression	Confidence Level
4	95%	4					11		16	10	95%
	90%	4					10		13	8	90%
5	95%	3	11		8		8		15	10	95%
	90%	2	10		7		7		12	8	90%
6	95%	3	11	5	7	4	8	11	12	10	95%
	90%	2	10	4	6	4	7	9	10	8	90%
7	95%	4	13	6	7	4	8	11	12	10	95%
	90%	4	11	5	6	4	7	9	10	8	90%
8	95%	4	9	7	8	4	8	11	12	10	95%
	90%	4	7	6	7	4	7	9	10	8	90%
9	95%	4	10	6	7	5	8	11	13	10	95%
	90%	4	9	5	6	4	7	9	11	8	90%
10	95%	4	11	6	7	4	7	13	14	12	95%
	90%	4	9	5	6	4	6	11	12	10	90%
11	95%	5	9	7	6	5	8	13	14	12	95%
	90%	4	8	6	5	4	7	11	12	10	90%
12	95%	5	8	6	7	4	7	13	12	12	95%
	90%	4	7	5	6	4	6	11	10	10	90%
13	95%	6	8	6	7	5	7	11	11	11	95%
	90%	5	7	5	6	4	6	9	10	10	90%
14	95%	7	6	6	7	6	8	11	13	11	95%
	90%	6	5	5	6	5	7	9	11	10	90%
15	95%	7	9	9	10	6	10	11	13	11	95%
	90%	6	8	7	8	5	8	9	11	10	90%
16	95%	7	8	7	9	6	8	11	14	11	95%
	90%	6	7	6	8	5	7	9	12	10	90%
17–19	95%	7	7	8	8	5	7	11	12	11	95%
	90%	6	6	7	7	4	6	9	10	10	90%

G

Table G.2. Confidence Interval Magnitudes for the Age-Based Composite Standard Scores

		Composite Standard Scores					
Age	Confidence Level	Reading	Mathematics	Written Language	Oral Language	Total	Confidence Level
4	95%				9		95%
	90%				7		90%
5	95%		8		9		95%
	90%		7		7		90%
6	95%	3	8	7	9	4	95%
	90%	2	7	6	7	4	90%
7	95%	3	9	7	9	4	95%
	90%	2	7	6	7	4	90%
8	95%	3	7	7	9	4	95%
	90%	2	6	6	7	4	90%
9	95%	3	7	7	9	4	95%
	90%	2	6	6	7	4	90%
10	95%	3	7	8	11	4	95%
	90%	2	6	7	9	4	90%
11	95%	4	7	8	11	4	95%
	90%	4	6	7	9	4	90%
12	95%	3	6	8	10	4	95%
	90%	2	5	7	9	4	90%
13	95%	4	5	7	9	3	95%
	90%	4	4	6	8	2	90%
14	95%	4	5	7	10	4	95%
	90%	4	4	6	8	4	90%
15	95%	5	7	8	11	4	95%
	90%	4	6	7	9	4	90%
16	95%	4	6	8	10	4	95%
	90%	4	5	7	9	4	90%
17–19	95%	4	5	7	11	4	95%
	90%	4	4	6	9	4	90%

Table G.3. Percentile Ranks, Normal Curve Equivalents, and Stanines Corresponding to the Age-Based Subtest and Composite Standard Scores

Standard Score	Percentile Rank	Normal Curve Equivalent	Stanine	Standard Score	Percentile Rank	Normal Curve Equivalent	Stanine
160				96	39	44	
159				95	37	43	
158				94	34	42	
157				93	32	40	
156				92	30	39	4
155				91	27	37	
154				90	25	36	
153				89	23	35	
152				88	21	33	
151				87	19	32	
150				86	18	30	
149	>99.9			85	16	29	3
148	99.9			84	14	28	
147	99.9			83	13	26	
146	99.9			82	12	25	
145	99.9			81	10	23	
144	99.8			80	9	22	
143	99.8			79	8	21	
142	99.7			78	7	19	
141	99.7			77	6	18	2
140	99.6			76	5	16	
139	99.5			75	5	15	
138	99			74	4	13	
137	99			73	4	12	
136	99	>99		72	3	11	
135	99	99		71	3	9	
134	99	98		70	2	8	
133	99	96	9	69	2	6	
132	98	95		68	2	5	
131	98	94		67	1	4	
130	98	92		66	1	2	1
129	97	91		65	1	1	
128	97	89		64	1	<1	
127	96	88		63	1		
126	96	87		62	1		
125	95	85		61	0.5		
124	95	84		60	0.4		
123	94	82		59	0.3		
122	93	81		58	0.3		
121	92	79	8	57	0.2		
120	91	78		56	0.2		
119	90	77		55	0.1		
118	88	75		54	0.1		
117	87	74		53	0.1		
116	86	72		52	0.1		
115	84	71		51	<0.1		
114	82	70	7	50			
113	81	68		49			
112	79	67		48			
111	77	65		47			
110	75	64		46			
109	73	63		45			
108	70	61		44			
107	68	60	6	43			
106	66	58		42			
105	63	57		41			
104	61	56		40			
103	58	54					
102	55	53					
101	53	51					
100	50	50					
99	47	49	5				
98	45	47					
97	42	46					

Table G.4. Age Equivalents Corresponding to the Subtest Total Raw Scores and Weighted Raw Scores

Subtest Total Raw Scores

Age Equiv.	Word Reading	Numerical Operations	Reading Comp[a]	Spelling	Pseudoword Decoding	Math Reasoning	Written Expression	Listening Comp	Oral Expression (PreK-3)[b]	Oral Expression (4-12)[c]	Age Equiv.
4:0	0–8	0–1		0	0	0–6	0	0–9	0–14	0–1	4:0
4:4	9–11	2		1–2	1–2	7		10	15–16	2	4:4
4:8	12–17	3–4		3	3	8–9	1	11	17	3–4	4:8
5:0	18–23	5		4	4	10	2	12	18	5–6	5:0
5:4	24–31	6		5–6	5	11–13		13	19–20	7	5:4
5:8	32–41	7		7–8	6–7	14–15	3–4	14	21–22	8–10	5:8
6:0	42–49	8	64–68	9–11	8–10	16–17	5	15	23	11–12	6:0
6:4	50–55	9	69–74	12–13	11–12	18–20	6	16	24	13	6:4
6:8	56–61	10	75–79	14–15	13–14	21–22		17	25–26	14–15	6:8
7:0	62–67	11	80–85	16–17	15–16	23–24	7	18	27	16–17	7:0
7:4	68–73	12–13	86–89	18–19	17–19	25–26	8	19	28	18	7:4
7:8	74–79	14	90–93	20–21	20–21	27–28	9	20	29	19–21	7:8
8:0	80–84	15–16	94–97	22	22–24	29–30	10–12	21	30–31	22–23	8:0
8:4	85–87	17	98–106	23–24	25–27	31–32	13	22	32	24	8:4
8:8	88–91	18	107–111	25	28–29	33–34	14–15	23	33–34	25–26	8:8
9:0	92–94	19	112–116	26	30–31	35	16–17		35–36	27	9:0
9:4	95–96	20–21	117–119	27–28	32–33	36–37	18	24	37	28	9:4
9:8	97–99	22	120	29	34	38–39		25	38	29	9:8
10:0	100–101	23	121–122	30	35	40	19		39–40		10:0
10:4	102–103	24–25	123–124	31	36	41		26	41		10:4
10:8	104	26		32	37	42–43	20		42–43		10:8
11:0	105–106	27	125	33	38–39	44	21	27	44–45	30	11:0
11:4	107–108	28	126		40	45–46		28	46		11:4
11:8	109	29	127–128	34	41	47	22		47–48	31	11:8
12:0	110–111	30	129–130	35	42	48	23	29	49–50		12:0
12:4	112	31–32	131–132	36	43	49–50	24		51		12:4
12:8	113	33	133–135			51	25	30	52–53	32	12:8
13:0	114	34	136–137	37	44		26		54–55		13:0
13:4		35	138–140	38		52	27		56		13:4
13:8	115		141–147		45	53		31	57		13:8
14:0	116–117	36–38	148–158	39		54	28	32	58–62	33	14:0
15:0	118–119	39	159–164	40	46	55	29	33	63–67	34	15:0
16:0	120	40	165–189	41		56	30	34	68–71	35	16:0
17:0–19:11	121–124	41	190–200	42–43	47–48	57	31	35	72–77	36–37	17:0–19:11
>19:11	125–131	42–54	201–233	44–53	49–55	58–67	32–55	36–41		38–68	>19:11

Note. For subtests not administered to Grades PreK or K, age equivalents are extrapolated.

[a] Based on weighted raw scores. Scores below 64 have an age equivalent of less than 6:0 years.

[b] Scores are for Ages 4:0–9:11 in Grades PreK–3.

[c] Scores are for Ages 9:0–19:11 in Grades 4–12.

G

WIAT–II Scores Predicted From the WPPSI–R, the WISC–III, and the WAIS–III Scores

Table H.1. WIAT–II Subtest and Composite Standard Scores Predicted From the WPPSI–R FSIQ Scores for Children Aged 4:0–6:11

FSIQ Score	Word Read	Num Ops	Read Comp	Spelling	Pseudowd Decod	Math Reason	Written Expr	Listen Comp	Oral Expr	Read	Math	Written Lang	Oral Lang	Total	FSIQ Score
					Subtest Standard Scores							Composite Standard Scores			
40															40
41	69	65	54	70	62	59	71	68	63	52	57	57	58	47	41
42	69	66	55	71	63	60	72	69	64	53	57	58	58	48	42
43	70	66	56	71	63	61	72	69	64	54	58	58	59	49	43
44	70	67	57	72	64	61	73	70	65	54	59	59	60	49	44
45	71	67	57	72	64	62	73	70	66	55	59	60	60	50	45
46	71	68	58	73	65	63	74	71	66	56	60	60	61	51	46
47	72	68	59	73	66	63	74	71	67	57	61	61	62	52	47
48	72	69	60	74	66	64	75	72	67	57	61	62	62	53	48
49	73	70	60	74	67	65	75	72	68	58	62	62	63	54	49
50	73	70	61	75	67	65	76	73	69	59	63	63	64	55	50
51	74	71	62	75	68	66	76	73	69	60	63	64	64	55	51
52	74	71	63	76	69	67	77	74	70	61	64	64	65	56	52
53	75	72	63	76	69	67	77	74	70	61	65	65	66	57	53
54	75	72	64	77	70	68	78	75	71	62	66	66	66	58	54
55	76	73	65	77	70	69	78	75	72	63	66	66	67	59	55
56	76	73	66	77	71	69	78	76	72	64	67	67	68	60	56
57	77	74	66	78	72	70	79	76	73	64	68	68	69	61	57
58	77	75	67	78	72	70	79	77	73	65	68	69	69	61	58
59	78	75	68	79	73	71	80	77	74	66	69	69	70	62	59
60	78	76	68	79	74	72	80	78	75	67	70	70	71	63	60
61	79	76	69	80	74	72	81	78	75	67	70	71	71	64	61
62	79	77	70	80	75	73	81	79	76	68	71	71	72	65	62
63	80	77	71	81	75	74	82	79	76	69	72	72	73	66	63
64	80	78	71	81	76	74	82	80	77	70	73	73	73	67	64
65	81	79	72	82	77	75	83	80	78	71	73	73	74	67	65
66	81	79	73	82	77	76	83	81	78	71	74	74	75	68	66
67	82	80	74	83	78	76	84	81	79	72	75	75	75	69	67
68	82	80	74	83	78	77	84	82	79	73	75	76	76	70	68
69	83	81	75	84	79	78	84	82	80	74	76	76	77	71	69
70	83	81	76	84	80	78	85	83	80	74	77	77	77	72	70
71	84	82	77	85	80	79	85	83	81	75	78	78	78	73	71
72	84	83	77	85	81	80	86	84	82	76	78	78	79	73	72
73	85	83	78	86	82	80	86	85	82	77	79	79	79	74	73
74	85	84	79	86	82	81	87	85	83	78	80	80	80	75	74
75	86	84	79	87	83	82	87	86	83	78	80	80	81	76	75
76	86	85	80	87	83	82	88	86	84	79	81	81	82	77	76
77	87	85	81	88	84	83	88	87	85	80	82	82	82	78	77
78	87	86	82	88	85	84	89	87	85	81	82	83	83	79	78
79	88	86	82	89	85	84	89	88	86	81	83	83	84	79	79
80	88	87	83	89	86	85	89	88	86	82	84	84	84	80	80
81	89	88	84	89	86	86	90	89	87	83	85	85	85	81	81
82	89	88	85	90	87	86	90	89	88	84	85	85	86	82	82
83	90	89	85	90	88	87	91	90	88	85	86	86	86	83	83
84	90	89	86	91	88	88	91	90	89	85	87	87	87	84	84
85	91	90	87	91	89	88	92	91	89	86	87	87	88	85	85
86	91	90	88	92	90	89	92	91	90	87	88	88	88	85	86
87	92	91	88	92	90	90	93	92	91	88	89	89	89	86	87
88	92	92	89	93	91	90	93	92	91	88	89	90	90	87	88
89	93	92	90	93	91	91	94	93	92	89	90	90	90	88	89
90	93	93	90	94	92	91	94	93	92	90	91	91	91	89	90
91	94	93	91	94	93	92	95	94	93	91	92	92	92	90	91
92	94	94	92	95	93	93	95	94	93	91	92	92	92	91	92
93	95	94	93	95	94	93	95	95	94	92	93	93	93	91	93
94	95	95	93	96	94	94	96	95	95	93	94	94	94	92	94
95	96	95	94	96	95	95	96	96	95	94	94	94	95	93	95
96	96	96	95	97	96	95	97	96	96	95	95	95	95	94	96
97	97	97	96	97	96	96	97	97	96	95	96	96	96	95	97
98	97	97	96	98	97	97	98	97	97	96	96	97	97	96	98
99	98	98	97	98	98	97	98	98	98	97	97	97	97	97	99
100	98	98	98	99	98	98	99	98	98	98	98	98	98	97	100

Note. FSIQ = Full Scale IQ. Based on the correlations between the WIAT–II standard scores and the WPPSI–R FSIQ across the three age ranges, and an adjustment for the difference between norming dates (refer to Chapter 7 of the *WIAT–II Examiner's Manual*). Presented in the order shown in the table, the average correlations for the nine WIAT–II subtests are .50, .56, .73, .48, .62, .66, .46, .52, and .59, and the average correlations for the five WIAT–II composites are .77, .70, .70, .68, and .86.

H

Table H.1. WIAT–II Subtest and Composite Standard Scores Predicted From the WPPSI–R FSIQ Scores for Children Aged 4:0–6:11 *(continued)*

	Subtest Standard Scores									Composite Standard Scores					
FSIQ Score	Word Read	Num Ops	Read Comp	Spelling	Pseudowd Decod	Math Reason	Written Expr	Listen Comp	Oral Expr	Read	Math	Written Lang	Oral Lang	Total	FSIQ Score
101	99	99	99	99	99	99	99	99	99	98	99	99	99	98	101
102	99	99	99	100	99	99	100	99	99	99	99	99	99	99	102
103	100	100	100	100	100	100	100	100	100	100	100	100	100	100	103
104	100	100	101	100	100	100	100	100	100	101	100	100	100	101	104
105	101	101	101	100	101	101	100	101	101	102	101	101	101	102	105
106	101	101	102	101	101	101	101	101	101	102	101	101	101	103	106
107	102	102	103	101	102	102	101	102	102	103	102	102	102	103	107
108	102	102	104	102	102	103	102	102	102	104	103	103	103	104	108
109	103	103	104	102	103	103	102	103	103	105	104	103	103	105	109
110	103	103	105	103	104	104	103	103	104	105	104	104	104	106	110
111	104	104	106	103	104	105	103	104	104	106	105	105	105	107	111
112	104	105	107	104	105	105	104	104	105	107	106	106	105	108	112
113	105	105	107	104	106	106	104	105	105	108	106	106	106	109	113
114	105	106	108	105	106	107	105	105	106	109	107	107	107	109	114
115	106	106	109	105	107	107	105	106	107	109	108	108	108	110	115
116	106	107	110	106	107	108	105	106	107	110	108	108	108	111	116
117	107	107	110	106	108	109	106	107	108	111	109	109	109	112	117
118	107	108	111	107	109	109	106	107	108	112	110	110	110	113	118
119	108	108	112	107	109	110	107	108	109	112	111	110	110	114	119
120	108	109	112	108	110	110	107	108	109	113	111	111	111	115	120
121	109	110	113	108	110	111	108	109	110	114	112	112	112	115	121
122	109	110	114	109	111	112	108	109	111	115	113	113	112	116	122
123	110	111	115	109	112	112	109	110	111	115	113	113	113	117	123
124	110	111	115	110	112	113	109	110	112	116	114	114	114	118	124
125	111	112	116	110	113	114	110	111	112	117	115	115	114	119	125
126	111	112	117	111	114	114	110	111	113	118	115	115	115	120	126
127	112	113	118	111	114	115	111	112	114	119	116	116	116	121	127
128	112	114	118	111	115	116	111	112	114	119	117	117	116	121	128
129	113	114	119	112	115	116	111	113	115	120	118	117	117	122	129
130	113	115	120	112	116	117	112	113	115	121	118	118	118	123	130
131	114	115	121	113	117	118	112	114	116	122	119	119	119	124	131
132	114	116	121	113	117	118	113	114	117	122	120	120	119	125	132
133	115	116	122	114	118	119	113	115	117	123	120	120	120	126	133
134	115	117	123	114	118	120	114	115	118	124	121	121	121	127	134
135	116	117	123	115	119	120	114	116	118	125	122	122	121	127	135
136	116	118	124	115	120	121	115	117	119	126	122	122	122	128	136
137	117	119	125	116	120	122	115	117	120	126	123	123	123	129	137
138	117	119	126	116	121	122	116	118	120	127	124	124	123	130	138
139	118	120	126	117	122	123	116	118	121	128	125	124	124	131	139
140	118	120	127	117	122	124	116	119	121	129	125	125	125	132	140
141	119	121	128	118	123	124	117	119	122	129	126	126	125	133	141
142	119	121	129	118	123	125	117	120	122	130	127	127	126	133	142
143	120	122	129	119	124	126	118	120	123	131	127	127	127	134	143
144	120	123	130	119	125	126	118	121	124	132	128	128	127	135	144
145	121	123	131	120	125	127	119	121	124	133	129	129	128	136	145
146	121	124	132	120	126	128	119	122	125	133	130	129	129	137	146
147	122	124	132	121	126	128	120	122	125	134	130	130	129	138	147
148	122	125	133	121	127	129	120	123	126	135	131	131	130	139	148
149	123	125	134	122	128	130	121	123	127	136	132	131	131	139	149
150	123	126	134	122	128	130	121	124	127	136	132	132	131	140	150
151	124	127	135	123	129	131	122	124	128	137	133	133	132	141	151
152	124	127	136	123	130	131	122	125	128	138	134	134	133	142	152
153	125	128	137	123	130	132	122	125	129	139	134	134	134	143	153
154	125	128	137	124	131	133	123	126	130	139	135	135	134	144	154
155	126	129	138	124	131	133	123	126	130	140	136	136	135	145	155
156	126	129	139	125	132	134	124	127	131	141	137	136	136	145	156
157	127	130	140	125	133	135	124	127	131	142	137	137	136	146	157
158	127	130	140	126	133	135	125	128	132	143	138	138	137	147	158
159	128	131	141	126	134	136	125	128	133	143	139	138	138	148	159
160	128	132	142	127	134	137	126	129	133	144	139	139	138	149	160

Note. FSIQ = Full Scale IQ. Based on the correlations between the WIAT–II standard scores and the WPPSI–R FSIQ across the three age ranges, and an adjustment for the difference between norming dates (refer to Chapter 7 of the *WIAT–II Examiner's Manual*). Presented in the order shown in the table, the average correlations for the nine WIAT–II subtests are .50, .56, .73, .48, .62, .66, .46, .52, and .59, and the average correlations for the five WIAT–II composites are .77, .70, .70, .68, and .86.

H

Table H.2. WIAT–II Subtest and Composite Standard Scores Predicted From the WPPSI–R VIQ Scores for Children Aged 4:0–6:11

	Subtest Standard Scores									Composite Standard Scores					
VIQ Score	Word Read	Num Ops	Read Comp	Spelling	Pseudowd Decod	Math Reason	Written Expr	Listen Comp	Oral Expr	Read	Math	Written Lang	Oral Lang	Total	VIQ Score
40															40
41															41
42															42
43															43
44															44
45															45
46	73	73	59	74	64	66	76	70	66	57	65	61	59	52	46
47	73	73	59	74	64	67	77	71	67	57	66	61	60	53	47
48	74	74	60	75	65	67	77	71	68	58	66	62	61	54	48
49	74	74	61	75	66	68	78	72	68	59	67	63	61	55	49
50	75	75	62	76	66	69	78	72	69	60	68	63	62	56	50
51	75	75	62	76	67	69	78	73	69	60	68	64	63	56	51
52	76	76	63	76	68	70	79	74	70	61	69	65	64	57	52
53	76	76	64	77	68	70	79	74	71	62	69	65	64	58	53
54	77	77	65	77	69	71	80	75	71	63	70	66	65	59	54
55	77	77	65	78	70	71	80	75	72	63	71	67	66	60	55
56	78	78	66	78	70	72	81	76	72	64	71	68	66	61	56
57	78	78	67	79	71	73	81	76	73	65	72	68	67	61	57
58	79	78	67	79	71	73	81	77	73	66	73	69	68	62	58
59	79	79	68	80	72	74	82	77	74	66	73	70	69	63	59
60	80	79	69	80	73	74	82	78	75	67	74	70	69	64	60
61	80	80	70	81	73	75	83	78	75	68	74	71	70	65	61
62	80	80	70	81	74	76	83	79	76	69	75	72	71	66	62
63	81	81	71	82	75	76	83	79	76	70	76	72	71	67	63
64	81	81	72	82	75	77	84	80	77	70	76	73	72	67	64
65	82	82	72	82	76	77	84	80	78	71	77	74	73	68	65
66	82	82	73	83	77	78	85	81	78	72	77	74	74	69	66
67	83	83	74	83	77	79	85	81	79	73	78	75	74	70	67
68	83	83	75	84	78	79	86	82	79	73	79	76	75	71	68
69	84	84	75	84	78	80	86	82	80	74	79	77	76	72	69
70	84	84	76	85	79	80	86	83	81	75	80	77	76	72	70
71	85	85	77	85	80	81	87	83	81	76	80	78	77	73	71
72	85	85	78	86	80	82	87	84	82	76	81	79	78	74	72
73	86	86	78	86	81	82	88	84	82	77	82	79	79	75	73
74	86	86	79	87	82	83	88	85	83	78	82	80	79	76	74
75	87	87	80	87	82	83	88	85	84	79	83	81	80	77	75
76	87	87	80	88	83	84	89	86	84	79	84	81	81	77	76
77	88	88	81	88	84	85	89	87	85	80	84	82	81	78	77
78	88	88	82	88	84	85	90	87	85	81	85	83	82	79	78
79	89	89	83	89	85	86	90	88	86	82	85	83	83	80	79
80	89	89	83	89	85	86	90	88	86	82	86	84	84	81	80
81	90	89	84	90	86	87	91	89	87	83	87	85	84	82	81
82	90	90	85	90	87	88	91	89	88	84	87	85	85	82	82
83	90	90	86	91	87	88	92	90	88	85	88	86	86	83	83
84	91	91	86	91	88	89	92	90	89	86	88	87	86	84	84
85	91	91	87	92	89	89	93	91	89	86	89	88	87	85	85
86	92	92	88	92	89	90	93	91	90	87	90	88	88	86	86
87	92	92	88	93	90	90	93	92	91	88	90	89	89	87	87
88	93	93	89	93	90	91	94	92	91	89	91	90	89	87	88
89	93	93	90	94	91	92	94	93	92	89	91	90	90	88	89
90	94	94	91	94	92	92	95	93	92	90	92	91	91	89	90
91	94	94	91	94	92	93	95	94	93	91	93	92	91	90	91
92	95	95	92	95	93	93	95	94	94	92	93	92	92	91	92
93	95	95	93	95	94	94	96	95	94	92	94	93	93	92	93
94	96	96	93	96	94	95	96	95	95	93	95	94	94	92	94
95	96	96	94	96	95	95	97	96	95	94	95	94	94	93	95
96	97	97	95	97	96	96	97	96	96	95	96	95	95	94	96
97	97	97	96	97	96	96	98	97	96	95	96	96	96	95	97
98	98	98	96	98	97	97	98	97	97	96	97	97	96	96	98
99	98	98	97	98	97	98	98	98	98	97	98	97	97	97	99
100	99	99	98	99	98	98	99	98	98	98	98	98	98	97	100

Note. VIQ = Verbal IQ. Based on the correlations between the WIAT–II standard scores and the WPPSI–R VIQ across the three age ranges, and an adjustment for the difference between norming dates (refer to Chapter 7 of the *WIAT–II Examiner's Manual*). Presented in the order shown in the table, the average correlations for the nine WIAT–II subtests are .48, .48, .72, .46, .63, .59, .41, .52, and .59, and the average correlations for the five WIAT–II composites are .76, .61, .69, .71, and .84.

Table H.2. WIAT–II Subtest and Composite Standard Scores Predicted From the WPPSI–R VIQ Scores for Children Aged 4:0–6:11 *(continued)*

	Subtest Standard Scores									Composite Standard Scores					
VIQ Score	Word Read	Num Ops	Read Comp	Spelling	Pseudowd Decod	Math Reason	Written Expr	Listen Comp	Oral Expr	Read	Math	Written Lang	Oral Lang	Total	VIQ Score
101	99	99	99	99	99	99	99	99	99	98	99	99	99	98	101
102	100	100	99	100	99	99	100	99	99	99	99	99	99	99	102
103	100	100	100	100	100	100	100	100	100	100	100	100	100	100	103
104	100	100	101	100	100	100	100	100	100	101	100	100	100	101	104
105	100	100	101	100	101	101	100	101	101	102	101	101	101	102	105
106	101	101	102	101	101	101	101	101	101	102	101	101	101	103	106
107	101	101	103	101	102	102	101	102	102	103	102	102	102	103	107
108	102	102	104	102	103	102	102	102	102	104	102	103	103	104	108
109	102	102	104	102	103	103	102	103	103	105	103	103	104	105	109
110	103	103	105	103	104	104	102	103	104	105	104	104	104	106	110
111	103	103	106	103	104	104	103	104	104	106	104	105	105	107	111
112	104	104	107	104	105	105	103	104	105	107	105	106	106	108	112
113	104	104	107	104	106	105	104	105	105	108	105	106	106	108	113
114	105	105	108	105	106	106	104	105	106	108	106	107	107	109	114
115	105	105	109	105	107	107	105	106	106	109	107	108	108	110	115
116	106	106	109	106	108	107	105	106	107	110	107	108	109	111	116
117	106	106	110	106	108	108	105	107	108	111	108	109	109	112	117
118	107	107	111	106	109	108	106	107	108	111	109	110	110	113	118
119	107	107	112	107	110	109	106	108	109	112	109	110	111	113	119
120	108	108	112	107	110	110	107	108	109	113	110	111	111	114	120
121	108	108	113	108	111	110	107	109	110	114	110	112	112	115	121
122	109	109	114	108	111	111	107	109	111	114	112	112	113	116	122
123	109	109	114	109	112	111	108	110	111	115	112	113	114	117	123
124	110	110	115	109	113	112	108	110	112	116	112	114	114	118	124
125	110	110	116	110	113	112	109	111	112	117	113	115	115	118	125
126	110	111	117	110	114	113	109	111	113	118	113	115	116	119	126
127	111	111	117	111	115	114	110	112	114	118	114	116	116	120	127
128	111	111	118	111	115	114	110	112	114	119	115	117	117	121	128
129	112	112	119	112	116	115	110	113	115	120	115	117	118	122	129
130	112	112	120	112	116	115	111	113	115	121	116	118	119	123	130
131	113	113	120	112	117	116	111	114	116	121	116	119	119	123	131
132	113	113	121	113	118	117	112	115	116	122	117	119	120	124	132
133	114	114	122	113	118	117	112	115	117	123	118	120	121	125	133
134	114	114	122	114	119	118	112	116	118	124	118	121	121	126	134
135	115	115	123	114	120	118	113	116	118	124	119	121	122	127	135
136	115	115	124	115	120	119	113	117	119	125	120	122	123	128	136
137	116	116	125	115	121	120	114	117	119	126	120	123	124	128	137
138	116	116	125	116	122	120	114	118	120	127	121	123	124	129	138
139	117	117	126	116	122	121	114	118	121	127	121	124	125	130	139
140	117	117	127	117	123	121	115	119	121	128	122	125	126	131	140
141	118	118	128	117	123	122	115	119	122	129	123	126	126	132	141
142	118	118	128	118	124	123	116	120	122	130	123	126	127	133	142
143	119	119	129	118	125	123	116	120	123	130	124	127	128	133	143
144	119	119	130	118	125	124	117	121	124	131	124	128	129	134	144
145	120	120	130	119	126	124	117	121	124	132	125	128	129	135	145
146	120	120	131	119	127	125	117	122	125	133	126	129	130	136	146
147	120	121	132	120	127	126	118	122	125	134	126	130	131	137	147
148	121	121	133	120	128	126	118	123	126	134	127	130	131	138	148
149	121	122	133	121	129	127	119	123	127	135	127	131	132	139	149
150	122	122	134	121	129	127	119	124	127	136	128	132	133	139	150
151	122	122	135	122	130	128	119	124	128	137	129	132	134	140	151
152	123	123	135	122	130	129	120	125	128	137	129	133	134	141	152
153	123	123	136	123	131	129	120	125	129	138	130	134	135	142	153
154	124	124	137	123	132	130	121	126	129	139	131	135	136	143	154
155	124	124	138	124	132	130	121	126	130	140	131	135	136	144	155
156	125	125	138	124	133	131	122	127	131	140	132	136	137	144	156
157	125	125	139	124	134	131	122	128	131	141	132	137	138	145	157
158	126	126	140	125	134	132	122	128	132	142	133	137	139	146	158
159	126	126	141	125	135	133	123	129	132	143	134	138	139	147	159
160	127	127	141	126	136	133	123	129	133	143	134	139	140	148	160

Note. VIQ = Verbal IQ. Based on the correlations between the WIAT–II standard scores and the WPPSI–R VIQ across the three age ranges, and an adjustment for the difference between norming dates (refer to Chapter 7 of the *WIAT–II Examiner's Manual*). Presented in the order shown in the table, the average correlations for the nine WIAT–II subtests are .48, .48, .72, .46, .63, .59, .41, .52, and .59, and the average correlations for the five WIAT–II composites are .76, .61, .69, .71, and .84.

Table H.3. WIAT–II Subtest and Composite Standard Scores Predicted From the WPPSI–R PIQ Scores for Children Aged 4:0–6:11

| | Subtest Standard Scores | | | | | | | | | Composite Standard Scores | | | | | |
PIQ Score	Word Read	Num Ops	Read Comp	Spelling	Pseudowd Decod	Math Reason	Written Expr	Listen Comp	Oral Expr	Read	Math	Written Lang	Oral Lang	Total	PIQ Score
40															40
41															41
42															42
43															43
44															44
45	78	72	71	81	77	68	79	79	75	74	67	73	79	69	45
46	78	73	72	81	77	69	80	80	76	74	67	73	80	69	46
47	78	73	72	81	78	70	80	80	76	75	68	74	80	70	47
48	79	74	73	82	78	70	80	81	77	75	68	74	80	71	48
49	79	74	73	82	79	71	81	81	77	76	69	75	81	71	49
50	80	75	74	82	79	71	81	81	78	76	70	75	81	72	50
51	80	75	74	83	79	72	82	82	78	76	70	76	82	72	51
52	80	76	75	83	80	72	82	82	78	77	71	76	82	73	52
53	81	76	75	83	80	73	82	82	79	77	71	77	82	73	53
54	81	77	76	84	81	74	83	83	79	78	72	77	83	74	54
55	82	77	76	84	81	74	83	83	80	78	73	78	83	74	55
56	82	78	77	84	81	75	83	83	80	79	73	78	83	75	56
57	82	78	77	85	82	75	84	84	81	79	74	79	84	75	57
58	83	79	78	85	82	76	84	84	81	80	74	79	84	76	58
59	83	79	78	85	83	76	85	85	82	80	75	80	85	77	59
60	84	80	79	86	83	77	85	85	82	81	76	80	85	77	60
61	84	80	79	86	83	77	85	85	82	81	76	80	85	78	61
62	84	81	80	86	84	78	86	86	83	82	77	81	86	78	62
63	85	81	80	87	84	79	86	86	83	82	77	81	86	79	63
64	85	82	81	87	85	79	86	86	84	82	78	82	86	79	64
65	86	82	81	88	85	80	87	87	84	83	79	82	87	80	65
66	86	83	82	88	86	80	87	87	85	83	79	83	87	80	66
67	86	83	82	88	86	81	87	88	85	84	80	83	87	81	67
68	87	84	83	89	86	81	88	88	85	84	80	84	88	81	68
69	87	84	83	89	87	82	88	88	86	85	81	84	88	82	69
70	88	85	84	89	87	83	89	89	86	85	81	85	89	83	70
71	88	85	84	90	88	83	89	89	87	86	82	85	89	83	71
72	88	86	85	90	88	84	89	89	87	86	83	86	89	84	72
73	89	86	85	90	88	84	90	90	88	87	83	86	90	84	73
74	89	87	86	91	89	85	90	90	88	87	84	87	90	85	74
75	90	87	86	91	89	85	90	90	89	88	84	87	90	85	75
76	90	88	87	91	90	86	91	91	89	88	85	88	91	86	76
77	90	88	87	92	90	86	91	91	89	88	86	88	91	86	77
78	91	89	88	92	91	87	92	92	90	89	86	89	92	87	78
79	91	89	88	92	91	88	92	92	90	89	87	89	92	87	79
80	92	90	89	93	91	88	92	92	91	90	87	90	92	88	80
81	92	90	89	93	92	89	93	93	91	90	88	90	93	89	81
82	92	91	90	93	92	89	93	93	92	91	89	91	93	89	82
83	93	91	90	94	93	90	93	93	92	91	89	91	93	90	83
84	93	92	91	94	93	90	94	94	93	92	90	92	94	90	84
85	94	92	91	94	93	91	94	94	93	92	90	92	94	91	85
86	94	93	92	95	94	92	94	94	93	93	91	93	94	91	86
87	94	93	92	95	94	92	94	94	93	93	91	93	94	92	87
88	94	93	93	95	94	92	95	95	94	94	92	93	95	92	88
89	95	94	93	95	95	93	95	95	94	94	92	94	95	93	89
90	95	94	94	96	95	93	96	96	95	94	93	94	96	93	90
91	96	95	94	96	95	94	96	96	95	95	93	95	96	94	91
92	96	95	95	97	96	94	96	96	96	95	94	95	96	95	92
93	96	96	95	97	96	95	97	97	96	96	95	96	97	95	93
94	97	96	96	97	97	95	97	97	96	96	95	96	97	96	94
95	97	97	96	98	97	96	97	97	97	97	96	97	97	96	95
96	98	97	97	98	98	97	98	98	97	97	96	97	98	97	96
97	98	98	97	98	98	97	98	98	98	98	97	98	98	97	97
98	98	98	98	99	98	98	99	99	98	98	98	98	99	98	98
99	99	99	98	99	99	98	99	99	99	99	98	99	99	98	99
100	99	99	99	99	99	99	99	99	99	99	99	99	99	99	100

Note. PIQ = Performance IQ. Based on the correlations between the WIAT–II standard scores and the WPPSI–R PIQ across the three age ranges, and an adjustment for the difference between norming dates (refer to Chapter 7 of the *WIAT–II Examiner's Manual*). Presented in the order shown in the table, the average correlations for the nine WIAT–II subtests are .40, .50, .51, .35, .41, .56, .37, .37, and .44, and the average correlations for the five WIAT–II composites are .46, .60, .49, .37, and .55.

H

Table H.3. WIAT–II Subtest and Composite Standard Scores Predicted From the WPPSI–R PIQ Scores for Children Aged 4:0–6:11 *(continued)*

PIQ Score	Word Read	Num Ops	Read Comp	Spelling	Pseudowd Decod	Math Reason	Written Expr	Listen Comp	Oral Expr	Read	Math	Written Lang	Oral Lang	Total	PIQ Score
	Subtest Standard Scores									Composite Standard Scores					
101	100	100	99	100	100	99	100	100	100	100	99	100	100	99	101
102	100	100	100	100	100	100	100	100	100	100	100	100	100	100	102
103	100	100	101	100	100	101	100	100	100	100	101	100	100	101	103
104	101	101	101	101	101	101	101	101	101	101	101	101	101	101	104
105	101	101	102	101	101	102	101	101	101	101	102	101	101	102	105
106	102	102	102	101	102	102	101	101	102	102	102	102	101	102	106
107	102	102	103	102	102	103	102	102	102	102	103	102	102	103	107
108	102	103	103	102	102	103	102	102	103	103	104	103	102	103	108
109	103	103	104	102	103	104	103	103	103	103	104	103	103	104	109
110	103	104	104	103	103	105	103	103	104	104	105	104	103	104	110
111	104	104	105	103	104	105	103	103	104	104	105	104	103	105	111
112	104	105	105	103	104	106	104	104	104	105	106	105	104	105	112
113	104	105	106	104	105	106	104	104	105	105	107	105	104	106	113
114	105	106	106	104	105	107	104	104	105	106	107	106	104	107	114
115	105	106	107	105	105	107	105	105	106	106	108	106	105	107	115
116	106	107	107	105	106	108	105	105	106	106	108	107	105	108	116
117	106	107	108	105	106	108	106	106	107	107	109	107	106	108	117
118	106	108	108	106	107	109	106	106	107	107	110	108	106	109	118
119	107	108	109	106	107	110	106	106	107	108	110	108	106	109	119
120	107	109	109	106	107	110	107	107	108	108	111	109	107	110	120
121	108	109	110	107	108	111	107	107	108	109	111	109	107	110	121
122	108	110	110	107	108	111	107	107	109	109	112	110	107	111	122
123	108	110	111	107	109	112	108	108	109	110	113	110	108	111	123
124	109	111	111	108	109	112	108	108	110	110	113	111	108	112	124
125	109	111	112	108	109	113	108	108	110	111	114	111	108	113	125
126	110	112	112	108	110	114	109	109	111	111	114	112	109	113	126
127	110	112	113	109	110	114	109	109	111	112	115	112	109	114	127
128	110	113	113	109	111	115	110	110	111	112	116	113	110	114	128
129	111	113	114	109	111	115	110	110	112	112	116	113	110	115	129
130	111	114	114	110	112	116	110	110	112	113	117	114	110	115	130
131	112	114	115	110	112	116	111	111	113	113	117	114	111	116	131
132	112	115	115	110	112	117	111	111	113	114	118	115	111	116	132
133	112	115	116	111	113	117	111	111	114	114	119	115	111	117	133
134	113	116	116	111	113	118	112	112	114	115	119	116	112	117	134
135	113	116	117	111	114	119	112	112	115	115	120	116	112	118	135
136	114	117	117	112	114	119	113	112	115	116	120	117	113	119	136
137	114	117	118	112	114	120	113	113	115	116	121	117	113	119	137
138	114	118	118	112	115	120	113	113	116	117	121	118	113	120	138
139	115	118	119	113	115	121	114	114	116	117	122	118	114	120	139
140	115	119	119	113	116	121	114	114	117	118	123	119	114	121	140
141	116	119	120	114	116	122	114	114	117	118	123	119	114	121	141
142	116	120	120	114	117	123	115	115	118	118	124	120	115	122	142
143	116	120	121	114	117	123	115	115	118	119	124	120	115	122	143
144	117	121	121	115	117	124	115	115	118	119	125	120	115	123	144
145	117	121	122	115	118	124	116	116	119	120	126	121	116	123	145
146	118	122	122	115	118	125	116	116	119	120	126	121	116	124	146
147	118	122	123	116	119	125	117	117	120	121	127	122	117	125	147
148	118	123	123	116	119	126	117	117	120	121	127	122	117	125	148
149	119	123	124	116	119	126	117	117	121	122	128	123	117	126	149
150	119	124	124	117	120	127	118	118	121	122	129	123	118	126	150
151	120	124	125	117	120	128	118	118	122	123	129	124	118	127	151
152	120	125	125	117	121	128	118	118	122	123	130	124	118	127	152
153	120	125	126	118	121	129	119	119	122	124	130	125	119	128	153
154	121	126	126	118	121	129	119	119	123	124	131	125	119	128	154
155	121	126	127	118	122	130	120	119	123	124	132	126	120	129	155
156	122	127	127	119	122	130	120	120	124	125	132	126	120	129	156
157	122	127	128	119	123	131	120	120	124	125	133	127	120	130	157
158	122	128	128	119	123	132	121	121	125	126	133	127	121	131	158
159	123	128	129	120	124	132	121	121	125	126	134	128	121	131	159
160	123	129	129	120	124	133	121	121	126	127	135	128	121	132	160

Note. PIQ = Performance IQ. Based on the correlations between the WIAT–II standard scores and the WPPSI–R PIQ across the three age ranges, and an adjustment for the difference between norming dates (refer to Chapter 7 of the *WIAT–II Examiner's Manual*). Presented in the order shown in the table, the average correlations for the nine WIAT–II subtests are .40, .50, .51, .35, .41, .56, .37, .37, and .44, and the average correlations for the five WIAT–II composites are .46, .60, .49, .37, and .55.

Table H.4. WIAT–II Subtest and Composite Standard Scores Predicted From the WISC–III FSIQ Scores for Children Aged 6:0–16:11

	Subtest Standard Scores										Composite Standard Scores					
FSIQ Score	Word Read	Num Ops	Read Comp	Spelling	Pseudowd Decod	Math Reason	Written Expr	Listen Comp	Oral Expr		Read	Math	Written Lang	Oral Lang	Total	FSIQ Score
40	62	63	60	67	69	53	66	58	70		60	55	64	58	52	40
41	63	64	61	68	69	54	67	58	71		61	56	65	58	53	41
42	63	65	61	68	70	55	67	59	71		61	57	65	59	54	42
43	64	65	62	69	70	55	68	59	72		62	57	66	60	55	43
44	65	66	63	69	71	56	68	60	72		63	58	66	60	55	44
45	65	66	63	70	71	57	69	60	73		63	59	67	61	56	45
46	66	67	64	70	72	58	70	61	73		64	59	68	62	57	46
47	66	67	65	71	72	58	70	62	74		65	60	68	62	58	47
48	67	68	65	71	73	59	71	62	74		65	61	69	63	58	48
49	68	69	66	72	73	60	71	63	75		66	62	69	64	59	49
50	68	69	66	72	74	61	72	64	75		67	62	70	64	60	50
51	69	70	67	73	74	61	72	64	75		67	63	70	65	61	51
52	69	70	68	73	75	62	73	65	76		68	64	71	66	61	52
53	70	71	68	74	75	63	73	66	76		68	64	72	66	62	53
54	71	71	69	74	76	64	74	66	77		69	65	72	67	63	54
55	71	72	70	75	76	64	74	67	77		70	66	73	68	64	55
56	72	73	70	75	77	65	75	68	78		70	67	73	68	64	56
57	72	73	71	76	77	66	75	68	78		71	67	74	69	65	57
58	73	74	72	76	78	67	76	69	79		72	68	74	70	66	58
59	74	74	72	77	78	67	77	70	79		72	69	75	70	67	59
60	74	75	73	77	79	68	77	71	80		73	69	75	71	67	60
61	75	76	73	78	79	69	78	71	80		73	70	76	72	68	61
62	75	76	74	78	80	70	78	72	81		74	71	77	72	69	62
63	76	77	75	79	80	70	79	73	81		75	72	77	73	70	63
64	77	77	75	80	81	71	79	73	82		75	72	78	74	70	64
65	77	78	76	80	81	72	80	74	82		76	73	78	74	71	65
66	78	78	77	81	82	73	80	75	83		77	74	79	75	72	66
67	78	79	77	81	82	73	81	75	83		77	74	79	76	73	67
68	79	80	78	82	83	74	81	76	83		78	75	80	76	74	68
69	80	80	78	82	83	75	82	77	84		79	76	81	77	74	69
70	80	81	79	83	84	76	82	77	84		79	77	81	78	75	70
71	81	81	80	83	84	76	83	78	85		80	77	82	78	76	71
72	81	82	80	84	85	77	83	79	85		80	78	82	79	77	72
73	82	83	81	84	85	78	84	79	86		81	79	83	80	77	73
74	83	83	82	85	86	78	85	80	86		82	79	83	80	78	74
75	83	84	82	85	86	79	85	81	87		82	80	84	81	79	75
76	84	84	83	86	87	80	86	82	87		83	81	85	82	80	76
77	84	85	84	86	87	81	86	82	88		84	82	85	83	80	77
78	85	85	84	87	88	81	87	83	88		84	82	86	83	81	78
79	86	86	85	87	88	82	87	84	89		85	83	86	84	82	79
80	86	87	85	88	89	83	88	84	89		85	84	87	85	83	80
81	87	87	86	88	89	84	88	85	90		86	84	87	85	83	81
82	87	88	87	89	90	84	89	86	90		87	85	88	86	84	82
83	88	88	87	90	90	85	89	86	91		87	86	89	87	85	83
84	89	89	88	90	91	86	90	87	91		88	86	89	87	86	84
85	89	90	89	91	91	87	90	88	92		89	87	90	88	86	85
86	90	90	89	91	92	87	91	88	92		89	88	90	89	87	86
87	90	91	90	92	92	88	91	89	92		90	89	91	89	88	87
88	91	91	91	92	93	89	92	90	93		91	89	91	90	89	88
89	92	92	91	93	93	90	93	90	93		91	90	92	91	89	89
90	92	92	92	93	94	90	93	91	94		92	91	93	91	90	90
91	93	93	92	94	94	91	94	92	94		92	91	93	92	91	91
92	93	94	93	94	95	92	94	92	95		93	92	94	93	92	92
93	94	94	94	95	95	93	95	93	95		94	93	94	93	92	93
94	95	95	94	95	96	93	95	94	96		94	94	95	94	93	94
95	95	95	95	96	96	94	96	95	96		95	94	95	95	94	95
96	96	96	96	96	97	95	96	95	97		96	95	96	95	95	96
97	96	97	96	97	97	96	97	96	97		96	96	97	96	95	97
98	97	97	97	97	98	96	97	97	98		97	96	97	97	96	98
99	98	98	97	98	98	97	98	97	98		97	97	98	97	97	99
100	98	98	98	98	99	98	98	98	99		98	98	98	98	98	100

Note. FSIQ = Full Scale IQ. Based on the correlations between the WIAT–II standard scores and the WISC–III FSIQ across the 11 age ranges, and an adjustment for the difference between norming dates (refer to Chapter 7 of the *WIAT–II Examiner's Manual*). Presented in the order shown in the table, the average correlations for the nine WIAT–II subtests are .60, .58, .63, .53, .50, .74, .53, .69, and .47, and the average correlations for the five WIAT–II composites are .63, .71, .57, .67, and .76.

Table H.4. WIAT–II Subtest and Composite Standard Scores Predicted From the WISC–III FSIQ Scores for Children Aged 6:0–16:11 *(continued)*

| | Subtest Standard Scores | | | | | | | | | Composite Standard Scores | | | | | |
FSIQ Score	Word Read	Num Ops	Read Comp	Spelling	Pseudowd Decod	Math Reason	Written Expr	Listen Comp	Oral Expr	Read	Math	Written Lang	Oral Lang	Total	FSIQ Score
101	99	99	99	99	99	99	99	99	99	99	99	99	99	98	101
102	99	99	99	99	100	99	99	99	100	99	99	99	99	99	102
103	100	100	100	100	100	100	100	100	100	100	100	100	100	100	103
104	101	101	101	101	100	101	101	101	100	101	101	101	101	101	104
105	101	101	101	101	101	101	101	101	101	101	101	101	101	102	105
106	102	102	102	102	101	102	102	102	101	102	102	102	102	102	106
107	102	102	103	102	102	103	102	103	102	103	103	102	103	103	107
108	103	103	103	103	102	104	103	103	102	103	104	103	103	104	108
109	104	103	104	103	103	104	103	104	103	104	104	103	104	105	109
110	104	104	104	104	103	105	104	105	103	104	105	104	105	105	110
111	105	105	105	104	104	106	104	105	104	105	106	105	105	106	111
112	105	105	106	105	104	107	105	106	104	106	106	105	106	107	112
113	106	106	106	105	105	107	105	107	105	106	107	106	107	108	113
114	107	106	107	106	105	108	106	108	105	107	108	106	107	108	114
115	107	107	108	106	106	109	106	108	106	108	109	107	108	109	115
116	108	108	108	107	106	110	107	109	106	108	109	107	109	110	116
117	108	108	109	107	107	110	107	110	107	109	110	108	109	111	117
118	109	109	109	108	107	111	108	110	107	109	111	109	110	111	118
119	110	109	110	108	108	112	109	111	108	110	111	109	111	112	119
120	110	110	111	109	108	113	109	112	108	111	112	110	111	113	120
121	111	110	111	109	109	113	110	112	108	111	113	110	112	114	121
122	111	111	112	110	109	114	110	113	109	112	114	111	113	114	122
123	112	112	113	111	110	115	111	114	109	113	114	111	113	115	123
124	113	112	113	111	110	116	111	114	110	113	115	112	114	116	124
125	113	113	114	112	111	116	112	115	110	114	116	113	115	117	125
126	114	113	115	112	111	117	112	116	111	115	116	113	115	117	126
127	114	114	115	113	112	118	113	116	111	115	117	114	116	118	127
128	115	115	116	113	112	119	113	117	112	116	118	114	117	119	128
129	116	115	116	114	113	119	114	118	112	116	118	115	117	120	129
130	116	116	117	114	113	120	114	118	113	117	119	115	118	120	130
131	117	116	118	115	114	121	115	119	113	118	120	116	119	121	131
132	117	117	118	115	114	122	115	120	114	118	121	117	120	122	132
133	118	117	119	116	115	122	116	121	114	119	121	117	120	123	133
134	119	118	120	116	115	123	117	121	115	120	122	118	121	123	134
135	119	119	120	117	116	124	117	122	115	120	123	118	122	124	135
136	120	119	121	117	116	124	118	123	116	121	123	119	122	125	136
137	120	120	122	118	117	125	118	123	116	121	124	119	123	126	137
138	121	120	122	118	117	126	119	124	117	122	125	120	124	126	138
139	122	121	123	119	118	127	119	125	117	123	126	121	124	127	139
140	122	122	123	119	118	127	120	125	117	123	126	121	125	128	140
141	123	122	124	120	119	128	120	126	118	124	127	122	126	129	141
142	123	123	125	120	119	129	121	127	118	125	128	122	126	130	142
143	124	123	125	121	120	130	121	127	119	125	128	123	127	130	143
144	125	124	126	122	120	130	122	128	119	126	129	123	128	131	144
145	125	124	127	122	121	131	122	129	120	127	130	124	128	132	145
146	126	125	127	123	121	132	123	129	120	127	131	125	129	133	146
147	126	126	128	123	122	133	123	130	121	128	131	125	130	133	147
148	127	126	128	124	122	133	124	131	121	128	132	126	130	134	148
149	128	127	129	124	123	134	125	132	122	129	133	126	131	135	149
150	128	127	130	125	123	135	125	132	122	130	133	127	132	136	150
151	129	128	130	125	124	136	126	133	123	130	134	127	132	136	151
152	129	129	131	126	124	136	126	134	123	131	135	128	133	137	152
153	130	129	132	126	125	137	127	134	124	132	136	129	134	138	153
154	131	130	132	127	125	138	127	135	124	132	136	129	134	139	154
155	131	130	133	127	126	139	128	136	125	133	137	130	135	139	155
156	132	131	134	128	126	139	128	136	125	133	138	130	136	140	156
157	132	131	134	128	127	140	129	137	125	134	138	131	136	141	157
158	133	132	135	129	127	141	129	138	126	135	139	131	137	142	158
159	134	133	135	129	128	142	130	138	126	135	140	132	138	142	159
160	134	133	136	130	128	142	130	139	127	136	141	132	138	143	160

Note. FSIQ = Full Scale IQ. Based on the correlations between the WIAT–II standard scores and the WISC–III FSIQ across the 11 age ranges, and an adjustment for the difference between norming dates (refer to Chapter 7 of the *WIAT–II Examiner's Manual*). Presented in the order shown in the table, the average correlations for the nine WIAT–II subtests are .60, .58, .63, .53, .50, .74, .53, .69, and .47, and the average correlations for the five WIAT–II composites are .63, .71, .57, .67, and .76.

Table H.5. WIAT-II Subtest and Composite Standard Scores Predicted From the WISC-III VIQ Scores for Children Aged 6:0–16:11

VIQ Score	Word Read	Num Ops	Read Comp	Spelling	Pseudowd Decod	Math Reason	Written Expr	Listen Comp	Oral Expr	Read	Math	Written Lang	Oral Lang	Total	VIQ Score
				Subtest Standard Scores								Composite Standard Scores			
40															40
41															41
42															42
43															43
44															44
45															45
46	63	67	62	68	69	58	69	60	73	61	59	66	61	55	46
47	64	67	62	68	69	58	70	60	73	62	60	67	61	56	47
48	65	68	63	69	70	59	70	61	74	62	61	67	62	57	48
49	65	69	64	70	70	60	71	62	74	63	62	68	63	58	49
50	66	69	65	70	71	61	71	63	75	64	62	68	63	58	50
51	67	70	65	71	72	61	72	63	75	64	63	69	64	59	51
52	67	70	66	71	72	62	72	64	76	65	64	70	65	60	52
53	68	71	67	72	73	63	73	65	76	66	65	70	66	61	53
54	69	72	67	72	73	64	73	65	77	66	65	71	66	62	54
55	69	72	68	73	74	64	74	66	77	67	66	71	67	62	55
56	70	73	69	74	74	65	75	67	78	68	67	72	68	63	56
57	70	73	69	74	75	66	75	68	78	69	67	73	68	64	57
58	71	74	70	75	75	67	76	68	79	69	68	73	69	65	58
59	72	75	71	75	76	67	76	69	79	70	69	74	70	66	59
60	72	75	71	76	77	68	77	70	80	71	70	75	71	66	60
61	73	76	72	77	77	69	77	70	80	71	70	75	71	67	61
62	74	76	73	77	78	70	78	71	81	72	71	76	72	68	62
63	74	77	73	78	78	70	78	72	81	73	72	76	73	69	63
64	75	77	74	78	79	71	79	73	82	73	72	77	73	70	64
65	76	78	75	79	79	72	80	73	82	74	73	78	74	70	65
66	76	79	75	79	80	73	80	74	83	75	74	78	75	71	66
67	77	79	76	80	80	74	81	75	83	76	75	79	75	72	67
68	78	80	77	81	81	74	81	75	84	76	75	79	76	73	68
69	78	80	77	81	82	75	82	76	84	77	76	80	77	74	69
70	79	81	78	82	82	76	82	77	85	78	77	81	78	74	70
71	80	82	79	82	83	77	83	78	85	78	78	81	78	75	71
72	80	82	80	83	83	77	83	78	85	79	78	82	79	76	72
73	81	83	80	83	84	78	84	79	86	80	79	82	80	77	73
74	82	83	81	84	84	79	84	80	86	80	80	83	80	78	74
75	82	84	82	85	85	80	85	81	87	81	80	84	81	78	75
76	83	85	82	85	85	80	86	81	87	82	81	84	82	79	76
77	84	85	83	86	86	81	86	82	88	83	82	85	82	80	77
78	84	86	84	86	87	82	87	83	88	83	83	85	83	81	78
79	85	86	84	87	87	83	87	83	89	84	83	86	84	82	79
80	86	87	85	87	88	83	88	84	89	85	84	87	85	82	80
81	86	88	86	88	88	84	88	85	90	85	85	87	85	83	81
82	87	88	86	89	89	85	89	86	90	86	86	88	86	84	82
83	88	89	87	89	89	86	89	86	91	87	86	88	87	85	83
84	88	89	88	90	90	86	90	87	91	87	87	89	87	86	84
85	89	90	88	90	91	87	91	88	92	88	88	90	88	86	85
86	90	91	89	91	91	88	91	88	92	89	88	90	89	87	86
87	90	91	90	91	92	89	92	89	93	90	89	91	89	88	87
88	91	92	90	92	92	89	92	90	93	90	90	92	90	89	88
89	91	92	91	93	93	90	93	91	94	91	91	92	91	90	89
90	92	93	92	93	93	91	93	91	94	92	91	93	92	90	90
91	93	93	92	94	94	92	94	92	95	92	92	93	92	91	91
92	93	94	93	94	94	92	94	93	95	93	93	94	93	92	92
93	94	95	94	95	95	93	95	94	96	94	93	95	94	93	93
94	95	95	95	95	96	94	96	94	96	94	94	95	94	94	94
95	95	96	95	96	96	95	96	95	97	95	95	96	95	94	95
96	96	96	96	97	97	95	97	96	97	96	96	96	96	95	96
97	97	97	97	97	97	96	97	96	98	97	96	97	96	96	97
98	97	98	97	98	98	97	98	97	98	97	97	98	97	97	98
99	98	98	98	98	98	98	98	98	99	98	98	98	98	98	99
100	99	99	99	99	99	98	99	99	99	99	99	99	99	98	100

Note. VIQ = Verbal IQ. Based on the correlations between the WIAT-II standard scores and the WISC-III VIQ across the 11 age ranges, and an adjustment for the difference between norming dates (refer to Chapter 7 of the *WIAT-II Examiner's Manual*). Presented in the order shown in the table, the average correlations for the nine WIAT-II subtests are .66, .59, .68, .57, .56, .76, .55, .72, and .48, and the average correlations for the five WIAT-II composites are .70, .72, .61, .70, and .80.

Table H.5. WIAT–II Subtest and Composite Standard Scores Predicted From the WISC–III VIQ Scores for Children Aged 6:0–16:11 *(continued)*

VIQ Score	Word Read	Num Ops	Read Comp	Spelling	Pseudowd Decod	Math Reason	Written Expr	Listen Comp	Oral Expr	Read	Math	Written Lang	Oral Lang	Total	VIQ Score
			Subtest Standard Scores									Composite Standard Scores			
101	99	99	99	99	99	99	99	99	100	99	99	99	99	99	101
102	100	100	100	100	100	100	100	100	100	100	100	100	100	100	102
103	100	100	101	100	100	100	100	100	100	101	100	100	100	101	103
104	101	101	101	101	101	101	101	101	100	101	101	101	101	102	104
105	101	101	102	101	101	102	101	101	101	102	101	101	101	102	105
106	102	102	103	102	102	102	102	102	101	103	102	102	102	103	106
107	103	102	103	102	102	103	102	103	102	104	103	102	103	104	107
108	103	103	104	103	103	104	103	104	102	104	104	103	104	105	108
109	104	104	105	103	103	105	103	104	103	105	104	104	104	106	109
110	105	104	105	104	104	105	104	105	103	106	105	104	105	106	110
111	105	105	106	105	104	106	104	106	104	106	106	105	106	107	111
112	106	105	107	105	105	107	105	106	104	107	107	105	106	108	112
113	107	106	108	106	106	108	106	107	105	108	107	106	107	109	113
114	107	107	108	106	106	108	106	108	105	108	108	107	108	110	114
115	108	107	109	107	107	109	107	109	106	109	109	107	108	110	115
116	109	108	110	107	107	110	107	109	106	110	109	108	109	111	116
117	109	108	110	108	108	111	108	110	107	111	110	108	110	112	117
118	110	109	111	109	108	111	108	111	107	111	111	109	111	113	118
119	110	109	112	109	109	112	109	112	108	112	112	110	111	114	119
120	111	110	112	110	109	113	109	112	108	113	112	110	112	114	120
121	112	111	113	110	110	114	110	113	109	113	113	111	113	115	121
122	112	111	114	111	111	114	111	114	109	114	114	112	113	116	122
123	113	112	114	111	111	115	111	114	110	115	114	112	114	117	123
124	114	112	115	112	112	116	112	115	110	115	115	113	115	118	124
125	114	113	116	113	112	117	112	116	111	116	116	113	115	118	125
126	115	114	116	113	113	117	113	117	111	117	117	114	116	119	126
127	116	114	117	114	113	118	113	117	112	118	117	115	117	120	127
128	116	115	118	114	114	119	114	118	112	118	118	115	118	121	128
129	117	115	118	115	115	120	114	119	113	119	119	116	118	122	129
130	118	116	119	115	115	120	115	119	113	120	120	116	119	122	130
131	118	117	120	116	116	121	116	120	114	120	120	117	120	123	131
132	119	117	120	117	116	122	116	121	114	121	121	118	120	124	132
133	120	118	121	117	117	123	117	122	115	122	122	118	121	125	133
134	120	118	122	118	117	123	117	122	115	122	122	119	122	126	134
135	121	119	123	118	118	124	118	123	115	123	123	119	122	126	135
136	122	120	123	119	118	125	118	124	116	124	124	120	123	127	136
137	122	120	124	119	119	126	119	125	116	125	125	121	124	128	137
138	123	121	125	120	120	126	119	125	117	125	125	121	125	129	138
139	124	121	125	121	120	127	120	126	117	126	126	122	125	130	139
140	124	122	126	121	121	128	120	127	118	127	127	122	126	130	140
141	125	123	127	122	121	129	121	127	118	127	128	123	127	131	141
142	126	123	127	122	122	130	122	128	119	128	128	124	127	132	142
143	126	124	128	123	122	130	122	129	119	129	129	124	128	133	143
144	127	124	129	123	123	131	123	130	120	129	130	125	129	134	144
145	128	125	129	124	123	132	123	130	120	130	130	125	129	134	145
146	128	125	130	125	124	133	124	131	121	131	131	126	130	135	146
147	129	126	131	125	125	133	124	132	121	132	132	127	131	136	147
148	130	127	131	126	125	134	125	132	122	132	133	127	132	137	148
149	130	127	132	126	126	135	125	133	122	133	133	128	132	138	149
150	131	128	133	127	126	136	126	134	123	134	134	129	133	138	150
151	131	128	133	128	127	136	127	135	123	134	135	129	134	139	151
152	132	129	134	128	127	137	127	135	124	135	135	130	134	140	152
153	133	130	135	129	128	138	128	136	124	136	136	130	135	141	153
154	133	130	135	129	128	139	128	137	125	136	137	131	136	142	154
155	134	131	136	130	129	139	129	137	125	137	138	132	137	142	155
156															156
157															157
158															158
159															159
160															160

Note. VIQ = Verbal IQ. Based on the correlations between the WIAT–II standard scores and the WISC–III VIQ across the 11 age ranges, and an adjustment for the difference between norming dates (refer to Chapter 7 of the *WIAT–II Examiner's Manual*). Presented in the order shown in the table, the average correlations for the nine WIAT–II subtests are .66, .59, .68, .57, .56, .76, .55, .72, and .48, and the average correlations for the five WIAT–II composites are .70, .72, .61, .70, and .80.

Table H.6. WIAT–II Subtest and Composite Standard Scores Predicted From the WISC–III PIQ Scores for Children Aged 6:0–16:11

| | Subtest Standard Scores | | | | | | | | | Composite Standard Scores | | | | | |
PIQ Score	Word Read	Num Ops	Read Comp	Spelling	Pseudowd Decod	Math Reason	Written Expr	Listen Comp	Oral Expr	Read	Math	Written Lang	Oral Lang	Total	PIQ Score
40															40
41															41
42															42
43															43
44															44
45															45
46	76	74	74	79	81	67	77	71	79	76	68	76	71	69	46
47	77	74	75	79	81	68	77	71	80	76	69	77	72	69	47
48	77	75	75	80	82	68	78	72	80	76	69	77	72	70	48
49	78	75	76	80	82	69	78	72	80	77	70	78	73	70	49
50	78	76	76	80	82	70	79	73	81	77	71	78	73	71	50
51	78	76	77	81	83	70	79	73	81	78	71	78	74	71	51
52	79	77	77	81	83	71	79	74	82	78	72	79	74	72	52
53	79	77	77	82	83	71	80	75	82	79	72	79	75	72	53
54	80	78	78	82	84	72	80	75	82	79	73	80	75	73	54
55	80	78	78	82	84	72	81	76	83	79	73	80	76	74	55
56	80	79	79	83	84	73	81	76	83	80	74	80	76	74	56
57	81	79	79	83	85	74	82	77	83	80	74	81	77	75	57
58	81	79	80	83	85	74	82	77	84	81	75	81	77	75	58
59	82	80	80	84	85	75	82	78	84	81	76	82	78	76	59
60	82	80	81	84	86	75	83	78	84	82	76	82	78	76	60
61	83	81	81	85	86	76	83	79	85	82	77	83	79	77	61
62	83	81	82	85	86	76	84	79	85	82	77	83	79	77	62
63	83	82	82	85	87	77	84	80	86	83	78	83	80	78	63
64	84	82	82	86	87	78	84	80	86	83	78	84	80	78	64
65	84	83	83	86	87	78	85	81	86	84	79	84	81	79	65
66	85	83	83	86	88	79	85	81	87	84	79	85	81	80	66
67	85	84	84	87	88	79	86	82	87	85	80	85	82	80	67
68	85	84	84	87	88	80	86	82	87	85	81	85	82	81	68
69	86	84	85	87	89	80	86	83	88	85	81	86	83	81	69
70	86	85	85	88	89	81	87	83	88	86	82	86	83	82	70
71	87	85	86	88	89	82	87	84	88	86	82	87	84	82	71
72	87	86	86	89	90	82	88	84	89	87	83	87	84	83	72
73	88	86	86	89	90	83	88	85	89	87	83	88	85	83	73
74	88	87	87	89	90	83	88	85	90	88	84	88	85	84	74
75	88	87	87	90	91	84	89	86	90	88	84	88	86	85	75
76	89	88	88	90	91	84	89	86	90	88	85	89	86	85	76
77	89	88	88	90	91	85	90	87	91	89	86	89	87	86	77
78	90	89	89	91	92	86	90	87	91	89	86	90	87	86	78
79	90	89	89	91	92	86	90	88	91	90	87	90	88	87	79
80	90	89	90	92	92	87	91	88	92	90	87	90	88	87	80
81	91	90	90	92	93	87	91	89	92	91	88	91	89	88	81
82	91	90	91	92	93	88	92	89	92	91	88	91	89	88	82
83	92	91	91	93	93	89	92	90	93	91	89	92	90	89	83
84	92	91	91	93	94	89	92	90	93	92	89	92	90	90	84
85	93	92	92	93	94	90	93	91	93	92	90	93	91	90	85
86	93	92	92	94	94	90	93	91	94	93	91	93	91	91	86
87	93	93	93	94	95	91	94	92	94	93	91	93	92	91	87
88	94	93	93	94	95	91	94	92	95	94	92	94	92	92	88
89	94	94	94	95	95	92	94	93	95	94	92	94	93	92	89
90	95	94	94	95	96	93	95	93	95	94	93	95	93	93	90
91	95	95	95	96	96	93	95	94	96	95	93	95	94	93	91
92	95	95	95	96	96	94	96	94	96	95	94	95	94	94	92
93	96	95	95	96	97	94	96	95	96	96	94	96	95	94	93
94	96	96	96	97	97	95	96	95	97	96	95	96	95	95	94
95	97	96	96	97	97	95	97	96	97	97	96	97	96	96	95
96	97	97	97	97	98	96	97	96	97	97	96	97	96	96	96
97	98	97	97	98	98	97	98	97	98	97	97	98	97	97	97
98	98	98	98	98	98	97	98	97	98	98	97	98	97	97	98
99	98	98	98	99	99	98	98	98	99	98	98	98	98	98	99
100	99	99	99	99	99	98	99	98	99	99	98	99	98	98	100

Note. PIQ = Performance IQ. Based on the correlations between the WIAT–II standard scores and the WISC–III PIQ across the 11 age ranges, and an adjustment for the difference between norming dates (refer to Chapter 7 of the *WIAT–II Examiner's Manual*). Presented in the order shown in the table, the average correlations for the nine WIAT–II subtests are .42, .46, .45, .37, .33, .58, .40, .51, and .36, and the average correlations for the five WIAT–II composites are .43, .56, .42, .51, and .55.

Table H.6. WIAT–II Subtest and Composite Standard Scores Predicted From the WISC–III PIQ Scores for Children Aged 6:0–16:11 *(continued)*

| | Subtest Standard Scores | | | | | | | | | Composite Standard Scores | | | | | |
PIQ Score	Word Read	Num Ops	Read Comp	Spelling	Pseudowd Decod	Math Reason	Written Expr	Listen Comp	Oral Expr	Read	Math	Written Lang	Oral Lang	Total	PIQ Score
101	99	99	99	99	99	99	99	99	99	99	99	99	99	99	101
102	100	100	100	100	100	99	100	99	100	100	99	100	99	99	102
103	100	100	100	100	100	100	100	100	100	100	100	100	100	100	103
104	100	100	100	100	100	101	100	101	100	100	101	100	101	101	104
105	101	101	101	101	101	101	101	101	101	101	101	101	101	101	105
106	101	101	101	101	101	102	101	102	101	101	102	101	102	102	106
107	102	102	102	101	101	102	102	102	101	102	102	102	102	102	107
108	102	102	102	102	102	103	102	103	102	102	103	102	103	103	108
109	102	103	103	102	102	103	102	103	102	103	103	102	103	103	109
110	103	103	103	103	102	104	103	104	103	103	104	103	104	104	110
111	103	104	104	103	103	105	103	104	103	103	104	103	104	104	111
112	104	104	104	103	103	105	104	105	103	104	105	104	105	105	112
113	104	105	105	104	103	106	104	105	104	104	106	104	105	106	113
114	105	105	105	104	104	106	104	106	104	105	106	105	106	106	114
115	105	105	105	104	104	107	105	106	104	105	107	105	106	107	115
116	105	106	106	105	104	107	105	107	105	106	107	105	107	107	116
117	106	106	106	105	105	108	106	107	105	106	108	106	107	108	117
118	106	107	107	106	105	109	106	108	105	106	108	106	108	108	118
119	107	107	107	106	105	109	106	108	106	107	109	107	108	109	119
120	107	108	108	106	106	110	107	109	106	107	109	107	109	109	120
121	107	108	108	107	106	110	107	109	107	108	110	107	109	110	121
122	108	109	109	107	106	111	108	110	107	108	111	108	110	110	122
123	108	109	109	107	107	112	108	110	107	109	111	108	110	111	123
124	109	110	109	108	107	112	108	111	108	109	112	109	111	112	124
125	109	110	110	108	107	113	109	111	108	109	112	109	111	112	125
126	110	111	110	108	108	113	109	112	108	110	113	110	112	113	126
127	110	111	111	109	108	114	110	112	109	110	113	110	112	113	127
128	110	111	111	109	108	114	110	113	109	111	114	110	113	114	128
129	111	112	112	110	109	115	110	113	109	111	114	111	113	114	129
130	111	112	112	110	109	116	111	114	110	112	115	111	114	115	130
131	112	113	113	110	109	117	111	114	110	112	116	112	114	115	131
132	112	113	113	111	110	117	112	115	110	112	116	112	115	116	132
133	112	114	114	111	110	117	112	115	111	113	117	112	115	117	133
134	113	114	114	111	110	118	112	116	111	113	117	113	116	117	134
135	113	115	114	112	111	118	113	116	112	114	118	113	116	118	135
136	114	115	115	112	111	119	113	117	112	114	118	114	117	118	136
137	114	116	115	113	111	120	114	117	112	115	119	114	117	119	137
138	115	116	116	113	112	120	114	118	113	115	119	115	118	119	138
139	115	116	116	113	112	121	114	118	113	115	120	115	118	120	139
140	115	117	117	114	112	121	115	119	113	116	121	115	119	120	140
141	116	117	117	114	113	122	115	119	114	116	121	116	119	121	141
142	116	118	118	114	113	122	116	120	114	117	122	116	120	122	142
143	117	118	118	115	113	123	116	120	114	117	122	117	120	122	143
144	117	119	118	115	114	124	116	121	115	118	123	117	121	123	144
145	117	119	119	115	114	124	117	121	115	118	123	117	121	123	145
146	118	120	119	116	114	125	117	122	116	118	124	118	122	124	146
147	118	120	120	116	115	125	118	122	116	119	124	118	122	124	147
148	119	121	120	117	115	126	118	123	116	119	125	119	123	125	148
149	119	121	121	117	115	126	118	123	117	120	126	119	123	125	149
150	120	121	121	117	116	127	119	124	117	120	126	120	124	126	150
151	120	122	122	118	116	128	119	124	117	121	127	120	124	126	151
152	120	122	122	118	116	128	120	125	118	121	127	120	125	127	152
153	121	123	123	118	117	129	120	126	118	121	128	121	125	128	153
154	121	123	123	119	117	129	121	126	118	122	128	121	126	128	154
155	122	124	123	119	117	130	121	127	119	122	129	122	126	129	155
156															156
157															157
158															158
159															159
160															160

Note. PIQ = Performance IQ. Based on the correlations between the WIAT–II standard scores and the WISC–III PIQ across the 11 age ranges, and an adjustment for the difference between norming dates (refer to Chapter 7 of the *WIAT–II Examiner's Manual*). Presented in the order shown in the table, the average correlations for the nine WIAT–II subtests are .42, .46, .45, .37, .33, .58, .40, .51, and .36, and the average correlations for the five WIAT–II composites are .43, .56, .42, .51, and .55.

Table H.7. WIAT–II Subtest and Composite Standard Scores Predicted from the WISC–III VCI Scores for Children Aged 6:0–16:11

VCI Score	Subtest Standard Scores									Composite Standard Scores					VCI Score
	Word Read	Num Ops	Read Comp	Spelling	Pseudowd Decod	Math Reason	Written Expr	Listen Comp	Oral Expr	Read	Math	Written Lang	Oral Lang	Total	
40															40
41															41
42															42
43															43
44															44
45															45
46															46
47															47
48															48
49															49
50	67	72	65	72	72	63	73	63	75	65	65	70	63	60	50
51	68	73	66	73	73	64	73	63	75	65	66	71	64	61	51
52	68	73	67	73	73	65	74	64	76	66	67	71	65	62	52
53	69	74	67	74	74	65	74	65	76	67	67	72	66	62	53
54	70	74	68	74	74	66	75	66	77	67	68	73	66	63	54
55	70	75	69	75	75	67	75	66	77	68	69	73	67	64	55
56	71	75	69	75	75	67	76	67	78	69	69	74	68	65	56
57	72	76	70	76	76	68	76	68	78	69	70	74	68	65	57
58	72	76	71	76	77	69	77	68	79	70	71	75	69	66	58
59	73	77	71	77	77	70	78	69	79	71	71	75	70	67	59
60	73	77	72	77	78	70	78	70	80	72	72	76	71	68	60
61	74	78	73	78	78	71	79	71	80	72	73	77	71	69	61
62	75	79	73	78	79	72	79	71	81	73	73	77	72	69	62
63	75	79	74	79	79	72	80	72	81	74	74	78	73	70	63
64	76	80	75	80	80	73	80	73	82	74	75	78	73	71	64
65	77	80	75	80	80	74	81	74	82	75	75	79	74	72	65
66	77	81	76	81	81	75	81	74	83	76	76	79	75	72	66
67	78	81	77	81	81	75	82	75	83	76	77	80	75	73	67
68	79	82	77	82	82	76	82	76	84	77	77	81	76	74	68
69	79	82	78	82	82	77	83	76	84	78	78	81	77	75	69
70	80	83	79	83	83	77	83	77	85	78	79	82	78	75	70
71	80	83	79	83	83	78	84	78	85	79	79	82	78	76	71
72	81	84	80	84	84	79	84	79	85	80	80	83	79	77	72
73	82	84	81	84	85	79	85	79	86	80	81	83	80	78	73
74	82	85	81	85	85	80	85	80	86	81	81	84	80	79	74
75	83	86	82	85	86	81	86	81	87	82	82	85	81	79	75
76	84	86	83	86	86	82	86	81	87	82	83	85	82	80	76
77	84	87	83	87	87	82	87	82	88	83	83	86	82	81	77
78	85	87	84	87	87	83	87	83	88	84	84	86	83	82	78
79	85	88	85	88	88	84	88	84	89	84	85	87	84	82	79
80	86	88	85	88	88	84	88	84	89	85	85	87	85	83	80
81	87	89	86	89	89	85	89	85	90	86	86	88	85	84	81
82	87	89	87	89	89	86	90	86	90	86	87	89	86	85	82
83	88	90	87	90	90	87	90	86	91	87	87	89	87	85	83
84	89	90	88	90	90	87	91	87	91	88	88	90	87	86	84
85	89	91	89	91	91	88	91	88	92	88	89	90	88	87	85
86	90	91	89	91	91	89	92	89	92	89	89	91	89	88	86
87	91	92	90	92	92	89	92	89	93	90	90	91	89	88	87
88	91	92	91	92	93	90	93	90	93	91	91	92	90	89	88
89	92	93	91	93	93	91	93	91	94	91	91	93	91	90	89
90	92	94	92	94	94	92	94	91	94	92	92	93	92	91	90
91	93	94	93	94	94	92	94	92	95	93	93	94	92	92	91
92	94	95	93	95	95	93	95	93	95	93	93	94	93	92	92
93	94	95	94	95	95	94	95	94	96	94	94	95	94	93	93
94	95	96	95	96	96	94	96	94	96	95	95	95	94	94	94
95	96	96	95	96	96	95	96	95	97	95	95	96	95	95	95
96	96	97	96	97	97	96	97	96	97	96	96	97	96	95	96
97	97	97	97	97	97	96	97	96	98	97	97	97	96	96	97
98	97	98	97	98	98	97	98	97	98	97	97	98	97	97	98
99	98	98	98	98	98	98	98	98	99	98	98	98	98	98	99
100	99	99	99	99	99	99	99	99	99	99	99	99	99	98	100

Note. VCI = Verbal Comprehension Index. Based on the correlations between the WIAT–II standard scores and the WISC–III VCI across the 11 age ranges, and an adjustment for the difference between norming dates (refer to Chapter 7 of the *WIAT–II Examiner's Manual*). Presented in the order shown in the table, the average correlations for the nine WIAT–II subtests are .63, .54, .67, .54, .53, .71, .52, .72, and .48, and the average correlations for the five WIAT–II composites are .68, .67, .57, .70, and .77.

H

Table H.7. WIAT–II Subtest and Composite Standard Scores Predicted From the WISC–III VCI Scores for Children Aged 6:0–16:11 *(continued)*

	Subtest Standard Scores									Composite Standard Scores					
VCI Score	Word Read	Num Ops	Read Comp	Spelling	Pseudowd Decod	Math Reason	Written Expr	Listen Comp	Oral Expr	Read	Math	Written Lang	Oral Lang	Total	VCI Score
101	99	99	99	99	99	99	99	99	100	99	99	99	99	99	101
102	100	100	100	100	100	100	100	100	100	100	100	100	100	100	102
103	100	100	101	100	100	100	100	100	100	101	100	100	100	101	103
104	101	101	101	101	101	101	101	101	100	101	101	101	101	102	104
105	101	101	102	101	101	101	101	101	101	102	101	101	101	102	105
106	102	102	103	102	102	102	102	102	101	103	102	102	102	103	106
107	103	102	103	102	102	103	102	103	102	103	103	102	103	104	107
108	103	103	104	103	103	104	103	104	102	104	103	103	104	105	108
109	104	103	105	103	103	104	103	104	103	105	104	103	104	105	109
110	104	104	105	104	104	105	104	105	104	105	105	104	105	106	110
111	105	104	106	104	104	106	104	106	104	106	105	105	106	107	111
112	106	105	107	105	105	106	105	106	104	107	106	105	106	108	112
113	106	105	107	105	105	107	105	107	105	107	107	106	107	108	113
114	107	106	108	106	106	108	106	108	105	108	107	106	108	109	114
115	108	106	109	106	106	108	106	109	106	109	108	107	108	110	115
116	108	107	109	107	107	109	107	109	106	109	109	107	109	111	116
117	109	108	110	108	107	110	107	110	107	110	109	108	110	112	117
118	109	108	111	108	108	111	108	111	107	111	110	109	111	112	118
119	110	109	111	109	109	111	108	111	108	112	111	109	111	113	119
120	111	109	112	109	109	112	109	112	108	112	111	110	112	114	120
121	111	110	113	110	110	113	109	113	109	113	112	110	113	115	121
122	112	110	113	110	110	113	110	114	109	114	113	111	113	115	122
123	113	111	114	111	111	114	110	114	110	114	113	111	114	116	123
124	113	111	115	111	111	115	111	115	110	115	114	112	115	117	124
125	114	112	115	112	112	116	112	116	111	116	115	113	115	118	125
126	115	112	116	112	112	116	112	116	111	116	115	113	116	118	126
127	115	113	117	113	113	117	113	117	112	117	116	114	117	119	127
128	116	113	117	113	113	118	113	118	112	118	117	114	118	120	128
129	116	114	118	114	114	118	114	119	113	118	117	115	118	121	129
130	117	114	119	115	114	119	114	119	113	119	118	115	119	121	130
131	118	115	119	115	115	120	115	120	114	120	119	116	120	122	131
132	118	116	120	116	115	121	115	121	114	120	119	117	120	123	132
133	119	116	121	116	116	121	116	121	115	121	120	117	121	124	133
134	120	117	121	117	117	122	116	122	115	122	121	118	122	125	134
135	120	117	122	117	117	123	117	123	115	122	121	118	122	125	135
136	121	118	123	118	118	123	117	124	116	123	122	119	123	126	136
137	121	118	123	118	118	124	118	124	116	124	123	119	124	127	137
138	122	119	124	119	119	125	118	125	117	124	123	120	125	128	138
139	123	119	125	119	119	125	119	126	117	125	124	121	125	128	139
140	123	120	125	120	120	126	119	126	118	126	125	121	126	129	140
141	124	120	126	120	120	127	120	127	118	126	125	122	127	130	141
142	125	121	127	121	121	128	120	128	119	127	126	122	127	131	142
143	125	121	127	122	121	128	121	129	119	128	127	123	128	131	143
144	126	122	128	122	122	129	121	129	120	128	127	123	129	132	144
145	127	123	129	123	122	130	122	130	120	129	128	124	129	133	145
146	127	123	129	123	123	130	122	131	121	130	129	125	130	134	146
147	128	124	130	124	123	131	123	132	121	131	129	125	131	135	147
148	128	124	131	124	124	132	124	132	122	131	130	126	132	135	148
149	129	125	131	125	125	133	124	133	122	132	131	126	132	136	149
150	130	125	132	125	125	133	125	134	123	133	131	127	133	137	150
151															151
152															152
153															153
154															154
155															155
156															156
157															157
158															158
159															159
160															160

Note. VCI = Verbal Comprehension Index. Based on the correlations between the WIAT–II standard scores and the WISC–III VCI across the 11 age ranges, and an adjustment for the difference between norming dates (refer to Chapter 7 of the *WIAT–II Examiner's Manual*). Presented in the order shown in the table, the average correlations for the nine WIAT–II subtests are .63, .54, .67, .54, .53, .71, .52, .72, and .48, and the average correlations for the five WIAT–II composites are .68, .67, .57, .70, and .77.

Table H.8. WIAT–II Subtest and Composite Standard Scores Predicted From the WISC–III POI Scores for Children Aged 6:0–16:11

	Subtest Standard Scores									Composite Standard Scores					
POI Score	Word Read	Num Ops	Read Comp	Spelling	Pseudowd Decod	Math Reason	Written Expr	Listen Comp	Oral Expr	Read	Math	Written Lang	Oral Lang	Total	POI Score
40															40
41															41
42															42
43															43
44															44
45															45
46															46
47															47
48															48
49															49
50	79	78	76	83	83	70	81	72	82	78	73	80	73	73	50
51	80	79	76	83	83	71	82	73	82	78	73	81	73	73	51
52	80	79	77	83	83	71	82	73	82	78	74	81	74	74	52
53	80	80	77	84	84	72	82	74	83	79	74	82	74	74	53
54	81	80	78	84	84	73	83	74	83	79	75	82	75	75	54
55	81	81	78	84	84	73	83	75	83	80	75	82	75	75	55
56	82	81	79	85	84	74	83	75	84	80	76	83	76	76	56
57	82	81	79	85	85	74	84	76	84	81	76	83	76	76	57
58	82	82	80	85	85	75	84	76	84	81	77	83	77	77	58
59	83	82	80	86	85	75	84	77	85	81	77	84	78	77	59
60	83	83	80	86	86	76	85	77	85	82	78	84	78	78	60
61	84	83	81	86	86	76	85	78	85	82	78	85	79	78	61
62	84	83	81	87	86	77	85	78	86	83	79	85	79	79	62
63	84	84	82	87	87	78	86	79	86	83	79	85	80	79	63
64	85	84	82	87	87	78	86	79	86	84	80	86	80	80	64
65	85	85	83	88	87	79	87	80	87	84	80	86	81	80	65
66	85	85	83	88	88	79	87	80	87	84	81	86	81	81	66
67	86	85	84	88	88	80	87	81	87	85	81	87	82	81	67
68	86	86	84	89	88	80	88	82	88	85	82	87	82	82	68
69	87	86	85	89	89	81	88	82	88	86	82	87	83	82	69
70	87	87	85	89	89	81	88	83	89	86	83	88	83	83	70
71	87	87	85	90	89	82	89	83	89	86	83	88	84	83	71
72	88	87	86	90	90	83	89	84	89	87	84	89	84	84	72
73	88	88	86	90	90	83	89	84	90	87	85	89	85	85	73
74	89	88	87	91	90	84	90	85	90	88	85	89	85	85	74
75	89	89	87	91	91	84	90	85	90	88	86	90	86	86	75
76	89	89	88	91	91	85	90	86	91	89	86	90	86	86	76
77	90	89	88	91	91	85	91	86	91	89	87	90	87	87	77
78	90	90	89	92	92	86	91	87	91	89	87	91	87	87	78
79	91	90	89	92	92	87	91	87	92	90	88	91	88	88	79
80	91	91	90	92	92	87	92	88	92	90	88	92	88	88	80
81	91	91	90	93	93	88	92	88	92	91	89	92	89	89	81
82	92	91	90	93	93	88	93	89	93	91	89	92	89	89	82
83	92	92	91	93	93	89	93	89	93	92	90	93	90	90	83
84	93	92	91	94	94	89	93	90	93	92	90	93	90	90	84
85	93	93	92	94	94	90	94	90	94	92	91	93	91	91	85
86	93	93	92	94	94	90	94	91	94	93	91	94	91	91	86
87	94	94	93	95	95	91	94	92	94	93	92	94	92	92	87
88	94	94	93	95	95	92	95	92	95	94	92	94	92	92	88
89	95	94	94	95	95	92	95	93	95	94	93	95	93	93	89
90	95	95	94	96	96	93	95	93	95	95	93	95	93	93	90
91	95	95	95	96	96	93	96	94	96	95	94	96	94	94	91
92	96	96	95	96	96	94	96	94	96	95	94	96	94	94	92
93	96	96	95	97	97	94	96	95	97	96	95	96	95	95	93
94	96	96	96	97	97	95	97	95	97	96	95	97	95	95	94
95	97	97	96	97	97	96	97	96	97	97	96	97	96	96	95
96	97	97	97	98	98	96	98	96	98	97	96	97	96	96	96
97	98	98	97	98	98	97	98	97	98	97	97	98	97	97	97
98	98	98	98	98	98	97	98	97	98	98	97	98	97	97	98
99	98	98	98	99	99	98	99	98	99	98	98	99	98	98	99
100	99	99	99	99	99	98	99	98	99	99	98	99	98	98	100

Note. POI = Perceptual Organization Index. Based on the correlations between the WIAT–II standard scores and the WISC–III POI across the 11 age ranges, and an adjustment for the difference between norming dates (refer to Chapter 7 of the *WIAT–II Examiner's Manual*). Presented in the order shown in the table, the average correlations for the nine WIAT–II subtests are .39, .41, .46, .33, .33, .56, .36, .53, and .35, and the average correlations for the five WIAT–II composites are .42, .52, .37, .51, and .52.

Table H.8. WIAT–II Subtest and Composite Standard Scores Predicted From the WISC–III POI Scores for Children Aged 6:0–16:11 *(continued)*

	Subtest Standard Scores										Composite Standard Scores					
POI Score	Word Read	Num Ops	Read Comp	Spelling	Pseudowd Decod	Math Reason	Written Expr	Listen Comp	Oral Expr		Read	Math	Written Lang	Oral Lang	Total	POI Score
101	99	99	99	99	99	99	99	99	99		99	99	99	99	99	101
102	100	100	100	100	100	99	100	99	100		100	99	100	99	99	102
103	100	100	100	100	100	100	100	100	100		100	100	100	100	100	103
104	100	100	100	100	100	101	100	101	100		100	101	100	101	101	104
105	101	101	101	101	101	101	101	101	101		101	101	101	101	101	105
106	101	101	101	101	101	102	101	102	101		101	102	101	102	102	106
107	102	102	102	101	101	102	101	102	101		102	102	101	102	102	107
108	102	102	102	102	102	103	102	103	102		102	103	102	103	103	108
109	102	102	103	102	102	103	102	103	102		103	103	102	103	103	109
110	103	103	103	102	102	104	102	104	102		103	104	103	104	104	110
111	103	103	104	103	103	104	103	104	103		103	104	103	104	104	111
112	104	104	104	103	103	105	103	105	103		104	105	103	105	105	112
113	104	104	105	103	103	106	104	105	103		104	105	104	105	105	113
114	104	104	105	104	104	106	104	106	104		105	106	104	106	106	114
115	105	105	105	104	104	107	104	106	104		105	106	104	106	106	115
116	105	105	106	104	104	107	105	107	105		105	107	105	107	107	116
117	105	106	106	105	105	108	105	107	105		106	107	105	107	107	117
118	106	106	107	105	105	108	105	108	105		106	108	106	108	108	118
119	106	106	107	105	105	109	106	108	106		107	108	106	108	108	119
120	107	107	108	106	106	110	106	109	106		107	109	106	109	109	120
121	107	107	108	106	106	110	106	110	106		108	109	107	109	109	121
122	107	108	109	106	106	111	107	110	107		108	110	107	110	110	122
123	108	108	109	107	107	111	107	111	107		108	110	107	110	110	123
124	108	109	110	107	107	112	107	111	107		109	111	108	111	111	124
125	109	109	110	107	107	112	108	112	108		109	111	108	111	111	125
126	109	109	110	108	108	113	108	112	108		110	112	109	112	112	126
127	109	110	111	108	108	113	109	113	108		110	112	109	112	112	127
128	110	110	111	108	108	114	109	113	109		111	113	109	113	113	128
129	110	111	112	109	109	115	109	114	109		111	113	110	113	113	129
130	111	111	112	109	109	115	110	114	109		111	114	110	114	114	130
131	111	111	113	109	109	116	110	115	110		112	114	110	114	114	131
132	111	112	113	109	110	116	110	115	110		112	115	111	115	115	132
133	112	112	114	110	110	117	111	116	110		113	115	111	115	115	133
134	112	113	114	110	110	117	111	116	111		113	116	111	116	116	134
135	113	113	115	110	111	118	111	117	111		114	117	112	116	117	135
136	113	113	115	111	111	119	112	117	112		114	117	112	117	117	136
137	113	114	115	111	111	119	112	118	112		114	118	113	117	118	137
138	114	114	116	111	112	120	112	118	112		115	118	113	118	118	138
139	114	115	116	112	112	120	113	119	113		115	119	113	118	119	139
140	115	115	117	112	112	121	113	120	113		116	119	114	119	119	140
141	115	115	117	112	113	121	113	120	113		116	120	114	119	120	141
142	115	116	118	113	113	122	114	121	114		116	120	114	120	120	142
143	116	116	118	113	113	122	114	121	114		117	121	115	120	121	143
144	116	117	119	113	114	123	115	122	114		117	121	115	121	121	144
145	116	117	119	114	114	124	115	122	115		118	122	115	121	122	145
146	117	117	120	114	114	124	115	123	115		118	122	116	122	122	146
147	117	118	120	114	115	125	116	123	115		119	123	116	122	123	147
148	118	118	120	115	115	125	116	124	116		119	123	117	123	123	148
149	118	119	121	115	115	126	116	124	116		119	124	117	124	124	149
150	118	119	121	115	116	126	117	125	116		120	124	117	124	124	150
151																151
152																152
153																153
154																154
155																155
156																156
157																157
158																158
159																159
160																160

Note. POI = Perceptual Organization Index. Based on the correlations between the WIAT–II standard scores and the WISC–III POI across the 11 age ranges, and an adjustment for the difference between norming dates (refer to Chapter 7 of the *WIAT–II Examiner's Manual*). Presented in the order shown in the table, the average correlations for the nine WIAT–II subtests are .39, .41, .46, .33, .33, .56, .36, .53, and .35, and the average correlations for the five WIAT–II composites are .42, .52, .37, .51, and .52.

H

Table H.9. WIAT–II Subtest and Composite Standard Scores Predicted From the WAIS–III FSIQ Scores for Individuals Aged 16:0–19:11

FSIQ Score	Subtest Standard Scores									Composite Standard Scores					FSIQ Score
	Word Read	Num Ops	Read Comp	Spelling	Pseudowd Decod	Math Reason	Written Expr	Listen Comp	Oral Expr	Read	Math	Written Lang	Oral Lang	Total	
40															40
41															41
42															42
43															43
44															44
45	62	59	63	63	68	56	68	58	73	59	55	63	57	53	45
46	63	60	64	64	68	57	68	59	74	60	56	64	58	54	46
47	63	61	64	65	69	57	69	59	74	61	57	64	59	55	47
48	64	61	65	65	70	58	69	60	75	62	58	65	60	56	48
49	65	62	66	66	70	59	70	61	75	62	59	66	60	56	49
50	65	63	66	67	71	60	71	62	76	63	59	66	61	57	50
51	66	63	67	67	71	61	71	62	76	64	60	67	62	58	51
52	67	64	68	68	72	61	72	63	77	65	61	68	63	59	52
53	67	65	68	69	73	62	72	64	77	65	62	68	64	60	53
54	68	66	69	69	73	63	73	65	78	66	63	69	64	61	54
55	69	66	70	70	74	64	73	65	78	67	63	70	65	62	55
56	69	67	70	71	74	65	74	66	78	67	64	70	66	62	56
57	70	68	71	71	75	65	75	67	79	68	65	71	67	63	57
58	71	69	72	72	75	66	75	68	79	69	66	72	67	64	58
59	72	69	72	73	76	67	76	69	80	70	67	72	68	65	59
60	72	70	73	73	77	68	76	69	80	70	67	73	69	66	60
61	73	71	74	74	77	69	77	70	81	71	68	74	70	67	61
62	74	72	74	75	78	69	78	71	81	72	69	74	71	68	62
63	74	72	75	75	78	70	78	72	82	73	70	75	71	68	63
64	75	73	76	76	79	71	79	72	82	73	71	76	72	69	64
65	76	74	76	77	80	72	79	73	83	74	72	76	73	70	65
66	76	75	77	77	80	73	80	74	83	75	72	77	74	71	66
67	77	75	78	78	81	74	81	75	84	76	73	78	74	72	67
68	78	76	78	79	81	74	81	75	84	76	74	78	75	73	68
69	78	77	79	79	82	75	82	76	85	77	75	79	76	73	69
70	79	78	80	80	82	76	82	77	85	78	76	80	77	74	70
71	80	78	80	81	83	77	83	78	86	79	76	80	77	75	71
72	81	79	81	81	84	78	84	79	86	79	77	81	78	76	72
73	81	80	82	82	84	78	84	79	87	80	78	82	79	77	73
74	82	81	82	83	85	79	85	80	87	81	79	83	80	78	74
75	83	81	83	83	85	80	85	81	88	82	80	83	81	79	75
76	83	82	84	84	86	81	86	82	88	82	80	84	81	79	76
77	84	83	84	85	87	82	86	82	89	83	81	85	82	80	77
78	85	84	85	85	87	82	87	83	89	84	82	85	83	81	78
79	85	84	86	86	88	83	88	84	90	84	83	86	84	82	79
80	86	85	87	87	88	84	88	85	90	85	84	87	84	83	80
81	87	86	87	87	89	85	89	85	91	86	85	87	85	84	81
82	88	87	88	88	89	86	89	86	91	87	85	88	86	85	82
83	88	87	89	89	90	86	90	87	92	87	86	89	87	85	83
84	89	88	89	89	91	87	91	88	92	88	87	89	88	86	84
85	90	89	90	90	91	88	91	88	93	89	88	90	88	87	85
86	90	90	91	91	92	89	92	89	93	90	89	91	89	88	86
87	91	90	91	91	92	90	92	90	94	90	89	91	90	89	87
88	92	91	92	92	93	90	93	91	94	91	90	92	91	90	88
89	92	92	93	93	94	91	94	92	95	92	91	93	91	91	89
90	93	93	93	93	94	92	94	92	95	93	92	93	92	91	90
91	94	93	94	94	95	93	95	93	96	93	93	94	93	92	91
92	94	94	95	95	95	94	95	94	96	94	93	95	94	93	92
93	95	95	95	95	96	94	96	95	97	95	94	95	95	94	93
94	96	96	96	96	96	95	96	95	97	96	95	96	95	95	94
95	97	96	97	97	97	96	97	96	98	96	96	97	96	96	95
96	97	97	97	97	98	97	98	97	98	97	97	97	97	97	96
97	98	98	98	98	98	98	98	98	99	98	98	98	98	97	97
98	99	99	99	99	99	98	99	98	99	99	98	99	98	98	98
99	99	99	99	99	99	99	99	99	100	99	99	99	99	99	99
100	100	100	100	100	100	100	100	100	100	100	100	100	100	100	100

Note. FSIQ = Full Scale IQ. Based on the correlations between the WIAT–II standard scores and the WAIS–III FSIQ across the four age ranges. Presented in the order shown in the table, the average correlations for the nine WIAT–II subtests are .69, .75, .67, .67, .59, .80, .59, .77, and .49, and the average correlations for the five WIAT–II composites are .74, .81, .67, .78, and .86.

H

Table H.9. WIAT–II Subtest and Composite Standard Scores Predicted From the WAIS–III FSIQ Scores for Individuals Aged 16:0–19:11 *(continued)*

	Subtest Standard Scores									Composite Standard Scores					
FSIQ Score	Word Read	Num Ops	Read Comp	Spelling	Pseudowd Decod	Math Reason	Written Expr	Listen Comp	Oral Expr	Read	Math	Written Lang	Oral Lang	Total	FSIQ Score
101	101	101	101	101	101	101	101	101	100	101	101	101	101	101	101
102	101	101	101	101	101	102	101	102	101	101	102	101	102	102	102
103	102	102	102	102	102	102	102	102	101	102	102	102	102	103	103
104	103	103	103	103	102	103	102	103	102	103	103	103	103	103	104
105	103	104	103	103	103	104	103	104	102	104	104	103	104	104	105
106	104	104	104	104	104	105	104	105	103	104	105	104	105	105	106
107	105	105	105	105	104	106	104	105	103	105	106	105	105	106	107
108	106	106	105	105	105	106	105	106	104	106	107	105	106	107	108
109	106	107	106	106	105	107	105	107	104	107	107	106	107	108	109
110	107	107	107	107	106	108	106	108	105	107	108	107	108	109	110
111	108	108	107	107	106	109	106	108	105	108	109	107	109	109	111
112	108	109	108	108	107	110	107	109	106	109	110	108	109	110	112
113	109	110	109	109	108	110	108	110	106	110	111	109	110	111	113
114	110	110	109	109	108	111	108	111	107	110	111	109	111	112	114
115	110	111	110	110	109	112	109	112	107	111	112	110	112	113	115
116	111	112	111	111	109	113	109	112	108	112	113	111	112	114	116
117	112	113	111	111	110	114	110	113	108	113	114	111	113	115	117
118	112	113	112	112	111	114	111	114	109	113	115	112	114	115	118
119	113	114	113	113	111	115	111	115	109	114	115	113	115	116	119
120	114	115	113	113	112	116	112	115	110	115	116	113	116	117	120
121	115	116	114	114	112	117	112	116	110	116	117	114	117	118	121
122	115	116	115	115	113	118	113	117	111	116	118	115	117	119	122
123	116	117	116	115	113	118	114	118	111	117	119	115	118	120	123
124	117	118	116	116	114	119	114	118	112	118	120	116	119	121	124
125	117	119	117	117	115	120	115	119	112	118	120	117	119	121	125
126	118	119	118	117	115	121	115	120	113	119	121	117	120	122	126
127	119	120	118	118	116	122	116	121	113	120	122	118	121	123	127
128	119	121	119	119	116	122	116	121	114	121	123	119	122	124	128
129	120	122	120	119	117	123	117	122	114	121	124	120	123	125	129
130	121	122	120	120	118	124	118	123	115	122	124	120	123	126	130
131	122	123	121	121	118	125	118	124	115	123	125	121	124	127	131
132	122	124	122	121	119	126	119	125	116	124	126	122	125	127	132
133	123	125	122	122	119	126	119	125	116	124	127	122	126	128	133
134	124	125	123	123	120	127	120	126	117	125	128	123	126	129	134
135	124	126	124	123	120	128	121	127	117	126	128	124	127	130	135
136	125	127	124	124	121	129	121	128	118	127	129	124	128	131	136
137	126	128	125	125	122	130	122	128	118	127	130	125	129	132	137
138	126	128	126	125	122	131	122	129	119	128	131	126	129	132	138
139	127	129	126	126	123	131	123	130	119	129	132	126	130	133	139
140	128	130	127	127	123	132	124	131	120	130	133	127	131	134	140
141	128	131	128	127	124	133	124	131	120	130	133	128	132	135	141
142	129	131	128	128	125	134	125	132	121	131	134	128	133	136	142
143	130	132	129	129	125	135	125	133	121	132	135	129	133	137	143
144	131	133	130	129	126	135	126	134	122	133	136	130	134	138	144
145	131	134	130	130	126	136	127	135	122	133	137	130	135	138	145
146	132	134	131	131	127	137	127	135	122	134	137	131	136	139	146
147	133	135	132	131	127	138	128	136	123	135	138	132	136	140	147
148	133	136	132	132	128	139	128	137	123	135	139	132	137	141	148
149	134	137	133	133	129	139	129	138	124	136	140	133	138	142	149
150	135	137	134	133	129	140	129	138	124	137	141	134	139	143	150
151	135	138	134	134	130	141	130	139	125	138	141	134	140	144	151
152	136	139	135	135	130	142	131	140	125	138	142	135	140	144	152
153	137	139	136	135	131	143	131	141	126	139	143	136	141	145	153
154	137	140	136	136	132	143	132	141	126	140	144	136	142	146	154
155	138	141	137	137	132	144	132	142	127	141	145	137	143	147	155
156															156
157															157
158															158
159															159
160															160

Note. FSIQ = Full Scale IQ. Based on the correlations between the WIAT–II standard scores and the WAIS–III FSIQ across the four age ranges. Presented in the order shown in the table, the average correlations for the nine WIAT–II subtests are .69, .75, .67, .67, .59, .80, .59, .77, and .49, and the average correlations for the five WIAT–II composites are .74, .81, .67, .78, and .86.

Table H.10. WIAT–II Subtest and Composite Standard Scores Predicted From the WAIS–III VIQ Scores for Individuals Aged 16:0–19:11

	Subtest Standard Scores									Composite Standard Scores					
VIQ Score	Word Read	Num Ops	Read Comp	Spelling	Pseudowd Decod	Math Reason	Written Expr	Listen Comp	Oral Expr	Read	Math	Written Lang	Oral Lang	Total	VIQ Score
40															40
41															41
42															42
43															43
44															44
45															45
46															46
47															47
48	63	63	62	66	69	62	70	58	77	60	61	66	60	57	48
49	63	64	63	67	69	63	71	59	77	60	62	67	61	58	49
50	64	65	64	68	70	64	71	60	78	61	63	67	62	59	50
51	65	66	65	68	70	64	72	60	78	62	63	68	62	60	51
52	66	66	65	69	71	65	73	61	79	63	64	69	63	60	52
53	66	67	66	70	72	66	73	62	79	63	65	69	64	61	53
54	67	68	67	70	72	67	74	63	80	64	66	70	65	62	54
55	68	68	67	71	73	67	74	64	80	65	66	71	65	63	55
56	68	69	68	72	73	68	75	64	81	66	67	71	66	64	56
57	69	70	69	72	74	69	75	65	81	67	68	72	67	64	57
58	70	70	70	73	75	69	76	66	81	67	69	73	68	65	58
59	71	71	70	74	75	70	77	67	82	68	69	73	68	66	59
60	71	72	71	74	76	71	77	68	82	69	70	74	69	67	60
61	72	73	72	75	76	72	78	68	83	70	71	74	70	68	61
62	73	73	72	75	77	72	78	69	83	70	72	75	71	69	62
63	73	74	73	76	78	73	79	70	84	71	72	76	72	69	63
64	74	75	74	77	78	74	79	71	84	72	73	76	72	70	64
65	75	75	75	77	79	75	80	72	84	73	74	77	73	71	65
66	76	76	75	78	79	75	81	73	85	74	75	78	74	72	66
67	76	77	76	79	80	76	81	73	85	74	75	78	75	73	67
68	77	78	77	79	81	77	82	74	86	75	76	79	75	74	68
69	78	78	78	80	81	77	82	75	86	76	77	80	76	74	69
70	78	79	78	81	82	78	83	76	87	77	78	80	77	75	70
71	79	80	79	81	82	79	83	77	87	77	78	81	78	76	71
72	80	80	80	82	83	80	84	77	88	78	79	82	78	77	72
73	81	81	80	83	84	80	85	78	88	79	80	82	79	78	73
74	81	82	81	83	84	81	85	79	88	80	81	83	80	79	74
75	82	82	82	84	85	82	86	80	89	81	81	84	81	79	75
76	83	83	83	84	86	83	86	81	89	81	82	84	82	80	76
77	84	84	83	85	86	83	87	81	90	82	83	85	82	81	77
78	84	85	84	86	87	84	87	82	90	83	84	86	83	82	78
79	85	85	85	86	87	85	88	83	91	84	84	86	84	83	79
80	86	86	86	87	88	85	89	84	91	84	85	87	85	83	80
81	86	87	86	88	89	86	89	85	92	85	86	88	85	84	81
82	87	87	87	88	89	87	90	85	92	86	87	88	86	85	82
83	88	88	88	89	90	88	90	86	92	87	87	89	87	86	83
84	89	89	88	90	90	88	91	87	93	88	88	90	88	87	84
85	89	89	89	90	91	89	91	88	93	88	89	90	88	88	85
86	90	90	90	91	92	90	92	89	94	89	90	91	89	88	86
87	91	91	91	92	92	91	93	89	94	90	90	91	90	89	87
88	91	92	91	92	93	91	93	90	95	91	91	92	91	90	88
89	92	92	92	93	93	92	94	91	95	91	92	93	92	91	89
90	93	93	93	94	94	93	94	92	96	92	93	93	92	92	90
91	94	94	93	94	95	93	95	93	96	93	93	94	93	93	91
92	94	94	94	95	95	94	95	94	96	94	94	95	94	93	92
93	95	95	95	95	96	95	96	94	97	95	95	95	95	94	93
94	96	96	96	96	96	96	97	95	97	95	96	96	95	95	94
95	96	96	96	97	97	96	97	96	98	96	96	97	96	96	95
96	97	97	97	97	98	97	98	97	98	97	97	97	97	97	96
97	98	98	98	98	98	98	98	98	99	98	98	98	98	98	97
98	99	99	99	99	99	99	99	98	99	98	99	99	98	98	98
99	99	99	99	99	99	99	99	99	100	99	99	99	99	99	99
100	100	100	100	100	100	100	100	100	100	100	100	100	100	100	100

Note. VIQ = Verbal IQ. Based on the correlations between the WIAT–II standard scores and the WAIS–III VIQ across the four age ranges. Presented in the order shown in the table, the average correlations for the nine WIAT–II subtests are .72, .70, .72, .65, .60, .73, .57, .81, and .44, and the average correlations for the five WIAT–II composites are .78, .75, .65, .77, and .83.

H

Table H.10. WIAT–II Subtest and Composite Standard Scores Predicted From the WAIS–III VIQ Scores for Individuals Aged 16:0–19:11 *(continued)*

	Subtest Standard Scores									Composite Standard Scores					
VIQ Score	Word Read	Num Ops	Read Comp	Spelling	Pseudowd Decod	Math Reason	Written Expr	Listen Comp	Oral Expr	Read	Math	Written Lang	Oral Lang	Total	VIQ Score
101	101	101	101	101	101	101	101	101	100	101	101	101	101	101	101
102	101	101	101	101	101	101	101	102	101	102	101	101	102	102	102
103	102	102	102	102	102	102	102	102	101	102	102	102	102	102	103
104	103	103	103	103	102	103	102	103	102	103	103	103	103	103	104
105	104	104	104	103	103	104	103	104	102	104	104	103	104	104	105
106	104	104	104	104	104	104	103	105	103	105	104	104	105	105	106
107	105	105	105	105	104	105	104	106	103	105	105	105	105	106	107
108	106	106	106	105	105	106	105	106	104	106	106	105	106	107	108
109	106	106	107	106	105	107	105	107	104	107	107	106	107	107	109
110	107	107	107	106	106	107	106	108	104	108	107	107	108	108	110
111	108	108	108	107	107	108	106	109	105	109	108	107	108	109	111
112	109	108	109	108	107	109	107	110	105	109	109	108	109	110	112
113	109	109	109	108	108	109	107	111	106	110	110	109	110	111	113
114	110	110	110	109	108	110	108	111	106	111	110	109	111	112	114
115	111	111	111	110	109	111	109	112	107	112	111	110	112	112	115
116	111	111	112	110	110	112	109	113	107	112	112	110	112	113	116
117	112	112	112	111	110	112	110	114	108	113	113	111	113	114	117
118	113	113	113	112	111	113	110	115	108	114	113	112	114	115	118
119	114	113	114	112	111	114	111	115	108	115	114	112	115	116	119
120	114	114	114	113	112	115	111	116	109	116	115	113	115	117	120
121	115	115	115	114	113	115	112	117	109	116	116	114	116	117	121
122	116	115	116	114	113	116	113	118	110	117	116	114	117	118	122
123	116	116	117	115	114	117	113	119	110	118	117	115	118	119	123
124	117	117	117	116	114	117	114	119	111	119	118	116	118	120	124
125	118	118	118	116	115	118	114	120	111	119	119	116	119	121	125
126	119	118	119	117	116	119	115	121	112	120	119	117	120	121	126
127	119	119	120	117	116	120	115	122	112	121	120	118	121	122	127
128	120	120	120	118	117	120	116	123	112	122	121	118	122	123	128
129	121	120	121	119	118	121	117	123	113	123	122	119	122	124	129
130	122	121	122	119	118	122	117	124	113	123	122	120	123	125	130
131	122	122	122	120	119	123	118	125	114	124	123	120	124	126	131
132	123	122	123	121	119	123	118	126	114	125	124	121	125	126	132
133	124	123	124	121	120	124	119	127	115	126	125	122	125	127	133
134	124	124	125	122	121	125	119	127	115	126	125	122	126	128	134
135	125	125	125	123	121	125	120	128	116	127	126	123	127	129	135
136	126	125	126	123	122	126	121	129	116	128	127	124	128	130	136
137	127	126	127	124	122	127	121	130	116	129	128	124	128	131	137
138	127	127	128	125	123	128	122	131	117	130	128	125	129	131	138
139	128	127	128	125	124	128	122	132	117	130	129	126	130	132	139
140	129	128	129	126	124	129	123	132	118	131	130	126	131	133	140
141	129	129	130	126	125	130	123	133	118	132	131	127	132	134	141
142	130	130	130	127	125	131	124	134	119	133	131	127	132	135	142
143	131	130	131	128	126	131	125	135	119	133	132	128	133	136	143
144	132	131	132	128	127	132	125	136	119	134	133	129	134	136	144
145	132	132	133	129	127	133	126	136	120	135	134	129	135	137	145
146	133	132	133	130	128	133	126	137	120	136	134	130	135	138	146
147	134	133	134	130	128	134	127	138	121	137	135	131	136	139	147
148	134	134	135	131	129	135	127	139	121	137	136	131	137	140	148
149	135	134	135	132	130	136	128	140	122	138	137	132	138	140	149
150	136	135	136	132	130	136	129	140	122	139	137	133	138	141	150
151	137	136	137	133	131	137	129	141	123	140	138	133	139	142	151
152	137	137	138	134	131	138	130	142	123	140	139	134	140	143	152
153	138	137	138	134	132	139	130	143	123	141	140	135	141	144	153
154	139	138	139	135	133	139	131	144	124	142	140	135	142	145	154
155	139	139	140	136	133	140	131	144	124	143	141	136	142	145	155
156															156
157															157
158															158
159															159
160															160

Note. VIQ = Verbal IQ. Based on the correlations between the WIAT–II standard scores and the WAIS–III VIQ across the four age ranges. Presented in the order shown in the table, the average correlations for the nine WIAT–II subtests are .72, .70, .72, .65, .60, .73, .57, .81, and .44, and the average correlations for the five WIAT–II composites are .78, .75, .65, .77, and .83.

Table H.11. WIAT–II Subtest and Composite Standard Scores Predicted From the WAIS–III PIQ Scores for Individuals Aged 16:0–19:11

	Subtest Standard Scores									Composite Standard Scores					
PIQ Score	Word Read	Num Ops	Read Comp	Spelling	Pseudowd Decod	Math Reason	Written Expr	Listen Comp	Oral Expr	Read	Math	Written Lang	Oral Lang	Total	PIQ Score
40															40
41															41
42															42
43															43
44															44
45															45
46															46
47	75	67	78	72	77	62	74	73	75	74	62	71	66	62	47
48	75	67	79	73	78	63	75	74	75	74	63	71	67	62	48
49	76	68	79	73	78	64	75	74	76	75	64	72	68	63	49
50	76	69	80	74	79	64	76	75	76	75	64	73	68	64	50
51	77	69	80	74	79	65	76	75	77	76	65	73	69	65	51
52	77	70	80	75	79	66	77	76	77	76	66	74	70	65	52
53	78	71	81	75	80	66	77	76	78	77	66	74	70	66	53
54	78	71	81	76	80	67	78	77	78	77	67	75	71	67	54
55	79	72	82	76	81	68	78	77	79	78	68	75	72	68	55
56	79	72	82	77	81	69	79	78	79	78	69	76	72	68	56
57	80	73	82	78	82	69	79	78	80	79	69	76	73	69	57
58	80	74	83	78	82	70	80	79	80	79	70	77	73	70	58
59	80	74	83	79	82	71	80	79	81	80	71	77	74	70	59
60	81	75	84	79	83	71	81	80	81	80	71	78	75	71	60
61	81	76	84	80	83	72	81	80	82	81	72	79	75	72	61
62	82	76	84	80	84	73	82	81	82	81	73	79	76	73	62
63	82	77	85	81	84	74	82	81	82	82	74	80	77	73	63
64	83	77	85	81	85	74	83	82	83	82	74	80	77	74	64
65	83	78	86	82	85	75	83	82	83	83	75	81	78	75	65
66	84	79	86	82	85	76	83	83	84	83	76	81	78	75	66
67	84	79	86	83	86	76	84	83	84	84	76	82	79	76	67
68	85	80	87	83	86	77	84	84	85	84	77	82	80	77	68
69	85	81	87	84	87	78	85	84	85	85	78	83	80	78	69
70	86	81	88	84	87	79	85	85	86	85	79	84	81	78	70
71	86	82	88	85	88	79	86	85	86	86	79	84	82	79	71
72	87	82	89	85	88	80	86	86	87	86	80	85	82	80	72
73	87	83	89	86	88	81	87	86	87	87	81	85	83	81	73
74	88	84	89	86	89	81	87	87	88	87	81	86	84	81	74
75	88	84	90	87	89	82	88	87	88	88	82	86	84	82	75
76	89	85	90	87	90	83	88	88	89	88	83	87	85	83	76
77	89	86	91	88	90	84	89	88	89	89	84	87	85	83	77
78	90	86	91	88	91	84	89	89	90	89	84	88	86	84	78
79	90	87	91	89	91	85	90	89	90	90	85	88	87	85	79
80	90	87	92	90	91	86	90	90	91	90	86	89	87	86	80
81	91	88	92	90	92	86	91	90	91	91	86	90	88	86	81
82	91	89	93	91	92	87	91	91	91	91	87	90	89	87	82
83	92	89	93	91	93	88	92	91	92	92	88	91	89	88	83
84	92	90	93	92	93	89	92	92	92	92	89	91	90	88	84
85	93	91	94	92	94	89	93	92	93	93	89	92	91	89	85
86	93	91	94	93	94	90	93	93	93	93	90	92	91	90	86
87	94	92	95	93	94	91	94	93	94	94	91	93	92	91	87
88	94	92	95	94	95	91	94	94	94	94	91	93	92	91	88
89	95	93	95	94	95	92	95	94	95	95	92	94	93	92	89
90	95	94	96	95	96	93	95	95	95	95	93	95	94	93	90
91	96	94	96	95	96	94	96	95	96	96	94	95	94	94	91
92	96	95	97	96	97	94	96	96	96	96	94	96	95	94	92
93	97	96	97	96	97	95	97	96	97	97	95	96	96	95	93
94	97	96	98	97	97	96	97	97	97	97	96	97	96	96	94
95	98	97	98	97	98	96	98	97	98	98	96	97	97	96	95
96	98	97	98	98	98	97	98	98	98	98	97	98	97	97	96
97	99	98	99	98	99	98	99	98	99	99	98	98	98	98	97
98	99	99	99	99	99	99	99	99	99	99	99	99	99	99	98
99	100	99	100	99	100	99	100	99	100	100	99	99	99	99	99
100	100	100	100	100	100	100	100	100	100	100	100	100	100	100	100

Note. PIQ = Performance IQ. Based on the correlations between the WIAT–II standard scores and the WAIS–III PIQ across the four age ranges. Presented in the order shown in the table, the average correlations for the nine WIAT–II subtests are .48, .63, .41, .52, .43, .72, .49, .50, and .47, and the average correlations for the five WIAT–II composites are .49, .72, .55, .63, and .72.

Table H.11. WIAT–II Subtest and Composite Standard Scores Predicted From the WAIS–III PIQ Scores for Individuals Aged 16:0–19:11 *(continued)*

	Subtest Standard Scores										Composite Standard Scores					
PIQ Score	Word Read	Num Ops	Read Comp	Spelling	Pseudowd Decod	Math Reason	Written Expr	Listen Comp	Oral Expr		Read	Math	Written Lang	Oral Lang	Total	PIQ Score
101	100	101	100	101	100	101	100	101	100		100	101	101	101	101	101
102	101	101	101	101	101	101	101	101	101		101	101	101	101	101	102
103	101	102	101	102	101	102	101	102	101		101	102	102	102	102	103
104	102	103	102	102	102	103	102	102	102		102	103	102	103	103	104
105	102	103	102	103	102	104	102	103	102		102	104	103	103	104	105
106	103	104	102	103	103	104	103	103	103		103	104	103	104	104	106
107	103	104	103	104	103	105	103	104	103		103	105	104	104	105	107
108	104	105	103	104	103	106	104	104	104		104	106	104	105	106	108
109	104	106	104	105	104	106	104	105	104		104	106	105	106	106	109
110	105	106	104	105	104	107	105	105	105		105	107	106	106	107	110
111	105	107	105	106	105	108	105	106	105		105	108	106	107	108	111
112	106	108	105	106	105	109	106	106	106		106	109	107	108	109	112
113	106	108	105	107	106	109	106	107	106		106	109	107	108	109	113
114	107	109	106	107	106	110	107	107	107		107	110	108	109	110	114
115	107	109	106	108	106	111	107	108	107		107	111	108	109	111	115
116	108	110	107	108	107	111	108	108	108		108	111	109	110	112	116
117	108	111	107	109	107	112	108	109	108		108	112	109	111	112	117
118	109	111	107	109	108	113	109	109	109		109	113	110	111	113	118
119	109	112	108	110	108	114	109	110	109		109	114	110	112	114	119
120	110	113	108	110	109	114	110	110	109		110	114	111	113	114	120
121	110	113	109	111	109	115	110	111	110		110	115	112	113	115	121
122	110	114	109	112	109	116	111	111	110		111	116	112	114	116	122
123	111	114	109	112	110	116	111	112	111		111	116	113	115	117	123
124	111	115	110	113	110	117	112	112	111		112	117	113	115	117	124
125	112	116	110	113	111	118	112	113	112		112	118	114	116	118	125
126	112	116	111	114	111	119	113	113	112		113	119	114	116	119	126
127	113	117	111	114	112	119	113	114	113		113	119	115	117	119	127
128	113	118	111	115	112	120	114	114	113		114	120	115	118	120	128
129	114	118	112	115	112	121	114	115	114		114	121	116	118	121	129
130	114	119	112	116	113	121	115	115	114		115	121	117	119	122	130
131	115	119	113	116	113	122	115	116	115		115	122	117	120	122	131
132	115	120	113	117	114	123	116	116	115		116	123	118	120	123	132
133	116	121	114	117	114	124	116	117	116		116	124	118	121	124	133
134	116	121	114	118	115	124	117	117	116		117	124	119	122	125	134
135	117	122	114	118	115	125	117	118	117		117	125	119	122	125	135
136	117	123	115	119	115	126	117	118	117		118	126	120	123	126	136
137	118	123	115	119	116	126	118	119	118		118	126	120	123	127	137
138	118	124	116	120	116	127	118	119	118		119	127	121	124	127	138
139	119	124	116	120	117	128	119	120	118		119	128	121	125	128	139
140	119	125	116	121	117	129	119	120	119		120	129	122	125	129	140
141	120	126	117	121	118	129	120	121	119		120	129	123	126	130	141
142	120	126	117	122	118	130	120	121	120		121	130	123	127	130	142
143	120	127	118	122	118	131	121	122	120		121	131	124	127	131	143
144	121	128	118	123	119	131	121	122	121		122	131	124	128	132	144
145	121	128	118	124	119	132	122	123	121		122	132	125	128	132	145
146	122	129	119	124	120	133	122	123	122		123	133	125	129	133	146
147	122	129	119	125	120	134	123	124	122		123	134	126	130	134	147
148	123	130	120	125	121	134	123	124	123		124	134	126	130	135	148
149	123	131	120	126	121	135	124	125	123		124	135	127	131	135	149
150	124	131	121	126	121	136	124	125	124		125	136	128	132	136	150
151	124	132	121	127	122	136	125	126	124		125	136	128	132	137	151
152	125	133	121	127	122	137	125	126	125		126	137	129	133	138	152
153	125	133	122	128	123	138	126	127	125		126	138	129	134	138	153
154	126	134	122	128	123	139	126	127	126		127	139	130	134	139	154
155	126	134	123	129	124	139	127	128	126		127	139	130	135	140	155
156																156
157																157
158																158
159																159
160																160

Note. PIQ = Performance IQ. Based on the correlations between the WIAT–II standard scores and the WAIS–III PIQ across the four age ranges. Presented in the order shown in the table, the average correlations for the nine WIAT–II subtests are .48, .63, .41, .52, .43, .72, .49, .50, and .47, and the average correlations for the five WIAT–II composites are .49, .72, .55, .63, and .72.

Table H.12. WIAT–II Subtest and Composite Standard Scores Predicted From the WAIS–III VCI Scores for Individuals Aged 16:0–19:11

VCI Score	Word Read	Num Ops	Read Comp	Spelling	Pseudowd Decod	Math Reason	Written Expr	Listen Comp	Oral Expr	Read	Math	Written Lang	Oral Lang	Total	VCI Score
			Subtest Standard Scores									Composite Standard Scores			
40															40
41															41
42															42
43															43
44															44
45															45
46															46
47															47
48															48
49															49
50	65	69	65	71	73	69	74	60	79	63	67	70	63	62	50
51	66	69	66	71	73	69	74	61	79	64	68	71	64	63	51
52	66	70	66	72	74	70	75	62	80	65	69	71	65	64	52
53	67	70	67	73	75	71	75	63	80	65	69	72	65	65	53
54	68	71	68	73	75	71	76	63	81	66	70	72	66	65	54
55	68	72	69	74	76	72	77	64	81	67	71	73	67	66	55
56	69	72	69	74	76	73	77	65	82	68	71	74	68	67	56
57	70	73	70	75	77	73	78	66	82	68	72	74	68	68	57
58	71	74	71	75	77	74	78	67	82	69	73	75	69	68	58
59	71	74	71	76	78	74	79	67	83	70	73	75	70	69	59
60	72	75	72	77	78	75	79	68	83	71	74	76	70	70	60
61	73	75	73	77	79	76	80	69	84	71	74	77	71	71	61
62	73	76	73	78	79	76	80	70	84	72	75	77	72	71	62
63	74	77	74	78	80	77	81	71	84	73	76	78	73	72	63
64	75	77	75	79	81	78	81	71	85	74	76	78	73	73	64
65	75	78	76	80	81	78	82	72	85	74	77	79	74	74	65
66	76	79	76	80	82	79	82	73	86	75	78	80	75	74	66
67	77	79	77	81	82	79	83	74	86	76	78	80	76	75	67
68	78	80	78	81	83	80	83	75	87	76	79	81	76	76	68
69	78	80	78	82	83	81	84	75	87	77	80	81	77	77	69
70	79	81	79	82	84	81	84	76	87	78	80	82	78	77	70
71	80	82	80	83	84	82	85	77	88	79	81	83	79	78	71
72	80	82	80	84	85	83	85	78	88	79	82	83	79	79	72
73	81	83	81	84	85	83	86	79	89	80	82	84	80	80	73
74	82	84	82	85	86	84	86	79	89	81	83	84	81	80	74
75	82	84	83	85	86	84	87	80	90	82	84	85	82	81	75
76	83	85	83	86	87	85	87	81	90	82	84	86	82	82	76
77	84	86	84	87	88	86	88	82	90	83	85	86	83	83	77
78	85	86	85	87	88	86	89	83	91	84	86	87	84	83	78
79	85	87	85	88	89	87	89	83	91	85	86	87	85	84	79
80	86	87	86	88	89	88	90	84	92	85	87	88	85	85	80
81	87	88	87	89	90	88	90	85	92	86	88	89	86	86	81
82	87	89	87	89	90	89	91	86	92	87	88	89	87	86	82
83	88	89	88	90	91	89	91	86	93	88	89	90	87	87	83
84	89	90	89	91	91	90	92	87	93	88	90	90	88	88	84
85	89	91	90	91	92	91	92	88	94	89	90	91	89	89	85
86	90	91	90	92	92	91	93	89	94	90	91	92	90	89	86
87	91	92	91	92	93	92	93	90	95	90	91	92	90	90	87
88	92	92	92	93	94	93	94	90	95	91	92	93	91	91	88
89	92	93	92	94	94	93	94	91	95	92	93	93	92	Total	89
90	93	94	93	94	95	94	95	92	96	93	93	94	93	92	90
91	94	94	94	95	95	94	95	93	96	93	94	95	93	93	91
92	94	95	94	95	96	95	96	94	97	94	95	95	94	94	92
93	95	96	95	96	96	96	96	94	97	95	95	96	95	95	93
94	96	96	96	96	97	96	97	95	97	96	96	96	96	95	94
95	96	97	97	97	97	97	97	96	98	96	97	97	96	96	95
96	97	97	97	98	98	98	98	97	98	97	97	98	97	97	96
97	98	98	98	98	98	98	98	98	99	98	98	98	98	98	97
98	99	99	99	99	99	99	99	98	99	99	99	99	99	98	98
99	99	99	99	99	99	99	99	99	100	99	99	99	99	99	99
100	100	100	100	100	100	100	100	100	100	100	100	100	100	100	100

Note. VCI = Verbal Comprehension Index. Based on the correlations between the WIAT–II standard scores and the WAIS–III VCI across the four age ranges. Presented in the order shown in the table, the average correlations for the nine WIAT–II subtests are .70, .63, .70, .59, .54, .62, .52, .80, and .42, and the average correlations for the five WIAT–II composites are .74, .65, .60, .74, and .75.

H

Table H.12. WIAT–II Subtest and Composite Standard Scores Predicted From the WAIS–III VCI Scores for Individuals Aged 16:0–19:11 (continued)

VCI Score	Word Read	Num Ops	Read Comp	Spelling	Pseudowd Decod	Math Reason	Written Expr	Listen Comp	Oral Expr	Read	Math	Written Lang	Oral Lang	Total	VCI Score
101	101	101	101	101	101	101	101	101	100	101	101	101	101	101	101
102	101	101	101	101	101	101	101	102	101	101	101	101	101	102	102
103	102	102	102	102	102	102	102	102	101	102	102	102	102	102	103
104	103	103	103	102	102	102	102	103	102	103	103	102	103	103	104
105	104	103	103	103	103	103	103	104	102	104	103	103	104	104	105
106	104	104	104	104	103	104	103	105	103	104	104	104	104	105	106
107	105	104	105	104	104	104	104	106	103	105	105	104	105	105	107
108	106	105	106	105	104	105	104	106	103	106	105	105	106	106	108
109	106	106	106	105	105	106	105	107	104	107	106	105	107	107	109
110	107	106	107	106	105	106	105	108	104	107	107	106	107	108	110
111	108	107	108	106	106	107	106	109	105	108	107	107	108	108	111
112	108	108	108	107	106	107	106	110	105	109	108	107	109	109	112
113	109	108	109	108	107	108	107	110	105	110	109	108	110	110	113
114	110	109	110	108	108	109	107	111	106	110	109	108	110	111	114
115	111	109	110	109	108	109	108	112	106	111	110	109	111	111	115
116	111	110	111	109	109	110	108	113	107	112	110	110	112	112	116
117	112	111	112	110	109	111	109	114	107	112	111	110	113	113	117
118	113	111	113	111	110	111	109	114	108	113	112	111	113	114	118
119	113	112	113	111	110	112	110	115	108	114	112	111	114	114	119
120	114	113	114	112	111	112	110	116	108	115	113	112	115	115	120
121	115	113	115	112	111	113	111	117	109	115	114	113	115	116	121
122	115	114	115	113	112	114	111	117	109	116	114	113	116	117	122
123	116	114	116	113	112	114	112	118	110	117	115	114	117	117	123
124	117	115	117	114	113	115	113	119	110	118	116	114	118	118	124
125	118	116	117	115	114	116	113	120	110	118	116	115	118	119	125
126	118	116	118	115	114	116	114	121	111	119	117	116	119	120	126
127	119	117	119	116	115	117	114	121	111	120	118	116	120	120	127
128	120	118	120	116	115	117	115	122	112	121	118	117	121	121	128
129	120	118	120	117	116	118	115	123	112	121	119	117	121	122	129
130	121	119	121	118	116	119	116	124	113	122	120	118	122	123	130
131	122	120	122	118	117	119	116	125	113	123	120	119	123	123	131
132	122	120	122	119	117	120	117	125	113	124	121	119	124	124	132
133	123	121	123	119	118	121	117	126	114	124	122	120	124	125	133
134	124	121	124	120	118	121	118	127	114	125	122	120	125	126	134
135	125	122	124	120	119	122	118	128	115	126	123	121	126	126	135
136	125	123	125	121	119	122	119	129	115	126	124	122	127	127	136
137	126	123	126	122	120	123	119	129	116	127	124	122	127	128	137
138	127	124	127	122	121	124	120	130	116	128	125	123	128	129	138
139	127	125	127	123	121	124	120	131	116	129	126	123	129	129	139
140	128	125	128	123	122	125	121	132	117	129	126	124	130	130	140
141	129	126	129	124	122	126	121	133	117	130	127	125	130	131	141
142	129	126	129	125	123	126	122	133	118	131	127	125	131	132	142
143	130	127	130	125	123	127	122	134	118	132	128	126	132	132	143
144	131	128	131	126	124	127	123	135	118	132	129	126	132	133	144
145	132	128	131	126	124	128	123	136	119	133	129	127	133	134	145
146	132	129	132	127	125	129	124	137	119	134	130	128	134	135	146
147	133	130	133	127	125	129	125	137	120	135	131	128	135	135	147
148	134	130	134	128	126	130	125	138	120	135	131	129	135	136	148
149	134	131	134	129	127	131	126	139	121	136	132	129	136	137	149
150	135	132	135	129	127	131	126	140	121	137	133	130	137	138	150
151															151
152															152
153															153
154															154
155															155
156															156
157															157
158															158
159															159
160															160

Note. VCI = Verbal Comprehension Index. Based on the correlations between the WIAT–II standard scores and the WAIS–III VCI across the four age ranges. Presented in the order shown in the table, the average correlations for the nine WIAT–II subtests are .70, .63, .70, .59, .54, .62, .52, .80, and .42, and the average correlations for the five WIAT–II composites are .74, .65, .60, .74, and .75.

Table H.13. WIAT–II Subtest and Composite Standard Scores Predicted From the WAIS–III POI Scores for Individuals Aged 16:0–19:11

POI Score	Word Read	Num Ops	Read Comp	Spelling	Pseudowd Decod	Math Reason	Written Expr	Listen Comp	Oral Expr	Read	Math	Written Lang	Oral Lang	Total	POI Score
40															40
41															41
42															42
43															43
44															44
45															45
46															46
47															47
48															48
49															49
50	81	65	84	77	82	60	78	75	66	78	60	74	65	62	50
51	81	66	84	77	82	61	78	76	67	78	61	75	66	62	51
52	82	66	84	78	82	62	79	76	68	79	61	75	66	63	52
53	82	67	85	78	83	63	79	77	68	79	62	76	67	64	53
54	82	68	85	79	83	64	80	77	69	79	63	76	68	65	54
55	83	69	85	79	84	64	80	78	70	80	64	77	68	65	55
56	83	69	86	79	84	65	81	78	70	80	65	77	69	66	56
57	84	70	86	80	84	66	81	79	71	81	65	78	70	67	57
58	84	71	86	80	85	67	81	79	72	81	66	78	70	68	58
59	84	71	87	81	85	68	82	80	72	82	67	79	71	68	59
60	85	72	87	81	85	68	82	80	73	82	68	79	72	69	60
61	85	73	87	82	86	69	83	81	74	83	69	80	73	70	61
62	86	73	88	82	86	70	83	81	74	83	69	80	73	71	62
63	86	74	88	83	86	71	84	82	75	83	70	81	74	72	63
64	86	75	88	83	87	72	84	82	76	84	71	81	75	72	64
65	87	76	89	84	87	72	84	83	76	84	72	82	75	73	65
66	87	76	89	84	88	73	85	83	77	85	73	82	76	74	66
67	87	77	89	85	88	74	85	84	78	85	73	83	77	75	67
68	88	78	90	85	88	75	86	84	78	86	74	84	77	75	68
69	88	78	90	86	89	75	86	85	79	86	75	84	78	76	69
70	89	79	90	86	89	76	87	85	80	87	76	85	79	77	70
71	89	80	91	86	89	77	87	86	81	87	77	85	80	78	71
72	89	80	91	87	90	78	88	86	81	88	77	86	80	78	72
73	90	81	91	87	90	79	88	87	82	88	78	86	81	79	73
74	90	82	92	88	91	79	88	87	83	88	79	87	82	80	74
75	90	83	92	88	91	80	89	88	83	89	80	87	82	81	75
76	91	83	92	89	91	81	89	88	84	89	81	88	83	82	76
77	91	84	93	89	92	82	90	89	85	90	82	88	84	82	77
78	92	85	93	90	92	83	90	89	85	90	82	89	85	83	78
79	92	85	93	90	92	83	91	90	86	91	83	89	85	84	79
80	92	86	93	91	93	84	91	90	87	91	84	90	86	85	80
81	93	87	94	91	93	85	92	91	87	92	85	90	87	85	81
82	93	87	94	92	93	86	92	91	88	92	86	91	87	86	82
83	94	88	94	92	94	87	92	92	89	92	86	91	88	87	83
84	94	89	95	93	94	87	93	92	89	93	87	92	89	88	84
85	94	90	95	93	95	88	93	93	90	93	88	92	89	88	85
86	95	90	95	93	95	89	94	93	91	94	89	93	90	89	86
87	95	91	96	94	95	90	94	94	91	94	90	93	91	90	87
88	95	92	96	94	96	91	95	94	92	95	90	94	92	91	88
89	96	92	96	95	96	91	95	95	93	95	91	94	92	92	89
90	96	93	97	95	96	92	96	95	93	96	92	95	93	92	90
91	97	94	97	96	97	93	96	96	94	96	93	95	94	93	91
92	97	94	97	96	97	94	96	96	95	96	94	96	94	94	92
93	97	95	98	97	97	94	97	97	95	97	94	96	95	95	93
94	98	96	98	97	98	95	97	97	96	97	95	97	96	95	94
95	98	97	98	98	98	96	98	98	97	98	96	97	96	96	95
96	98	97	99	98	99	97	98	98	97	98	97	98	97	97	96
97	99	98	99	99	99	98	99	99	98	99	98	98	98	98	97
98	99	99	99	99	99	98	99	99	99	99	98	99	99	98	98
99	100	99	100	100	100	99	100	100	99	100	99	99	99	99	99
100	100	100	100	100	100	100	100	100	100	100	100	100	100	100	100

Note. POI = Perceptual Organization Index. Based on the correlations between the WIAT–II standard scores and the WAIS–III POI across the four age ranges. Presented in the order shown in the table, the average correlations for the nine WIAT–II subtests are .38, .70, .33, .47, .37, .79, .44, .50, and .67, and the average correlations for the five WIAT–II composites are .45, .80, .52, .70, and .77.

Table H.13. WIAT–II Subtest and Composite Standard Scores Predicted From the WAIS–III POI Scores for Individuals Aged 16:0–19:11 *(continued)*

	Subtest Standard Scores									Composite Standard Scores					
POI Score	Word Read	Num Ops	Read Comp	Spelling	Pseudowd Decod	Math Reason	Written Expr	Listen Comp	Oral Expr	Read	Math	Written Lang	Oral Lang	Total	POI Score
101	100	101	100	100	100	101	100	100	101	100	101	101	101	101	101
102	101	101	101	101	101	102	101	101	101	101	102	101	101	102	102
103	101	102	101	101	101	102	101	101	102	101	102	102	102	102	103
104	102	103	101	102	101	103	102	102	103	102	103	102	103	103	104
105	102	103	102	102	102	104	102	102	103	102	104	103	104	104	105
106	102	104	102	103	102	105	103	103	104	103	105	103	104	105	106
107	103	105	102	103	103	106	103	103	105	103	106	104	105	105	107
108	103	106	103	104	103	106	104	104	105	104	106	104	106	106	108
109	103	106	103	104	103	107	104	104	106	104	107	105	106	107	109
110	104	107	103	105	104	108	104	105	107	104	108	105	107	108	110
111	104	108	104	105	104	109	105	105	107	105	109	106	108	108	111
112	105	108	104	106	104	109	105	106	108	105	110	106	108	109	112
113	105	109	104	106	105	110	106	106	109	106	110	107	109	110	113
114	105	110	105	107	105	111	106	107	109	106	111	107	110	111	114
115	106	110	105	107	105	112	107	107	110	107	112	108	111	112	115
116	106	111	105	107	106	113	107	108	111	107	113	108	111	112	116
117	106	112	106	108	106	113	108	108	111	108	114	109	112	113	117
118	107	113	106	108	107	114	108	109	112	108	114	109	113	114	118
119	107	113	106	109	107	115	108	109	113	108	115	110	113	115	119
120	108	114	107	109	107	116	109	110	113	109	116	110	114	115	120
121	108	115	107	110	108	117	109	110	114	109	117	111	115	116	121
122	108	115	107	110	108	117	110	111	115	110	118	111	115	117	122
123	109	116	107	111	108	118	110	111	115	110	118	112	116	118	123
124	109	117	108	111	109	119	111	112	116	111	119	112	117	118	124
125	110	117	108	112	109	120	111	112	117	111	120	113	118	119	125
126	110	118	108	112	109	121	112	113	117	112	121	113	118	120	126
127	110	119	109	113	110	121	112	113	118	112	122	114	119	121	127
128	111	120	109	113	110	122	112	114	119	112	123	114	120	122	128
129	111	120	109	114	111	123	113	114	119	113	123	115	120	122	129
130	111	121	110	114	111	124	113	115	120	113	124	115	121	123	130
131	112	122	110	114	111	125	114	115	121	114	125	116	122	124	131
132	112	122	110	115	112	125	114	116	122	114	126	116	123	125	132
133	113	123	111	115	112	126	115	116	122	115	127	117	123	125	133
134	113	124	111	116	112	127	115	117	123	115	127	118	124	126	134
135	113	124	111	116	113	128	116	117	124	116	128	118	125	127	135
136	114	125	112	117	113	128	116	118	124	116	129	119	125	128	136
137	114	126	112	117	114	129	116	118	125	117	130	119	126	128	137
138	114	127	112	118	114	130	117	119	126	117	131	120	127	129	138
139	115	127	113	118	114	131	117	119	126	117	131	120	127	130	139
140	115	128	113	119	115	132	118	120	127	118	132	121	128	131	140
141	116	129	113	119	115	132	118	120	128	118	133	121	129	132	141
142	116	129	114	120	115	133	119	121	128	119	134	122	130	132	142
143	116	130	114	120	116	134	119	121	129	119	135	122	130	133	143
144	117	131	114	121	116	135	119	122	130	120	135	123	131	134	144
145	117	131	115	121	116	136	120	122	130	120	136	123	132	135	145
146	118	132	115	121	117	136	120	123	131	121	137	124	132	135	146
147	118	133	115	122	117	137	121	123	132	121	138	124	133	136	147
148	118	134	116	122	118	138	121	124	132	121	139	125	134	137	148
149	119	134	116	123	118	139	122	124	133	122	139	125	134	138	149
150	119	135	116	123	118	140	122	125	134	122	140	126	135	138	150
151															151
152															152
153															153
154															154
155															155
156															156
157															157
158															158
159															159
160															160

Note. POI = Perceptual Organization Index. Based on the correlations between the WIAT–II standard scores and the WAIS–III POI across the four age ranges. Presented in the order shown in the table, the average correlations for the nine WIAT–II subtests are .38, .70, .33, .47, .37, .79, .44, .50, and .67, and the average correlations for the five WIAT–II composites are .45, .80, .52, .70, and .77.

I

Predicted-Achievement Method

Differences Required for Statistical Significance and Differences Obtained by Linking Samples

Differences Required for Statistical Significance

Differences Obtained by Linking Samples

Table I.1. Differences Between Predicted and Actual Subtest and Composite Standard Scores Required for Statistical Significance Using the WPPSI–R Scores

Subtests	p	FSIQ	VIQ	PIQ
Word Reading	0.05	5.10	5.20	5.32
	0.01	6.71	6.85	7.01
Numerical Operations	0.05	11.86	11.81	12.11
	0.01	15.61	15.55	15.94
Reading Comprehension	0.05	6.68	6.97	6.62
	0.01	8.79	9.18	8.71
Spelling	0.05	8.27	8.35	8.30
	0.01	10.89	10.99	10.92
Pseudoword Decoding	0.05	5.51	5.89	5.39
	0.01	7.25	7.75	7.10
Math Reasoning	0.05	9.83	9.85	10.18
	0.01	12.94	12.97	13.41
Written Expression	0.05	10.94	10.94	11.03
	0.01	14.40	14.41	14.52
Listening Comprehension	0.05	14.47	14.56	14.48
	0.01	19.05	19.16	19.06
Oral Expression	0.05	10.35	10.49	10.41
	0.01	13.63	13.81	13.71

Composites	p	FSIQ	VIQ	PIQ
Reading	0.05	6.16	6.51	5.66
	0.01	8.11	8.57	7.45
Mathematics	0.05	8.81	8.75	9.23
	0.01	11.60	11.52	12.15
Written Language	0.05	8.29	8.51	8.27
	0.01	10.91	11.21	10.88
Oral Language	0.05	9.69	9.99	9.34
	0.01	12.76	13.15	12.29
Total	0.05	6.53	6.90	6.15
	0.01	8.60	9.08	8.10

Note. FSIQ = Full Scale IQ; VIQ = Verbal IQ; PIQ = Performance IQ.

I

Table I.2. Differences Between Predicted and Actual Subtest and Composite Standard Scores Required for Statistical Significance Using the WISC–III Scores

Subtests	p	FSIQ	VIQ	PIQ	VCI	POI
Word Reading	0.05	6.51	7.01	6.37	7.13	6.41
	0.01	8.58	9.23	8.39	9.38	8.44
Numerical Operations	0.05	11.05	11.16	11.17	11.13	11.11
	0.01	14.54	14.69	14.71	14.65	14.62
Reading Comprehension	0.05	7.36	7.79	7.24	7.98	7.46
	0.01	9.69	10.25	9.54	10.51	9.83
Spelling	0.05	7.88	8.20	7.84	8.23	7.85
	0.01	10.37	10.79	10.32	10.83	10.33
Pseudoword Decoding	0.05	6.09	6.46	5.91	6.53	5.97
	0.01	8.01	8.51	7.78	8.60	7.86
Math Reasoning	0.05	9.29	9.61	9.41	9.68	9.55
	0.01	12.22	12.65	12.38	12.74	12.57
Written Expression	0.05	11.82	11.96	11.84	11.99	11.83
	0.01	15.56	15.74	15.58	15.78	15.58
Listening Comprehension	0.05	13.57	13.81	13.56	13.94	13.75
	0.01	17.87	18.18	17.85	18.35	18.10
Oral Expression	0.05	11.07	11.23	11.10	11.40	11.12
	0.01	14.57	14.78	14.61	15.00	14.63

Composites

	p	FSIQ	VIQ	PIQ	VCI	POI
Reading	0.05	5.87	6.47	5.60	6.64	5.74
	0.01	7.73	8.52	7.38	8.74	7.56
Mathematics	0.05	8.67	8.93	8.86	8.93	8.85
	0.01	11.41	11.76	11.66	11.75	11.64
Written Language	0.05	8.35	8.63	8.35	8.69	8.36
	0.01	10.99	11.36	11.00	11.43	11.01
Oral Language	0.05	10.44	10.74	10.45	10.97	10.63
	0.01	13.74	14.14	13.76	14.45	13.99
Total	0.05	6.45	6.99	6.42	7.19	6.43
	0.01	8.50	9.21	8.45	9.46	8.47

Note. FSIQ = Full Scale IQ; VIQ = Verbal IQ; PIQ = Performance IQ; VCI = Verbal Comprehension Index; POI = Perceptual Organization Index.

Table I.2. Differences Between Predicted and Actual Subtest and Composite Standard Scores Required for Statistical Significance Using the WISC–III Scores (*continued*)

Subtests	p	FSIQ	VIQ	PIQ	VCI	POI
Word Reading	0.05	7.05	7.49	7.10	7.63	6.97
	0.01	9.29	9.85	9.34	10.04	9.18
Numerical Operations	0.05	8.56	8.85	8.77	8.83	8.54
	0.01	11.26	11.64	11.54	11.63	11.24
Reading Comprehension	0.05	7.69	8.11	7.85	8.31	7.79
	0.01	10.12	10.68	10.33	10.93	10.25
Spelling	0.05	8.40	8.67	8.41	8.72	8.23
	0.01	11.06	11.41	11.08	11.48	10.83
Pseudoword Decoding	0.05	6.02	6.46	6.00	6.58	6.00
	0.01	7.93	8.51	7.90	8.66	7.90
Math Reasoning	0.05	9.04	9.35	9.39	9.37	9.27
	0.01	11.90	12.30	12.37	12.34	12.20
Written Expression	0.05	11.47	11.64	11.57	11.68	11.38
	0.01	15.10	15.32	15.23	15.38	14.97
Listening Comprehension	0.05	13.42	13.67	13.61	13.84	13.60
	0.01	17.67	17.99	17.91	18.21	17.90
Oral Expression	0.05	11.73	11.77	11.81	11.80	11.78
	0.01	15.44	15.50	15.54	15.53	15.51

Composites

	p	FSIQ	VIQ	PIQ	VCI	POI
Reading	0.05	6.36	6.97	6.42	7.19	6.37
	0.01	8.37	9.18	8.45	9.46	8.38
Mathematics	0.05	7.16	7.57	7.53	7.57	7.26
	0.01	9.42	9.96	9.91	9.96	9.56
Written Language	0.05	8.30	8.59	8.40	8.65	8.15
	0.01	10.93	11.31	11.06	11.39	10.72
Oral Language	0.05	10.76	10.99	10.96	11.14	10.95
	0.01	14.16	14.47	14.42	14.66	14.41
Total	0.05	5.95	6.67	6.19	6.85	5.91
	0.01	7.84	8.78	8.15	9.02	7.78

Note. FSIQ = Full Scale IQ; VIQ = Verbal IQ; PIQ = Performance IQ; VCI = Verbal Comprehension Index; POI = Perceptual Organization Index.

Table I.3. Differences Between Predicted and Actual Subtest and Composite Standard Scores Required for Statistical Significance Using the WAIS–III Scores

Subtests	p	FSIQ	VIQ	PIQ	VCI	POI
Word Reading	0.05	7.46	7.81	7.55	8.29	7.21
	0.01	9.82	10.28	9.93	10.92	9.49
Numerical Operations	0.05	8.14	8.30	8.70	8.51	9.02
	0.01	10.71	10.93	11.45	11.20	11.87
Reading Comprehension	0.05	8.50	8.87	8.41	9.26	8.18
	0.01	11.19	11.67	11.07	12.19	10.77
Spelling	0.05	9.46	9.60	9.71	9.77	9.54
	0.01	12.45	12.64	12.79	12.87	12.55
Pseudoword Decoding	0.05	6.59	6.87	6.76	7.05	6.53
	0.01	8.68	9.04	8.90	9.28	8.60
Math Reasoning	0.05	8.79	8.88	9.56	8.98	9.92
	0.01	11.57	11.69	12.59	11.82	13.06
Written Expression	0.05	11.02	11.12	11.25	11.25	11.15
	0.01	14.50	14.64	14.81	14.80	14.67
Listening Comprehension	0.05	13.72	13.98	13.72	14.34	13.70
	0.01	18.05	18.40	18.05	18.88	18.04
Oral Expression	0.05	11.66	11.68	11.97	11.78	12.53
	0.01	15.34	15.38	15.75	15.51	16.49

Composites

	p	FSIQ	VIQ	PIQ	VCI	POI
Reading	0.05	5.61	6.18	5.65	6.73	5.42
	0.01	7.38	8.13	7.43	8.86	7.13
Mathematics	0.05	7.19	7.34	8.09	7.53	8.58
	0.01	9.47	9.66	10.65	9.92	11.30
Written Language	0.05	8.50	8.68	8.88	8.89	8.75
	0.01	11.19	11.42	11.69	11.71	11.52
Oral Language	0.05	11.31	11.52	11.69	11.86	11.93
	0.01	14.89	15.17	15.39	15.61	15.71
Total	0.05	6.02	6.39	6.99	6.83	7.28
	0.01	7.92	8.42	9.20	8.99	9.59

Note. FSIQ = Full Scale IQ; VIQ = Verbal IQ; PIQ = Performance IQ; VCI = Verbal Comprehension Index; POI = Perceptual Organization Index.

Table I.4. Differences Between Predicted and Actual Subtest and Composite Standard Scores Obtained by Various Percentages of Children in the WPPSI–R Linking Sample Based on FSIQ Scores

Subtests	25	20	15	10	5	4	3	2	1
				Percentage[a]					
Word Reading	9	11	13	16	21	23	24	26	30
Numerical Operations	8	10	13	16	20	22	23	25	29
Reading Comprehension	7	9	11	13	17	18	19	21	24
Spelling	9	11	14	17	22	23	25	27	31
Pseudoword Decoding	8	10	12	15	19	21	22	24	27
Math Reasoning	8	9	12	14	19	20	21	23	26
Written Expression	9	11	14	17	22	23	25	27	31
Listening Comprehension	9	11	13	16	21	22	24	26	30
Oral Expression	8	10	12	15	20	21	23	25	28
Composites									
Reading	6	8	10	12	16	17	18	19	22
Mathematics	7	9	11	14	18	19	20	22	25
Written Language	7	9	11	14	18	19	20	22	25
Oral Language	7	9	11	14	18	19	21	22	25
Total	5	7	8	10	13	14	15	16	18

Note. FSIQ = Full Scale IQ.

[a] Percentage of children whose obtained achievement standard score was below their predicted-achievement score by the specified amount or more.

Table I.5. Differences Between Predicted and Actual Subtest and Composite Standard Scores Obtained by Various Percentages of Children in the WPPSI–R Linking Sample Based on VIQ Scores

Subtests	25	20	15	10	5	4	3	2	1
				Percentage[a]					
Word Reading	9	11	14	17	22	23	25	27	31
Numerical Operations	9	11	14	17	22	23	25	27	31
Reading Comprehension	7	9	11	13	17	18	19	21	24
Spelling	9	11	14	17	22	23	25	27	31
Pseudoword Decoding	8	10	12	15	19	20	22	24	27
Math Reasoning	8	10	12	15	20	21	23	25	28
Written Expression	9	11	14	17	22	24	25	28	32
Listening Comprehension	9	11	13	16	21	22	24	26	30
Oral Expression	8	10	13	15	20	21	23	25	28
Composites									
Reading	7	8	10	12	16	17	18	20	23
Mathematics	8	10	12	15	19	21	22	24	28
Written Language	7	9	11	14	18	19	20	22	25
Oral Language	7	9	11	13	17	18	20	22	24
Total	6	7	9	11	13	14	15	17	19

Note. VIQ = Verbal IQ.

[a] Percentage of children whose obtained achievement standard score was below their predicted-achievement score by the specified amount or more.

Table I.6. Differences Between Predicted and Actual Subtest and Composite Standard Scores Obtained by Various Percentages of Children in the WPPSI–R Linking Sample Based on PIQ Scores

Subtests	Percentage[a]								
	25	20	15	10	5	4	3	2	1
Word Reading	9	11	14	17	22	24	26	28	32
Numerical Operations	9	11	13	17	21	23	24	27	30
Reading Comprehension	9	11	13	16	21	22	24	26	30
Spelling	9	12	14	18	23	24	26	29	33
Pseudoword Decoding	9	11	14	17	22	24	25	28	32
Math Reasoning	8	10	13	16	20	22	23	25	29
Written Expression	9	12	14	18	23	24	26	28	32
Listening Comprehension	9	12	14	18	23	24	26	28	32
Oral Expression	9	11	14	17	22	23	25	27	31
Composites									
Reading	9	11	14	17	22	23	25	27	31
Mathematics	8	10	12	15	20	21	23	25	28
Written Language	9	11	13	17	21	23	24	27	30
Oral Language	9	12	14	18	23	24	26	28	32
Total	8	10	13	16	21	22	24	26	29

Note. PIQ = Performance IQ.

[a] Percentage of children whose obtained achievement standard score was below their predicted-achievement score by the specified amount or more.

Table I.7. Differences Between Predicted and Actual Subtest and Composite Standard Scores Obtained by Various Percentages of Children in the WISC–III Linking Sample Based on FSIQ Scores

Subtests	Percentage[a]								
	25	20	15	10	5	4	3	2	1
Word Reading	8	10	12	15	20	21	22	25	28
Numerical Operations	8	10	13	16	20	21	23	25	28
Reading Comprehension	8	10	12	15	19	20	22	24	27
Spelling	9	11	13	16	21	22	24	26	30
Pseudoword Decoding	9	11	13	16	21	23	24	26	30
Math Reasoning	7	8	10	13	17	18	19	21	23
Written Expression	8	11	13	16	21	22	24	26	29
Listening Comprehension	7	9	11	14	18	19	20	22	25
Oral Expression	9	11	14	17	22	23	25	27	31
Composites									
Reading	8	10	12	15	19	20	22	24	27
Mathematics	7	9	11	13	17	18	20	22	25
Written Language	8	10	13	16	20	21	23	25	29
Oral Language	7	9	11	14	18	19	21	23	26
Total	7	8	10	13	16	17	18	20	23

Note. FSIQ = Full Scale IQ.

[a] Percentage of children whose obtained achievement standard score was below their predicted-achievement score by the specified amount or more.

Table I.8. Differences Between Predicted and Actual Subtest and Composite Standard Scores Obtained by Various Percentages of Children in the WISC–III Linking Sample Based on VIQ Scores

	Percentage[a]								
Subtests	25	20	15	10	5	4	3	2	1
Word Reading	8	9	12	14	19	20	21	23	26
Numerical Operations	8	10	12	15	20	21	23	25	28
Reading Comprehension	7	9	11	14	18	19	21	22	26
Spelling	8	10	13	16	20	21	23	25	29
Pseudoword Decoding	8	10	13	16	20	22	23	25	29
Math Reasoning	7	8	10	13	16	17	18	20	23
Written Expression	8	10	13	16	20	22	23	25	29
Listening Comprehension	7	9	11	13	17	18	20	21	24
Oral Expression	9	11	13	17	22	23	25	27	30
Composites									
Reading	7	9	11	14	18	19	20	22	25
Mathematics	7	9	11	13	17	18	19	21	24
Written Language	8	10	12	15	20	21	22	24	28
Oral Language	7	9	11	14	18	19	20	22	25
Total	6	8	9	12	15	16	17	18	21

Note. VIQ = Verbal IQ.

[a] Percentage of children whose obtained achievement standard score was below their predicted-achievement score by the specified amount or more.

Table I.9. Differences Between Predicted and Actual Subtest and Composite Standard Scores Obtained by Various Percentages of Children in the WISC–III Linking Sample Based on PIQ Scores

	Percentage[a]								
Subtests	25	20	15	10	5	4	3	2	1
Word Reading	9	11	14	17	22	24	25	28	32
Numerical Operations	9	11	14	17	22	23	25	27	31
Reading Comprehension	9	11	14	17	22	23	25	27	31
Spelling	9	12	14	18	23	24	26	28	32
Pseudoword Decoding	9	12	15	18	23	25	26	29	33
Math Reasoning	8	10	13	16	20	21	23	25	28
Written Expression	9	11	14	17	22	24	26	28	32
Listening Comprehension	9	11	13	16	21	22	24	26	30
Oral Expression	9	12	14	18	23	24	26	28	32
Composites									
Reading	9	11	14	17	22	24	25	28	31
Mathematics	8	10	13	16	20	22	23	25	29
Written Language	9	11	14	17	22	24	25	28	32
Oral Language	9	11	13	16	21	22	24	26	30
Total	8	10	13	16	21	22	23	26	29

Note. PIQ = Performance IQ.

[a] Percentage of children whose obtained achievement standard score was below their predicted-achievement score by the specified amount or more.

Table I.10. Differences Between Predicted and Actual Subtest and Composite Standard Scores Obtained by Various Percentages of Children in the WISC–III Linking Sample Based on VCI Scores

	Percentage[a]								
Subtests	**25**	**20**	**15**	**10**	**5**	**4**	**3**	**2**	**1**
Word Reading	8	10	12	15	19	20	22	24	27
Numerical Operations	8	10	13	16	21	22	24	26	29
Reading Comprehension	8	9	12	14	18	19	21	23	26
Spelling	8	10	13	16	21	22	24	26	29
Pseudoword Decoding	8	11	13	16	21	22	24	26	29
Math Reasoning	7	9	11	14	17	19	20	22	25
Written Expression	9	11	13	16	21	22	24	26	30
Listening Comprehension	7	9	11	13	17	18	20	21	24
Oral Expression	9	11	13	17	22	23	25	27	30
Composites									
Reading	7	9	11	14	18	19	21	23	26
Mathematics	8	9	12	14	18	20	21	23	26
Written Language	8	10	13	16	20	21	23	25	29
Oral Language	7	9	11	14	18	19	20	22	25
Total	7	8	10	12	16	17	18	20	22

Note. VCI = Verbal Comprehension Index.

[a] Percentage of children whose obtained achievement standard score was below their predicted-achievement score by the specified amount or more.

Table I.11. Differences Between Predicted and Actual Subtest and Composite Standard Scores Obtained by Various Percentages of Children in the WISC–III Linking Sample Based on POI Scores

	Percentage[a]								
Subtests	**25**	**20**	**15**	**10**	**5**	**4**	**3**	**2**	**1**
Word Reading	9	11	14	17	23	24	26	28	32
Numerical Operations	9	11	14	17	22	24	26	28	32
Reading Comprehension	9	11	14	17	22	23	25	27	31
Spelling	9	12	15	18	23	25	26	29	33
Pseudoword Decoding	9	12	15	18	23	25	26	29	33
Math Reasoning	8	10	13	16	20	22	23	25	29
Written Expression	9	12	14	18	23	24	26	29	32
Listening Comprehension	9	11	13	16	21	22	24	26	30
Oral Expression	9	12	14	18	23	24	26	29	33
Composites									
Reading	9	11	14	17	22	24	25	28	31
Mathematics	9	11	13	16	21	22	24	26	30
Written Language	9	12	14	18	23	24	26	28	32
Oral Language	9	11	13	16	21	22	24	26	30
Total	9	11	13	16	21	22	24	26	30

Note. POI = Perceptual Organization Index.

[a] Percentage of children whose obtained achievement standard score was below their predicted-achievement score by the specified amount or more.

Table I.12. Differences Between Predicted and Actual Subtest and Composite Standard Scores Obtained by Various Percentages of Individuals in the WAIS–III Linking Sample Based on FSIQ Scores

Subtests	Percentage[a]								
	25	20	15	10	5	4	3	2	1
Word Reading	7	9	11	14	18	19	20	22	25
Numerical Operations	7	8	10	13	17	18	19	21	23
Reading Comprehension	7	9	11	14	18	19	21	23	26
Spelling	8	9	12	14	18	19	21	23	26
Pseudoword Decoding	8	10	13	15	20	21	23	25	28
Math Reasoning	6	8	9	11	15	16	17	18	21
Written Expression	8	10	13	15	20	21	23	25	28
Listening Comprehension	7	8	10	12	16	17	18	20	22
Oral Expression	9	11	13	17	21	23	24	27	30
Composites									
Reading	7	8	11	13	17	18	19	21	24
Mathematics	6	7	9	11	14	15	16	18	20
Written Language	7	9	11	14	18	19	21	23	26
Oral Language	6	8	10	12	16	17	18	19	22
Total	5	7	8	10	13	14	15	16	18

Note. FSIQ = Full Scale IQ.

[a] Percentage of individuals whose obtained achievement standard score was below their predicted-achievement score by the specified amount or more.

Table I.13. Differences Between Predicted and Actual Subtest and Composite Standard Scores Obtained by Various Percentages of Individuals in the WAIS–III Linking Sample Based on VIQ Scores

Subtests	Percentage[a]								
	25	20	15	10	5	4	3	2	1
Word Reading	7	9	11	13	17	18	20	21	24
Numerical Operations	7	9	11	14	18	19	20	22	25
Reading Comprehension	7	9	11	13	17	18	19	21	24
Spelling	8	10	12	15	19	20	21	23	27
Pseudoword Decoding	8	10	12	15	20	21	22	24	28
Math Reasoning	7	9	11	13	17	18	19	21	24
Written Expression	8	10	13	16	20	21	23	25	29
Listening Comprehension	6	7	9	11	14	15	17	18	21
Oral Expression	9	11	14	17	22	23	25	27	31
Composites									
Reading	6	8	10	12	16	17	18	19	22
Mathematics	7	8	10	13	16	17	19	20	23
Written Language	8	9	12	14	19	20	21	23	26
Oral Language	6	8	10	12	16	17	18	20	22
Total	6	7	9	11	14	15	16	17	20

Note. VIQ = Verbal IQ.

[a] Percentage of individuals whose obtained achievement standard score was below their predicted-achievement score by the specified amount or more.

Table I.14. Differences Between Predicted and Actual Subtest and Composite Standard Scores Obtained by Various Percentages of Individuals in the WAIS–III Linking Sample Based on PIQ Scores

	Percentage[a]								
Subtests	**25**	**20**	**15**	**10**	**5**	**4**	**3**	**2**	**1**
Word Reading	9	11	14	17	22	23	25	27	31
Numerical Operations	8	10	12	15	19	20	22	24	27
Reading Comprehension	9	11	14	17	22	24	26	28	32
Spelling	9	11	13	16	21	22	24	26	30
Pseudoword Decoding	9	11	14	17	22	24	25	28	31
Math Reasoning	7	9	11	13	17	18	20·	21	24
Written Expression	9	11	13	17	21	23	24	27	30
Listening Comprehension	9	11	13	16	21	23	24	26	30
Oral Expression	9	11	14	17	22	23	25	27	31
Composites									
Reading	9	11	13	17	21	23	24	27	30
Mathematics	7	9	11	13	17	18	20	21	24
Written Language	8	10	13	16	21	22	23	26	29
Oral Language	8	10	12	15	19	20	22	24	27
Total	7	9	11	13	17	18	19	21	24

Note. PIQ = Performance IQ.

[a] Percentage of individuals whose obtained achievement standard score was below their predicted-achievement score by the specified amount or more.

Table I.15. Differences Between Predicted and Actual Subtest and Composite Standard Scores Obtained by Various Percentages of Individuals in the WAIS–III Linking Sample Based on VCI Scores

	Percentage[a]								
Subtests	**25**	**20**	**15**	**10**	**5**	**4**	**3**	**2**	**1**
Word Reading	7	9	11	14	18	19	20	22	25
Numerical Operations	8	10	12	15	19	20	22	24	27
Reading Comprehension	7	9	11	14	18	19	20	22	25
Spelling	8	10	13	15	20	21	23	25	28
Pseudoword Decoding	8	10	13	16	21	22	24	26	29
Math Reasoning	8	10	12	15	19	20	22	24	27
Written Expression	9	11	13	16	21	22	24	26	30
Listening Comprehension	6	8	9	12	15	16	17	19	21
Oral Expression	9	11	14	17	22	24	25	28	32
Composites									
Reading	7	9	11	13	17	18	19	21	24
Mathematics	8	9	12	14	19	20	21	23	26
Written Language	8	10	12	15	20	21	22	25	28
Oral Language	7	8	11	13	17	18	19	21	24
Total	7	8	10	13	16	17	19	20	23

Note. VCI = Verbal Comprehension Index.

[a] Percentage of individuals whose obtained achievement standard score was below their predicted-achievement score by the specified amount or more.

Table I.16. Differences Between Predicted and Actual Subtest and Composite Standard Scores Obtained by Various Percentages of Individuals in the WAIS–III Linking Sample Based on POI Scores

Subtests	Percentage[a]								
	25	20	15	10	5	4	3	2	1
Word Reading	9	11	14	18	23	24	26	28	32
Numerical Operations	7	9	11	14	18	19	20	22	25
Reading Comprehension	9	12	15	18	23	25	26	29	33
Spelling	9	11	14	17	22	23	25	27	31
Pseudoword Decoding	9	12	14	18	23	24	26	28	32
Math Reasoning	6	8	10	12	15	16	17	19	21
Written Expression	9	11	14	17	22	23	25	27	31
Listening Comprehension	9	11	13	17	21	23	24	27	30
Oral Expression	7	9	11	14	18	19	21	23	26
Composites									
Reading	9	11	14	17	22	23	25	27	31
Mathematics	6	8	9	11	15	16	17	18	21
Written Language	9	11	13	16	21	22	24	26	30
Oral Language	7	9	11	14	18	19	20	22	25
Total	7	8	10	12	16	17	18	20	22

Note. POI = Perceptual Organization Index.

[a] Percentage of individuals whose obtained achievement standard score was below their predicted-achievement score by the specified amount or more.

Simple-Difference Method

Differences Required for Statistical Significance and Differences Obtained by Linking Samples

**Differences Required
for Statistical Significance**

**Differences Obtained
by Linking Samples**

Table J.1. Differences Between Ability and Actual Subtest and Composite Standard Scores Required for Statistical Significance Using the WPPSI–R Scores

Ages 4:0–6:11

Subtests	p	FSIQ	VIQ	PIQ
Word Reading	0.05	7.20	7.78	9.30
	0.01	9.48	10.24	12.24
Numerical Operations	0.05	12.82	13.15	14.10
	0.01	16.87	17.31	18.56
Reading Comprehension	0.05	7.78	8.32	9.75
	0.01	10.24	10.95	12.84
Spelling	0.05	9.75	10.18	11.39
	0.01	12.84	13.41	14.99
Pseudoword Decoding	0.05	7.20	7.78	9.30
	0.01	9.48	10.24	12.24
Math Reasoning	0.05	10.79	11.18	12.29
	0.01	14.20	14.72	16.17
Written Expression	0.05	12.12	12.47	13.47
	0.01	15.96	16.42	17.73
Listening Comprehension	0.05	15.33	15.61	16.41
	0.01	20.17	20.54	21.61
Oral Expression	0.05	11.39	11.76	12.82
	0.01	14.99	15.48	16.87

Composites

Composites	p	FSIQ	VIQ	PIQ
Reading	0.05	7.20	7.78	9.30
	0.01	9.48	10.24	12.24
Mathematics	0.05	9.75	10.18	11.39
	0.01	12.84	13.41	14.99
Written Language	0.05	9.30	9.75	11.00
	0.01	12.24	12.84	14.48
Oral Language	0.05	10.60	11.00	12.12
	0.01	13.95	14.48	15.96
Total	0.05	7.20	7.78	9.30
	0.01	9.48	10.24	12.24

Note. FSIQ = Full Scale IQ; VIQ = Verbal IQ; PIQ = Performance IQ.

Table J.2. Differences Between Ability and Actual Subtest and Composite Standard Scores Required for Statistical Significance Using the WISC–III Scores

Subtests	p	FSIQ	VIQ	PIQ	VCI	POI
		Ages 6:0–11:11				
Word Reading	0.05	7.73	8.27	9.71	8.77	10.15
	0.01	10.17	10.88	12.78	11.55	13.35
Numerical Operations	0.05	12.34	12.69	13.67	13.02	13.98
	0.01	16.25	16.70	18.00	17.15	18.41
Reading Comprehension	0.05	9.00	9.47	10.75	9.91	11.14
	0.01	11.84	12.46	14.15	13.05	14.67
Spelling	0.05	9.56	10.01	11.23	10.43	11.61
	0.01	12.59	13.17	14.78	13.73	15.28
Pseudoword Decoding	0.05	7.94	8.46	9.88	8.96	10.31
	0.01	10.45	11.14	13.00	11.80	13.57
Math Reasoning	0.05	10.24	10.65	11.81	11.05	12.17
	0.01	13.48	14.03	15.54	14.55	16.02
Written Expression	0.05	13.07	13.40	14.33	13.72	14.63
	0.01	17.21	17.64	18.87	18.06	19.26
Listening Comprehension	0.05	14.42	14.72	15.58	15.01	15.85
	0.01	18.98	19.38	20.50	19.76	20.86
Oral Expression	0.05	12.38	12.73	13.71	13.06	14.02
	0.01	16.30	16.75	18.04	17.19	18.45

Composites

	p	FSIQ	VIQ	PIQ	VCI	POI
Reading	0.05	7.27	7.85	9.35	8.38	9.81
	0.01	9.58	10.33	12.31	11.03	12.91
Mathematics	0.05	9.84	10.27	11.46	10.68	11.83
	0.01	12.95	13.52	15.09	14.06	15.58
Written Language	0.05	9.89	10.32	11.51	10.73	11.88
	0.01	13.02	13.58	15.15	14.12	15.63
Oral Language	0.05	11.46	11.83	12.88	12.19	13.21
	0.01	15.08	15.57	16.95	16.04	17.39
Total	0.05	7.78	8.32	9.75	8.82	10.18
	0.01	10.24	10.95	12.84	11.61	13.41

Note. FSIQ = Full Scale IQ; VIQ = Verbal IQ; PIQ = Performance IQ; VCI = Verbal Comprehension Index; POI = Perceptual Organization Index.

Table J.2. Differences Between Ability and Actual Subtest and Composite Standard Scores Required for Statistical Significance Using the WISC–III Scores (*continued*)

Subtests	p	FSIQ	VIQ	PIQ	VCI	POI
Word Reading	0.05	8.56	9.05	10.79	9.52	10.79
	0.01	11.27	11.92	14.21	12.53	14.21
Numerical Operations	0.05	9.71	10.15	11.73	10.57	11.73
	0.01	12.79	13.36	15.44	13.91	15.44
Reading Comprehension	0.05	8.87	9.35	11.04	9.80	11.04
	0.01	11.68	12.30	14.54	12.90	14.54
Spelling	0.05	9.86	10.29	11.85	10.70	11.85
	0.01	12.98	13.54	15.60	14.09	15.60
Pseudoword Decoding	0.05	7.94	8.46	10.31	8.96	10.31
	0.01	10.45	11.14	13.57	11.80	13.57
Math Reasoning	0.05	9.90	10.33	11.88	10.74	11.88
	0.01	13.03	13.59	15.64	14.13	15.64
Written Expression	0.05	12.49	12.83	14.11	13.16	14.11
	0.01	16.44	16.89	18.58	17.32	18.58
Listening Comprehension	0.05	14.05	14.36	15.52	14.66	15.52
	0.01	18.50	18.90	20.42	19.29	20.42
Oral Expression	0.05	12.94	13.27	14.52	13.59	14.52
	0.01	17.04	17.47	19.11	17.90	19.11

Composites

	p	FSIQ	VIQ	PIQ	VCI	POI
Reading	0.05	7.13	7.72	9.70	8.26	9.70
	0.01	9.39	10.16	12.77	10.87	12.77
Mathematics	0.05	8.25	8.76	10.55	9.24	10.55
	0.01	10.86	11.53	13.88	12.16	13.88
Written Language	0.05	9.64	10.08	11.67	10.50	11.67
	0.01	12.70	13.27	15.36	13.82	15.36
Oral Language	0.05	11.66	12.03	13.39	12.38	13.39
	0.01	15.35	15.83	17.62	16.30	17.62
Total	0.05	7.04	7.63	9.64	8.18	9.64
	0.01	9.27	10.05	12.68	10.77	12.68

Note. FSIQ = Full Scale IQ; VIQ = Verbal IQ; PIQ = Performance IQ; VCI = Verbal Comprehension Index; POI = Perceptual Organization Index.

Table J.3. Differences Between Ability and Actual Subtest and Composite Standard Scores Required for Statistical Significance Using the WAIS–III Scores

Subtests	p	FSIQ	VIQ	PIQ	VCI	POI
		Ages 16:0–19:11				
Word Reading	0.05	8.32	8.82	10.18	9.75	10.18
	0.01	10.95	11.61	13.41	12.84	13.41
Numerical Operations	0.05	8.82	9.30	10.60	10.18	10.60
	0.01	11.61	12.24	13.95	13.41	13.95
Reading Comprehension	0.05	9.30	9.75	11.00	10.60	11.00
	0.01	12.24	12.84	14.48	13.95	14.48
Spelling	0.05	10.18	10.60	11.76	11.39	11.76
	0.01	13.41	13.95	15.48	14.99	15.48
Pseudoword Decoding	0.05	7.78	8.32	9.75	9.30	9.75
	0.01	10.24	10.95	12.84	12.24	12.84
Math Reasoning	0.05	9.30	9.75	11.00	10.60	11.00
	0.01	12.24	12.84	14.48	13.95	14.48
Written Expression	0.05	11.76	12.12	13.15	12.82	13.15
	0.01	15.48	15.96	17.31	16.87	17.31
Listening Comprehension	0.05	14.10	14.40	15.28	14.99	15.28
	0.01	18.56	18.96	20.11	19.73	20.11
Oral Expression	0.05	12.47	12.82	13.79	13.47	13.79
	0.01	16.42	16.87	18.15	17.73	18.15

Composites

	p	FSIQ	VIQ	PIQ	VCI	POI
Reading	0.05	6.57	7.20	8.82	8.32	8.82
	0.01	8.65	9.48	11.61	10.95	11.61
Mathematics	0.05	7.78	8.32	9.75	9.30	9.75
	0.01	10.24	10.95	12.84	12.24	12.84
Written Language	0.05	9.30	9.75	11.00	10.60	11.00
	0.01	12.24	12.84	14.48	13.95	14.48
Oral Language	0.05	11.76	12.12	13.15	12.82	13.15
	0.01	15.48	15.96	17.31	16.87	17.31
Total	0.05	6.57	7.20	8.82	8.32	8.82
	0.01	8.65	9.48	11.61	10.95	11.61

Note. FSIQ = Full Scale IQ; VIQ = Verbal IQ; PIQ = Performance IQ; VCI = Verbal Comprehension Index; POI = Perceptual Organization Index.

Table J.4. Differences Between Ability and Actual Subtest and Composite Standard Scores Obtained by Various Percentages of Children in the WPPSI–R Linking Sample Based on FSIQ Scores

	Percentage[a]								
Subtests	**25**	**20**	**15**	**10**	**5**	**4**	**3**	**2**	**1**
Word Reading	10	12	15	19	24	26	28	30	35
Numerical Operations	9	12	14	18	23	24	26	29	32
Reading Comprehension	7	9	11	14	18	19	21	22	25
Spelling	10	13	16	19	25	27	29	31	35
Pseudoword Decoding	9	11	14	17	22	23	25	27	31
Math Reasoning	8	10	13	16	20	22	23	25	29
Written Expression	10	13	16	20	25	27	29	32	36
Listening Comprehension	10	12	15	19	24	26	28	30	34
Oral Expression	9	11	14	17	22	24	25	28	31
Composites									
Reading	7	8	10	13	17	18	19	21	23
Mathematics	8	10	12	15	19	20	22	24	27
Written Language	8	10	12	15	19	20	22	24	27
Oral Language	8	10	12	15	20	21	22	24	28
Total	5	7	8	10	13	14	15	17	19

Note. FSIQ = Full Scale IQ.

[a] Percentage of children whose actual achievement standard score was below their FSIQ by the specified amount or more.

Table J.5. Differences Between Ability and Actual Subtest and Composite Standard Scores Obtained by Various Percentages of Children in the WPPSI–R Linking Sample Based on VIQ Scores

	Percentage[a]								
Subtests	**25**	**20**	**15**	**10**	**5**	**4**	**3**	**2**	**1**
Word Reading	10	13	16	19	25	27	29	31	36
Numerical Operations	10	13	16	19	25	27	29	31	35
Reading Comprehension	8	9	12	14	18	19	21	23	26
Spelling	10	13	16	20	25	27	29	32	36
Pseudoword Decoding	9	11	13	16	21	22	24	26	30
Math Reasoning	9	11	14	17	22	23	25	28	31
Written Expression	11	13	17	20	26	28	30	33	38
Listening Comprehension	10	12	15	19	24	26	27	30	34
Oral Expression	9	11	14	17	22	24	25	28	32
Composites									
Reading	7	9	11	13	17	18	19	21	24
Mathematics	9	11	14	17	22	23	25	27	31
Written Language	8	10	12	15	19	21	22	24	27
Oral Language	8	9	12	14	19	20	21	23	26
Total	6	7	9	11	14	15	16	18	20

Note. VIQ = Verbal IQ.

[a] Percentage of children whose actual achievement standard score was below their VIQ by the specified amount or more.

Table J.6. Differences Between Ability and Actual Subtest and Composite Standard Scores Obtained by Various Percentages of Children in the WPPSI–R Linking Sample Based on PIQ Scores

	Percentage[a]								
Subtests	**25**	**20**	**15**	**10**	**5**	**4**	**3**	**2**	**1**
Word Reading	11	13	17	21	27	28	31	33	38
Numerical Operations	10	12	15	19	25	26	28	31	35
Reading Comprehension	10	12	15	19	24	26	28	30	34
Spelling	11	14	17	22	28	30	32	35	40
Pseudoword Decoding	11	13	17	20	27	28	30	33	38
Math Reasoning	9	12	14	18	23	24	26	29	32
Written Expression	11	14	17	21	27	29	31	34	39
Listening Comprehension	11	14	17	21	28	29	31	34	39
Oral Expression	11	13	16	20	26	27	30	32	37
Composites									
Reading	10	13	16	20	25	27	29	32	36
Mathematics	9	11	14	17	22	23	25	27	31
Written Language	10	12	16	19	25	26	28	31	35
Oral Language	11	14	17	21	27	29	31	34	39
Total	10	12	15	18	23	25	27	29	33

Note. PIQ = Performance IQ.

[a] Percentage of children whose actual achievement standard score was below their PIQ by the specified amount or more.

Table J.7. Differences Between Ability and Actual Subtest and Composite Standard Scores Obtained by Various Percentages of Children in the WISC–III Linking Sample Based on FSIQ Scores

	Percentage[a]								
Subtests	**25**	**20**	**15**	**10**	**5**	**4**	**3**	**2**	**1**
Word Reading	9	11	14	17	22	23	25	27	31
Numerical Operations	9	11	14	17	22	24	26	28	32
Reading Comprehension	9	11	13	16	21	22	24	26	30
Spelling	10	12	15	18	24	25	27	30	34
Pseudoword Decoding	10	12	15	19	25	26	28	31	35
Math Reasoning	7	9	11	14	18	19	20	22	25
Written Expression	10	12	15	18	24	25	27	29	34
Listening Comprehension	8	10	12	15	20	21	22	24	28
Oral Expression	10	13	16	19	25	27	29	31	36
Composites									
Reading	9	11	13	16	21	22	24	26	30
Mathematics	8	10	12	15	19	20	21	23	27
Written Language	9	11	14	18	23	24	26	28	32
Oral Language	8	10	13	15	20	21	23	25	28
Total	7	9	11	13	17	18	20	21	24

Note. FSIQ = Full Scale IQ.

[a] Percentage of children whose actual achievement standard score was below their FSIQ by the specified amount or more.

Table J.8. Differences Between Ability and Actual Subtest and Composite Standard Scores Obtained by Various Percentages of Children in the WISC–III Linking Sample Based on VIQ Scores

Subtests	Percentage[a]								
	25	20	15	10	5	4	3	2	1
Word Reading	8	10	13	16	20	22	23	25	29
Numerical Operations	9	11	14	17	22	24	25	28	31
Reading Comprehension	8	10	12	15	20	21	22	24	28
Spelling	9	11	14	18	23	24	26	28	32
Pseudoword Decoding	9	12	14	18	23	24	26	29	33
Math Reasoning	7	9	11	13	17	18	20	21	24
Written Expression	9	12	15	18	23	25	26	29	33
Listening Comprehension	8	9	12	14	18	20	21	23	26
Oral Expression	10	13	16	19	25	26	28	31	35
Composites									
Reading	8	10	12	15	19	20	22	24	27
Mathematics	8	9	12	14	18	19	21	23	26
Written Language	9	11	14	17	22	23	25	27	31
Oral Language	8	10	12	15	19	20	22	24	27
Total	6	8	10	12	16	17	18	19	22

Note. VIQ = Verbal IQ.

[a] Percentage of children whose actual achievement standard score was below their VIQ by the specified amount or more.

Table J.9. Differences Between Ability and Actual Subtest and Composite Standard Scores Obtained by Various Percentages of Children in the WISC–III Linking Sample Based on PIQ Scores

Subtests	Percentage[a]								
	25	20	15	10	5	4	3	2	1
Word Reading	11	13	17	20	26	28	30	33	37
Numerical Operations	10	13	16	20	26	27	29	32	36
Reading Comprehension	10	13	16	20	26	27	29	32	36
Spelling	11	14	17	21	27	29	31	34	39
Pseudoword Decoding	11	14	18	22	28	30	32	35	40
Math Reasoning	9	11	14	18	23	24	26	28	32
Written Expression	11	13	17	21	27	28	31	33	38
Listening Comprehension	10	12	15	19	24	26	28	30	34
Oral Expression	11	14	17	21	28	29	32	34	39
Composites									
Reading	11	13	16	20	26	28	30	33	37
Mathematics	9	12	15	18	23	25	26	29	33
Written Language	11	13	17	20	26	28	30	33	37
Oral Language	10	12	15	19	24	26	28	30	34
Total	9	12	15	18	23	25	26	29	33

Note. PIQ = Performance IQ.

[a] Percentage of children whose actual achievement standard score was below their PIQ by the specified amount or more.

Table J.10. Differences Between Ability and Actual Subtest and Composite Standard Scores Obtained by Various Percentages of Children in the WISC–III Linking Sample Based on VCI Scores

Subtests	25	20	15	10	5	4	3	2	1
				Percentage[a]					
Word Reading	9	11	13	16	21	22	24	26	30
Numerical Operations	10	12	15	18	24	25	27	29	33
Reading Comprehension	8	10	13	16	20	21	23	25	28
Spelling	10	12	15	18	24	25	27	29	33
Pseudoword Decoding	10	12	15	18	24	25	27	29	34
Math Reasoning	8	10	12	15	19	20	21	23	27
Written Expression	10	12	15	19	24	25	27	30	34
Listening Comprehension	8	9	12	14	19	20	21	23	26
Oral Expression	10	13	16	19	25	26	28	31	35
Composites									
Reading	8	10	12	15	20	21	23	25	28
Mathematics	8	10	13	16	20	21	23	25	28
Written Language	9	11	14	18	23	24	26	28	32
Oral Language	8	10	12	15	19	20	22	24	27
Total	7	9	11	13	17	18	19	21	24

Note. VCI = Verbal Comprehension Index.

[a] Percentage of children whose actual achievement standard score was below their VCI by the specified amount or more.

Table J.11. Differences Between Ability and Actual Subtest and Composite Standard Scores Obtained by Various Percentages of Children in the WISC–III Linking Sample Based on POI Scores

Subtests	25	20	15	10	5	4	3	2	1
				Percentage[a]					
Word Reading	11	14	17	21	27	29	31	34	38
Numerical Operations	11	13	17	21	27	28	30	33	38
Reading Comprehension	10	13	16	20	26	27	29	32	36
Spelling	11	14	18	22	28	30	32	35	40
Pseudoword Decoding	11	14	18	22	28	30	32	35	40
Math Reasoning	9	12	14	18	23	24	26	29	33
Written Expression	11	14	17	21	28	29	32	35	39
Listening Comprehension	10	12	15	18	24	25	27	30	34
Oral Expression	11	14	17	22	28	30	32	35	40
Composites									
Reading	11	13	16	20	26	28	30	33	37
Mathematics	10	12	15	19	24	26	28	30	34
Written Language	11	14	17	21	27	29	31	34	39
Oral Language	10	12	15	19	24	26	28	30	34
Total	10	12	15	19	24	26	28	30	34

Note. POI = Perceptual Organization Index.

[a] Percentage of children whose actual achievement standard score was below their POI by the specified amount or more.

Table J.12. Differences Between Ability and Actual Subtest and Composite Standard Scores Obtained by Various Percentages of Individuals in the WAIS–III Linking Sample Based on FSIQ Scores

Subtests	Percentage[a]								
	25	20	15	10	5	4	3	2	1
Word Reading	8	10	12	15	19	20	22	24	27
Numerical Operations	7	9	11	14	18	19	20	22	25
Reading Comprehension	8	10	12	15	20	21	23	25	28
Spelling	8	10	13	16	20	21	23	25	28
Pseudoword Decoding	9	11	14	17	22	24	26	28	32
Math Reasoning	6	8	10	12	16	17	18	19	22
Written Expression	9	11	14	17	22	24	25	28	32
Listening Comprehension	7	9	11	13	17	18	19	21	24
Oral Expression	10	12	16	19	25	26	28	31	35
Composites									
Reading	7	9	11	14	18	19	20	22	25
Mathematics	6	8	10	12	15	16	17	19	21
Written Language	8	10	13	15	20	21	23	25	28
Oral Language	7	8	10	13	17	18	19	21	23
Total	6	7	8	10	13	14	15	17	19

Note. FSIQ = Full Scale IQ.

[a] Percentage of individuals whose actual achievement standard score was below their FSIQ by the specified amount or more.

Table J.13. Differences Between Ability and Actual Subtest and Composite Standard Scores Obtained by Various Percentages of Individuals in the WAIS–III Linking Sample Based on VIQ Scores

Subtests	Percentage[a]								
	25	20	15	10	5	4	3	2	1
Word Reading	8	9	12	14	19	20	21	23	26
Numerical Operations	8	10	12	15	19	20	22	24	27
Reading Comprehension	8	9	12	14	18	19	21	23	26
Spelling	8	10	13	16	21	22	24	26	29
Pseudoword Decoding	9	11	14	17	22	23	25	27	31
Math Reasoning	7	9	11	14	18	19	21	23	26
Written Expression	9	11	14	18	23	24	26	28	32
Listening Comprehension	6	8	10	12	15	16	17	19	22
Oral Expression	10	13	16	20	26	27	29	32	37
Composites									
Reading	7	8	10	13	17	18	19	21	23
Mathematics	7	9	11	14	18	19	20	22	25
Written Language	8	10	13	16	20	22	23	25	29
Oral Language	7	9	11	13	17	18	19	21	24
Total	6	7	9	11	15	16	17	18	21

Note. VIQ = Verbal IQ.

[a] Percentage of individuals whose actual achievement standard score was below their VIQ by the specified amount or more.

Table J.14. Differences Between Ability and Actual Subtest and Composite Standard Scores Obtained by Various Percentages of Individuals in the WAIS–III Linking Sample Based on PIQ Scores

Subtests	Percentage[a]								
	25	20	15	10	5	4	3	2	1
Word Reading	10	13	16	19	25	27	29	31	36
Numerical Operations	9	11	13	16	21	23	24	26	30
Reading Comprehension	11	13	17	21	27	28	30	33	38
Spelling	10	12	15	19	24	25	27	30	34
Pseudoword Decoding	11	13	16	20	26	28	30	33	37
Math Reasoning	8	9	12	14	19	20	21	23	26
Written Expression	10	13	16	19	25	26	28	31	35
Listening Comprehension	10	12	15	19	24	26	28	30	35
Oral Expression	10	13	16	19	25	27	29	31	36
Composites									
Reading	10	12	15	19	25	26	28	31	35
Mathematics	8	9	12	14	19	20	21	23	26
Written Language	9	12	15	18	23	25	27	29	33
Oral Language	9	11	13	16	21	22	24	26	30
Total	8	9	12	14	18	20	21	23	26

Note. PIQ = Performance IQ.

[a] Percentage of individuals whose actual achievement standard score was below their PIQ by the specified amount or more.

Table J.15. Differences Between Ability and Actual Subtest and Composite Standard Scores Obtained by Various Percentages of Individuals in the WAIS–III Linking Sample Based on VCI Scores

Subtests	Percentage[a]								
	25	20	15	10	5	4	3	2	1
Word Reading	8	10	12	15	19	20	22	24	27
Numerical Operations	9	11	13	16	21	22	24	26	30
Reading Comprehension	8	10	12	15	19	20	22	24	27
Spelling	9	11	14	17	22	24	26	28	32
Pseudoword Decoding	10	12	15	18	23	25	27	29	33
Math Reasoning	9	11	13	16	21	23	24	27	30
Written Expression	10	12	15	19	24	25	27	30	34
Listening Comprehension	7	8	10	12	16	17	18	20	22
Oral Expression	11	13	17	20	26	28	30	33	37
Composites									
Reading	7	9	11	14	18	19	20	22	25
Mathematics	8	10	13	16	20	22	23	25	29
Written Language	9	11	14	17	22	23	25	27	31
Oral Language	7	9	11	14	18	19	20	22	25
Total	7	9	11	13	17	18	20	22	25

Note. VCI = Verbal Comprehension Index.

[a] Percentage of individuals whose actual achievement standard score was below their VCI by the specified amount or more.

Table J.16. Differences Between Ability and Actual Subtest and Composite Standard Scores Obtained by Various Percentages of Individuals in the WAIS–III Linking Sample Based on POI Scores

Subtests	Percentage[a]								
	25	20	15	10	5	4	3	2	1
Word Reading	11	14	17	21	27	29	31	34	39
Numerical Operations	8	10	12	15	19	20	22	24	27
Reading Comprehension	11	14	18	22	28	30	32	35	40
Spelling	10	13	16	20	25	27	29	32	36
Pseudoword Decoding	11	14	17	21	28	29	31	34	39
Math Reasoning	7	8	10	12	16	17	18	20	23
Written Expression	10	13	16	20	26	27	29	32	37
Listening Comprehension	10	12	15	19	25	26	28	31	35
Oral Expression	8	10	13	15	20	21	23	25	28
Composites									
Reading	10	13	16	20	26	27	29	32	36
Mathematics	6	8	10	12	17	16	18	19	22
Written Language	10	12	15	19	24	26	28	30	34
Oral Language	8	10	12	15	19	20	22	24	27
Total	7	9	11	13	17	18	19	21	24

Note. POI = Perceptual Organization Index.

[a] Percentage of individuals whose actual achievement standard score was below their POI by the specified amount or more.

K Supplemental Tables

Table K.1. Differences Between Composite Standard Scores Required for Statistical Significance by Grade: Fall[a]

		Composites						
Grade	Significance Levels	Reading/ Math	Reading/ Oral Lang	Reading/ Written Lang	Math/ Oral Lang	Math/ Written Lang	Oral Lang/ Written Lang	Significance Levels
PreK (Age 5)	.15							.15
	.05							.05
K	.15							.15
	.05							.05
1	.15	8.09	7.48	5.71	10.13	8.91	8.36	.15
	.05	11.01	10.18	7.77	13.79	12.12	11.38	.05
2	.15	7.48	7.48	5.29	9.65	8.08	8.08	.15
	.05	10.18	10.18	7.20	13.14	10.99	10.99	.05
3	.15	5.71	8.09	6.83	8.91	7.78	9.66	.15
	.05	7.77	11.01	9.29	12.12	10.59	13.15	.05
4	.15	5.71	8.08	6.83	9.41	8.36	10.13	.15
	.05	7.77	11.00	9.30	12.81	11.38	13.79	.05
5	.15	5.29	8.08	6.11	9.16	7.48	9.66	.15
	.05	7.19	11.00	8.32	12.47	10.18	13.15	.05
6	.15	6.11	8.37	7.16	8.91	7.78	9.66	.15
	.05	8.31	11.40	9.75	12.12	10.59	13.15	.05
7	.15	5.71	7.78	6.10	8.63	7.16	8.90	.15
	.05	7.77	10.59	8.31	11.75	9.74	12.11	.05
8	.15	5.29	7.48	6.10	8.08	6.83	8.63	.15
	.05	7.20	10.18	8.31	10.99	9.29	11.75	.05
9	.15	5.72	8.37	6.48	8.64	6.83	9.17	.15
	.05	7.78	11.40	8.82	11.77	9.29	12.47	.05
10	.15	5.71	8.91	6.10	9.66	7.16	9.90	.15
	.05	7.77	12.12	8.31	13.14	9.74	13.47	.05
11	.15	5.29	8.90	6.48	8.90	6.48	9.65	.15
	.05	7.21	12.12	8.82	12.12	8.82	13.14	.05
12	.15	5.29	8.37	6.10	8.91	6.83	9.41	.15
	.05	7.20	11.39	8.31	12.12	9.29	12.81	.05
All Grades	.15	6.09	8.13	6.30	9.14	7.57	9.29	.15
	.05	8.29	11.06	8.58	12.45	10.30	12.64	.05

Note. Differences required for statistical significance are based on the standard error of measurement for each composite at each grade and calculated with the following formula:

$$\text{Difference Score} = Z\sqrt{SE_{M_a}^2 + SE_{M_b}^2}$$

where Z is the normal curve value associated with the desired significance level and SE_{M_a} and SE_{M_b} are the standard errors of measurement of the two composite standard scores.

[a] For Grades 9–12, the standardization sample consisted of cases from both Fall and Spring.

Table K.2. Differences Between Composite Standard Scores Required for Statistical Significance by Grade: Spring[a]

Grade	Significance Levels	Reading/ Math	Reading/ Oral Lang	Reading/ Written Lang	Math/ Oral Lang	Math/ Written Lang	Oral Lang/ Written Lang	Significance Levels
				Composites				
PreK (Age 5)	.15							.15
	.05							.05
K	.15							.15
	.05							.05
1	.15	7.78	7.48	6.10	9.89	8.90	8.63	.15
	.05	10.59	10.18	8.31	13.46	12.11	11.75	.05
2	.15	6.83	7.78	5.71	9.41	7.78	8.63	.15
	.05	9.29	10.59	7.77	12.80	10.59	11.75	.05
3	.15	6.48	8.09	6.83	9.42	8.36	9.66	.15
	.05	8.82	11.01	9.29	12.82	11.38	13.15	.05
4	.15	6.48	8.09	6.83	9.42	8.36	9.66	.15
	.05	8.82	11.01	9.29	12.82	11.38	13.15	.05
5	.15	6.10	9.41	6.83	10.35	8.08	10.79	.15
	.05	8.31	12.81	9.29	14.09	10.99	14.69	.05
6	.15	4.83	7.48	5.71	8.36	6.83	8.90	.15
	.05	6.57	10.18	7.77	11.38	9.29	12.11	.05
7	.15	5.71	7.48	6.10	8.36	7.16	8.63	.15
	.05	7.77	10.18	8.31	11.38	9.74	11.75	.05
8	.15	4.83	6.83	5.71	7.79	6.83	8.36	.15
	.05	6.57	9.30	7.77	10.60	9.29	11.38	.05
9	.15	5.72	8.37	6.48	8.64	6.83	9.17	.15
	.05	7.78	11.40	8.82	11.77	9.29	12.47	.05
10	.15	5.71	8.91	6.10	9.66	7.16	9.90	.15
	.05	7.77	12.12	8.31	13.14	9.74	13.47	.05
11	.15	5.29	8.90	6.48	8.90	6.48	9.65	.15
	.05	7.21	12.12	8.82	12.12	8.82	13.14	.05
12	.15	5.29	8.37	6.10	8.91	6.83	9.41	.15
	.05	7.20	11.39	8.31	12.12	9.29	12.81	.05
All Grades	.15	6.10	8.13	6.27	9.20	7.61	9.31	.15
	.05	8.31	11.06	8.53	12.52	10.35	12.67	.05

Note. Differences required for statistical significance are based on the standard error of measurement for each composite at each grade and calculated with the following formula:

$$\text{Difference Score} = Z\sqrt{SE_{M_a}^{2} + SE_{M_b}^{2}}$$

where Z is the normal curve value associated with the desired significance level and SE_{M_a} and SE_{M_b} are the standard errors of measurement of the two composite standard scores.

[a] For Grades 9–12, the standardization sample consisted of cases from both Fall and Spring.

Table K.3. Differences Between Composite Standard Scores Required for Statistical Significance by Age

		Composites						
Age	Significance Levels	Reading/ Math	Reading/ Oral Lang	Reading/ Written Lang	Math/ Oral Lang	Math/ Written Lang	Oral Lang/ Written Lang	Significance Levels
4	.15							.15
	.05							.05
5	.15							.15
	.05							.05
6	.15	6.11	6.83	5.71	8.64	7.79	8.36	.15
	.05	8.32	9.30	7.77	11.76	10.60	11.38	.05
7	.15	6.83	6.83	5.71	9.16	8.36	8.36	.15
	.05	9.30	9.30	7.77	12.47	11.38	11.38	.05
8	.15	5.29	6.83	5.71	8.08	7.16	8.36	.15
	.05	7.19	9.30	7.77	11.00	9.74	11.38	.05
9	.15	5.71	6.83	5.71	8.36	7.47	8.36	.15
	.05	7.77	9.30	7.77	11.38	10.17	11.38	.05
10	.15	5.71	8.08	6.11	9.41	7.79	9.66	.15
	.05	7.77	11.00	8.32	12.81	10.60	13.15	.05
11	.15	5.71	8.37	6.48	9.16	7.48	9.66	.15
	.05	7.77	11.39	8.82	12.47	10.18	13.15	.05
12	.15	4.83	7.79	6.11	8.64	7.17	9.42	.15
	.05	6.57	10.61	8.32	11.77	9.75	12.82	.05
13	.15	4.83	7.48	6.10	7.79	6.48	8.63	.15
	.05	6.58	10.18	8.31	10.60	8.82	11.75	.05
14	.15	4.83	7.78	6.10	8.08	6.48	8.90	.15
	.05	6.58	10.59	8.31	10.99	8.82	12.11	.05
15	.15	6.48	8.90	6.83	9.65	7.79	9.90	.15
	.05	8.82	12.12	9.30	13.14	10.60	13.47	.05
16	.15	5.29	8.09	6.48	8.64	7.17	9.42	.15
	.05	7.20	11.01	8.82	11.77	9.75	12.82	.05
17–19	.15	4.83	8.37	6.10	8.64	6.48	9.41	.15
	.05	6.58	11.39	8.31	11.76	8.82	12.81	.05
All Ages	.15	5.64	7.71	6.11	8.74	7.37	9.05	.15
	.05	7.68	10.50	8.32	11.90	10.03	12.32	.05

Note. Differences required for statistical significance are based on the standard error of measurement for each composite at each age and calculated with the following formula:

$$\text{Difference Score} = Z\sqrt{SE_{M_a}^2 + SE_{M_b}^2}$$

where Z is the normal curve value associated with the desired significance level and SE_{M_a} and SE_{M_b} are the standard errors of measurement of the two composite standard scores.

Table K.4. Cumulative Percentages of the Grade-Based Standardization Sample Obtaining Various Composite Score Discrepancies

	Composites												
Discrepancy	Reading/ Mathematics		Reading/ Oral Lang		Reading/ Written Lang		Mathematics/ Oral Lang		Mathematics/ Written Lang		Oral Language/ Written Lang		Discrepancy
	R<M	R>M	R<OL	R>OL	R<WL	R>WL	M<OL	M>OL	M<WL	M>WL	OL<WL	OL>WL	
≥40	0.4	0.3	0.3	0.4	0.0	0.1	0.4	0.5	0.2	0.4	0.3	0.5	≥40
39	0.4	0.3	0.5	0.5	0.0	0.1	0.4	0.5	0.2	0.4	0.3	0.5	39
38	0.5	0.3	0.6	0.6	0.0	0.1	0.5	0.6	0.2	0.5	0.4	0.6	38
37	0.5	0.5	0.7	0.7	0.0	0.2	0.6	0.7	0.3	0.6	0.5	0.7	37
36	0.6	0.5	0.8	0.8	0.0	0.2	0.8	0.7	0.4	0.7	0.7	0.8	36
35	0.8	0.5	0.9	0.9	0.0	0.3	1.1	0.8	0.4	0.7	0.8	1.1	35
34	0.9	0.6	1.1	1.0	0.0	0.4	1.3	0.9	0.5	0.7	1.1	1.3	34
33	0.9	0.7	1.3	1.2	0.0	0.5	1.4	1.0	0.6	0.9	1.1	1.5	33
32	1.2	1.0	1.5	1.5	0.0	0.6	1.7	1.3	0.7	1.1	1.2	1.8	32
31	1.3	1.2	2.0	1.8	0.1	0.8	2.0	1.4	0.7	1.1	1.5	2.0	31
30	1.6	1.5	2.4	1.9	0.3	0.8	2.3	1.6	0.9	1.3	1.8	2.3	30
29	2.0	1.5	2.8	2.4	0.4	0.9	2.5	1.8	1.1	1.6	2.1	2.7	29
28	2.3	1.7	3.2	2.8	0.4	1.1	3.0	2.1	1.2	1.9	2.5	3.4	28
27	2.5	2.2	3.3	3.0	0.7	1.4	3.4	2.5	1.5	2.2	3.0	3.9	27
26	3.1	2.5	3.6	3.3	0.8	1.7	3.6	3.0	2.0	2.7	3.5	4.3	26
25	3.6	2.8	4.1	3.6	1.1	1.9	4.3	3.6	2.2	2.9	3.9	5.2	25
24	4.3	3.4	5.0	4.2	1.6	2.4	5.0	4.1	2.8	3.4	4.5	6.1	24
23	4.8	4.0	5.7	4.7	2.1	2.6	6.0	4.5	3.6	4.0	5.0	7.1	23
22	5.5	4.7	6.4	5.4	2.5	3.1	6.6	5.3	4.3	4.6	5.5	8.0	22
21	6.2	5.6	7.5	6.0	2.7	3.4	7.4	5.8	4.9	5.6	6.5	9.1	21
20	7.6	6.1	8.7	7.2	3.2	3.8	8.2	7.0	5.4	6.7	7.7	9.9	20
19	8.3	7.1	10.3	7.7	4.0	4.3	8.9	8.0	6.3	7.8	8.9	11.1	19
18	9.6	8.0	11.3	8.7	4.7	4.9	10.2	9.2	7.3	9.0	10.1	12.2	18
17	10.6	9.1	12.5	9.8	5.7	5.6	11.5	10.5	8.8	10.2	11.5	13.5	17
16	11.9	10.5	14.3	10.7	7.1	6.5	12.9	12.1	11.0	11.4	12.8	15.2	16
15	13.6	12.0	16.1	12.1	8.2	8.1	14.3	13.9	12.1	12.7	14.7	16.3	15
14	15.5	13.3	17.9	13.6	9.9	9.4	15.9	15.4	13.8	14.9	16.2	18.0	14
13	17.9	14.4	20.1	14.8	11.8	11.0	17.6	17.9	15.7	16.4	17.8	19.9	13
12	19.8	16.4	21.7	16.5	14.3	13.1	19.7	19.8	17.9	18.5	19.5	21.4	12
11	21.8	18.1	23.6	18.6	17.1	14.8	21.8	21.6	20.2	21.1	21.7	23.4	11
10	24.4	20.4	26.6	20.4	20.4	16.8	24.6	23.9	22.9	23.5	24.1	25.9	10
9	26.8	22.4	29.4	22.6	23.2	18.9	26.8	26.1	25.4	25.7	26.2	28.0	9
8	29.3	25.2	31.6	24.4	26.2	21.6	29.5	28.6	27.9	28.3	28.7	30.4	8
7	32.4	27.7	34.3	26.6	29.4	24.1	32.5	31.1	30.1	30.8	31.3	32.8	7
6	35.8	30.1	36.9	29.5	32.1	26.8	35.3	32.6	32.8	33.1	33.8	35.2	6
5	39.4	33.5	40.2	32.8	35.5	29.6	38.1	35.1	36.4	36.2	36.4	37.7	5
4	42.1	36.7	42.7	35.5	38.8	33.7	41.1	37.7	39.2	39.2	38.7	40.9	4
3	44.7	39.7	45.8	38.3	42.5	37.6	43.5	41.0	41.9	42.3	41.6	44.0	3
2	47.9	42.8	49.0	40.9	46.6	41.4	46.7	44.4	45.2	45.5	44.3	46.9	2
1	51.1	46.0	52.4	44.2	50.7	45.5	49.7	47.2	48.1	49.0	47.4	49.7	1
0													0
Mean	10.8	10.3	11.4	10.9	8.8	8.8	11.3	11.1	10.3	10.6	11.4	12.0	Mean
SD	8.0	8.0	8.5	8.6	6.2	7.1	8.5	8.2	7.4	7.9	8.3	8.9	SD
Median	9.0	8.0	10.0	9.0	8.0	7.0	9.0	10.0	9.0	9.0	10.0	10.0	Median

Note. M = Mathematics composite; R = Reading composite; OL = Oral Language composite; WL = Written Language composite.

Table K.5. Cumulative Percentages of the Age-Based Standardization Sample Obtaining Various Composite Score Discrepancies

	Composites												
Discrepancy	Reading/ Mathematics		Reading/ Oral Lang		Reading/ Written Lang		Mathematics/ Oral Lang		Mathematics/ Written Lang		Oral Language/ Written Lang		Discrepancy
	R<M	R>M	R<OL	R>OL	R<WL	R>WL	M<OL	M>OL	M<WL	M>WL	OL<WL	OL>WL	
≥40	0.4	0.4	0.3	0.4	0.0	0.1	0.2	0.6	0.1	0.3	0.3	0.1	≥40
39	0.5	0.4	0.3	0.4	0.0	0.2	0.4	0.7	0.1	0.4	0.4	0.3	39
38	0.5	0.4	0.4	0.4	0.0	0.2	0.4	0.7	0.1	0.4	0.4	0.3	38
37	0.6	0.5	0.5	0.5	0.0	0.2	0.5	0.8	0.2	0.6	0.6	0.4	37
36	0.6	0.5	0.6	0.7	0.0	0.3	0.6	0.9	0.2	0.6	0.7	0.6	36
35	0.7	0.5	0.7	0.8	0.0	0.4	0.7	1.0	0.2	0.7	0.9	0.7	35
34	0.8	0.6	0.8	0.8	0.0	0.5	0.8	1.1	0.4	0.8	1.1	0.9	34
33	1.0	0.6	0.9	1.0	0.0	0.5	1.0	1.2	0.4	0.9	1.2	1.2	33
32	1.2	0.6	1.2	1.1	0.1	0.5	1.3	1.4	0.6	1.1	1.3	1.4	32
31	1.5	0.7	1.6	1.4	0.1	0.7	1.4	1.6	0.8	1.3	1.8	1.6	31
30	1.7	1.1	1.9	1.6	0.2	0.8	1.9	2.0	1.1	1.3	2.0	1.8	30
29	1.9	1.4	2.3	2.2	0.3	0.8	2.1	2.3	1.3	1.5	2.3	2.3	29
28	2.3	1.6	2.7	2.3	0.4	1.1	2.5	2.5	1.5	1.9	2.9	2.7	28
27	2.9	2.0	3.3	2.7	0.6	1.2	2.9	3.0	1.7	2.3	3.5	3.4	27
26	3.3	2.1	3.5	3.3	0.8	1.4	3.3	3.5	2.0	2.6	3.9	4.0	26
25	3.7	2.5	4.0	3.7	1.0	1.8	3.7	4.1	2.3	3.2	4.2	4.6	25
24	4.6	3.2	4.5	4.6	1.3	2.0	4.5	5.0	2.9	3.7	5.0	5.3	24
23	5.2	3.6	5.1	5.5	1.7	2.3	5.2	5.8	3.3	4.3	5.6	5.9	23
22	5.8	4.4	5.8	6.4	1.9	2.9	6.1	6.4	3.9	5.0	6.2	7.1	22
21	7.0	5.2	6.7	7.2	2.6	3.4	7.1	7.3	4.6	5.8	7.2	8.0	21
20	7.9	5.7	8.2	7.8	3.3	3.9	8.0	8.4	5.4	6.4	8.3	9.3	20
19	9.3	6.9	9.7	8.4	3.9	4.2	8.9	9.6	6.4	7.3	9.2	10.2	19
18	10.1	7.9	10.2	9.2	4.6	4.7	10.1	10.5	7.3	8.8	10.5	11.7	18
17	11.3	9.2	12.1	10.0	5.5	5.4	11.1	11.8	8.5	9.6	11.6	12.6	17
16	12.4	10.0	13.4	11.6	6.6	6.3	12.5	13.0	9.6	11.1	12.8	13.8	16
15	13.8	11.5	14.6	13.3	8.4	7.3	13.7	14.9	11.3	12.7	14.4	15.4	15
14	15.2	13.0	16.7	14.8	10.0	9.0	15.2	17.0	13.1	14.4	16.3	17.4	14
13	17.0	14.6	18.1	16.8	12.4	10.6	17.0	18.8	14.3	16.6	18.1	19.1	13
12	18.8	16.1	20.2	19.2	14.5	12.8	18.9	20.7	16.4	18.2	19.9	20.7	12
11	21.2	18.3	21.8	21.2	16.6	14.4	21.3	22.7	18.6	20.4	22.3	21.9	11
10	24.1	20.0	23.7	22.8	19.4	16.5	23.2	24.9	22.1	22.7	24.8	23.7	10
9	27.3	22.2	26.5	24.5	23.6	19.1	25.6	27.6	24.3	25.6	27.4	25.9	9
8	29.4	24.4	29.2	27.4	26.7	21.6	28.1	30.2	27.8	28.6	30.3	28.3	8
7	32.3	27.5	31.7	29.7	30.3	24.1	30.7	33.1	30.0	31.7	32.8	31.1	7
6	35.3	30.3	34.9	32.1	33.2	27.0	33.4	35.4	32.6	33.8	35.3	33.4	6
5	38.9	33.2	37.5	35.3	36.8	30.2	36.4	37.8	36.0	36.5	37.5	36.1	5
4	41.5	35.6	40.0	38.6	40.7	33.8	39.1	40.4	39.2	39.6	41.2	38.6	4
3	44.5	39.1	42.8	41.7	43.6	37.2	41.9	43.5	41.6	43.0	44.2	41.9	3
2	47.1	42.0	46.1	44.6	47.7	40.4	45.0	46.1	44.7	46.6	46.5	44.7	2
1	51.1	45.2	48.7	48.3	51.6	44.0	48.1	48.4	47.3	49.4	49.2	47.9	1
0													0
Mean	10.9	10.3	11.4	10.9	8.7	8.9	11.1	11.7	10.2	10.6	11.5	11.6	Mean
SD	8.2	7.8	8.3	8.4	6.0	7.0	8.3	8.4	7.3	7.9	8.4	8.7	SD
Median	9.0	8.0	9.0	9.0	8.0	7.0	9.0	10.0	9.0	9.0	10.0	9.0	Median

Note. M = Mathematics composite; R = Reading composite; OL = Oral Language composite; WL = Written Language composite.

Table K.6. Differences Between Single Subtest Standard Scores and Averages of Subtest Standard Scores Required for Statistical Significance and Differences Obtained by the Cumulative Percentages of the Grade-Based Standardization Sample: Fall[a]

	Significance Level		Cumulative Percentage				
	.15	.05	1	2	5	10	25
9 SUBTESTS							
Word Reading	6.90	8.00	24.78	21.11	17.11	13.00	8.67
Numerical Operations	11.61	13.47	28.22	25.11	20.44	17.11	11.78
Reading Comprehension	9.50	11.01	22.56	20.22	16.89	13.78	9.67
Spelling	9.40	10.90	23.11	20.33	16.11	13.33	9.00
Pseudoword Decoding	6.69	7.76	30.33	26.22	20.11	16.33	11.22
Math Reasoning	9.57	11.10	26.33	21.89	17.11	14.67	9.89
Written Expression	12.61	14.62	25.56	22.56	19.67	16.22	11.33
Listening Comprehension	14.44	16.75	26.44	24.00	19.78	16.11	11.11
Oral Expression	12.89	14.95	32.11	28.11	23.89	20.33	13.78
6 SUBTESTS							
Word Reading	6.71	7.86	27.67	23.50	17.50	13.83	9.17
Numerical Operations	10.49	12.29	25.50	23.00	18.67	15.67	10.83
Spelling	8.69	10.17	24.00	21.67	17.17	14.17	9.50
Math Reasoning	8.83	10.34	21.83	19.33	16.00	13.50	9.33
Listening Comprehension	12.85	15.05	26.33	22.83	19.33	16.00	10.83
Oral Expression	11.55	13.53	30.50	27.50	22.83	18.83	13.00
4 SUBTESTS							
Word Reading	6.60	7.98	27.25	23.50	18.50	14.75	10.00
Math Reasoning	8.05	9.73	21.75	19.00	16.75	13.50	9.50
Listening Comprehension	11.00	13.30	22.50	19.75	16.75	13.75	9.50
Oral Expression	10.03	12.12	26.50	24.25	20.50	16.75	11.50

Note. The differences required for statistical significance are based on the average standard errors of measurement across all grades and calculated with the following formula provided by Davis (1959):

$$\text{Difference Score} = Z\sqrt{(SE_{M_t})^2/K^2 + [(K-2)/K](SE_{M_i})^2}$$

where Z is the normal curve value associated with the desired significance level derived with the Bonferroni correction for multiple comparisons, K is the number of subtests in comparison, $SE_{M_t}^2$ is the sum of the squared standard errors of measurement for all subtests in the comparison and $SE_{M_i}^2$ is the squared standard error of measurement for the subtest of interest.

[a] For Grades 9–12, the standardization sample consisted of cases from both Fall and Spring.

Table K.7. Differences Between Single Subtest Standard Scores and Averages of Subtest Standard Scores Required for Statistical Significance and Differences Obtained by the Cumulative Percentages of the Grade-Based Standardization Sample: Spring[a]

	Significance Level		Cumulative Percentage				
	.15	.05	1	2	5	10	25
9 SUBTESTS							
Word Reading	7.02	8.14	23.33	20.44	15.89	12.67	8.56
Numerical Operations	11.48	13.31	28.44	24.67	20.44	16.00	10.78
Reading Comprehension	9.47	10.98	20.67	18.11	15.44	13.33	9.11
Spelling	9.37	10.86	23.67	19.78	16.00	13.22	9.33
Pseudoword Decoding	6.58	7.63	26.78	23.11	19.33	16.22	10.89
Math Reasoning	9.75	11.31	24.67	22.11	18.00	14.78	10.44
Written Expression	12.61	14.63	25.56	23.78	19.89	16.22	10.89
Listening Comprehension	14.75	17.10	27.78	25.00	19.56	16.22	10.56
Oral Expression	12.89	14.95	32.00	28.00	23.00	19.78	13.44
6 SUBTESTS							
Word Reading	6.82	7.99	24.83	21.50	16.83	13.83	9.33
Numerical Operations	10.39	12.17	26.67	23.33	19.00	15.33	10.33
Spelling	8.67	10.16	24.00	21.17	17.50	14.33	10.00
Math Reasoning	8.98	10.52	22.50	20.17	16.50	13.67	9.83
Listening Comprehension	13.12	15.36	26.33	22.50	18.83	15.50	10.33
Oral Expression	11.57	13.54	30.17	28.00	23.33	19.33	13.17
4 SUBTESTS							
Word Reading	6.71	8.12	26.00	22.25	17.75	14.50	10.25
Math Reasoning	8.20	9.91	23.75	20.00	17.00	13.75	9.75
Listening Comprehension	11.23	13.58	24.00	20.00	17.00	13.50	9.25
Oral Expression	10.07	12.17	28.00	25.00	20.75	17.25	11.75

Note. The differences required for statistical significance are based on the average standard errors of measurement across all grades and calculated with the following formula provided by Davis (1959):

$$\text{Difference Score} = Z\sqrt{(SE_{M_t})^2/K^2 + [(K-2)/K](SE_{M_i})^2}$$

where Z is the normal curve value associated with the desired significance level derived with the Bonferroni correction for multiple comparisons, K is the number of subtests in comparison, $SE_{M_t}^2$ is the sum of the squared standard errors of measurement for all subtests in the comparison and $SE_{M_i}^2$ is the squared standard error of measurement for the subtest of interest.

[a] For Grades 9–12, the standardization sample consisted of cases from both Fall and Spring.

Table K.8. Differences Between Single Subtest Standard Scores and Averages of Subtest Standard Scores Required for Statistical Significance and Differences Obtained by the Cumulative Percentages of the Age-Based Standardization Sample

	Significance Level		Cumulative Percentage				
	.15	.05	1	2	5	10	25
9 SUBTESTS							
Word Reading	6.61	7.67	22.44	20.22	16.56	13.00	8.89
Numerical Operations	10.75	12.47	27.78	24.78	20.22	17.00	11.22
Reading Comprehension	7.97	9.25	21.67	19.67	16.33	13.33	9.22
Spelling	8.88	10.30	22.11	18.78	15.44	12.56	8.78
Pseudoword Decoding	6.42	7.44	26.11	23.11	18.89	15.67	10.89
Math Reasoning	9.54	11.06	24.67	22.33	17.56	14.56	10.00
Written Expression	12.52	14.52	26.67	22.67	19.22	15.89	11.00
Listening Comprehension	14.59	16.92	27.78	24.44	20.00	16.33	10.89
Oral Expression	12.20	14.15	31.22	27.33	22.56	18.33	13.00
6 SUBTESTS							
Word Reading	6.46	7.57	24.00	20.83	17.17	13.50	9.33
Numerical Operations	9.76	11.44	26.50	23.33	19.33	15.67	10.33
Spelling	8.24	9.65	22.83	19.67	16.17	13.50	9.00
Math Reasoning	8.77	10.27	22.50	19.67	16.33	13.50	9.17
Listening Comprehension	12.95	15.17	25.33	23.33	19.00	15.50	10.50
Oral Expression	10.96	12.84	30.33	27.00	21.83	17.67	12.33
4 SUBTESTS							
Word Reading	6.43	7.77	25.75	22.25	18.00	14.75	10.25
Math Reasoning	8.01	9.68	21.75	19.00	16.00	13.25	9.50
Listening Comprehension	11.08	13.39	22.75	20.25	16.50	13.50	9.25
Oral Expression	9.59	11.60	27.50	23.25	19.25	16.00	11.00

Note. The differences required for statistical significance are based on the average standard errors of measurement across all ages and calculated with the following formula provided by Davis (1959):

$$\text{Difference Score} = Z\sqrt{(SE_{M_t})^2/K^2 + [(K-2)/K](SE_{M_i})^2}$$

where Z is the normal curve value associated with the desired significance level derived with the Bonferroni correction for multiple comparisons, K is the number of subtests in comparison, $SE_{M_t}^2$ is the sum of the squared standard errors of measurement for all subtests in the comparison and $SE_{M_i}^2$ is the squared standard error of measurement for the subtest of interest.

Table K.9. Differences Between Subtest Standard Scores Required for Statistical Significance of the Grade-Based Standardization Sample: Fall[a]

Subtests	Word Reading	Numerical Operations	Reading Comp	Spelling	Pseudoword Decoding	Math Reasoning	Written Expression	Listening Comp	Oral Expression
Word Reading		8.51	7.17	7.11	5.48	7.22	9.15	10.35	9.33
Numerical Operations	11.58		9.61	9.57	8.43	9.65	11.17	12.17	11.32
Reading Comp	9.76	13.09		8.40	7.07	8.49	10.19	11.28	10.35
Spelling	9.68	13.03	11.43		7.01	8.44	10.15	11.24	10.31
Pseudoword Decoding	7.46	11.47	9.63	9.55		7.12	9.08	10.28	9.26
Math Reasoning	9.82	13.13	11.56	11.49	9.70		10.22	11.31	10.39
Written Expression	12.46	15.21	13.87	13.81	12.36	13.91		12.63	11.81
Listening Comp	14.09	16.57	15.35	15.30	14.00	15.39	17.19		12.76
Oral Expression	12.71	15.41	14.09	14.03	12.61	14.14	16.08	17.37	

Note. Differences between subtest standard scores required for significance at the .15 level appear above the diagonal in the screened area, and differences significant at the .05 level appear below the diagonal. The differences required for statistical significance are based on the average standard errors of measurement across all grades for each subtest and calculated with the following formula:

$$\text{Difference Score} = Z\sqrt{SE_{M_a}^2 + SE_{M_b}^2}$$

where Z is the normal curve value associated with the desired significance level and SE_{M_a} and SE_{M_b} are the standard errors of measurement of the two subtest standard scores.

[a] For Grades 9–12, the standardization sample consisted of cases from both Fall and Spring.

Table K.10. Differences Between Subtest Standard Scores Required for Statistical Significance of the Grade-Based Standardization Sample: Spring[a]

Subtests	Word Reading	Numerical Operations	Reading Comp	Spelling	Pseudoword Decoding	Math Reasoning	Written Expression	Listening Comp	Oral Expression
Word Reading		8.46	7.19	7.13	5.47	7.37	9.19	10.58	9.37
Numerical Operations	11.52		9.52	9.47	8.29	9.65	11.10	12.28	11.25
Reading Comp	9.79	12.95		8.36	7.00	8.56	10.17	11.44	10.34
Spelling	9.71	12.89	11.38		6.94	8.51	10.13	11.41	10.29
Pseudoword Decoding	7.45	11.29	9.52	9.44		7.18	9.04	10.45	9.22
Math Reasoning	10.04	13.14	11.66	11.59	9.77		10.30	11.56	10.46
Written Expression	12.51	15.11	13.84	13.79	12.30	14.02		12.79	11.81
Listening Comp	14.40	16.72	15.58	15.53	14.22	15.73	17.41		12.92
Oral Expression	12.76	15.32	14.07	14.01	12.55	14.24	16.08	17.59	

Note. Differences between subtest standard scores required for significance at the .15 level appear above the diagonal in the screened area, and differences significant at the .05 level appear below the diagonal. The differences required for statistical significance are based on the average standard errors of measurement across all grades for each subtest and calculated with the following formula:

$$\text{Difference Score} = Z\sqrt{SE_{M_a}^2 + SE_{M_b}^2}$$

where Z is the normal curve value associated with the desired significance level and SE_{M_a} and SE_{M_b} are the standard errors of measurement of the two subtest standard scores.

[a] For Grades 9–12, the standardization sample consisted of cases from both Fall and Spring.

Table K.11. Differences Between Subtest Standard Scores Required for Statistical Significance of the Age-Based Standardization Sample

Subtests	Word Reading	Numerical Operations	Reading Comp	Spelling	Pseudoword Decoding	Math Reasoning	Written Expression	Listening Comp	Oral Expression
Word Reading		7.91	6.17	6.73	5.25	7.14	9.05	10.40	8.84
Numerical Operations	10.76		8.48	8.89	7.83	9.21	10.76	11.92	10.59
Reading Comp	8.39	11.54		7.39	6.07	7.76	9.55	10.84	9.36
Spelling	9.15	12.10	10.06		6.64	8.21	9.92	11.17	9.73
Pseudoword Decoding	7.14	10.66	8.26	9.04		7.05	8.99	10.35	8.78
Math Reasoning	9.71	12.53	10.57	11.18	9.60		10.21	11.42	10.02
Written Expression	12.32	14.65	13.01	13.51	12.23	13.89		12.71	11.47
Listening Comp	14.16	16.22	14.76	15.21	14.09	15.55	17.30		12.56
Oral Expression	12.04	14.41	12.74	13.25	11.95	13.64	15.61	17.10	

Note. Differences between subtest standard scores required for significance at the .15 level appear above the diagonal in the screened area, and differences significant at the .05 level appear below the diagonal. The differences required for statistical significance are based on the average standard errors of measurement across all ages for each subtest and calculated with the following formula:

$$\text{Difference Score} = Z\sqrt{SE_{M_a}^2 + SE_{M_b}^2}$$

where Z is the normal curve value associated with the desired significance level and SE_{M_a} and SE_{M_b} are the standard errors of measurement of the two subtest standard scores.

Table K.12. Cumulative Percentages of Intersubtest and Composite Scatter for the Standardization Sample

Comprehensive Battery

Scatter	Grade PreK	Ages 4–5	Grade K	Ages 5–6	Grades 1–12	Ages 6–19	Scatter
≥65	0.0	0.0	1.0	0.0	0.5	0.6	≥65
64	0.0	0.0	1.3	0.0	0.5	0.6	64
63	0.0	0.0	1.3	0.0	0.5	0.7	63
62	0.0	0.0	2.0	0.5	0.6	0.7	62
61	0.0	0.0	2.0	0.9	0.6	0.8	61
60	0.0	0.0	2.0	0.9	0.8	0.9	60
59	0.0	0.0	2.0	0.9	0.9	1.1	59
58	0.0	0.0	2.0	0.9	1.0	1.4	58
57	0.0	0.0	2.0	0.9	1.5	1.6	57
56	0.0	0.0	2.0	1.4	1.8	1.6	56
55	0.0	0.0	2.0	1.4	2.4	1.9	55
54	0.0	0.2	2.0	1.8	2.8	2.2	54
53	0.0	0.2	2.7	1.8	3.0	2.6	53
52	0.5	0.2	2.7	1.8	3.6	3.0	52
51	0.5	0.2	3.3	1.8	4.1	3.5	51
50	1.0	0.2	4.0	1.8	4.6	4.0	50
49	1.0	0.2	4.3	1.8	5.1	4.4	49
48	1.0	0.4	5.3	2.3	5.7	5.0	48
47	1.0	0.4	5.7	2.3	6.5	5.9	47
46	1.0	0.4	5.7	2.7	7.5	7.1	46
45	1.5	0.9	5.7	3.6	8.8	7.8	45
44	1.5	0.9	5.7	5.0	10.0	8.7	44
43	2.0	1.1	5.7	5.0	11.1	10.1	43
42	2.5	1.8	7.0	5.0	12.2	11.3	42
41	2.5	2.2	8.0	5.4	14.0	12.8	41
40	2.5	2.2	10.3	5.9	15.8	14.4	40
39	3.0	3.6	11.0	7.2	17.7	16.1	39
38	3.5	4.4	12.3	8.1	19.6	18.0	38
37	3.5	5.3	14.0	10.8	21.4	20.1	37
36	6.0	6.4	17.0	12.2	24.2	22.8	36
35	7.5	8.0	19.3	14.0	27.0	25.1	35
34	8.0	9.8	21.3	14.4	29.9	27.6	34
33	9.5	11.3	24.0	18.0	33.5	31.6	33
32	13.0	13.3	25.3	20.3	36.5	34.5	32
31	14.0	15.8	27.3	22.5	39.9	38.3	31
30	17.5	18.4	29.7	27.0	43.9	42.0	30
29	20.0	19.6	32.3	27.9	48.0	46.1	29
28	21.0	20.9	34.0	31.5	52.3	50.4	28
27	26.5	23.8	36.7	34.2	57.1	54.7	27
26	28.0	27.6	38.7	36.9	61.2	58.6	26
25	30.5	28.9	43.3	39.2	65.2	62.8	25
24	34.5	31.3	49.0	42.8	70.1	67.7	24
23	38.5	35.3	51.7	48.6	74.6	72.7	23
22	42.0	40.0	56.7	50.5	78.4	76.9	22
21	44.5	42.9	59.7	52.7	82.8	81.6	21
20	47.5	46.7	62.7	56.8	86.2	84.8	20
19	51.0	52.7	68.3	63.1	89.0	88.5	19
18	57.5	60.0	73.0	66.7	91.3	91.2	18
17	62.5	66.0	77.3	73.9	93.4	93.3	17
16	66.5	68.4	83.0	78.4	95.2	94.7	16
15	72.0	71.6	84.3	80.2	96.3	96.4	15
14	77.5	76.4	85.7	83.3	97.4	97.5	14
13	83.0	81.1	90.3	87.4	98.4	98.4	13
12	87.0	84.2	93.0	90.1	98.9	99.1	12
11	88.0	88.4	94.7	93.2	99.5	99.5	11
10	88.5	90.4	97.0	95.5	99.8	99.8	10
9	93.0	92.4	98.3	97.7	99.9	100.0	9
8	94.5	94.4	98.7	98.6	99.9	100.0	8
7	96.5	96.0	99.0	99.1	100.0	100.0	7
6	99.0	98.0	99.3	99.1	100.0	100.0	6
5	99.5	99.1	99.7	99.5	100.0	100.0	5
4	100.0	99.6	99.7	99.5	100.0	100.0	4
3	100.0	99.6	99.7	99.5	100.0	100.0	3
2	100.0	99.8	99.7	99.5	100.0	100.0	2
1	100.0	100.0	99.7	99.5	100.0	100.0	1
0	100.0	100.0	99.7	99.5	100.0	100.0	0
Mean	20.5	20.4	25.1	23.4	29.6	29.1	Mean
SD	9.0	9.0	11.7	10.3	10.2	10.1	SD
Median	19.0	19.0	23.0	22.0	28.0	28.0	Median

Table K.13. Intercorrelations of the WIAT–II Subtest and Composite Standard Scores and the Wechsler IQ Scores by Age

Age 4	WIAT–II Subtests									WIAT–II Composites				
	Word Reading	Numerical Operations	Reading Comprehension	Spelling	Pseudoword Decoding	Math Reasoning	Written Expression	Listening Comprehension	Oral Expression	Reading	Mathematics	Written Language	Oral Language	Total
WIAT–II Subtests														
Word Reading														
Numerical Operations														
Reading Comprehension														
Spelling														
Pseudoword Decoding														
Math Reasoning	0.48													
Written Expression														
Listening Comprehension	0.32					0.57							0.54	
Oral Expression	0.36					0.57		0.54					0.54	
WIAT–II Composites														
Reading														
Mathematics														
Written Language														
Oral Language	0.38					0.63		0.87	0.88					
Total														
Wechsler IQ Scores														
FSIQ	0.45					0.66		0.50	0.53				0.59	
VIQ	0.37					0.61		0.52	0.50				0.58	
PIQ	0.43					0.58		0.36	0.45				0.48	
Mean	100.57					100.53		99.96	100.12				99.16	
SD	14.16					13.89		13.96	13.92				14.53	

Note. FSIQ = Full Scale IQ; VIQ = Verbal IQ; PIQ = Performance IQ. The correlation of a composite with one of its contributing subtests, (e.g., the Oral Language composite with the Listening Comprehension subtest) was corrected by removing the subtest score from the composite score in order to control for inflated correlations. Corrected correlations appear above the diagonal, in the screened area. For children aged 4:0–4:11, the WPPSI–R scores were used. Ability correlations were corrected for the variability of the WPPSI–R scores (Guilford & Fruchter, 1978).

Table K.13. Intercorrelations of the WIAT–II Subtest and Composite Standard Scores and the Wechsler IQ Scores by Age *(continued)*

Age 5	WIAT–II Subtests									WIAT–II Composites				
	Word Reading	Numerical Operations	Reading Comprehension	Spelling	Pseudoword Decoding	Math Reasoning	Written Expression	Listening Comprehension	Oral Expression	Reading	Mathematics	Written Language	Oral Language	Total
WIAT–II Subtests														
Word Reading														
Numerical Operations	0.66										0.65			
Reading Comprehension														
Spelling	0.84	0.66												
Pseudoword Decoding														
Math Reasoning	0.66	0.65		0.63							0.65			
Written Expression														
Listening Comprehension	0.50	0.36		0.41		0.58							0.59	
Oral Expression	0.51	0.49		0.54		0.64	0.59						0.59	
WIAT–II Composites														
Reading														
Mathematics	0.72	0.90		0.70		0.91	0.49	0.62						
Written Language														
Oral Language	0.55	0.47		0.52		0.68	0.88	0.89		0.63				
Total														
Wechsler IQ Scores														
FSIQ	0.40	0.56		0.21		0.71	0.52	0.61		0.71			0.63	
VIQ	0.39	0.47		0.24		0.58	0.48	0.62		0.58			0.62	
PIQ	0.31	0.50		0.14		0.66	0.42	0.46		0.66			0.47	
Mean	97.96	99.08		97.56		98.81	98.40	99.38		100.37			97.84	
SD	15.24	13.57		13.02		14.72	13.94	15.32		14.14			15.37	

Note. FSIQ = Full Scale IQ; VIQ = Verbal IQ; PIQ = Performance IQ. The correlation of a composite with one of its contributing subtests, (e.g., the Mathematics composite with the Mathematics Reasoning subtest) was corrected by removing the subtest score from the composite score in order to control for inflated correlations. Corrected correlations appear above the diagonal, in the screened area. For children aged 5:0–5:11, the WPPSI–R scores were used. Ability correlations were corrected for the variability of the WPPSI–R scores (Guilford & Fruchter, 1978).

Table K.13. Intercorrelations of the WIAT–II Subtest and Composite Standard Scores and the Wechsler IQ Scores by Age (continued)

Age 6	WIAT–II Subtests									WIAT–II Composites				
	Word Reading	Numerical Operations	Reading Comprehension	Spelling	Pseudoword Decoding	Math Reasoning	Written Expression	Listening Comprehension	Oral Expression	Reading	Mathematics	Written Language	Oral Language	Total
WIAT–II Subtests														
Word Reading										0.85				0.82
Numerical Operations	0.62										0.58			0.68
Reading Comprehension	0.75	0.62								0.75				0.82
Spelling	0.83	0.58	0.79									0.57		0.80
Pseudoword Decoding	0.77	0.48	0.67	0.77						0.78				0.72
Math Reasoning	0.70	0.58	0.68	0.64	0.63						0.58			0.81
Written Expression	0.54	0.41	0.55	0.57	0.51	0.51						0.57		0.63
Listening Comprehension	0.45	0.30	0.41	0.40	0.29	0.54	0.30						0.56	0.52
Oral Expression	0.54	0.34	0.56	0.49	0.52	0.58	0.47	0.56					0.56	0.71
WIAT–II Composites														
Reading	0.93	0.60	0.85	0.87	0.92	0.73	0.54	0.34	0.57					0.80
Mathematics	0.75	0.87	0.72	0.70	0.63	0.90	0.54	0.48	0.53	0.75				0.81
Written Language	0.81	0.56	0.77	0.89	0.75	0.69	0.88	0.39	0.57	0.83	0.72			0.81
Oral Language	0.55	0.36	0.55	0.50	0.45	0.62	0.44	0.89	0.88	0.53	0.56	0.55		0.59
Total	0.87	0.73	0.86	0.87	0.82	0.85	0.68	0.56	0.74	0.93	0.88	0.89	0.73	
Wechsler IQ Scores														
FSIQ	0.58	0.51	0.51	0.56	0.36	0.81	0.32	0.56	0.76	0.50	0.75	0.50	0.75	0.81
VIQ	0.53	0.44	0.49	0.54	0.39	0.79	0.38	0.61	0.78	0.49	0.70	0.50	0.79	0.71
PIQ	0.54	0.50	0.43	0.49	0.26	0.69	0.18	0.40	0.61	0.42	0.69	0.42	0.57	0.78
Mean	99.98	100.23	98.34	99.03	99.03	99.54	99.92	100.38	100.29	100.07	99.59	101.50	99.88	101.51
SD	14.24	12.87	15.36	14.19	13.91	14.35	14.35	15.60	14.60	17.05	14.09	14.84	16.11	15.42

Note. FSIQ = Full Scale IQ; VIQ = Verbal IQ; PIQ = Performance IQ. The correlation of a composite with one of its contributing subtests, (e.g., the Reading composite with the Word Reading subtest) was corrected by removing the subtest score from the composite score in order to control for inflated correlations. Corrected correlations appear above the diagonal, in the screened area. For children aged 6:0–16:11, the WISC–III scores were used. Ability correlations were corrected for the variability of the WISC–III scores (Guilford & Fruchter, 1978).

Table K.13. Intercorrelations of the WIAT–II Subtest and Composite Standard Scores and the Wechsler IQ Scores by Age *(continued)*

Age 7	WIAT–II Subtests									WIAT–II Composites				
WIAT–II Subtests	Word Reading	Numerical Operations	Reading Comprehension	Spelling	Pseudoword Decoding	Math Reasoning	Written Expression	Listening Comprehension	Oral Expression	Reading	Mathematics	Written Language	Oral Language	Total
Word Reading										0.91				0.88
Numerical Operations	0.53										0.53			0.52
Reading Comprehension	0.85	0.55								0.81				0.85
Spelling	0.81	0.58	0.74									0.47		0.76
Pseudoword Decoding	0.77	0.40	0.68	0.71						0.77				0.66
Math Reasoning	0.65	0.53	0.64	0.59	0.52						0.53			0.68
Written Expression	0.48	0.38	0.60	0.47	0.42	0.42						0.47		0.56
Listening Comprehension	0.58	0.31	0.59	0.51	0.44	0.62	0.49						0.62	0.69
Oral Expression	0.58	0.39	0.63	0.49	0.44	0.58	0.49	0.62					0.62	0.64
WIAT–II Composites														
Reading	0.95	0.51	0.89	0.82	0.91	0.63	0.52	0.57	0.56					0.80
Mathematics	0.68	0.86	0.68	0.66	0.53	0.89	0.44	0.51	0.54	0.67				0.70
Written Language	0.74	0.55	0.77	0.86	0.66	0.58	0.86	0.59	0.54	0.78	0.63			0.80
Oral Language	0.65	0.39	0.68	0.56	0.49	0.66	0.53	0.89	0.90	0.63	0.59	0.62		0.67
Total	0.91	0.60	0.88	0.82	0.78	0.75	0.66	0.73	0.69	0.93	0.81	0.87	0.79	
Wechsler IQ Scores														
FSIQ	0.68	0.71	0.75	0.67	0.54	0.81	0.59	0.72	0.48	0.70	0.81	0.71	0.74	0.84
VIQ	0.75	0.73	0.77	0.69	0.60	0.80	0.62	0.79	0.49	0.76	0.81	0.74	0.79	0.87
PIQ	0.49	0.59	0.60	0.53	0.38	0.69	0.46	0.53	0.38	0.52	0.68	0.56	0.56	0.69
Mean	101.13	99.78	99.50	101.80	100.12	100.72	97.92	99.80	100.85	100.62	100.25	99.52	99.71	100.44
SD	15.44	13.15	16.23	14.05	15.58	14.87	13.80	14.72	15.73	18.15	14.17	13.45	16.38	14.74

Note. FSIQ = Full Scale IQ; VIQ = Verbal IQ; PIQ = Performance IQ. The correlation of a composite with one of its contributing subtests, (e.g., the Reading composite with the Word Reading subtest) was corrected by removing the subtest score from the composite score in order to control for inflated correlations. Corrected correlations appear above the diagonal, in the screened area. For children aged 6:0–16:11, the WISC–III scores were used. Ability correlations were corrected for the variability of the WISC–III scores (Guilford & Fruchter, 1978).

Table K.13. Intercorrelations of the WIAT–II Subtest and Composite Standard Scores and the Wechsler IQ Scores by Age *(continued)*

Age 8

	WIAT–II Subtests									WIAT–II Composites				
	Word Reading	Numerical Operations	Reading Comprehension	Spelling	Pseudoword Decoding	Math Reasoning	Written Expression	Listening Comprehension	Oral Expression	Reading	Mathematics	Written Language	Oral Language	Total
WIAT–II Subtests														
Word Reading										0.86				0.82
Numerical Operations	0.52										0.63			0.60
Reading Comprehension	0.72	0.51								0.70				0.81
Spelling	0.79	0.56	0.64									0.70		0.82
Pseudoword Decoding	0.82	0.45	0.61	0.78						0.77				0.73
Math Reasoning	0.62	0.63	0.66	0.60	0.55						0.63			0.75
Written Expression	0.63	0.52	0.55	0.70	0.63	0.55						0.70		0.74
Listening Comprehension	0.56	0.31	0.65	0.49	0.48	0.60	0.44						0.60	0.64
Oral Expression	0.54	0.39	0.66	0.52	0.47	0.55	0.52	0.60					0.60	0.64
WIAT–II Composites														
Reading	0.92	0.55	0.83	0.82	0.91	0.67	0.65	0.61	0.60					0.83
Mathematics	0.62	0.91	0.65	0.63	0.55	0.90	0.59	0.50	0.51	0.67				0.70
Written Language	0.75	0.57	0.62	0.91	0.76	0.61	0.92	0.49	0.55	0.79	0.65			0.81
Oral Language	0.61	0.38	0.73	0.57	0.53	0.64	0.54	0.89	0.89	0.68	0.56	0.58		0.69
Total	0.85	0.69	0.84	0.87	0.81	0.81	0.78	0.71	0.72	0.93	0.82	0.89	0.80	
Wechsler IQ Scores														
FSIQ	0.66	0.49	0.68	0.60	0.62	0.78	0.58	0.72	0.69	0.71	0.70	0.62	0.77	0.78
VIQ	0.70	0.43	0.72	0.65	0.68	0.80	0.57	0.71	0.67	0.77	0.68	0.64	0.75	0.78
PIQ	0.47	0.46	0.48	0.42	0.41	0.58	0.46	0.59	0.59	0.47	0.57	0.48	0.64	0.61
Mean	101.35	100.77	101.05	101.28	100.69	100.84	101.11	101.62	100.97	100.57	100.97	101.32	100.92	101.35
SD	14.11	15.01	14.00	14.07	16.06	14.46	15.53	15.03	14.47	16.00	15.29	15.57	15.75	15.66

Note. FSIQ = Full Scale IQ; VIQ = Verbal IQ; PIQ = Performance IQ. The correlation of a composite with one of its contributing subtests, (e.g., the Reading composite with the Word Reading subtest) was corrected by removing the subtest score from the composite score in order to control for inflated correlations. Corrected correlations appear above the diagonal, in the screened area. For children aged 6:0–16:11, the WISC–III scores were used. Ability correlations were corrected for the variability of the WISC–III scores (Guilford & Fruchter, 1978).

Table K.13. Intercorrelations of the WIAT–II Subtest and Composite Standard Scores and the Wechsler IQ Scores by Age *(continued)*

| Age 9 | WIAT–II Subtests | | | | | | | | | WIAT–II Composites | | | | |
	Word Reading	Numerical Operations	Reading Comprehension	Spelling	Pseudoword Decoding	Math Reasoning	Written Expression	Listening Comprehension	Oral Expression	Reading	Mathematics	Written Language	Oral Language	Total
WIAT–II Subtests														
Word Reading										0.78				0.71
Numerical Operations	0.50										0.66			0.63
Reading Comrehension	0.66	0.56								0.64				0.75
Spelling	0.76	0.58	0.63									0.64		0.75
Pseudoword Decoding	0.78	0.42	0.60	0.69						0.78				0.70
Math Reasoning	0.56	0.66	0.63	0.63	0.55						0.66			0.74
Written Expression	0.56	0.49	0.55	0.64	0.57	0.54						0.64		0.64
Listening Comprehension	0.47	0.41	0.50	0.47	0.43	0.60	0.38						0.58	0.59
Oral Expression	0.40	0.32	0.57	0.41	0.39	0.49	0.39	0.58					0.58	0.47
WIAT–II Composites														
Reading	0.91	0.53	0.80	0.78	0.91	0.62	0.63	0.50	0.45					0.77
Mathematics	0.57	0.90	0.64	0.66	0.53	0.91	0.55	0.54	0.43	0.63				0.71
Written Language	0.72	0.57	0.62	0.91	0.69	0.63	0.90	0.46	0.42	0.78	0.66			0.76
Oral Language	0.53	0.41	0.61	0.50	0.49	0.63	0.44	0.88	0.89	0.56	0.55	0.51		0.59
Total	0.77	0.72	0.79	0.82	0.78	0.81	0.74	0.68	0.59	0.89	0.83	0.87	0.74	
Wechsler IQ Scores														
FSIQ	0.51	0.37	0.60	0.46	0.44	0.67	0.39	0.51	0.37	0.56	0.57	0.47	0.51	0.62
VIQ	0.62	0.40	0.65	0.51	0.53	0.68	0.41	0.60	0.46	0.66	0.59	0.50	0.61	0.71
PIQ	0.27	0.25	0.41	0.31	0.23	0.52	0.29	0.28	0.17	0.30	0.43	0.33	0.28	0.37
Mean	100.94	100.78	100.89	100.50	101.98	100.75	101.54	100.08	100.26	101.11	100.67	101.48	98.85	100.63
SD	14.49	14.24	12.45	14.36	14.98	14.61	14.87	14.62	14.84	14.15	14.93	15.06	16.58	13.82

Note. FSIQ = Full Scale IQ; VIQ = Verbal IQ; PIQ = Performance IQ. The correlation of a composite with one of its contributing subtests, (e.g., the Reading composite with the Word Reading subtest) was corrected by removing the subtest score from the composite score in order to control for inflated correlations. Corrected correlations appear above the diagonal, in the screened area. For children aged 6:0–16:11, the WISC–III scores were used. Ability correlations were corrected for the variability of the WISC–III scores (Guilford & Fruchter, 1978).

Age 10	WIAT–II Subtests									WIAT–II Composites				
	Word Reading	Numerical Operations	Reading Comprehension	Spelling	Pseudoword Decoding	Math Reasoning	Written Expression	Listening Comprehension	Oral Expression	Reading	Mathematics	Written Language	Oral Language	Total
WIAT–II Subtests														
Word Reading										0.85				0.79
Numerical Operations	0.57										0.67			0.63
Reading Comprehension	0.70	0.57								0.67				0.80
Spelling	0.84	0.57	0.68									0.72		0.79
Pseudoword Decoding	0.80	0.48	0.57	0.77						0.75				0.72
Math Reasoning	0.59	0.67	0.67	0.62	0.53						0.67			0.71
Written Expression	0.68	0.53	0.64	0.72	0.67	0.59						0.72		0.76
Listening Comprehension	0.52	0.39	0.60	0.47	0.51	0.58	0.55						0.49	0.65
Oral Expression	0.34	0.32	0.55	0.39	0.31	0.43	0.35	0.49					0.49	0.47
WIAT–II Composites														
Reading	0.93	0.59	0.83	0.85	0.88	0.67	0.76	0.59	0.44					0.83
Mathematics	0.61	0.90	0.67	0.63	0.54	0.92	0.61	0.53	0.41	0.68				0.70
Written Language	0.80	0.55	0.70	0.92	0.77	0.63	0.92	0.55	0.38	0.86	0.64			0.82
Oral Language	0.48	0.39	0.66	0.47	0.47	0.58	0.53	0.85	0.87	0.58	0.54	0.54		0.60
Total	0.83	0.69	0.84	0.84	0.79	0.79	0.82	0.71	0.62	0.92	0.82	0.90	0.76	
Wechsler IQ Scores														
FSIQ	0.65	0.56	0.63	0.53	0.54	0.75	0.60	0.80	0.65	0.69	0.71	0.61	0.82	0.78
VIQ	0.64	0.53	0.66	0.57	0.51	0.75	0.60	0.81	0.62	0.66	0.68	0.63	0.80	0.77
PIQ	0.54	0.50	0.45	0.38	0.44	0.60	0.48	0.65	0.57	0.58	0.61	0.47	0.69	0.64
Mean	100.10	100.64	100.08	100.09	100.59	100.15	99.39	100.59	100.44	99.12	100.10	100.11	99.84	98.67
SD	14.78	14.91	12.88	15.17	15.23	15.26	15.53	14.28	14.89	14.75	15.58	15.64	14.94	14.47

Note. FSIQ = Full Scale IQ; VIQ = Verbal IQ; PIQ = Performance IQ. The correlation of a composite with one of its contributing subtests, (e.g., the Reading composite with the Word Reading subtest) was corrected by removing the subtest score from the composite score in order to control for inflated correlations. Corrected correlations appear above the diagonal, in the screened area. For children aged 6:0–16:11, the WISC–III scores were used. Ability correlations were corrected for the variability of the WISC–III scores (Guilford & Fruchter, 1978).

Table K.13. Intercorrelations of the WIAT–II Subtest and Composite Standard Scores and the Wechsler IQ Scores by Age *(continued)*

Age 11	WIAT–II Subtests									WIAT–II Composites				
WIAT–II Subtests	Word Reading	Numerical Operations	Reading Comprehension	Spelling	Pseudoword Decoding	Math Reasoning	Written Expression	Listening Comprehension	Oral Expression	Reading	Mathematics	Written Language	Oral Language	Total
Word Reading										0.81				0.83
Numerical Operations	0.51										0.64			0.68
Reading Comprehension	0.65	0.55								0.64				0.74
Spelling	0.82	0.54	0.55									0.76		0.76
Pseudoword Decoding	0.75	0.42	0.54	0.67						0.71				0.62
Math Reasoning	0.57	0.64	0.64	0.56	0.44						0.64			0.74
Written Expression	0.68	0.56	0.59	0.76	0.56	0.57						0.76		0.75
Listening Comprehension	0.54	0.51	0.61	0.46	0.33	0.54	0.52						0.45	0.66
Oral Expression	0.38	0.33	0.43	0.29	0.23	0.40	0.35	0.45					0.45	0.53
WIAT–II Composites														
Reading	0.92	0.57	0.84	0.78	0.84	0.63	0.70	0.59	0.43					0.81
Mathematics	0.59	0.90	0.64	0.60	0.46	0.91	0.63	0.58	0.40	0.65				0.74
Written Language	0.80	0.59	0.60	0.94	0.65	0.59	0.93	0.53	0.35	0.79	0.65			0.77
Oral Language	0.54	0.49	0.61	0.45	0.32	0.55	0.50	0.84	0.86	0.60	0.58	0.51		0.66
Total	0.87	0.76	0.80	0.82	0.70	0.79	0.81	0.75	0.63	0.92	0.84	0.87	0.79	
Wechsler IQ Scores														
FSIQ	0.61	0.62	0.60	0.57	0.54	0.74	0.57	0.67	0.42	0.63	0.73	0.60	0.62	0.74
VIQ	0.69	0.64	0.65	0.61	0.53	0.79	0.60	0.70	0.47	0.69	0.77	0.64	0.66	0.79
PIQ	0.40	0.47	0.43	0.39	0.42	0.53	0.43	0.49	0.27	0.42	0.52	0.43	0.43	0.47
Mean	99.74	101.05	100.94	99.17	101.07	100.62	98.68	100.76	100.30	99.87	100.77	98.74	100.05	99.65
SD	14.61	14.63	14.90	15.18	14.64	15.33	15.03	14.06	14.44	15.57	15.75	15.98	14.75	15.01

Note. FSIQ = Full Scale IQ; VIQ = Verbal IQ; PIQ = Performance IQ. The correlation of a composite with one of its contributing subtests, (e.g., the Reading composite with the Word Reading subtest) was corrected by removing the subtest score from the composite score in order to control for inflated correlations. Corrected correlations appear above the diagonal, in the screened area. For children aged 6:0–16:11, the WISC–III scores were used. Ability correlations were corrected for the variability of the WISC–III scores (Guilford & Fruchter, 1978).

Table K.13. Intercorrelations of the WIAT–II Subtest and Composite Standard Scores and the Wechsler IQ Scores by Age *(continued)*

Age 12

	WIAT–II Subtests									WIAT–II Composites				
	Word Reading	Numerical Operations	Reading Comprehension	Spelling	Pseudoword Decoding	Math Reasoning	Written Expression	Listening Comprehension	Oral Expression	Reading	Mathematics	Written Language	Oral Language	Total
WIAT–II Subtests														
Word Reading										0.85				0.77
Numerical Operations	0.57										0.72			0.71
Reading Comprehension	0.73	0.57								0.73				0.79
Spelling	0.78	0.59	0.67									0.74		0.80
Pseudoword Decoding	0.80	0.48	0.65	0.73						0.77				0.70
Math Reasoning	0.59	0.72	0.63	0.62	0.56						0.72			0.77
Written Expression	0.56	0.54	0.60	0.74	0.55	0.52						0.74		0.74
Listening Comprehension	0.52	0.50	0.61	0.50	0.51	0.62	0.50						0.46	0.65
Oral Expression	0.32	0.37	0.37	0.44	0.30	0.43	0.43	0.46					0.46	0.50
WIAT–II Composites														
Reading	0.94	0.60	0.87	0.79	0.88	0.64	0.60	0.63	0.35					0.77
Mathematics	0.63	0.92	0.65	0.64	0.55	0.93	0.56	0.61	0.42	0.67				0.76
Written Language	0.72	0.60	0.68	0.92	0.69	0.61	0.93	0.53	0.47	0.74	0.64			0.81
Oral Language	0.48	0.52	0.58	0.53	0.46	0.62	0.53	0.85	0.86	0.56	0.61	0.58		0.63
Total	0.82	0.78	0.82	0.85	0.75	0.82	0.81	0.73	0.60	0.89	0.86	0.89	0.77	
Wechsler IQ Scores														
FSIQ	0.63	0.66	0.63	0.58	0.54	0.73	0.58	0.72	0.34	0.68	0.74	0.62	0.61	0.79
VIQ	0.62	0.65	0.55	0.59	0.56	0.67	0.53	0.78	0.37	0.70	0.71	0.58	0.68	0.81
PIQ	0.50	0.50	0.57	0.43	0.39	0.62	0.51	0.49	0.22	0.50	0.60	0.51	0.39	0.58
Mean	99.38	99.82	100.21	100.53	99.05	100.16	100.15	101.85	99.49	98.57	99.91	100.52	100.22	99.78
SD	15.72	15.24	15.52	15.24	15.14	16.05	15.75	14.07	14.06	16.43	16.59	16.09	14.41	14.96

Note. FSIQ = Full Scale IQ; VIQ = Verbal IQ; PIQ = Performance IQ. The correlation of a composite with one of its contributing subtests, (e.g., the Reading composite with the Word Reading subtest) was corrected by removing the subtest score from the composite score in order to control for inflated correlations. Corrected correlations appear above the diagonal, in the screened area. For children aged 6:0–16:11, the WISC–III scores were used. Ability correlations were corrected for the variability of the WISC–III scores (Guilford & Fruchter, 1978).

Table K.13. Intercorrelations of the WIAT–II Subtest and Composite Standard Scores and the Wechsler IQ Scores by Age *(continued)*

Age 13	WIAT–II Subtests									WIAT–II Composites				
	Word Reading	Numerical Operations	Reading Comprehension	Spelling	Pseudoword Decoding	Math Reasoning	Written Expression	Listening Comprehension	Oral Expression	Reading	Mathematics	Written Language	Oral Language	Total
WIAT–II Subtests														
Word Reading										0.79				0.80
Numerical Operations	0.59										0.72			0.74
Reading Comprehension	0.64	0.61								0.62				0.77
Spelling	0.78	0.61	0.56									0.72		0.75
Pseudoword Decoding	0.77	0.49	0.52	0.64						0.70				0.63
Math Reasoning	0.64	0.72	0.66	0.56	0.52						0.72			0.82
Written Expression	0.61	0.66	0.60	0.72	0.46	0.64						0.72		0.76
Listening Comprehension	0.62	0.58	0.62	0.52	0.48	0.70	0.49						0.56	0.73
Oral Expression	0.43	0.39	0.48	0.39	0.26	0.52	0.47	0.56					0.56	0.50
WIAT–II Composites														
Reading	0.91	0.64	0.83	0.77	0.85	0.70	0.63	0.65	0.43					0.80
Mathematics	0.65	0.93	0.68	0.63	0.54	0.92	0.70	0.68	0.50	0.71				0.81
Written Language	0.75	0.68	0.63	0.91	0.57	0.65	0.93	0.55	0.45	0.75	0.71			0.78
Oral Language	0.60	0.56	0.63	0.52	0.42	0.68	0.55	0.88	0.88	0.62	0.67	0.58		0.68
Total	0.84	0.81	0.81	0.82	0.70	0.85	0.81	0.78	0.59	0.90	0.89	0.88	0.80	
Wechsler IQ Scores														
FSIQ	0.47	0.51	0.50	0.28	0.40	0.69	0.53	0.68	0.46	0.52	0.65	0.48	0.66	0.71
VIQ	0.56	0.56	0.60	0.36	0.48	0.73	0.57	0.71	0.49	0.62	0.69	0.55	0.69	0.80
PIQ	0.31	0.39	0.31	0.16	0.26	0.56	0.40	0.55	0.35	0.33	0.52	0.34	0.52	0.48
Mean	99.57	99.44	99.04	100.06	101.37	98.89	99.37	99.40	100.21	99.47	99.07	100.13	98.93	99.45
SD	15.47	15.97	14.90	15.05	15.25	15.62	16.73	15.65	15.13	15.79	16.80	16.72	16.36	15.80

Note. FSIQ = Full Scale IQ; VIQ = Verbal IQ; PIQ = Performance IQ. The correlation of a composite with one of its contributing subtests, (e.g., the Reading composite with the Word Reading subtest) was corrected by removing the subtest score from the composite score in order to control for inflated correlations. Corrected correlations appear above the diagonal, in the screened area. For children aged 6:0–16:11, the WISC–III scores were used. Ability correlations were corrected for the variability of the WISC–III scores (Guilford & Fruchter, 1978).

Age 14	WIAT–II Subtests									WIAT–II Composites				
WIAT–II Subtests	Word Reading	Numerical Operations	Reading Comprehension	Spelling	Pseudoword Decoding	Math Reasoning	Written Expression	Listening Comprehension	Oral Expression	Reading	Mathematics	Written Language	Oral Language	Total
WIAT–II Subtests														
Word Reading										0.82				0.71
Numerical Operations	0.48										0.76			0.63
Reading Comprehension	0.69	0.58								0.68				0.79
Spelling	0.78	0.63	0.64									0.70		0.78
Pseudoword Decoding	0.79	0.42	0.60	0.71						0.76				0.61
Math Reasoning	0.47	0.76	0.63	0.61	0.43						0.76			0.72
Written Expression	0.57	0.63	0.64	0.70	0.53	0.59						0.70		0.72
Listening Comprehension	0.66	0.49	0.70	0.57	0.56	0.54	0.54						0.48	0.69
Oral Expression	0.35	0.43	0.46	0.40	0.24	0.37	0.51	0.48					0.48	0.52
WIAT–II Composites														
Reading	0.92	0.48	0.85	0.78	0.87	0.50	0.59	0.71	0.40					0.71
Mathematics	0.51	0.95	0.65	0.67	0.46	0.92	0.67	0.57	0.47	0.54				0.67
Written Language	0.72	0.68	0.69	0.91	0.64	0.64	0.93	0.59	0.50	0.73	0.72			0.78
Oral Language	0.58	0.53	0.66	0.55	0.45	0.53	0.60	0.85	0.87	0.64	0.60	0.62		0.69
Total	0.76	0.73	0.84	0.82	0.66	0.78	0.76	0.77	0.63	0.86	0.81	0.87	0.82	
Wechsler IQ Scores														
FSIQ	0.47	0.60	0.70	0.32	0.56	0.76	0.38	0.70	0.37	0.69	0.71	0.36	0.65	0.81
VIQ	0.60	0.61	0.79	0.42	0.65	0.76	0.42	0.71	0.34	0.80	0.72	0.43	0.65	0.86
PIQ	0.22	0.47	0.47	0.14	0.35	0.60	0.27	0.55	0.33	0.43	0.57	0.21	0.53	0.60
Mean	100.69	101.21	99.36	101.32	100.88	100.67	101.07	100.59	99.98	98.50	101.17	101.35	99.63	99.31
SD	15.36	16.74	14.44	14.23	14.70	14.81	15.43	15.30	15.19	15.18	16.91	15.78	15.66	14.02

Note. FSIQ = Full Scale IQ; VIQ = Verbal IQ; PIQ = Performance IQ. The correlation of a composite with one of its contributing subtests, (e.g., the Reading composite with the Word Reading subtest) was corrected by removing the subtest score from the composite score in order to control for inflated correlations. Corrected correlations appear above the diagonal, in the screened area. For children aged 6:0–16:11, the WISC–III scores were used. Ability correlations were corrected for the variability of the WISC–III scores (Guilford & Fruchter, 1978).

Table K.13. Intercorrelations of the WIAT–II Subtest and Composite Standard Scores and the Wechsler IQ Scores by Age (continued)

Age 15	WIAT–II Subtests									WIAT–II Composites				
WIAT–II Subtests	Word Reading	Numerical Operations	Reading Comprehension	Spelling	Pseudoword Decoding	Math Reasoning	Written Expression	Listening Comprehension	Oral Expression	Reading	Mathematics	Written Language	Oral Language	Total
Word Reading										0.83				0.69
Numerical Operations	0.41										0.73			0.59
Reading Comprehension	0.60	0.37								0.59				0.69
Spelling	0.68	0.42	0.46									0.60		0.63
Pseudoword Decoding	0.81	0.24	0.51	0.59						0.75				0.52
Math Reasoning	0.47	0.73	0.52	0.41	0.33						0.73			0.70
Written Expression	0.48	0.55	0.49	0.60	0.33	0.55						0.60		0.71
Listening Comprehension	0.53	0.50	0.67	0.45	0.45	0.61	0.52						0.29	0.70
Oral Expression	0.11	0.23	0.37	0.20	0.12	0.27	0.33	0.29					0.29	0.32
WIAT–II Composites														
Reading	0.92	0.36	0.82	0.66	0.87	0.50	0.45	0.60	0.24					0.62
Mathematics	0.47	0.93	0.47	0.45	0.31	0.92	0.58	0.59	0.27	0.46				0.61
Written Language	0.66	0.54	0.54	0.89	0.51	0.54	0.89	0.54	0.32	0.63	0.58			0.72
Oral Language	0.38	0.45	0.63	0.40	0.34	0.55	0.52	0.79	0.81	0.51	0.54	0.53		0.63
Total	0.76	0.68	0.76	0.74	0.64	0.77	0.75	0.77	0.50	0.83	0.78	0.83	0.79	
Wechsler IQ Scores														
FSIQ	0.62	0.67	0.73	0.58	0.35	0.76	0.61	0.70	0.25	0.60	0.75	0.63	0.59	0.73
VIQ	0.71	0.71	0.81	0 65	0.49	0.80	0.71	0.80	0.22	0.74	0.79	0.72	0.63	0.82
PIQ	0.44	0.53	0.55	0.40	0.23	0.60	0.40	0.50	0.21	0.46	0.60	0.43	0.45	0 55
Mean	100.74	100.15	100.02	100.98	101.29	100.76	99.30	99.42	99.87	99.86	100.13	99.94	98.79	98.59
SD	14.81	14.89	13.97	13.79	14.00	14.30	14.36	14.36	14.54	15.01	15.23	14.27	13.93	13.63

Note. FSIQ = Full Scale IQ; VIQ = Verbal IQ; PIQ = Performance IQ. The correlation of a composite with one of its contributing subtests, (e.g., the Reading composite with the Word Reading subtest) was corrected by removing the subtest score from the composite score in order to control for inflated correlations. Corrected correlations appear above the diagonal, in the screened area. For children aged 6:0–16:11, the WISC–III scores were used. Ability correlations were corrected for the variability of the WISC–III scores (Guilford & Fruchter, 1978).

Table K.13. Intercorrelations of the WIAT–II Subtest and Composite Standard Scores and the Wechsler IQ Scores by Age *(continued)*

Age 16	WIAT–II Subtests									WIAT–II Composites				
WIAT–II Subtests	Word Reading	Numerical Operations	Reading Comprehension	Spelling	Pseudoword Decoding	Math Reasoning	Written Expression	Listening Comprehension	Oral Expression	Reading	Mathematics	Written Language	Oral Language	Total
Word Reading										0.84				0.80
Numerical Operations	0.58										0.72			0.68
Reading Comprehension	0.67	0.55								0.60				0.72
Spelling	0.77	0.68	0.64									0.71		0.84
Pseudoword Decoding	0.82	0.53	0.48	0.72						0.71				0.69
Math Reasoning	0.63	0.72	0.60	0.66	0.49						0.72			0.66
Written Expression	0.62	0.63	0.57	0.71	0.52	0.54						0.71		0.70
Listening Comprehension	0.66	0.44	0.66	0.61	0.49	0.60	0.55						0.50	0.67
Oral Expression	0.40	0.46	0.51	0.45	0.30	0.44	0.48	0.50					0.50	0.48
WIAT–II Composites														
Reading	0.92	0.59	0.83	0.79	0.86	0.58	0.65	0.66	0.40					0.79
Mathematics	0.65	0.93	0.62	0.72	0.55	0.92	0.63	0.56	0.49	0.63				0.68
Written Language	0.74	0.69	0.64	0.91	0.63	0.64	0.93	0.62	0.49	0.76	0.72			0.81
Oral Language	0.60	0.52	0.68	0.61	0.45	0.59	0.59	0.87	0.86	0.62	0.60	0.64		0.66
Total	0.83	0.75	0.78	0.87	0.75	0.74	0.80	0.75	0.59	0.90	0.81	0.90	0.78	
Wechsler IQ Scores														
FSIQ	0.61	0.67	0.70	0.60	0.47	0.69	0.56	0.78	0.53	0.69	0.72	0.61	0.77	0.78
VIQ	0.66	0.75	0.76	0.62	0.62	0.83	0.62	0.75	0.52	0.77	0.86	0.65	0.75	0.86
PIQ	0.41	0.41	0.46	0.43	0.18	0.33	0.37	0.66	0.41	0.42	0.34	0.42	0.64	0.46
Mean	98.45	100.17	100.56	101.03	100.80	100.66	100.07	100.60	101.01	99.21	100.49	100.74	100.17	99.47
SD	16.08	15.84	14.86	14.04	15.20	14.60	15.77	14.64	14.04	15.61	15.95	15.56	14.87	15.11

Note. FSIQ = Full Scale IQ; VIQ = Verbal IQ; PIQ = Performance IQ. The correlation of a composite with one of its contributing subtests, (e.g., the Reading composite with the Word Reading subtest) was corrected by removing the subtest score from the composite score in order to control for inflated correlations. Corrected correlations appear above the diagonal, in the screened area. For children aged 6:0–16:11, the WISC–III scores were used. Ability correlations were corrected for the variability of the WISC–III scores (Guilford & Fruchter, 1978).

Table K.13. Intercorrelations of the WIAT–II Subtest and Composite Standard Scores and the Wechsler IQ Scores by Age *(continued)*

Age 17–19	WIAT–II Subtests									WIAT–II Composites				Total
	Word Reading	Numerical Operations	Reading Comprehension	Spelling	Pseudoword Decoding	Math Reasoning	Written Expression	Listening Comprehension	Oral Expression	Reading	Mathematics	Written Language	Oral Language	Total
WIAT–II Subtests														
Word Reading										0.73				0.81
Numerical Operations	0.58										0.80			0.79
Reading Comprehension	0.67	0.67								0.68				0.78
Spelling	0.69	0.72	0.63									0.73		0.84
Pseudoword Decoding	0.72	0.51	0.61	0.64						0.71				0.73
Math Reasoning	0.61	0.80	0.71	0.62	0.58						0.80			0.81
Written Expression	0.66	0.63	0.54	0.73	0.56	0.61						0.73		0.75
Listening Comprehension	0.62	0.58	0.71	0.64	0.51	0.61	0.42						0.23	0.68
Oral Expression	0.29	0.36	0.43	0.36	0.26	0.37	0.45	0.23					0.23	0.48
WIAT–II Composites														
Reading	0.87	0.66	0.88	0.72	0.85	0.70	0.61	0.70	0.45					0.83
Mathematics	0.62	0.94	0.73	0.70	0.57	0.95	0.66	0.62	0.39	0.72				0.80
Written Language	0.76	0.72	0.62	0.92	0.64	0.66	0.93	0.56	0.48	0.70	0.72			0.78
Oral Language	0.59	0.59	0.72	0.63	0.48	0.62	0.55	0.79	0.77	0.71	0.64	0.65		0.78
Total	0.78	0.83	0.82	0.82	0.75	0.83	0.79	0.74	0.62	0.91	0.87	0.85	0.85	
Wechsler IQ Scores														
FSIQ	0.68	0.73	0.73	0.70	0.52	0.82	0.65	0.80	0.50	0.77	0.82	0.72	0.81	0.88
VIQ	0.70	0.69	0.75	0.65	0.53	0.74	0.60	0.82	0.46	0.78	0.75	0.67	0.78	0.85
PIQ	0.47	0.64	0.51	0.60	0.40	0.76	0.61	0.58	0.50	0.57	0.75	0.66	0.71	0.79
Mean	99.33	98.51	99.16	99.81	100.46	98.61	98.62	100.03	99.20	99.36	98.40	98.65	98.94	100.40
SD	14.82	16.72	16.40	14.92	14.13	16.87	16.51	15.03	14.48	14.76	17.95	16.70	13.61	15.07

Note. FSIQ = Full Scale IQ; VIQ = Verbal IQ; PIQ = Performance IQ. The correlation of a composite with one of its contributing subtests, (e.g., the Reading composite with the Word Reading subtest) was corrected by removing the subtest score from the composite score in order to control for inflated correlations. Corrected correlations appear above the diagonal, in the screened area. For individuals aged 17:0–19:11, the WAIS–III scores were used. Ability correlations were corrected for the variability of the WAIS–III scores (Guilford & Fruchter, 1978).

References

Davis, F. B. (1959). Interpretation of differences among averages and individual test scores. *Journal of Educational Psychology,* *50*(4), 162–170.

Guilford, J. P., & Fruchter, B. (1978). *Fundamental statistics in psychology and education* (6th ed.). New York: McGraw-Hill.

Wechsler, D. (1989). *Wechsler Preschool and Primary Scale of Intelligence–Revised.* San Antonio, TX: The Psychological Corporation.

Wechsler, D. (1991). *Wechsler Intelligence Scales for Children–Third Edition.* San Antonio, TX: The Psychological Corporation.

Wechsler, D. (1992). *Wechsler Individual Achievement Test.* San Antonio, TX: The Psychological Corporation.

Wechsler, D. (1997). *Wechsler Adult Intelligence Scale–Third Edition.* San Antonio, TX: The Psychological Corporation.